THE CANADIAN WOMAN'S
LEGAL GUIDE

The Canadian WOMAN'S Legal Guide

M.J. Dymond, editor

1987
Doubleday Canada Limited, Toronto, Ontario

Copyright © 1987 by Doubleday Canada Limited
All rights reserved
First edition

Cover design by Dragon's Eye Press
Typeset by Q Composition
Printed and bound in Canada by John Deyell Company

Published by arrangement with Doubleday and Company, Inc. and
Nelson Doubleday Inc.

Canadian Cataloguing in Publication Data

Main entry under title:

The Canadian woman's legal guide

Includes index.
ISBN 0-385-25066-5

1. Law – Canada – Popular works. 2. Women – Legal status,
laws, etc. – Canada. I. Dymond, Mary Joy.

KE450.W6C36 1987   349.71'02'4042   C86-094926-5

CONTENTS

PREFACE

The Canadian Woman's Legal Guide has been written by twenty different lawyers, all women and all Canadian, representing a tremendous amount of expertise right across the country. The authors are all accomplished and distinguished individuals who share a commitment to making the law more accessible to women. Most of these lawyers are active in community legal education, either through writing and public speaking or through their participation in community activities and volunteer organizations. Many have also been involved in the push for law reform that has resulted in so many changes to our laws, especially the law relating to women, over the past twenty years. You will no doubt recognize the names of many contributors, several of whom are nationally known for the contributions they have made to the law and to our justice system. It has been an honour to work with them in preparing this guide.

This book covers a wide range of topics and is designed to give you as much information as possible about your rights in the marketplace, in the family, at work, and in the legal system. Knowledge of the law should not and need not be an exclusive preserve of lawyers. The more you know about the law, the better able you will be to protect your rights and prevent legal problems from arising.

Although we have tried to present a legal guide which is as comprehensive as possible, the nature of the law, its complexity, flexibility, provincial variations, and constant evolution may necessitate your seeking professional legal advice. If you do need expert legal advice, this guide should help you decide when, how, and where to find it.

A very important part of *The Canadian Woman's Legal Guide* is the Resource Guide found at the back of the book. If you wish to find out more about a particular area of the law or require help with a legal problem, the list of further sources of information and further reading provided for each chapter should be of assistance.

We hope that you will find this book an informative and practical source of legal information. We also hope that, by reading it, you will recognize the need for further reform and join us in working to improve our laws and system of justice for the women of Canada.

M.J. Dymond

PART ONE

Women as Consumers—
Your Rights in the
Marketplace

CHAPTER 1

WOMEN AND CREDIT

Beverly Mills Stetson

Beverly Mills Stetson is the Executive Director of the Community Legal Information Association of Prince Edward Island. She obtained her law degree at Dalhousie University in Halifax and practised law in Charlottetown for a number of years. She is co-author of How to Do Your Own Divorce *on P.E.I. and other legal information brochures and is a member of the Association of Women and the Law. Beverly Mills Stetson is a member of the Bar of Prince Edward Island.*

IN THE PAST most ordinary citizens used cash to conduct their personal and business affairs, and "neither a borrower nor a lender be" was a motto to live by. With the prosperity of recent times the role of credit has changed. Most people now use credit at least to acquire such major items as homes, automobiles, and education. Businesses and professions need credit to begin and meet operating costs.

With women now taking an increased role in economic life, they need to understand how credit works and what its limitations are. Financial institutions have great resources, legal expertise, and knowledge. Dealing with them can be intimidating. This chapter will help you learn more about credit and how to deal with financial institutions when borrowing money.

THE CONTRACT OF CREDIT

The first thing to understand about credit is that all agreements to lend money or to provide a credit card are contracts, whether written or not. When you get a loan from your bank to buy a new car, use your Visa card, or even borrow money from your mother to get you through until pay day, you have entered a contract with the lender. We'll assume, for the purposes of this article, that the lender is a bank or other institution and that there is a written agreement or contract setting out the terms of the loan.

The borrower and lender are considered by our laws to have included all the agreed terms in the contract and to have bargained equally, even if in practical terms there is no real choice for the borrower. Once a contract is formed, both parties are bound by the promises they have made. If one wants to get out of the contract, the other can sue. The court can enforce the contract by ordering the party to go through with the contract or to pay damages or the amount of money the other person lost.

The documents you sign when applying for a loan or a charge card are contracts. They may be long or short, written in legal or plain language; but whether they look like legal documents or not, they are still contracts. They are usually in a "standard form," printed in advance by the lender with no input from the borrower, and are designed to protect the lender. From the institution's point of view, a standard-form contract is the best way of handling routine loans and ensuring that its own interests are met. It would be expensive and time consuming to negotiate and write out a new contract with every borrower.

A typical credit contract contains terms about the amount to be received by the borrower, the goods or services purchased, and the amount of interest charged (the cost of borrowing), and sets out the arrangements for repayment.

FINANCIAL INSTITUTIONS AND CREDIT

Lending money is a big business in Canada today and many institutions are in the market—banks, trust companies, credit unions, insurance companies, caisses populaires, finance companies, credit card companies, and department stores. Banks are given their charters by Parliament and are governed by the federal *Bank Act*, which regulates their operations. Other financial institutions and lenders may be regulated by either federal or provincial legislation. Each institution offers a number of services on a variety of terms. It does pay to check the options available and to ensure that the institution you are dealing with is a reputable one.

THE BASIC FACTS ABOUT CREDIT

Credit is a kind of contract by which the bank or lender allows its customer to borrow money or use a credit card to purchase goods or services as they are needed, and to repay the price at a future time with interest. The amount borrowed is called the "principal," and the extra amount you pay is the "interest" or the cost of the loan.

Pros and Cons of Credit

Credit is a convenience; it allows you to make purchases now and pay for them later. It lets you take advantage of special sales or unexpected expenses. It relieves you from carrying a lot of cash around. It can help you keep track of your purchases by the written statements you receive.

Some people find credit difficult to control, however. You may be more inclined to purchase items you don't really need. You may have trouble making your payments. A special sale may end up costing you more, once interest and carrying charges are added. Credit cards can be lost or stolen, and you could be responsible for someone else's charges. Credit is a debt; it does cost money, and it can get out of control.

Handling Credit

The amount of interest charged and the terms of repayment may vary from lender to lender, so compare before deciding which institution to approach. Keep control of credit and your budget. Use common sense about the number of credit cards you need and how often you use them. Find out the total cost and consider whether another form of credit may be more suitable for your purpose. Use your credit card to purchase goods and services from reputable merchants only. Keep track of all your credit purchases—save your receipts and check them against your monthly statements. Make the largest down payment possible. Keep your payment period as short as possible, and make your payments promptly to avoid additional charges.

Kinds of Loans

Loans may be divided into two kinds: secured loans and unsecured loans. When you obtain a secured loan, you put up an item—a car, furniture, your home, etc.—as "collateral" or "security" for the loan. This gives the lender added protection to guarantee payment of the debt. The lender can seize and sell the goods without taking court action. A secured loan also acquires priority over unsecured loans.

When you get an unsecured loan, the lender is relying on your promise to pay without any additional protection. The lender can't seize your goods or land without first taking court action.

Whether secured or not, a loan may take a variety of forms, and may offer different rates of interest and terms for repayment. The following are typical kinds of credit transactions.

Personal Loans

The lender lends you money, and you sign a contract promising to pay it back at an agreed rate of interest and at agreed times. You may be asked to have someone co-sign (or guarantee) the loan if it is a large amount or if you have an inadequate credit rating. Often credit unions and co-operatives offer the best terms or lower interest rates and a choice of repayment periods. Banks and trust companies usually have higher rates, and finance companies ask for very high interest rates.

Demand Loans

For this kind of loan, repayment may be required at any time (on demand) by the bank, although usually payments are made over time, as arranged when the loan was made. Partial or full payment may usually be made without penalty.

Conditional Sales Contracts

This type of loan is generally available from stores to finance the purchase of goods "on time." You get possession of the goods and may use them, but you don't own them until you have made your last payment. If you don't pay as agreed, the store may repossess the goods. You sign a conditional sales contract and a promissory note, which are registered in a public registry. The contract may be sold by the store to a lender, often a finance company. These kinds of contracts are governed by legislation in each province.

Mortgages

This is usually a long-term loan made by a bank or similar institution for the purchase of real property. A land mortgage can also be "collateral" or security for a loan made for another purpose.

Chattel Mortgages

Legally, "chattels" are movable objects, such as furniture, cars, and boats. A mortgage is put on a chattel as security for a loan. You give the lender a legal right or interest in the object. The lender will have the right to seize the object and sell it if you don't pay as agreed.

You will sign a chattel-mortgage document and a promissory note, which is registered and becomes a "lien" or charge against the object. The document may also contain other conditions; for example, it may stipulate that you cannot remove the object from the province permanently, or sell it, and that you are to keep it free from other legal claims. Each province has laws governing chattel mortgages.

Charge Cards

These are available from stores and on various repayment terms. Among these might be: a thirty-day account, requiring repayment in thirty days from the date of billing; an instalment plan, requiring equal payments including interest for a number of months; and all-purpose accounts, allowing payments to be made in full or paid over a period of time. The features of each and the interest charged vary with the retailer.

Life-Insurance Loans

Some life insurance policies allow you to borrow money at a low interest rate. If your policy has surrender value, or equity, money can be borrowed from the insurance company. The value of the policy is reduced by the amount of the loan until it is repaid.

Tax Discounters

This is a form of loan by which you, as a taxpayer, sell your income-tax refund to a tax discounter before you file your tax return. If you are qualified to receive a refund, the discount buys the return by giving you a portion of the refund (at least 85 percent) in cash immediately. The government then sends the entire refund to the tax discounter. The discounter must give you the extra amount received if the eventual refund is larger than you expected. The agreement you sign must show the amount of refund due, the amount given to you, and the amount kept.

Pawnbrokers

A pawnbroker will give you money for an item of value that you wish to pawn. The money will be a small portion of the value of the item. You can recover the item after paying back the loan plus a high rate of interest. If you don't pay, the item is sold.

Credit Cards

Canadians are among the heaviest users of credit cards in the world. Over 90 percent of eligible adults hold them. One half of credit-card charges are paid off before the due date and are therefore interest-free. The other half are subject to monthly interest charges at a rate much higher than you would pay for a personal bank loan. Credit-card misuse is the major cause of personal bankruptcy. People are tempted to use these cards to buy things they can't afford or don't need. The credit card is an expensive form of borrowing money unless the account is paid in full each month.

A credit card offers a form of "variable credit," making credit available in advance to you to use from month to month when you need to purchase goods or services. It can also be used as a source of short-term loans. When you use your credit card you are post-poning payment until you receive your statement in the mail. You may either make a partial payment of at least a minimum amount (which depends on the balance owing) or pay the full amount. No interest is charged if the full amount is paid by the due date (though some companies now charge a user fee, even to customers who pay in full each month). If you don't pay the full amount, interest is added every month to the outstanding balance. The interest on credit cards is high, usually between 18 and 28 percent a year.

Credit cards may also be used to obtain cash advances from a branch of your bank by using the banking machine or approaching a teller. Some cards allow you to get cash advances in other ways. A cash advance is a loan, and it costs more than using the card for purchases because interest charges begin immediately instead of at the payment due date.

Each card will have a limit to the amount that can be charged. Card holders start with a low credit limit. Your limit may increase after a time if you are using the card regularly, appear to need a higher limit, and have a good payment record.

It is advisable to take certain precautions when using your credit cards. Make sure that the clerk gives your card back to you, and check to see that the card you receive is yours and not someone else's. If you receive an uninvited card in the mail, don't feel you have to accept it. You may return it to the sender or carefully cut it in half and dispose of it. You are not responsible for it unless you requested the card in writing or accept it by using it.

If your card is lost or stolen you must report it to the card company immediately. Most companies have twenty-four hour toll-free telephone service for this purpose, listed in most telephone directories. You should request a new card immediately, as this could take a few weeks. Any charges made on your card by a thief or finder may be your responsibility if you haven't reported the loss. You may be responsible for the first $50 charged to your account even if you have reported it. Report the lost or stolen card to the police.

It is a good idea to have a list of your credit cards in a safe place, including their numbers and information about where and how lost or stolen cards are to be reported.

HOW TO APPLY FOR CREDIT

You have the right to ask questions, have them answered, and take time to consider your options before making an actual application for credit. You may comparison shop for credit in the same way you would if you were thinking of buying a new appliance. Interest rates and terms of payment do vary.

You will be asked to fill out an application form whenever you request credit privileges. Remember that this is a contract. Make sure you read the entire agreement and understand it before signing and that you fill in each blank. Never sign a blank form. Obtain a copy of the signed agreement. You may take the form with you before signing it to give yourself time to think about it or to consult your lawyer if you wish. Usually there is a clause on the form in which you are giving your permission to the lender to obtain credit information about you from a credit agency or other lender. It also gives the lender permission to give information about your account in the future to these agencies.

When deciding whether to give you credit, the lender will consider your financial history, your assets, and your ability to pay. The lender may ask you for documentation or a statement of your earnings. The lender may find out more about you from a credit bureau or other lenders, or from public records such as the registry of court judgments or bankruptcies.

If you are refused credit, ask your lender the reason. Sometimes a lender is reluctant to answer this question. Ask to see someone with higher authority. Your application may be refused if you have had debt problems in the past, if you do not have sufficient collateral to offer as security for the loan, or if the lender feels you don't have the ability to make monthly payments over the term of the loan. Once you understand why you don't qualify, you may be able to take steps to improve your situation so that you may qualify at another time. You might apply for a smaller loan, pay off debts and then reapply, or apply elsewhere. You should carefully consider the cost before going to another institution that charges much higher interest rates or has harsher terms. You might improve your position by establishing a separate credit rating, if you don't have one or if your spouse's bad credit history is affecting you. If you think you may have been refused because the lender has discriminated against you, you might be able to obtain assistance from your provincial human rights commission.

Business Loans

Many women report difficulty in obtaining business loans, even though studies show that women have recently been more successful in starting businesses than men. It is important to be prepared with complete information about your business proposal when approaching your lender. You should carefully consider both your ability to repay and the type of security the lender requires for the loan. Before signing a contract for a business loan, seek legal advice and perhaps the advice of an accountant to ensure that the business is assuming a realistic debt load and that you understand the ramifications of the contract. If you are in partnership with your spouse or another person, make sure the legal aspects of the business accurately reflect that relationship and the role and obligations you have agreed on.

Co-signing a Loan

Women are often asked to co-sign loan and credit applications for their spouses or children. This is *not* just a formality by which you give your permission for the loan. Co-signing means that you fully guarantee the loan. The lender obtains additional security for the loan, since two people are liable, rather than one. If the borrower does not make payments, you will be asked to do so. By co-signing you are equally responsible for paying the entire loan, not just half of it. You could also be asked to pay late-payment charges or collection and court costs. You can be sued if you don't pay.

On the other hand, co-signing for a loan may be one way of establishing a good credit record. It can mean that you have been acknowledged by the lender as a partner in an enterprise, such as a family farm or small business.

Recent matrimonial property legislation in every province has had an impact on lenders. Because family assets are now divided between the spouses if they separate, a lender will want you to co-sign the contract before it will accept a family asset (a car, for example) as security for your spouse's personal loan. Often lenders want the major family asset—the home—given as security for a spouse's business loans. You should carefully consider and seek legal advice before encumbering family assets for the benefit of one spouse only.

Wives are often under a lot of pressure to co-sign because needed loans may not otherwise be available to their husbands. Sometimes, however, the banks have no basis for this request and may approve the loan anyway. There is no law that requires you to co-sign. If you don't want to be equally responsible for the loan, it may be possible to sign a waiver saying you give permission to secure the family asset under the loan and that your rights to a share in the asset will stand second in line to the lender's rights.

You are entitled to get independent legal advice before signing. This means that you get advice from a lawyer who is not acting for your spouse or for the lender. In this way you can find out how the contract affects your interests and what your options may be. You may wish to have your husband agree, in writing, that he will be solely responsible for the loan or that he will give you shares in the business. You may discuss options for your protection with your lawyer. In some cases the lending institution will want to protect itself by insisting that you do get your own legal advice. Your lawyer will be asked for a certificate indicating that you have received independent legal advice; the lender is thus assured that you knew what you signed and that you weren't forced to sign the documents by your spouse's influence.

If you are asked to co-sign or guarantee your spouse's loans you may want to consider whether your income and assets should be kept free from creditors' claims. This is an opportunity for you and your spouse to discuss with one another what each of you is prepared to contribute to individual or joint business enterprises and what steps should be taken to protect one another. Ensure that the legal steps are taken to reflect this understanding.

Before co-signing for anyone you should make sure that you are willing and able to repay the loan if called upon to do so. You should ask the same questions of the borrower as the bank will. Know the risk you are taking.

You should save your receipts if you, as co-signer, are required to make payments. You may want to take steps to recover this from the borrower by seeking legal advice or going to Small Claims Court.

CREDIT AND DISCRIMINATION

Women are entitled to be considered for a loan on the same basis as men in similar economic circumstances. If you have established your own separate credit rating, you should not be denied credit because you are now separated, divorced, or widowed. Banks, credit-card companies, and other federal institutions must comply with federal human rights legislation, which forbids discrimination on the grounds of race, national or ethnic origin, colour, religion, age, sex, marital status, or conviction for an offence for which a pardon has been granted. Other lenders, such as credit unions, loan companies, and stores, must follow provincial human rights codes, which also prohibit discrimination based on sex or marital status.

You may feel that you are discriminated against as a woman if you are refused a loan or a credit card or if you must get your spouse or parent to co-sign. If a man in the same position would not have to meet the same requirement, then it is discrimination. Lenders are entitled, however, to refuse a loan based on your own credit worthiness.

Some problems women have faced that may indicate discrimination include:

- Single or married women with their own income may have difficulty in obtaining credit in their own names.
- Women may have difficulty in obtaining loans for businesses or professions, especially if it is a non-traditional area for women, such as farming.
- A married woman with her own income may have to give financial information about her spouse in order to obtain a loan.
- A wife's earnings may be reduced or discounted by a lender in determining eligibility for a mortgage because the lender feels the woman's earning capacity will be affected by child rearing or that it is not as reliable as her husband's.
- A wife's credit rating may be reduced by her spouse's poor credit record.
- Women may be asked questions about their plans to have children or their family-planning methods.
- Divorced, separated, or widowed women may have difficulty establishing or re-establishing their credit rating even if they previously had their own separate rating.
- Spousal or child-support payments may not be included in calculating income, even when they can be verified as reliable.

Because of human rights legislation most major lenders now have policies or guidelines requiring their employees not to discriminate.

Women's relationships with financial institutions have improved; but with hundreds of branches and employees, individual attitudes and prejudices may affect decisions.

If you feel that you have been discriminated against by a lender, contact your local human rights commission.

Credit and Marital Status

A lender must decide whether to lend you money or grant you credit based on your circumstances and not discriminate against you because of your marital status, whether you are married, separated, divorced, or living in a common-law relationship. If you rely solely on your spouse's income, the lender may request your spouse to co-sign the contract to make your spouse responsible for the debt if you fail to pay. While this may be distasteful to you, it is not discriminatory if a man in similar circumstances would have to meet the same requirement.

Your spouse may have credit cards and may have given you a card in your own name. This does not mean that you have established your own account with the credit-card company. You have been given permission to use your spouse's card. Your spouse is responsible for paying the charges and may end your use of the card by notifying the credit-card company.

Although we often don't like to recognize it, marriage is a business relationship as well as a romantic one. A wise woman takes steps to protect herself. This will be especially important if you become separated or widowed. It makes good sense to establish your own separate credit rating and history, and to have experience in handling money matters and your family budget. Know your family's income, assets, and liabilities. You should make sure that you and your spouse obtain sufficient life insurance to cover major debts, such as a mortgage.

If you and your spouse separate, one of the matters that will need to be settled is payment of debts. You are not responsible for a debt unless you have signed the loan contract or the credit-card application. However, you may be asked to share responsibility for a debt if it was acquired for family purposes. While you are settling matters with your spouse, make sure payments are being made on debts that have family assets as security. Responsibility for debts should be negotiated and made part of your separation agreement.

If your spouse dies, you are not personally responsible for his debts unless you have co-signed the loan contract. However, any assets left in your husband's estate must be used to pay his outstanding debts before any inheritance can be paid. If there is insufficient money to pay your spouse's debts a lender may ask you to take on that responsibility. Get legal advice to understand what your obligations are.

YOUR CREDIT RATING

Most people will need to borrow money, acquire a credit card, or charge purchases at some point in their lives. To be eligible you must possess a good credit record indicating that you are financially responsible. If you are single and have regular income from employment, you will probably have no difficulty in establishing a credit record. If you do not have income, establishing a credit rating may be more difficult.

If you are married, it is important to have your own credit rating, separate from your spouse's, so that if your spouse's rating falls, yours will remain intact. Your own rating may give you the opportunity to obtain credit to start up your own business or other endeavour. Your rating may enhance your family's ability to obtain loans or mortgages. If you separate or if your spouse dies, you will have access to credit without waiting to build up an independent rating.

The following steps are all ways you can obtain and maintain a credit rating and credit history. Make regular deposits in your own savings account, even if you don't earn a salary. Pay utility and other bills regularly and on time. Get a small personal loan and pay it back on time. Open charge accounts in your own name and use them properly. If you get a student loan, repay it promptly. Obtain your own credit cards on your own account; reject courtesy cards on your spouse's account, since your use will influence your spouse's credit record, not your own. Make yourself known to bank officials by transacting business at your bank regularly and seeking their advice as needed.

You may lose a previous credit rating if you marry and change your surname. Some lenders maintain credit records in a husband's name only. If you obtain a joint loan with your spouse, the lender may combine both credit records. If your spouse has a bad credit rating it could harm yours as well. You should check with your lender and your credit agency to see if you have a separate credit record.

Credit-Reporting Agencies

Credit agencies or bureaus are private businesses that collect credit and personal information about individuals and sell this information to their members. Members are stores, employers, and such lenders as banks. The agencies gather information about charge accounts and loans from members and about court judgments, bankruptcies, chattel mortgages, conditional sales contracts, mortgages, and deeds from public registries. All agencies are regulated by provincial legislation that also covers your right to access to this information, the kind of information that may be included in a report, or the interval after which certain things—bankruptcy or a judgment, for example—should be removed from a report. Credit agencies do not make the decision whether to grant credit; they only give a credit report to a member.

If you notify your credit agency that you want all information about you kept in a separate file in your own name, the agency must comply. It's a good idea to check your credit record at a credit agency if you are not sure about your standing, if your marital status has changed, or if you've been refused credit because of a bad credit report. Check the yellow pages for names of the credit-reporting agencies in your area, or ask your lender which agency it uses.

It is important that your record at a credit agency be accurate. Under provincial legislation you have the right to be told what is in your file at a credit agency and to have errors corrected. You may also be told the source of information and the names of any companies that have requested information about you recently. The consumer services department of your provincial government can provide information about the laws governing credit-reporting agencies in your province.

FAILURE TO PAY—WHAT THE LENDER MAY DO

If you do not pay your debts there are many things a lender may do to collect, depending on the nature of the transaction and what the credit contract provides.

The first step a lender usually takes is to write you a "demand" letter, which acts as notice to you that you are in default. The lender may then take additional steps, depending on the nature of the loan.

If the loan is secured by a mortgage, the lender may sell the land and buildings on it by a mortgage sale or foreclosure. Other secured loans, such as conditional sales contracts or chattel mortgages, allow the lender to seize or repossess items given as security for the loan. The lender then may sell these items, following what has been established by law as the proper procedure for doing so. If this does not yield enough money to cover the amount of the debt and the expenses of repossession and sale, the lender may sue you for the balance. If more than is needed to cover the debt and expenses is realized from the sale, the lender will usually be required to pay you the surplus.

If the loan is unsecured, the lender must commence a court action against you. Goods cannot be seized until the court action has commenced. A lender commences a court action by filing documents in court and giving you notice by delivering or serving them on you. If the lender wins in court or if you don't file a defence to the court action within the prescribed time, the lender obtains a court judgment against you; this gives the lender additional means to collect the debt. The lender could, for instance, get a court order permitting the sheriff to seize and sell your land or your personal property or take money from your bank accounts. Certain items that the law deems necessary for survival are exempt from seizure.

A lender who has won a court action could take steps to garnishee your wages. If the court agrees, your employer is ordered to pay a portion of your wages into court to pay the debt. Some kinds of income, such as social assistance, cannot be garnisheed.

A lender may prefer to turn your debt over to a collection agency. These agencies charge a percentage of the debt as the fee for collecting it. They are governed by legislation in each province and again must follow an established "proper" procedure in dealing with you and your debt. For instance in many provinces the collection agency cannot harass or threaten you or telephone you between certain hours, and is restricted in communicating with your employers, friends, or neighbours.

Check with your provincial consumer affairs department, a legal-information service, or your lawyer to see what is permitted in your province and what legal steps the lender must follow before it can take these actions. Consumer Services can also be a source of help if you are being harassed by your lender or by a collection agency.

Unpaid support payments are also a debt. Many of the steps a lender can take to collect an overdue debt are available to you if you are entitled to receive support payments for yourself or your children. There are usually enforcement offices in the Family Court in your province to assist you in collecting this debt. In many cases your husband may be called into court to attempt to explain why he is not paying, and you may ask that his assets be seized or his wages garnisheed, or that a jail sentence be imposed.

HELP FOR THE DEBTOR

Unexpected events can affect you financially. If you are unable to pay your debts on time you should not ignore the situation and wait for the lender to call you. It may be better to contact the lender immediately and explain your circumstances. Sometimes it is possible to work out an arrangement to give you extra time or to reduce payments while you overcome your financial difficulties. Often, though not always, a lender who understands your situation will be reasonable.

If you are having financial difficulties, try to reduce your living expenses or increase your income by additional employment. Stop all further borrowing and do not use your credit cards. Take courses on budgeting and money management to help you learn the skills you need to avoid credit problems.

Another possibility is to get assistance from a credit-counselling service in your area. Such a service can help you work out a budget and a schedule for payments with your creditors, or suggest other options such as consolidating your loans into one.

Each province has a program (an ''orderly payment of debts'' program, for example) to assist debtors who are in trouble. This is usually administered by your provincial consumer affairs department. An application is made to the courts to consolidate your debts, and you pay one affordable monthly payment, which is then sent to your creditors. Your creditors must first agree to the arrangement.

A final solution is bankruptcy. This is only possible for people who are in very serious financial difficulty. Bankruptcy is a legal process, regulated by the federal government through the federal Department of Consumer and Corporate Affairs. Bankruptcy proceedings will cost you money and the loss of your assets and will affect your credit rating for at least six years. But this last resort will, if successful, provide you with a fresh start.

You may declare bankruptcy, if you qualify; or, you could be forced into bankruptcy by your creditors. Either way, an appointed trustee takes control of most of your assets and sells those that are not necessary for your survival. Your income above a basic amount for necessities is paid to the trustee as well. The trustee pays the money so raised to your creditors. You must pay the trustee's fees and expenses. Some debts—such as support payments, or debts for necessities—cannot be discharged by a bankruptcy. For more information on bankruptcy, contact the federal Department of Consumer and Corporate Affairs. (See the federal government listings in your phone directory.)

Women's relationship with credit and financial institutions has evolved over time with the ever-changing role of women in Canadian history. It is the responsibility of financial institutions to respond to the changing needs of women. It is the responsibility of women to understand credit and financial services and to use them wisely and well.

CHAPTER 2

CONSUMER PROTECTION

Sandra Hornung

Sandra Hornung is the Adult Program Co-ordinator for the Public Legal Education Association of Saskatchewan. She obtained her law degree from the University of Saskatchewan and has been active in several community organizations in Regina and Saskatoon. She is the author of Consumer Power: A Guide to the Basics of Consumer Law and Consumer Credit in Saskatchewan.

CONSUMER AWARENESS is the key to consumer protection. Consumer awareness means shopping wisely, becoming knowledgable about available products and services, and considering all facts before buying. Consumer awareness also means knowing where to find out about the legislation that exists within a province, understanding the legislation, knowing the situations the legislation applies to, and using the legislation to protect against marketplace rip-offs.

There are legal implications every time you purchase a product or a service. Buying a chocolate bar, buying an automobile, getting a haircut, hiring a lawyer, and signing a lease to rent an apartment are all contracts. And contracts cannot be broken easily. Most provinces in Canada have legislation to protect the consumer from unfair business practices and defective products. But the legislation, which varies from province to province, cannot protect the consumer who is unaware of it. For example, if your washing machine quits two days after the warranty expires you may still be able to seek a remedy from the original dealer provided you know about the provincial legislation that imposes implied or statutory warranties on every consumer product.

There are other methods of resolving grievances where there is no legislation to protect the consumer. Complaining effectively, seeking assistance from consumer-protection agencies or organizations, and going to Small Claims Court are avenues open to you if you want to take the time and energy to pursue your claim.

Although you have rights in the market place as a consumer, you have responsibilities as well. It is your responsibility to know the terms of the contract you are entering into, to inform yourself about consumer-protection laws, and to communicate in an honest and fair manner any dissatisfaction with a business. Businesses generally respond in a favourable way to consumer complaints because they need the goodwill of their customers.

This chapter cannot cover all of the variations in provincial legislation across Canada, but it does deal with some of the most common consumer complaints that our laws attempt to remedy. Included at the end of the chapter is some practical advice—on effective consumer complaining and on seeking help within your province—that will increase your consumer awareness.

PURCHASING PRODUCTS AND SERVICES

Buying a soft drink from a vending machine or getting a haircut are contracts, just as signing a loan agreement with the bank is a contract. Everyday consumer transactions are contracts and cannot be cancelled or altered merely because you change your mind about a product or a service. If you refuse to perform your part of a contract, you can be sued in a court of law.

A contract is a legally binding agreement between two or more people (parties) by which one party promises to do something and the other promises to do something in return (for example, pay for a service). The contract must be clear about who the parties are, what the subject matter is, and what is given in exchange. Because a contract is enforceable in court, it is especially important for the consumer to know and understand when there is a contract and what the terms of the contract are.

Retail Purchases

Buying something in a store is a contract, and you do not have the right to return an item because you decide you do not need it or because you do not like the colour. Whether you get a refund, exchange, or credit note depends on store policy; there is no automatic right to return an item where there is no breach of warranty. However, if a store displays a sign stating its refund policy, it must comply with that policy if the consumer complies with the conditions of the policy. For example, if a store posts a sign that says "Refunds within three days with receipt," the store must give a refund if you return an item within the three-day period and have the receipt, whatever the reason for return. You should check a store's refund policy before making your purchase, and only shop at businesses that do have reasonable policies.

Door-to-Door Purchases

Door-to-door sales are another problematic area of consumer purchasing because of the high-pressure sales tactics used by the salespeople. These "direct sellers" include encyclopedia and vacuum-cleaner salespeople as well as people selling home improvement materials and/or services (for example, siding, insulation, or furnace cleaning). Also included are sales at "home parties" where people gather to hear a sales pitch and to order products.

Always ask to see the door-to-door salesperson's provincial licence and, if in doubt, contact your provincial government's consumer affairs department. A reputable seller will return a second or third time to make a sale, so there is no need to rush into a sale or to sign an agreement or contract to get rid of a salesperson.

As with any contract, it is important to know and understand the contract before signing it. All provinces have legislation to allow for a "cooling-off" period that applies to direct sellers or door-to-door salespeople. Cooling-off periods range from three to ten days, depending on the province, and allow the consumer to cancel the contract within that time and receive a full refund. The legislation states the number of days within which the seller must refund the money and sets out the format for cancelling the contract. Usually this is by way of a registered letter.

This legislation is useless, however, if the salesperson has left the province and cannot be found. It is good consumer practice to have the salesperson return after you have had time to verify his or her licence with the department of consumer affairs and to check the company's reputation with the Better Business Bureau. Then, if you are sure you wish to purchase the product, the chance that problems will arise later is minimized. Never pay for goods not yet received. The best idea is to pay for goods only after receipt and examination of them.

Mail-Order Purchases

Consumers also often misunderstand contracts with book, record, or tape clubs. By signing the tear-off card in a magazine advertisement, you are entering into a contract, and you must be prepared to perform your part of that agreement. If you agree to purchase one item every month for the next twelve months, you must do so. Although you are not responsible for returning unsolicited goods, you are responsible for returning goods received under a contract that you have signed. For example, with clubs that send you the monthly special selection if you do not make another choice by a particular date, you are responsible for the item's safe return if you choose not to keep it. If the goods are lost on the return trip, you must pay for them.

Consumer Services

Purchasing consumer services often results in many consumer complaints. Difficulties with memberships in health clubs, dating agencies, and training courses are fairly common. Consumers may change their minds about wanting the service after they have signed the contract and, perhaps, paid the money. Some provinces have legislation that allows for cancellation of contracts with these types of businesses within a time period (up to fourteen days), and the consumer gets a full refund less handling fees and fees for any services used. But that provincial legislation only applies to businesses licenced in the province. Some businesses may not be required to be licenced in a province before operating there. Chances for recovery from businesses not licenced within the province are slim because provincial legislation does not apply to them. For a business licenced outside the province, the consumer can only sue for breach of a contract—a very difficult and expensive method of recovery.

Legal Services

Purchasing professional services often presents problems for the consumer. It is difficult to choose a lawyer if you have never used one or do not know any. Some but not all provinces have lawyer-referral services. The best referral service is word of mouth. Ask friends or co-workers to recommend a good lawyer and read Chapter 20 for more information about lawyers and the legal system.

If you have a complaint about the service received from or the fees charged by a lawyer, you can seek help. Every provincial law society has a disciplinary committee to deal with situations in which a lawyer has done something unethical. If you feel you have been unfairly billed, you should first discuss the situation with your lawyer. If the problem cannot be resolved, you should contact the law society and ask to have the bill taxed or reviewed by an independent officer of the court.

Read the Contract

Whether purchasing products or services, your best protection is to read and understand the contracts you enter into. Most businesses today use standard-form contracts for ease of handling and costs. Many consumers do not read these contracts before signing because the terms are too technical, or the contracts are too long, or the small print makes the contract physically difficult to read. Even if you do not read or understand the contract, you are responsible for what you sign. Occasionally, though, a court may hold that you are not responsible for unusually onerous terms in a contract that were not brought to your attention.

You should not sign any contract if you do not understand or agree with any terms. You can make alterations to a standard-form contract by crossing out some of the terms and initialling the change. Another way to change a contract is to add a "Subject to . . ." clause. Some businesses will not accept changes to a standard-form contract. The consumer has two choices: accept the contract as it is, or go elsewhere. The chances are that going elsewhere means the same type of contract. The best way to protect yourself is to read and understand the contract or to leave it.

Purchasing Defective Products

What happens if you purchase a product and take it home only to find that it is defective and that the warranty or guarantee does not cover what you expected it would?

In order to get a defective product repaired, you should understand that there are different kinds of warranties: the written warranties given by the manufacturer or the seller of the product, the statutory warranties imposed by legislation in some provinces, and additional written warranties. If you read the warranty before purchasing a product and know the warranties imposed by the laws of the province, you will have less trouble with defective products than if you are uninformed of your legal rights.

Express Warranties

Express warranties are promises or statements about a product or its performance made by a seller or a manufacturer to the consumer. These warranties may be made verbally, in writing, or in advertising. Although an oral promise by a salesperson may be binding even if it contradicts the written warranty, the consumer should try to get all statements of warranty in writing.

A salesperson's *opinion* about a product (called a "sales puff") is not binding. For example, when a salesperson says the automobile is "the best on the market," we know the statement is a sales pitch and not legally binding. But the dealer who says the car is six years old, has 55,000 kilometres on it, and has a new transmission is warranting those facts, and you should be able to rely on that statement. If you later discover that the car really has 155,000 kilometres on it, you can expect to collect damages from the dealer.

It is important to read and understand the warranties made by the manufacturer and seller. Express warranties are usually limited by expiry dates or by statements like "parts not labour" or "transportation costs not included." Knowing that a product is guaranteed is not enough. You must ask, "Guaranteed for what?" Also, a "lifetime guarantee" is insufficient if the guarantee is for the lifetime of the product instead of for your lifetime. Once the product quits working, its life is over.

When purchasing consumer products, it is important to compare

warranties as well as prices. The reputation of the seller or manufacturer who gives the warranty is also important. A warranty is
useless if the warrantor has left town and cannot be found.

Statutory or Implied Warranties

In most provinces, the legislatures have enacted laws that provide
some warranties on every consumer product sold by a dealer. A
consumer product is usually any new or used product purchased for
personal, family, or household purposes. A statutory warranty cannot be denied or ignored by a manufacturer or seller. Even though
an express warranty expires or the store has a no-refund policy in
effect, the consumer can demand a full refund if there is a breach
of these statutory warranties.

Statutory warranties differ from province to province (see the
section on getting assistance to determine how to find the laws of
a particular province). Some of the most common statutory warranties include the following:

Good Title

The consumer gets a guarantee that the seller has a right to sell the
goods and that the consumer will enjoy quiet possession of them,
(that is, that no one else will assert a claim to them).

Description

The goods purchased must match the description on the outside of
the package, or, if ordered from a catalogue, must match the description in the catalogue. It is a good idea to inspect mailed items
right away and store-bought items at the store if possible. Practically,
it is always more difficult to return a defective item than it is to
purchase a defect-free one to begin with.

Acceptable Quality

This warranty covers hidden defects only. It does not cover defects
drawn to your attention before the contract of sale was made, or
defects you should have noticed upon reasonable examination of
the product. For example, a packaged shirt that has sleeves of
different lengths is not of acceptable quality and you can expect to
return it for a full refund. But if a clerk says the hem of a skirt is

coming undone and you still buy the skirt, you cannot then return it on that account, since you made the contract knowing of the defect. Similarly, you would not be expected to notice a defect in the motor of a lawnmower but would be expected to notice a bent handle if the lawnmower was fully assembled in the store.

Because it is more difficult to determine acceptable quality of secondhand goods than of new goods, it is best to get secondhand dealers to make all warranties in writing.

Sales items marked "seconds" or "substandard" are not expected to have the same quality as new items. However, when regular stock is offered at reduced prices, the consumer can expect the same quality as new.

Fit for Purpose

The statutory warranty of fit for purpose means that a product must be fit for its ordinary purpose. If the item has more than one purpose and the salesperson says it is fit for the consumer's particular purpose, the consumer should be able to rely on that statement. For example, you may want to buy paint for some wooden lawn furniture. In the store, you find some paint marked "General Use" and the salesclerk tells you that the paint is suitable for outdoor use. You are entitled to rely on that statement and, if the paint turns out to be unsuitable for outdoor use, you may return it and expect to get a refund or damages. But if you do not ask the clerk or the clerk does not know if the paint is suitable for your particular purpose and you buy it anyway, you cannot get a remedy for a breach of the warranty of fit for purpose if the paint turns out to be unsuitable for exterior use.

Statutory warranties vary from province to province, and the legislation does not always include sales of services. You should check the laws in your province to see what warranties are implied and to what purchases they apply. Then if a manufacturer's warranty has expired, you can use your knowledge of statutory or implied warranties to resolve a consumer complaint.

Additional Written Warranties

Sometimes manufacturers give additional written warranties on a product. These are the warranties that fall out of the box and that you must complete and mail for the warranty to take effect. Again, these warranties may contain some limitations and may therefore be not worth accepting. You should read and understand the terms before signing and mailing these warranties. Remember, the additional written warranty cannot limit or exclude the statutory or implied warranties of your province.

Some examples of limitations to watch for are terms like these:

- ''For guarantee to be effective the purchaser must complete and return detachable portion of this card within fourteen days of purchase.'' If you neglect to return the card within the time limit, you will not be able to claim under this warranty for repairs.
- ''The customer is liable for any labour, postal, or carrying charges.'' This may greatly reduce the value of the warranty. If you live in Alberta and have to return a new refrigerator to Ontario for repair under the warranty, this warranty is worth nothing.
- ''The manufacturer's decisions about alleged defects are final.'' This means the manufacturer gets to decide whether to repair under the warranty or not. You could still go to court but, depending on the defect and the value of the product, it may not be worth it.
- ''This guarantee excludes all liability to compensate for loss or damages, however caused.'' This means you cannot claim against the manufacturer for the manufacturer's negligence. You should not accept a warranty that includes this type of statement.

You can cross out the terms of the guarantee or warranty you do not agree with, but manufacturers will not usually accept any alterations to their warranties. You must read and understand these warranties. If the warranty limits recovery in any way, do not sign or mail it.

Remedies for Breach of Statutory Warranties

Remedies depend upon provincial laws. The same legislation that imposes the implied warranties determines who is responsible for remedying the defect—the seller, the manufacturer, or both—and what remedies are available. Sometimes, if the product cannot be repaired, you may be able to reject the goods and get a refund if the defect is discovered within a reasonable time. If the product is repairable, you may have to give the seller or manufacturer a reasonable amount of time to repair the item—at no cost to the consumer. The type of remedy available also depends on the product. Manufacturers may replace defective coffee pots but will never replace a defective automobile.

The warrantor (the seller or manufacturer) is usually responsible for the costs of assembly or disassembly unless you agreed in writing beforehand to pay these costs (for example, if that was a term in the additional written warranty that you signed and mailed in).

In some provinces, if you are injured while using a consumer product, you may sue the manufacturer for personal injury occurring as a result of defects in the product. In the event that you suffer injuries from using a consumer product, you should obtain professional legal advice as soon as possible.

PURCHASING AUTOMOBILES

Major purchases like automobiles often give rise to major consumer complaints. Because the purchase of an automobile involves considerable expense, it is especially important for you to comparison shop, to check with consumer reports for information on the different types of vehicles and the frequency of repairs, and to check with other consumers about the performance of the automobile and the adequacy of the dealer's service. If you are financing the purchase of an automobile you should know and understand the terms of credit (see Chapter 1).

Buying a New Automobile

One of the problems you may face when purchasing a new automobile is understanding the warranty. New car warranties are made to sell cars, not to repair them. Hence, many consumers are surprised to find that the manufacturer's warranty does not cover the expenses they expected it would. Automobile warranties, as with product warranties, usually cover only defective parts and not labour or damages that result from the defect (consequential damages). Therefore, when the car is in the service centre for repairs, you pay labour charges (often the most substantial part of the bill), plus your own travelling expenses while the vehicle is in the shop, plus your own towing charges (if any). Also, if the defect in the car caused an accident, the warranty covers only the repair of the defect and not the dented fenders that may have resulted.

New car warranties (express warranties) are often full of legal jargon that is difficult for the consumer to understand. But you are entitled to have the warranty fully explained by the dealer before making your purchase. It is a good idea to prepare a checklist of questions before talking to a dealer. Then, after comparison shopping, you will be able to make a more informed decision about which automobile to buy.

A checklist may include, among other things:

a) consumer reports
   • frequency and cost of repairs
   • average cost of maintenance
   • gas mileage
b) the warranty
   • labour coverage
   • parts coverage
   • consequential damages (car rental, towing, dented fenders)
   • expiry date (in months or kilometres)
   • frequency with which periodic maintenance checks are required for the warranty to be effective

The provincial statutory or implied warranties that apply to products also apply to automobiles. A manufacturer or dealer cannot limit or exclude these warranties. Hence, if the manufacturer's warranty expires in twelve months, you may still be able to recover for some defects after the twelve-month period if there is a breach of a statutory warranty. Suppose that something major goes wrong with the motor after fourteen months of normal use but the manufacturer's warranty expired after twelve months. You may be able to get the motor repaired under the statutory warranty of acceptable quality, because a motor is expected to last for a much longer period and it is a defect you could not reasonably have been expected to detect upon examination of the vehicle.

Occasionally, a manufacturer extends the length of the warranty for some defects. For example, suppose a particular model of car has a defect in the transmission. After a number of consumer complaints, the manufacturer "extends" the warranty past the original expiry date for the transmission system on that model. However, only the consumer who knows about the extended warranty can take advantage of it. Therefore, when something goes wrong with a new vehicle, you should always check for a manufacturer's extended warranty before taking it to a local mechanic and getting it repaired. If there is a major defect that you must get repaired immediately, you can later check with the manufacturer and get your money back. Any dealership will know if there is an extended warranty for a particular defect.

When problems arise with a new automobile, it is advisable to return to the original dealer, if possible, to have the defects corrected. Getting warranty work done by an independent mechanic may invalidate the warranty. If you have moved, you can go to the nearest dealer for your car make. If the dealer is not prepared to fix the defect under warranty or denies there is a defect, try to get the dealer to agree to an independent examination by another mechanic (for a price). You can then present the dealer with a written statement of what needs to be done. If the dealer will not agree to an independent examination, try some of the suggested techniques on complaining effectively discussed at the end of this chapter.

Buying a Used Automobile

Although there are some unscrupulous used-car dealers around, you can prevent most misfortunes by shopping wisely. Check consumer reports for the track record of many models of used vehicles. Before purchasing a used automobile, get it checked by a reliable mechanic. Although you will have to pay for this check, having it done can prevent a lot of problems in the future. If you cannot get such a check, add a term to the bill of sale that says: "Subject to mechanic's approval." Anyone selling a used automobile should not object to such a term unless there is something to hide.

Dealers often write "As is" on the contract of sale. This means the person buying the vehicle is aware of its mechanical condition. The term is used by the dealer to hold the consumer responsible for all damages or injuries caused by mechanical defects. You may still be able to collect for damages for defects if you can show the defect was serious enough that the dealer must have known about it at the time of the sale. However, generally you will have to go to court to collect for damages on an "As is" sale.

Remember that statutory or implied warranties apply to all consumer sales; this includes used automobiles when sold by a dealer. However, it is difficult to determine the "acceptable quality" of a used car. Ask the dealer to warrant, in writing, statements made about the condition of the automobile—for example, by writing the number of "original" miles or kilometres, or the condition of the motor, on the bill of sale.

Consumer-protection laws apply only to consumer sales by a dealer and not to private sales. Therefore, when buying privately, you must use extra caution. Getting a mechanic's approval and checking for liens is essential. A bill of sale that says "clear of liens" does not mean the vehicle cannot be repossessed if a former owner had a lien registered against the vehicle. The bill of sale is a contract between the buyer and the seller, so if the information on it is incorrect, the buyer may sue the seller (who may or may not be available when the vehicle is being repossessed). But the buyer cannot use the bill of sale to prevent a third party from repossessing the automobile. Some provinces have a registry system where liens must be registered by the automobile serial number. You are responsible for checking the registry or you may suffer the consequences. By checking available information in your province, you can determine whether there is a registry system for liens and how to check the vehicle you are purchasing. It is good practice not to depend on a loans manager or anyone else to check for liens; ultimately you are the one who will suffer if the delegated person forgets to check.

Repairing an Automobile

Before getting repair work done, shop around for a reliable mechanic. Check the consumer-complaint records of the Better Business Bureau, and ask neighbours and friends to recommend a reliable mechanic. For major repair work, it is a good idea to get estimates, but be aware that estimates are often low.

You should never sign blank order forms and should always insist on being notified before work not requested is done by the mechanic. It is a good practice to write "No further work without telephone authorization" on the service order.

When you are dissatisfied with the repair work, you should return to the same shop and demand that the work be redone. Most shops are concerned with their reputations and will try to satisfy you. Even when you are dissatisfied with the quality of repair, you still have to pay the bill or the garage may register a lien against your vehicle (which means the car may eventually be seized and sold). Find out the provincial laws through the consumer affairs department of your provincial government. Follow the guidelines for effective complaining provided below and, if necessary, get help from other agencies, organizations, or government departments. For a small repair bill, the consumer may go to Small Claims Court. For larger problems, you might require the services of a professional.

COMPLAINING EFFECTIVELY

Do complain, and complain at once. Although prevention is the key to consumer protection, problems do occur. If you follow use and care instructions properly and problems still arise, you have a responsibility to yourself and to other consumers to inform the business of your complaint. Make your complaint as quickly as possible. If you cannot return the defective product at once, telephone the business to let them know what has happened and when you are available. If you know your rights and responsibilities and those of the business, you will not be easily put off.

Get facts together and keep records. Always keep the original bill, receipt, warranty, and any letters you have written to the business. If personal or telephone contact is made, keep a record of the calls or contacts, the dates of each, and the details of each. Following up letters with personal contact allows the business to think of you as a real person. Having the information readily available eases discussions of the problem.

Talk or write to the appropriate person. It is a good idea to talk to the salesperson first, as that person may feel a sense of responsibility towards you. However, you may need to go directly to the manager if the salesperson seems unwilling or unable to resolve the matter.

Be specific and be polite. In writing or talking to the businessperson, clearly state the problem, the result you expect, and how soon you expect it. Being nasty or losing your temper may make you feel good, but it puts the other person on the defensive, and you may end up fighting a battle of personalities instead of resolving the issue.

Have a plan of action. Organize your action. Go to the salesperson or manager first. If you do not get any results, write to the president of the company and give a review of the entire complaint process to date. If you still do not get appropriate results, decide on the next step, which may be to contact a consumer group, a government agency, the media, Small Claims Court, or a lawyer. Your plan of action will depend on your particular situation. An organized plan of action is preferable to the scattergun approach of contacting every available source right away and sitting back and waiting for something to happen.

Do not give up. Some businesses may try to discourage you by giving you the runaround—by blaming the manufacturer (who in turn blames the seller), by not responding to your complaint, by using legal terms that no one can understand, by using the legal system for one-sided interpretation of the law, by blaming the consumer for the defect, by offering partial refunds, or by saying ''it's company policy.'' Do not accept a solution to your complaint that is less than appropriate and reasonable in the circumstances. Once you accept an offer of settlement, you cannot go back for more later. Knowing your legal rights and using appropriate agencies helps balance the power between the consumer and the business.

The Costs of Complaining

A defective toaster may warrant going to Small Claims Court but may not justify hiring a lawyer to sue the manufacturer. In addition to financial costs, there are physical and emotional costs of complaining. Waiting a year and a half to get house siding repaired is reasonable, but such a delay may not be appropriate for a defective iron. You may have to return to a business several times or write many letters before you are satisfied. If it is necessary and worth it—do it!

GETTING ASSISTANCE

Becoming an informed consumer takes time and energy: it involves more than reading a book or two. Consumers generally buy on impulse, sign contracts without reading them, and do not know how to handle a consumer problem when it occurs. Regardless of where you live, there are many community resources available to you.

Public libraries are a useful source of consumer information, covering everything from addresses of consumer groups and government agencies to copies of federal and provincial legislation. The library will also have books on the complaint process, including sample letters of complaint.

The *Consumers' Association of Canada* has publications containing valuable information on consumer products and services. The association provides self-help information and can direct you to the appropriate organization or agency for help with a particular problem.

Most provinces have *public legal education or information associations* that provide consumers with useful information and education on the laws and the legal system. These non-profit, non-government organizations offer assistance in the form of booklets, pamphlets, and free law classes that help people to become informed consumers.

The *Better Business Bureau* works to respect and protect the rights of both the consumer and the business. It may help resolve legitimate complaints and can give complaint reports on businesses.

Each *provincial government* has a department of consumer affairs that supplies information and self-help guides to encourage competent and confident consumers. These departments administer the consumer legislation for the province and can provide the names of the statutes that affect you.

The *federal government's* Department of Consumer and Corporate Affairs administers laws dealing with health, safety, and other standards.

Small Claims Court is an informal and inexpensive method of resolving disputes without the aid of a lawyer; the court staff and judge provide assistance in presenting claims if a lawyer is not present. Contact the nearest Provincial Court to get the information needed to take a claim to small claims court. The maximum amounts of a claim that can be settled in Small Claims Court vary from province to province (from $3,000 to $10,000).

Professional assistance may be required if the problem involves a major consumer purchase or personal injury that justifies the expense of expert legal advice.

CHAPTER 3

HOUSING AND REAL ESTATE

Thelma Costello

Thelma Costello is a graduate of Dalhousie Law School and a member of the Nova Scotia Barristers' Society. She has been Executive Director of the Public Legal Education Society of Nova Scotia since 1982. The PLE Society provides information and resources on the law to Nova Scotians.

THIS CHAPTER DEALS WITH the law of "real property," the area of law that covers buying, selling, renting, and leasing land and buildings. This area of law takes up many hardcover volumes in most law libraries, but is dealt with here in relatively few pages. The information in this chapter is general and intended to provide a framework to help you find further information when you need it. Only the law relating to residential (as opposed to commercial) property is explained. You'll learn about renting an apartment, boarding, renting public housing, joining a non-profit co-op, and buying a house or condominium.

RENTING

When you decide to rent a house, an apartment, or a room in a rooming house, you enter into a contract with the landlord. The contract need not be in writing, but when it is, it is called a *lease*. In its simplest form a rental agreement or lease states that you have the right to exclusive use of a specified house or apartment for a certain period of time in exchange for a payment of rent to the landlord.

The relationship between landlords and tenants has its origins in the English feudal system. In the past, tenants have usually been the losers in disputes with landlords, but that has changed in recent years with the passing in most provinces of laws governing relations between landlords and tenants. In your province the law may be called the *Residential Tenancies Act* or the *Landlord and Tenant Act*. In Quebec, the Civil Code governs this area. Usually these laws are administered by the provincial departments of consumer affairs, and often a mediation service as well as a board or tribunal to settle disputes has been established by the government.

Before signing a lease or agreeing to rent an apartment or house, be sure you understand what is expected of you, and what you can expect from the landlord. Some of the rights and responsibilities are set out in law and cannot be altered, while others are created by mutual agreement between you and your landlord. For example, most provinces require that the landlord keep the premises in a reasonable state of repair, but whether the landlord must paint the premises or shampoo the rugs before a new tenant moves in often depends on the agreement made with each tenant. The premises may still be in a reasonable state of repair even though the paint is an ugly, institutional green and the carpets are stained.

Before entering into a lease, you should carefully inspect the premises. It's a good idea to make a written list of the condition they're in, noting repairs needed, damage from previous tenants, and wear and tear. (Does the toilet flush properly? Are there marks on the walls? Do the appliances work?) Both you and the landlord should sign the list, so if any dispute arises later about who caused damage, it can be resolved quickly.

The Tenant's Rights

Once you sign a lease and move in, you have the right to exclusive use of the premises. Unless you agree otherwise, the landlord must give you (usually) twenty-four hours' notice, in writing, before entering the premises. If you've given notice to move out or if there is an emergency such as a fire, the landlord may enter, without written notice, to show the apartment to prospective tenants or to handle the emergency.

You are entitled to have premises that are kept in a good state of repair (in practice the definition of "good" depends on where you live, but the standard is not generally very high), and to enjoy them without interference by other tenants or the landlord.

Your landlord must give you notice in writing (''notice to quit'') in order to evict you. The amount of notice depends upon the terms of your lease, or, if you have no lease, upon how often you pay rent. If your lease is for a fixed period (such as January 1 to December 31) you cannot be evicted as long as you do not breach any of the terms of the lease. However, unless you take some steps to renew the lease, the landlord can expect vacant possession on the last day.

Your lease may contain special provisions for ending it before the term is up. Read it carefully! If you have no lease, the notice that you are entitled to receive depends upon whether you pay rent on a weekly or monthly basis. If your rent is in arrears, the notice-to-quit period will be drastically shortened, perhaps to almost nothing.

In some provinces there are guidelines governing rent increases. Check to see if your province has rent-control or rent-review laws. In provinces with such laws, a landlord might be able to raise the rent by only a certain percentage and must apply to a board or tribunal for permission to raise it further. Even if your province does not have rent control or rent review, it may have laws that do not allow rent increases more often than once every twelve months. And, in many provinces, the landlord must give up to three months' notice of any rent increase.

Whether you have a right to sublet your apartment depends on the conditions in your lease. Subletting occurs when you have someone take over a portion of your lease (e.g., you go away for three months during the summer and return to your apartment in the fall), or when you move out entirely and someone else moves in. You may still be responsible for the apartment and for the rent payments should the person who sublets default. Most leases require that you get the landlord's permission before subletting. Your landlord can't unreasonably withhold consent, but can expect you to find a new tenant who will take good care of the property and pay the rent promptly.

A final and very important right you have is the right not to be discriminated against because of your race, religion, creed, colour, ethnic origin, sex, disability, or, in many provinces, source of income. Only Quebec and Ontario prohibit discrimination on the basis of sexual orientation. Human rights laws in most provinces don't allow landlords to refuse to rent apartments just because they don't like the colour of your skin or your racial origin. Unfortunately, in many provinces landlords can refuse to rent to you because you have children. Age is not a prohibited ground of discrimination in most provinces, so human rights laws cannot stop landlords from insisting on adult-only buildings. Only Quebec, Manitoba, and the Northwest Territories prohibit discrimination on the basis of age. And at the time of writing, Ontario was proposing to change the law so that landlords cannot discriminate against families with children. Check with your provincial human rights commission for further information about your province's protections.

Your rights as a tenant are tempered by responsibilities. You must keep your premises clean, pay your rent on time, repair damage you or your friends may have caused, and meet any other obligations you and your landlord may have agreed upon. You must give written notice if you plan to move. If your lease is for a fixed period, such as a year, you are obliged to pay the rent for the full year regardless of whether you actually live there. You can attempt to sublet if you must vacate, and the landlord is obliged to make reasonable efforts to let the premises and reduce the loss if you move out, but in the final analysis, you are responsible for the whole term of the agreement.

The Landlord's Rights

The landlord's rights mirror the tenant's duties. The landlord is entitled to expect the premises to be looked after, the rent to be paid on time, and the tenant to behave in a reasonable fashion. The landlord also has the right to request a security deposit, which often amounts to a portion of the monthly rent or the last month's rent in advance and is intended to cover damage or rent arrears. The maximum security deposit that can be charged is set out in your province's legislation. Usually the security deposit must be paid back with interest, and the landlord must have permission from the residential tenancies office (or the courts) to apply the deposit to damages or rent arrears.

The landlord also has responsibilities. In some provinces, for example, the landlord must give the tenant a copy of the lease and a copy of the relevant provincial legislation covering landlords and tenants. The landlord must abide by rent-review or rent-control guidelines where they exist, and must maintain the premises in good repair and ensure that essential services (heat, electricity, water) are maintained (unless you have agreed to pay separately for these items).

Insurance

The landlord will insure the property for damage resulting from fire or storms. However, the landlord's insurance will not cover your personal possessions as a tenant, nor will it cover expenses you may incur if you are forced to live elsewhere while your apartment is repaired or cleaned. You should arrange your own insurance to cover these situations.

BOARDING

If you decide to board with a family or friend, different rules apply from those applicable to tenants.

Usually, residential tenancies or landlord and tenant laws do not apply to boarders and lodgers. The law views boarders as "licensees" who are given a personal right to use property in a special manner. The main difference is that a boarder does not have the sole right to occupy the premises to the exclusion of all others. As a result of this fundamental difference, the legal protections given to tenants do not apply to boarders. Do not confuse "boarding" with having a room in a rooming house. If you have an exclusive right to even a part of a building, you are a tenant, and have all of a tenant's protections.

Boarders are usually subject to "house rules," which may be quite arbitrary. Some provinces do not extend human rights protections to boarders where the premises rented consist of a room in a private house.

PUBLIC HOUSING

Public housing is accommodation established to provide low-cost rental units to families, senior citizens, or other special groups. Public housing is generally administered by housing authorities set up by a municipality or province. Subsidies are shared by Canada Mortgage and Housing Corporation (a federal Crown corporation), the province, and the municipality.

Rent charges are subsidized so that you pay 25 percent of your income for rent. Housing units are allocated to applicants on a point system. The system takes into consideration a number of factors, including the condition and adequacy of your present accommodation and the rent you are currently paying in relation to your income.

Even though you are a tenant in public housing, you will probably not be covered by your province's rent-review or rent-control legislation, should it exist. You also may not be subject to your residential tenancies or landlord and tenant laws. Some provinces say that the lease you have with the housing authority, even if it conflicts with the landlord and tenant legislation (for example, with respect to notice-to-quit provisions) will govern the situation. You should, of course, read your lease with the housing authority very carefully before you sign it.

In a recent case in Newfoundland the court said that it was contrary to the *Charter of Rights and Freedoms* to exempt persons in subsidized rental housing from certain specific benefits in that province's *Landlord and Tenant Act* that are given to people in non-subsidized rental situations. If the ruling is upheld by the higher courts, it may affect public-housing laws across Canada.

NON-PROFIT CONTINUING HOUSING CO-OPERATIVES

A co-operative is a special type of corporation, adaptable to virtually any type of business. Housing co-operatives are in the business of owning and operating housing units for the benefit of their members. In Canada they have developed into a very specialized form of home ownership that in many respects is closer to a tenancy.

Almost all housing co-operatives operate with the assistance of a Canada Mortgage and Housing Corporation (CMHC) subsidy program. This scheme depends upon a co-operative's non-profit status and an intention to continue in operation for an indefinite term.

The following discussion is restricted to non-profit continuing housing co-operatives of the CMHC-supported type.

Housing co-ops have the following characteristics:

- The CMHC program allows a co-operative to obtain financing for 100 percent of its start-up, purchase, capital, and other "front end" costs.
- The members of the co-operative do not invest any personal funds other than a membership fee. The co-operative "rents" its units to members at operating cost. The rent usually includes all operating costs, a maintenance allowance, and a reserve or contingency allowance.
- The "rent" will vary from time to time as operating expenses change. The co-op sets an annual budget and determines the rent for each unit accordingly.
- The "rent" is based on a scale that varies with family income. There are fixed limits at the high and low ends of the scale. The high end of the co-op rent scale is approximately equal to the market rentals for similar units. Ideally, even the low-income co-op members should not pay more than 25 percent of their gross income for rent. This ideal is not achieved by all co-ops, but most come very close to it.
- Members cannot be evicted as long as they pay the rent and abide by the rules and regulations of the co-op.
- There can be no distribution of an operating surplus to the membership, except through a reduced rent in the next year.
- Management and financial control are provided by a board of directors elected by the membership from their number.
- Individual members do not share in any increase in the value of the property. A new member taking the place of a departing member is not required to "buy" the membership or pay any more than the fee required of any other member. If the co-operative is wound up, the profits on sale of the property are given to another co-op or to a charity. This general rule regarding non-participation in the equity or surplus of the co-operative by individual members also holds true when the mortgage is ultimately paid off. The "rent" may decrease because of the reduced operating cost, but no other change takes place.
- Individual members do not have any personal liability for the mortgage or other debts of the co-operative beyond the obligation to pay rent.

- A co-operative may require the payment of a refundable security or damage deposit.

A person wishing to become involved in a co-operative housing project may join an existing co-op or take part in the establishment of a new one. Co-op housing projects may renovate existing buildings or construct new ones. Co-op homes take every form: single family dwellings, town houses, flats, and apartment buildings.

The development of a co-operative housing project is a complex undertaking, usually completed with technical assistance from the CMHC and an independent housing-consultant group specializing in the field.

Co-op housing is aimed at low- and middle-income people. It is an attractive alternative to renting because of its relatively low cost and security of tenure. It may require a substantial input of time from members to manage the co-op's affairs.

OWNERSHIP

Traditionally, home ownership has meant owning a single family dwelling, or a duplex. This is still the ultimate housing goal for many of us, but now there are several other home-ownership options, including condominiums, home-ownership corporations, co-ownership agreements, and housing co-operatives. This section describes the ins and outs of each, particularly how to go about buying, what precisely you will own, and the rights and responsibilities that are associated with the property. This section deals only with purchasing a completed home. The issues and concerns related to new home construction could take another entire chapter. If you are selling a home, keep in mind the concerns of the purchaser, especially the need for you to pass on clear title.

Title
There are various forms of legal ownership (called "title").

Tenancy in Common
This is one of the simplest forms of joint ownership. You and any number of people, related or unrelated, may own a piece of property as tenants in common. Each joint owner has the right to possession

and use of the entire property. In effect, you have an undivided part interest. When you die, your share passes to your estate. The value of your share will usually be in proportion to your payments for the property, although you may make an agreement (in writing) with the other tenants to allow for a different division.

Joint Tenancy

A joint tenancy is basically the same as a tenancy in common, except that it has a right of survivorship. This means that if you die, your joint tenant or tenants will automatically inherit your share. It will not go into your estate. This is the most common form of title used by husbands and wives, although matrimonial property legislation in most provinces secures both spouses' interest in the matrimonial home (and other assets) even if title is held by one spouse alone.

Matrimonial Property Laws

Family law reforms affecting matrimonial property have had a significant effect on married persons' property rights. In provinces where reforms have been instituted, it is virtually impossible for the spouse who holds title to the matrimonial home to sell or encumber it without the consent of the other spouse. Generally, both spouses must sign all documents relating to the sale or mortgaging of a matrimonial home.

The proceeds from the sale of property considered to be matrimonial property usually can be "traced" by the courts so that a spouse cannot be deprived of his or her rightful share. (See Chapter 7, "Separation and Divorce," for further information on the effect on matrimonial property of marriage dissolution.)

The Deed

Title is set out in the deed, which is the formal document transferring title to the property. The deed states the names of the sellers (the "grantors") and the buyers (the "grantees"). It indicates whether the grantees are taking title as "joint tenants" or as "tenants in common." Deeds always contain a legal description of the property setting out the boundary lines.

The most common forms of deeds are "warranty" and "quit

claim." In a warranty deed, the grantors guarantee to the grantees that they have both good title to the property and the right to sell it. The grantors in a quit-claim deed provide no guarantee. They simply say that they are releasing any rights they may have to the grantees without any statement about how extensive those rights may be.

Types of Home Ownership

Freehold

This is the simplest kind of home ownership to describe and is familiar to most people. It means that you own a particular piece of land and everything that is attached to it (the most important attachment is the house, of course!). In law, it is referred to as a "freehold." The owner is responsible for all costs associated with the property, including mortgage, taxes, insurance, maintenance, repairs, etc. As an owner you may do what you want with the property (subject to local land-use laws); you may finance it, sell it, rent it, alter the buildings to suit yourself, or tear them down and build new ones (again, subject to local land-use laws). This type of home ownership is still the most common in Canada, but in areas where land costs are very high, the following forms of ownership are becoming much more common.

Condominiums

Condominiums, though a new and increasingly popular type of home ownership in Canada, have existed for years in Europe and the United States. They are usually in the form of apartments or town houses and are unique in two ways:
1. The condominium property is divided into two types of space. The separate units or apartments are individually owned. The common areas, such as driveways, elevators, and hallways, are owned in common by all unit owners.
2. The unit owners manage the property by forming a corporation. The individual owners are all shareholders. Each owner has a vote in the corporation.

In British Columbia, condominiums are referred to as "strata titles" and in Quebec as "co-ownership immovables."

The owners elect a board of directors to manage the property. The board usually hires a manager to look after the day-to-day work necessary for the upkeep of the property (such as common-area cleaning and lawn cutting). The board is responsible for seeing that repairs are done on the property and for insuring the property; it also manages any mortgage that may cover the building as a whole (but not the mortgages on individual units).

As a condominium owner you are responsible for the mortgage payments on your unit, the unit property taxes, insurance on the contents of the unit, and a monthly "condominium fee." This fee covers the costs of the mortgage and taxes on the common property of the building, common electricity costs, insurance on the building, maintenance, management, and a "reserve and contingency fund." The reserve and contingency fund is required by law to be at a fixed level to protect the owners from sudden and unforeseen expenses. When you sell your unit, the amount you have put into the reserve fund is added to the selling price so that you get back the unused portion of your contribution. The corporation can sue you if you do not pay the condominium fee.

Each unit owner gets a document with all the rules and regulations of the condominium corporation. Usually, this document must be approved by the province's registrar of condominums (or equivalent), and the condominium project itself must be registered. Remember that the rules are made by the vote of the owners, so if you do not like them, you have the right to attempt to have them changed.

Home-Ownership Corporations

A home-ownership corporation (sometimes called a co-op) is a corporation that owns a residential property, usually an apartment building. The shares of the corporation are owned by the residents of the building, one share per apartment. The value of each share is equal to the value of the apartment to which it is assigned. As a shareholder, you sign a lease that gives you an exclusive right to occupy one of the apartments in the building and the right to use the common areas of the building. The lease continues indefinitely, but it can be terminated if any of its terms are broken.

The corporation is managed by the shareholder/occupants according to a shareholder's agreement in the same way as any other company. A board of directors elected by the shareholders is responsible for day-to-day management, maintenance, and so on.

The home-ownership corporation takes out a mortgage (often called a blanket mortgage) on the whole property. You are required to make a monthly payment to cover your share of the blanket mortgage and the maintenance fee that covers taxes, heat, common electricity, insurance, administrative costs, and a reserve and contingency fund for sudden or unforeseen expenses. Reserve and contingency funds may not be required by law, but provision for such funds is usually made in the lease or shareholders' agreement.

As with a condominium, you are responsible for maintaining and insuring your own unit.

The home-ownership corporation is very similar to a condominium in many ways, but there is a fundamental difference. A shareholder in a home-ownership corporation does not own any land. You have no deed and pay no direct property taxes; you own only a share in a company. Much of the security and protection available to those who own land or a regular condominium unit are not given to shareholders. Be sure you understand what you are paying for and what your rights and responsibilities are.

Co-ownership Agreements

The sharing of a single house by two or more owners has always been very common. The co-owners have usually been spouses who depend upon their matrimonial relationship to resolve financial and property-management issues. However, many single women now see the joint purchase of a house or condominium as an attractive idea, since they might not individually be able to afford to buy. A co-ownership arrangement looks attractive because it allows you to get out of the apartment-rental market and into home ownership at only a portion of the cost of purchasing a single-owner property.

Co-ownership arrangements potentially offer considerable benefits, but careful thought and planning must be devoted to details before the investment is made. The comments that follow address small co-ownership arrangements, such as those involving only two or three parties. The same principles apply to large-scale co-ownerships, but the practical problems are considerably greater if more parties are involved.

Co-owners usually own the property directly, in their personal capacities. Their respective shares or interests will be characterized legally as a "tenancy in common," which allows each share to be transferred to the owner's heirs on death.

This type of ownership arrangement does not give, in law, an exclusive right to a physically defined part of the property. Rather, each co-owner has an "undivided interest" in the whole property. The rights of exclusive possession of certain areas and the common responsibilities of the co-owners must be handled by way of a separate agreement.

The costs of purchasing the property as co-owners will be the same as for an ordinary real-estate transaction, except that the expenses of preparing the agreement must be added in.

If the co-owners mortgage the property, each will be responsible for the whole mortgage debt. The mortgage company will have its choice of looking to everyone together or to any one of the individuals to make good a default. The co-owners do not have the option of mortgaging each of their interests separately, as condominium owners do, nor are they protected by any "limited liability."

Co-owners should discuss and agree upon several aspects of their relationship, and ask a lawyer to prepare a written agreement before the property is purchased. This agreement is limited only by the foresight and ingenuity of the parties, but should at a minimum cover the topics in the following checklist:

TERMS OF A CO-OWNERSHIP AGREEMENT

a) relative contributions to the down payment and initial costs
b) proportions of ownership held by each party
c) the rights of each party to exclusive occupancy of a portion of the property
d) rights and obligations with respect to common areas
e) decision-making procedures
f) budgeting, contributions to operating costs, and financial management
g) maintenance and renovations

h)   the degree of freedom each of you may have to sell your share
i)   the possibility of, and terms of, a forced or voluntary "buy-out" of one party by the remaining parties
j)   a method for fixing the price in the event of a buy-out or a sale of the whole property
k)   sharing of profit (or loss) upon sale
l)   possibility of, and terms of, any subletting by one or more parties to an outsider
m)   insurance provisions and liability for third-party injuries
n)   your liability in the event of failure to meet your share of costs or responsibilities and the corresponding remedies of the remaining parties
o)   a procedure for resolving differences of opinion

If the management of the property is to proceed by consensus or unanimous agreement, differences may be resolved by referring the problem to an independent third person. If the co-owners cannot agree on a third party, each may nominate a person, and those nominees will choose an appropriate person. However, it is probably fair to comment that if the relationship between the co-owners has deteriorated so badly that they cannot even agree on an arbitrator, the final decision will not be very helpful.

The relationship between co-owners is often more personal than businesslike. The process of discussion and reaching a co-ownership agreement is, in itself, a useful exercise in preventing later misunderstanding.

The most troublesome problems will likely arise in discussions about buy-outs and sale of property. These areas should be carefully thought out when the agreement is drafted.

Your investment in a co-ownership arrangement is reasonably secure and stands a good chance of appreciating in value as long as all of the parties remain in agreement about when to sell. However, it is difficult if not impossible to sell a partial interest in a house without the co-operation and consent of the remaining co-owners. If you wish to leave you may find that your investment, though secure, is difficult to liquidate. One of the major problems of co-ownership is in achieving a balance between the interests of the person who wishes to sell out and those of the person who wants to stay on.

It is possible and sometimes advisable to purchase the property through an incorporated company, an incorporated co-operative, or a partnership; this will result in a legal structure very similar to a home-ownership corporation. Such a structure may be unnecessarily complicated for a two, or three-party agreement, but as the number of parties becomes larger the use of a corporate vehicle makes sense. It provides a relatively rigid management and financial structure. If there are more than two or three units in the property, if the parties anticipate a regular turnover in their number, or if there are a few co-owners of a relatively large apartment complex renting some units to outside tenants, a corporate entity might be the answer.

Financing Your Purchase

The Cost of Buying a Home

It is important to understand what is involved in a house purchase.

The following table illustrates the typical cost of purchasing a modest, detached bungalow in a suburb (or a property of similar value):

Table 3:1   Typical Cost of House Purchase

House price	$87,500
Closing costs	
• legal fees	1,000
• survey	175
• deed transfer tax (1%)	875
• moving costs	750
• mortgage-insurance-application fee	250
• mortgage-insurance premium (at 2.5%)	1,950
Total Cost of House	$92,500
Maximum Mortgage Available*	$79,950 (includes mortgage-insurance premium)

Down payment required $12,550

---

*for a high-ratio mortgage (a mortgage for over 75 percent
of the value of the property)

Arranging a Mortgage

Most buyers of a home have to borrow a substantial portion of the
cost. This loan is called a "mortgage." The institution that lends
you the money (usually a bank or trust company) is the "mortgagee." You are called the borrower or "mortgagor," and you transfer
the title to your home to the mortgagee on the condition that once
the loan is repaid the title is transferred back to you. The mortgagee
keeps the title to the house as security while you repay the loan.
Although the mortgagee has title to your home, you can use and
occupy the house while you are repaying the loan.

A mortgage loan has three characteristics:

1. *Term.* The term is the period of time a borrower has before the
   lender can demand the principal balance owing on the loan. The
   term is usually between one and five years and the interest rate
   is normally established for this term. Legally, at the end of the
   term, the lender is entitled to ask you to repay the entire amount
   of the mortgage loan that is outstanding. However, this rarely
   happens. It is obviously to the advantage of the lender to keep
   you as a borrower for a new term at the current interest rate, if
   you agree.

   A mortgage term may be closed or open. A "closed-term"
   mortgage is one that cannot be paid off in advance or before the
   term expires. If you are permitted to pay off the loan in advance,
   you may have to pay a penalty fee. An "open-term" mortgage
   provides for the prepayment of the loan without a penalty. Open-
   term mortgages usually have higher interest rates than closed-
   term ones. They are attractive if you expect to sell your home
   before the term ends or if you expect interest rates to fall during
   the period of the mortgage.

2. *Amortization period.* This is the period of time required to reduce
   the debt to zero assuming a fixed level of monthly payments.
   Amortization periods are usually between twenty and thirty years.
   The shorter the amortization period, the higher the monthly payments will be and the less the total amount of interest paid.

3. *Interest rate*. This is a charge for borrowing money. It is generally a percentage of the amount borrowed. The rate is affected by the size of the amount borrowed and the length of time over which it is borrowed.

Your monthly mortgage payments are based on how much it would cost per month to pay back the principal (the amount borrowed) plus the interest over the complete repayment period.

You may wish to take over payment of the vendor's mortgage instead of getting your own loan. This is called "assuming" the mortgage. This may be useful if the interest rate on the vendor's mortgage is lower than those currently available.

If you assume the vendor's mortgage, you may still need to borrow money to pay the difference between the purchase price of the property and the existing mortgage. Your loan is called a "second mortgage," and you will have to make two payments, one on the assumed mortgage and the other on your second mortgage. (You might also take out a second mortgage to cover the cost of renovating or repairing your house.)

Generally, it is best to have a large down payment on your house and a short term for repayment. This will make your monthly payments higher, but the saving in interest will be substantial.

When you are buying a house you must consider how large a down payment you can make and how much you can afford in monthly repayments. In the examples given below the following assumptions have been made.
1. The purchase price of the house is $80,000.
2. The mortgage interest rate is 12 percent.
3. The maximum you can afford to repay monthly is $850.
4. You have savings of $15,000 with which to make a down payment.

Table 3:2 shows the difference a large down payment can make to the overall amount.

Striking the Deal

A home is usually the largest purchase you will make, and the need for professional assistance can't be emphasized too much. You should definitely hire a lawyer to ensure that you have legal title to the home and that your offer has all the important terms. Your lawyer will prepare all the documents, deal with the financial in-

Table 3:2   20-Year Mortgage Term

	With $10,000 Down Payment	With $15,000 Down Payment
	$	$
Amount of mortgage	70,000.00	65,000.00
Monthly repayments	770.70	715.65
Total repayments over mortgage term	184,968.00	171,756.00
Deposit	10,000.00	15,000.00
Total overall cost	194,968.00	186,756.00

Table 3:3 shows the savings that can be made by shortening the mortgage term to fifteen years and increasing the monthly payments.

Table 3:3   15-Year Mortgage Term

	With $10,000 Down Payment	With $15,000 Down Payment
	$	$
Amount of mortgage	70,000.00	65,000.00
Monthly repayments	840.00	740.00
Total repayments over mortgage term	151,200.00	140,400.00
Deposit	10,000.00	15,000.00
Total overall cost	161,200.00	155,400.00

stitution, work with the other party to close the deal formally, and handle the transfer of funds.

In provinces where there is a registry system (see ''Title Searching'' later in this chapter) the lawyer's most important function is to provide a certificate of title. In provinces with a land-titles system, the government provides a certificate of title. The institution you go to for your mortgage will demand it, and if you later sell, you will need to prove you have clear title to pass on. If you don't, and your lawyer certified title when you bought, you may be able to sue the law firm to recover the loss that might result from your inability to sell.

A real-estate agent can help you find a house. But bear in mind that the agent is working for the seller and receives a commission on the sale of the house. Therefore, you should check out the condition of the house or have an appraiser or friend who knows about furnaces, plumbing, and the like do it for you rather than rely on any claims made by the seller or the agent.

Offer to Purchase
The standard form used when you make an offer to buy a home is called an "offer to purchase." The contents of this form should include:
- identification of the buyer and seller
- identification of the property
- date of closing
- price offered
- amount of deposit
- list of extras included in the purchase price (carpets, drapes, etc.)
- any conditions that restrict the offer (e.g., the offer may be subject to selling your current home or to your getting a mortgage)

Your offer may be a "conditional offer," which means that your offer to purchase property depends on whether some other event takes place. For example, you may wish to sell your present home first or get financing at a certain interest rate before the contract becomes binding. If the conditional offer is accepted, the contract becomes binding once the conditions are fulfilled. Any conditions must be written into the offer.

Have your lawyer check over your offer *before* you sign it, even if only over the phone. Once the vendor (seller) accepts your offer by signing it, the terms or conditions in the offer cannot be changed except with the consent of both you and the vendor. All terms or conditions *must* be in writing. Verbal terms are not binding in a contract for the sale of real estate.

After the vendor has accepted your offer to purchase, the document is called an "agreement of purchase and sale." In the agreement, you, the buyer, agree to buy the property and the vendor agrees to sell it subject to certain conditions.

Buyer Beware

Here are a few things that you should be careful of:

1. You are buying what is described in the offer to purchase. Any "extras" or things not attached to the house (curtains, appliances) that are to be part of the sale should be written into the offer, so that there can be no misunderstanding later.

2. Arrange for an inspection of the house for any defects before you make an offer. You are legally protected against defects only if the real-estate agent or the vendor deliberately misled you about the condition of the property. The agent or the vendor must not make any misleading statements about the property. For example, the agent or vendor should not tell you that a home has been completely rewired if only the ground-floor rooms have been rewired. If you have been misled, you may take legal action and sue the agent or the vendor for damages.

   However, unless you have been deliberately misled, you are responsible for finding any defects in the property. You should take into account the cost of any necessary repairs before you make your offer to purchase.

3. You must get "clear title" to the property when you buy it, which means the vendor must sell the property free of any claims or mortgages. These must be paid off before the property is transferred to you. The standard-form purchase-and-sale agreement usually contains a clause stating that the sale is subject to availability of clear title.

4. Zoning by-laws enacted by the municipality may restrict the use of your home. Check these regulations before you make an offer. These by-laws might prohibit you from making certain renovations or having a boarder or using the house for commercial purposes.

The Deposit

If your offer is accepted by the vendor and you both sign the agreement, you will pay a deposit (usually 10 percent of the purchase price) to the vendor or to the real-estate agent. The deposit will be held in trust until the sale is complete.

Closing the Deal

Once all the conditions you set out in your offer are met, the sale of the house can be completed. This is called the "closing." On the closing date specified in the agreement of purchase and sale, the buyer must pay the outstanding purchase price to the vendor. The vendor transfers ownership of the house to the buyer by delivering the deed and the keys. The deed must then be registered in the buyer's name at the registry of deeds.

The costs involved in closing include the lawyer's fees, the fees for a title search on the house and for the registration of the deed, and the deed transfer tax. You may have to share with the vendor some of the costs that are computed annually. Your lawyer can make "adjustments" by calculating the annual charges (such as municipal taxes) and dividing them between you and the vendor. For example, if you close the deal on the first of March, the vendor would pay municipal taxes for the first two months while you would pay for the remaining ten months.

Title Searching

The most crucial aspect in any property transaction is the title search. Without clear title a property is next to impossible to sell, and generally impossible to mortgage. Clear title means that no one else has any claims against the property you wish to purchase.

Title documents and claims against real property must be registered in each province with a central agency. In Canada there are two methods of recording interests in land—the land-titles system and the registry system. The registry system prevails in the eastern provinces, Quebec, part of Ontario, and Manitoba. In the other provinces, the remaining part of Ontario, and the Northwest Territories the land-titles system prevails.

The land-registry system is older and more complicated than the land-titles system, but the bottom line with both is that *any* claims against land must be registered with the appropriate agency or the claim will be useless. Claims include liens, judgments, and mortgages.

Your lawyer should ensure that any questions about the validity of title are cleared up prior to closing.

Surveys

A recent survey of the property you wish to buy is usually required by the institution lending you the purchase money. If you have any questions about the extent of the property, the location of the boundaries, and whether there are any encroachments onto the property or onto an adjoining property, you should call in a surveyor or request a survey from the vendor. If there is no recent survey available, who will pay for a new one is a point for negotiation between you and the vendor.

There are two kinds of survey—a location survey and a boundary survey. The location survey tells you that the buildings are entirely within the boundaries of the property, but does not define the boundaries exactly. A boundary survey provides a detailed description of the size of the lot, the exact location of the boundaries, and whether there are any encroachments such as easements, rights of way, fences, mutual driveways, hedges, or widened roadways.

Your lender will most often be interested in obtaining a location certificate rather than a full boundary survey. If you are buying a condominium, a survey is not required, since the registry office will already have a survey for the whole complex.

A survey will not tell you the condition of the buildings or the relative value of the property. Also, don't confuse the survey certificate with the certificate of title. They are entirely different documents for different purposes.

Taking Possession

The closing is complete. Now you're a proud owner and ready to move in! Your lawyer will have obtained the keys (or some other mutually agreeable arrangement will have been made to get the keys to you).

You should make an inspection to ensure that no fixtures were taken (one vendor tried to take the rosebushes out of the garden, and another removed the wall-to-wall carpeting!) and that any extras included in the purchase price (such as dishwasher or drapes) are in the house. In some provinces it is common to inspect just prior to closing, preferably after the vendors have moved their furniture out.

You'll have to arrange for the electricity, telephone, water, cable TV, and oil or gas to be uninterrupted but transferred to your name.

The post office will re-route your mail for a certain period of time for a small fee, until your friends and creditors record your change of address.

Ownership of a home brings with it special responsibilities. Make sure your insurance covers more than just protection against fire or theft. It should provide protection if a neighbour or friend is injured on your property, perhaps by slipping on ice or tripping over a loose board on the porch.

Your mortgage company will require that the house be insured for the full replacement value of the buildings. If you do not pay the insurance, the company can step in, pay the premiums, charge you interest on the amount paid, and look to you for the premiums.

In some municipalities you may be required to keep your yard tidy (i.e., free of old car bodies, junk heaps, or other "unsightly trash"), and some developments have "restrictive covenants." A restrictive covenant is basically a rule that goes with the property, if you buy the property you must obey the rule. Examples would be the banning of clotheslines or restrictions on the kinds of fences allowed or rules about exterior finishes of buildings.

Most of these matters should be checked out prior to purchase, so you aren't faced with surprises.

A Final Word

Ask a lot of questions! And don't be afraid to say you don't understand the answers! Ask for answers in easy-to-understand language. Lawyers, bankers, surveyors, appraisers, and real-estate agents have languages all their own that are usually unintelligible to someone outside their field. They are *all* profiting from your decision to buy a home, so don't be afraid to make them earn their fee. You'll be more comfortable with your decision and happier in your new home if you take the time to understand what must be done and why.

CHAPTER 4

WOMEN AND HEALTH

Mary Marshall

Mary Marshall has practised in the health law area since her call to the Ontario Bar in 1982. She has lectured at the Bar Admission course, and has participated in other Law Society educational sessions. In addition, she has been active in doing research and writing and in giving lectures for health care consumers and professionals. She has served as a volunteer board member for a number of groups involved in health issues with particular attention to mental health, and women and health.

FOR TOO LONG women have been deprived of a voice in their own health care. The situation has begun to change as women educate themselves and express their desire for new policies and procedures in this area. This chapter discusses the law as it pertains to women and health, so that women can be more aware of legal issues that directly affect their physical and mental well-being. First, we examine issues of general concern, including the Canadian health-care system and your rights as a patient within that system. Second, some issues of special concern to women—such as women's health products and the law relating to various aspects of childbirth—are considered. Great strides have been made in reproductive technology, and there now have been a number of live births resulting from artificial insemination by donor. On the other hand, women are still struggling for reproductive freedom, and the right to choose to have an abortion remains a controversial topic. Many health products, including contraceptives, can have adverse health consequences, and women are demanding more information so that they can make a truly informed choice. The situation is constantly changing, and it is crucial that we remain abreast of these concerns and developments in the legal regulation of reproductive issues.

THE CANADIAN HEALTH-CARE SYSTEM

Until relatively recently, health services in Canada were paid for the same way as any other commodity. This began to change in the 1950s and 60s with the introduction of a national program for medical insurance. The federal government offered to provide the provinces with 50 percent of the yearly costs of basic insured health services. In return the provinces agreed to insure basic hospital and medical services and also to provide health plans that met certain conditions pertaining to universality, comprehensiveness, accessibility, and public administration. Persons unable to pay premiums charged by a province would have a right to financial assistance.

A major step towards universality was taken in 1984. In that year the federal government passed the *Canada Health Act*. This legislation allows the federal government to deduct one dollar in transfer payments for each one dollar of extra-billing or user fees allowed by a province. The provinces were given until April 1, 1987 to stop extra billing and user fees and retrieve the money. As of July 1986, only two provinces, Alberta and New Brunswick, allow extra billing. In Ontario, the *Health Care Accessibility Act* was passed into law on June 20, 1986. This legislation forbids charging a patient more than the Ontario Health Insurance Plan, regardless of whether a doctor remains in the provincial plan.

The Alberta government reached an agreement with the Alberta Medical Association to end extra billing as of October 1, 1986. The Alberta government will also be advising hospitals across the province to discontinue the ten-dollar admission charge they now levy. The provincial legislation that forbids extra billing also provides for penalties if doctors charge more than the regulated rates.

Despite the advances made by the *Canada Health Act*, there are still a number of problems in health-care accessibility. The act includes the provision that "a province must insure all insured health services provided by hospitals, medical practitioners or dentists and where the law of the province so permits, similar or additional services rendered by other health care practitioners." Nursing, chiropractic, and other non-medical services are not automatically covered under the legislative change; however, a significant financial barrier to insuring these services is removed. It is likely that any effort by the provincial governments to include these services would be strongly resisted by the provincial medical associations.

YOUR RIGHTS AS A PATIENT

The law in Canada has developed a number of principles determining the rights of individuals in the health-care system. These relate to your rights as a patient to be informed about your medical treatments, to refuse treatment if you so choose, and to have the confidentiality of your medical records protected. Recent developments in the laws relating to mental health and prescription drugs have also afforded new rights to the patient.

Consent to Treatment

The general rule is that a patient must consent to any medical treatment before it is provided. In 1980, the Supreme Court of Canada set the basic rules for consent to treatment. In order for a consent to be valid, it must be an informed consent, the consent must be given voluntarily, and the consenting person must have the capacity to consent. In addition, the consent must relate to the specific treatment and to the person performing the treatment.

How much information is required? And of what type? Basically, the Supreme Court of Canada tried to strike a balance. A person needs to have enough information to know what he or she is consenting to and to understand some of the problems that may arise. On the other hand, the explanation should not be so lengthy or so frightening that a person will be deterred from undertaking a necessary treatment. It is a question of fact in each case. The court will look at each situation to determine whether objectively a person should have received more information and whether this particular patient asked questions indicating that more information was required than is needed by the average patient. After providing information, a doctor may ask a patient to sign a consent form. The patient may make changes to this form provided they are agreed to by the health provider.

There are some exceptions to the general rule that a patient must provide consent to treatment. Provinces have legislation requiring that patients be treated for communicable diseases whether the patient agrees or not. A health-care provider can give treatment in a life-threatening emergency where a patient is incapable of giving consent. Special rules apply in the case of a minor or a mentally incompetent person. Generally, the health-care provider must obtain substitute consent. In the case of a minor, consent is obtained from a parent or guardian. The nearest relative or guardian provides substitute consent for a mentally incompetent person. Also, special rules apply for mental-health facilities. The governing provincial legislation should be consulted.

If proper consent is not obtained, a doctor may be sued for negligence or battery. Most commonly a patient sues a doctor for negligence because the doctor did not give the patient sufficient information about the risks of the operation. For example, several negligence suits have reached the courts in which women have argued that their cosmetic surgeons did not give them sufficient information about the extent of scarring before performing the surgery. These are difficult cases to prove because it is usually the patient's word against the doctor's.

Access to Medical Records
Courts in Canada have consistently held that medical records are the property of the hospital. The hospital has an obligation to keep your medical information confidential. You may complain to a physician's governing body if your doctor releases information to a third party without your consent.

In general, it is within the hospital's discretion to decide whether to release information to you, or your personal representative. The situation is different if a court action, such as a claim for damages for medical malpractice, is started. At that time the rules governing court procedure may be used to compel the hospital to release the records.

There are provincial statutes that override the confidentiality requirements and require health-care providers to report certain information. For example, in Ontario a physician is obliged to report to the appropriate government authorities a patient who is abusing a child, a patient with a communicable disease, or a patient who is physically incapable of driving.

Mental Health

Women use the mental-health-care system more than men. Women outnumber men among depressives by more than two to one; women attempt suicide three times as often as men (although men succeed three times as often as women); and women have a much greater incidence of hysteria, phobia, and psychosomatic illness (including anorexia nervosa, which is almost exclusively a women's problem). Women take mood-altering drugs in general, and tranquillizers in particular, two to three times as often as men. The largest single group prescribed tranquillizers is unemployed women over thirty-five.

Research indicates that the status of women in society has a marked influence on their mental health. The highest rate of depression (the most prevalent women's mental-health problem) is found among working-class women. The incidence decreases with employment and also with involvement in other activities outside the home. Depression also correlates highly with other chronic problems, including poverty, wife battery, single parenthood, and the need to work while carrying all household responsibilities. Given these facts and statistics, the laws governing mental-health services are of particular concern to women.

Historically, these laws were designed to promote two purposes. First, society needs to be protected from "dangerous" people with psychiatric problems. Second, psychiatric patients need to be protected and cared for in an "asylum" because they are not able to look after themselves. The laws are based on these premises even though many psychiatric patients fall into neither category. Provincial mental-health legislation therefore has provisions governing involuntary confinement in a psychiatric hospital, forcible administration of treatment, and management of property during the patient's stay in the hospital.

Every province has legislation with procedures for involuntarily committing psychiatric patients. All the provinces agree that people should be confined who are mentally ill and who are suicidal, or who are physically assaultive towards others. Some provinces have additional criteria. In Ontario, you may be involuntarily committed if you have a mental disorder that will likely result in "imminent and serious physical impairment of the person." In Newfoundland, you may be certified if you are suffering from a mental disorder that requires hospitalization in the interests of your own safety, the safety of others, or the safety of property. In Saskatchewan, you may be involuntarily committed if you suffer from a mental disorder, are unable to understand and make an informed decision regarding the need for treatment or care or supervision, and are likely to cause harm to yourself or to others or to suffer substantial mental or physical deterioration.

In every province, the patient may be brought to the hospital for an assessment by order of a judge or a justice of the peace. In addition, your doctor may take steps to have you involuntarily committed. Most provinces also grant the police authority to bring a person to a psychiatric facility for examination by a physician.

Many persons are concerned about their rights once they are in the hospital. Will I be able to refuse treatment? Will I be able to pay bills and keep on managing my finances? What do I do if I think I shouldn't be in the hospital?

Every province has different guidelines. In Saskatchewan, the medical officer has full authority to determine the care and treatment to be provided to the patient. In Newfoundland, there is no treatment unless the patient consents, or, if the patient is incapable of providing consent, the next of kin or the Public Trustee agrees. In Ontario, psychosurgery may not be given to involuntarily committed psychiatric patients. If a patient is competent and refuses to consent to treatment, the doctor may apply to a review board to obtain consent. If a patient is incompetent, the doctor must first try to obtain a substitute consent from a family member. If there is no family member, or if the family member refuses, the doctor may apply to a review board.

The legislation across Canada varies widely. The governing act in each province should be obtained and examined carefully to determine when a doctor may override a patient's refusal. Many hospitals also distribute booklets or leaflets that explain patients' rights in an understandable form.

The legislation also deals with such matters as who will manage the patient's funds. In Ontario, the Public Trustee manages your funds if the doctor decides that you are incompetent. In Prince Edward Island, the Official Trustee assumes responsibility over the estate of incompetent patients in psychiatric facilities. Again, the legislation generally outlines who should assume control of the patient's assets.

Most provincial legislation provides an avenue for appealing the initial decision to confine the patient in a psychiatric hospital. In Ontario, the patient, or someone acting for the patient, applies to a review board. Similarly, a patient in Alberta applies to a review panel for cancellation of a certificate. In British Columbia, the application is to a judge of the Supreme Court. In Nova Scotia, a patient or next of kin or the Public Trustee may apply to a judge of the County Court.

Prescription Drugs

The major concerns with regard to prescription drugs lie in the areas of safety, understanding, and price. Fifty percent of drugs sold in Canada today have never passed modern tests to prove their safety or effectiveness. Most drugs are prescribed by their brand name as opposed to the generic name (e.g., Valium, as opposed to diazepam) thereby guaranteeing certain drug companies the sales of these drugs when other companies may be producing the same drugs at a much lower cost to the public. Research prepared for the Canadian Federation of University Women (CFUW) found that Canadian prescription drug prices are among the highest in developed countries. The CFUW concluded that drugs are currently priced at "several times the price they can be made available for." In addition, Canadian doctors are inadequately informed about the drugs they prescribe. Much of their information comes from the drug companies themselves, and many researchers allege that these companies will misinform doctors about serious side effects in order to maintain profits. These problems are being addressed at both the federal and provincial levels. In 1985, the federal Eastman Commission made a number of recommendations that would ensure the safety of prescription drugs. The commission suggested clear specifications for new drug submissions. It also recommended that the Health Protection Branch require greater control over new drugs and impose post-market studies on manufacturers as a condition for marketing. It was recommended that an expert committee, with support from the Health Protection Branch, be established to make the final judgment on approval for new drug submissions. With direct reference to public understanding, it was recommended that prescriptions be stated in "layman's" terms with clear instructions and a complete list of contents.

In conjunction with safety and comprehension, the issue of cost is also a matter of public concern. This is certainly an area in which the public has encountered confusion. In Ontario the *Drug Benefit Act, 1986*, gives the government the right to set the price of drugs, after discussion with the appropriate bodies. This will help the government to save money on the cost of giving free drug prescriptions to seniors and the needy. According to the *Prescription Drug Cost Regulation Act, 1986*, pharmacists are required to itemize drug labels revealing the price of the drug and the dispensing fee. Pharmacists will have to give consumers cheaper generic drugs unless a doctor specifies that a patient must have a certain brand-name product.

WOMEN'S HEALTH PRODUCTS

In 1980, there were reports of deaths from toxic shock syndrome. The sharp rise in the incidence of toxic shock syndrome from 1977 to 1980 coincided with the marketing of "superabsorbent" tampons. Rely, a brand name manufactured by Procter and Gamble, was associated with 71 percent of the cases. It was found to contain polyester foam chopped into tiny cubes, as well as carboxymethylcellulose, an absorbent organic material. Rely was pulled off the market in August 1980. However, in the ensuing publicity, many questions were raised about the testing, labelling, and marketing of women's health products. This section will examine these issues with regard to the health effects of feminine-hygiene products, pregnancy drugs, and birth-control products.

Feminine-Hygiene Products

Health Effects

1. *Tampons.* Tampon use has been associated with a number of problems.
   a) Tampon use has been linked with toxic shock syndrome. Toxic shock syndrome is a serious disease, with death resulting in a reported 7.8 percent of the cases.
   b) According to a report by Women's Health International, pressure imparted by tampons against the vaginal wall or over-drying of adjacent tissue may result in small ulcerations to the tissue.
   c) Bacteria may be introduced into the vagina by the method of insertion of the tampon. Withdrawal strings can act as "wicks" through which bacteria are transmitted to the vagina.
2. *Vaginal Sprays.* Spraying chemicals on the fragile membranes of the vaginal area can cause irritation and inflammation. There are no cleansing properties in vaginal sprays. Ingredients in the spray may make the vaginal environment vulnerable to other organisms.
3. *Vaginal Douches.* There is controversy about the health benefits of douching.
   a) Some reports suggest that interference with the vagina's normal secretions may enhance its susceptibility to infection.
   b) Douching during pregnancy can be dangerous. The effects of high pressure and air introduced into the uterus are potentially very hazardous. Any chemical poses a potential danger to the developing fetus. The douching liquid may carry an infection into the uterus and inner fetal membrane resulting in possible abortion or fetal death.

Testing, Labelling, and Monitoring

1. *Tampons.* As of May 27, 1981, tampons are classified as medical devices under the federal *Food and Drugs Act*. Under the legislation, data from studies attesting to the safety and efficacy of a new medical device must be submitted to the Health Protection Branch prior to sale. Special warnings regarding toxic shock syndrome are required on tampon packages. However, manu-

facturers are not required to report adverse reactions or consumer complaints. The Adverse Drug Reaction Reporting Program, which is the only formal monitoring mechanism, is seldom used for non-drug health products. Thus, despite the known hazard, there is no monitoring system in force with respect to the use of tampons. Ingredients are not listed on packaging, and may include acetic acid, polyvinyl alcohol, ethers, methylcellulose, phenol, sodium salt, paraffin oils, talc, polyurethane foam, and carboxylic acid salts.

2. *Vaginal Sprays.* Vaginal sprays are classified as ''cosmetics'' under the federal *Food and Drugs Act.* No pre-market evidence of safety or efficacy is required for cosmetics. The manufacturers need only notify the Health Protection Branch of the name of the cosmetic, its purpose, ingredients, and directions for use, within ten days of placing it on the market.

The label is required to include the name of the product, the manufacturer, and ''adequate directions for safe use.'' An additional requirement in the regulations is that vaginal deodorant sprays must carry a warning that the product not be applied to irritated skin, that it should not be used when using sanitary napkins, and that it should be discontinued if a rash or irritation develops.

3. *Vaginal Douches.* No warnings appear on commercial products regarding the dangers of douching during pregnancy. The testing and monitoring required under the *Food and Drugs Act* is the same as for vaginal sprays.

Use of Drugs During Pregnancy

Studies have shown that all drugs taken by a pregnant woman cross the placenta, and that fetal development is extremely sensitive to a wide range of substances. Much of this concern arose from the fact that two drugs prescribed to women, Thalidomide and diethylstilbestrol (DES), were later discovered to have had severe adverse effects on their offspring.

DES was hailed as a wonder drug in the 1940s and given to thousands of North American women and to women all over the world to prevent miscarriages. DES daughters face a number of possible health effects, including cancer, structural abnormalities in the reproductive organs, infertility, ectopic pregnancies, miscarriages, and premature births. The most common problem DES daughters face is difficulty in conceiving and carrying a pregnancy to term. Studies have found that DES sons also have a number of health abnormalities. More DES sons have undescended testicles, which greatly increases the risk of testicular cancer. They also have more sperm abnormalities, which may reduce fertility.

DES action groups have formed across Canada. These groups are encouraging Health and Welfare Canada to undertake a national public-education campaign through advertising, to establish a registry for DES exposed people, to support an information centre for doctors, and to tighten new drug laws.

A third drug, the anti-nausea medicine Benedictin, has recently been withdrawn from the market by the manufacturer. In 1980, the United States Food and Drug Administration (FDA) panel heard evidence that a number of studies linked Benedictin with birth defects in the offspring of women taking it during pregnancy. These studies have shown a small but statistically significant association between Benedictin and cleft palate, cleft lip, and congenital heart and limb disorder. However, many other studies failed to find evidence of an association between Benedictin and increased risk of birth defects.

The FDA panel concluded that existing data did not show an association between Benedictin and an increased risk of birth defects in humans, but noted a "residual uncertainty" in the available information and recommended further epidemiological studies. The Canadian Health Protection Branch arrived at the same conclusion.

In June 1983, the manufacturer of Benedictin announced that it would cease production of the drug as a result of "the publicity surrounding the hundreds of 'unjustified' lawsuits . . . and the increase in insurance premiums." At that time, two actions in the United States had resulted in damages being awarded for $750,000 and $20,000. The drug was not withdrawn from the drugstore shelves, but the manufacturer stated that it would request doctors not to prescribe it to new patients. Spokespersons for Health and Welfare Canada commented that the drugs were safe and that no connection had been found between physical abnormalities and Benedictin.

Birth-Control Products

The legislation with regard to birth control is integral to a discussion of women and health. When considering such a wide subject, it is necessary to break it down into subtopics. We will examine intrauterine devices (specifically the Dalkon Shield), Depo-Provera, oral contraceptives, and various other methods of birth control.

The Dalkon Shield

The Dalkon Shield, an intrauterine device (IUD) designed and manufactured by A.H. Robins, was removed from the market in 1975. An IUD works by causing a slight irritation in the uterine lining that prevents the implantation of the fertilized egg. While the Dalkon Shield was designed according to this same theory, it became linked with Pelvic Inflammatory Disease (PID), which can lead to sterility. Complaints about PID and other problems began to arise in the United States, culminating in the reported connection between the Dalkon Shield and numerous septic (spontaneous) abortions as well as the deaths of sixteen American women. Problems were caused by the Dalkon Shield's multifilament tail. While other IUDs had a solid, single strand for a tail, the Dalkon Shield's tail was composed of 200-450 filaments twisted together and coated with a sheath. It was believed that the tail acted as a wick, pulling bacteria up from the vagina and into the uterus.

When the product was pulled from the shelves, neither Canadian nor American governments demanded recall. None the less, the explosion of complaints led A.H. Robins to remove the device from the market. In Canada it is estimated that, between 1971 and 1974, 125,000 Dalkon Shields were sold.

In 1980 it was discovered that, six years after the device had been taken off the market, many Canadian women were still using the Dalkon Shield. Health and Welfare Canada issued warnings to physicians across the country.

While the findings in the early 1980s were shocking, it was even more surprising that A.H. Robins initiated a national information program in 1985. The campaign in the United States involved ads in 177 daily newspapers and 13 minority papers, television and radio commercials, and letters to 185,000 physicians. The Dalkon

Shield Removal Program was implemented in Canada through the Medical Offices of Health. Warnings about the device appeared in the *Globe and Mail*, the *Toronto Sun*, and the *Toronto Star*. Robins urged women to have the Dalkon Shield removed, agreeing to pay for costs incurred in the removal. However, many women did not know what type of IUD they were using.

In Canada, there have been no reports of lawsuits. However, in the United States there are thousands pending against A.H. Robins, and the company has set up a $614-million-dollar litigation fund. Judges in the United States have been very critical of the actions of senior officials of A.H. Robins. Robins continued to market the Dalkon Shield for a number of years after it was aware of the problems with the design. On February 29, 1984, Federal District Court Judge Miles W. Lord delivered the following remarks to senior staff of A.H. Robins Company:

> Under your direction your company has continued to allow women, tens of thousands of them, to wear this device—a deadly depth charge in their wombs, ready to explode at any time . . . We simply do not know how many women are still wearing these devices because your company is not willing to find out. The only conceivable reasons that you have not recalled this product are that it would hurt your balance sheet and alert women who have already been harmed that you may be liable for their injuries. You have taken the bottom line as your guiding beacon and the low road as your route. That is corporate irresponsibility at its meanest.

The Dalkon Shield is not the only IUD to cause women to experience infection, PID, and septic abortions. A group in Vancouver is lobbying to remove the Copper 7 from the market. While many lawsuits have been launched against the manufacturer, G.D. Searle, very few have been successful. The company claims that the device is effective in preventing pregnancy and that it is perfectly safe.

Depo-Provera
In November 1985, the Canadian Coalition on Depo-Provera protested to federal authorities over the licensing of Depo-Provera for use in birth control.

Depo-Provera is an injectable drug that is a synthetic copy of progesterone. If injected every three months, it acts as a contraceptive. Depo-Provera prevents both ovulation and menstrual bleeding by disrupting a woman's normal hormone pattern. It is currently used in the treatment of endometriosis and cervical cancer. In mental-health institutions it is also used for the treatment of sexual deviants to reduce sex drive. The World Health Organization and more than eighty countries use Depo-Provera for various therapeutic treatments.

In 1981, the Canadian and Ontario Association for the Mentally Retarded demanded that a ban be placed on the drug. This was a result of the death from breast cancer of three mentally retarded women who were being treated with Depo-Provera. After extensive investigation, Dr. R.A. Farmer, Co-ordinator of Medical Services for the Ministry of Community and Social Services in Ontario, found that there was little evidence to support a connection between Depo-Provera and the development of breast cancer. He also found that Depo-Provera was very effective as a long-acting injectable contraceptive. It is capable of preventing menstruation which, in profoundly retarded women, allows them to "continue their program development without interruption and to maintain a level of personal hygiene under very difficult and trying circumstances." Dr. Farmer recommended use of this drug both as a contraceptive and as a method to prevent menstruation among institutionalized women.

In the United States, however, the use of Depo-Provera as a contraceptive was stopped after lengthy hearings and public debates.

Oral Contraceptives

A serious concern in the area of oral contraception is that of consumer information. In April 1982, Carol Rosenberg of Toronto died of a blood clot connected with oral contraception. The inquest jury made a series of recommendations in August 1983, generally calling for greater written warnings to be made available to the consumer. Changes to the information distributed with the pills were suggested, stressing the importance of "layman's terms." The patient, stated the jury, should be warned of the physical changes and dangers that can occur after the patient begins taking the pill. Further recommendations suggested that the physician should provide the patient with specific information that would allow her to make an informed judgment.

Ms. Rosenberg's death contributed to the realization that public information regarding oral contraceptives needed revision. A Report on Oral Contraceptives was published by Health and Welfare Canada in September 1985. The report made many recommendations and observations. It identified the surprising evidence that, in many cases, oral contraceptives actually reduce the chance of contracting both some forms of cancer and Pelvic Inflammatory Disease. The studies revealed that the high-risk groups are: women who smoke, women with diabetes or high blood pressure, women over thirty-five, and women suffering from obesity. One of the most pertinent recommendations of the report was the need for extensive revision of the written material available to users.

In December 1985, the information distributed with oral contraception was published in its new format. Paradoxically, however, physicians are now concerned that the warnings are so detailed that patients may become confused and unnecessarily frightened. According to the government guidelines stated in the 1985 Report on Oral Contraceptives, the physician is now required to explain all of the dangers. Prior to this regulation, prescription and use were governed by the patient's medical history alone. Many physicians feel that this extensive information detracts from the professionalism of the doctor and may lead a woman to avoid using the pill when, in fact, it would be a perfectly safe choice.

These warnings will become essential in view of a landmark Ontario Court of Appeal decision in which a woman successfully sued Ortho Pharmaceutical (Canada) Ltd. The plaintiff in that case suffered a stroke at age twenty-three that left her paralysed. She had recently started taking oral contraceptives manufactured and distributed by the defendant, Ortho Pharmaceutical (Canada) Ltd. The plaintiff claimed that the defendant failed to warn her about the risk of stroke. The plaintiff was a non-smoker and in excellent health before the stroke. The Court of Appeal upheld the decision of the trial judge that the use of oral contraceptives probably caused or, at the very least, materially contributed to her stroke. The plaintiff was awarded substantial damages because Ortho Pharmaceutical (Canada) Ltd. had failed to warn consumers and their doctors adequately about the risk of a stroke.

Other Methods of Birth Control

Other methods of contraception include condoms, cervical caps, sponges, and a variety of new innovations. Each of these is addressed briefly below.

1. In a study conducted by Price Watch, in January 1981, "Contraceptive Shields" by Ortho, and "Ramses" by Julius Schmid were found to be the only condoms to meet Canadian Regulations. The condom is the only contraceptive device controlled by the federal government under the *Medical Devices Regulation Act* (oral contraceptives are controlled under the *Food and Drug Act*).

2. Health and Welfare Canada produced an unpublished study in 1984 on cervical caps. The study found that the caps may cause cervical damage and that they must be replaced every six months. The cervical cap does not require federal pre-marketing and, therefore, safety and quality are not regulated. The Bureau of Medical Devices study revealed that more durable and chemically resistant material may be necessary to improve safety.

3. A new sponge, patented under the name "Today," was introduced in the United States in 1983. At that time the company also sought Canadian approval for the device from the Federal Health Protection Branch. The sponge was found to be 85 percent effective, but the tests were not extensive enough to discount the danger of toxic shock syndrome.

4. According to an April 1, 1986 report in the *Toronto Star*, the latest advance in birth control is the Norplant. This "long-acting subcutaneous implant" is being developed in the United States. The implant is a time-releasing capsule containing synthetic progesterone that is said to last five years after a three-minute injection into the upper arm. However, insurance companies are reluctant to cover the implant after the millions of dollars claimed by women harmed by the Dalkon Shield.

5. Another innovation is the pregnancy vaccine that is currently being developed and tested in Australia and India. The vaccine works by blocking the access of sperm to the egg. Researchers suggest that the vaccine may be ready for use in as little as ten years.

6. The last area to be considered in connection with birth control is sex education. An Ontario Medical Association Report dated June 1981 examined teenage pregnancies and sex education in Ontario. It found that the school was the most important source of information and that sex education in schools had resulted in a decrease in the number of teenage pregnancies and abortions.

WOMEN AND CHILDBIRTH

The law relating to women and childbirth is currently undergoing dramatic and fascinating change as technology develops new means of intervention in the reproductive process and as women become more vocal about their rights to choose whether or not to have children and their right to deliver children with dignity. In the next few years we may expect to see a number of new developments in the law relating to midwifery, artificial insemination, surrogate motherhood, and abortion.

Midwifery

In October 1984, Daniel McLaughlin-Harris died two days after his birth began on Toronto Island. The birth was complicated because the baby was post-mature and became wedged in the birth canal. An inquest jury found that despite the expertise of three midwives attending the birth, the lack of sophisticated equipment and the thirty-minute transportation time to the hospital caused the death of the baby from asphyxia.

The jury made several recommendations. The jury felt quite strongly that midwifery should be legalized under the *Health Disciplines Act.* This would give a specific description of midwifery as well as penalties for unlicensed practitioners. The jury believed that midwifery should be recognized as a profession that is integral to our health-care system. Under legalization, it would be necessary to establish a governing body as well as a training or certification program. Training and standards of conduct would be established by the International Federation of Obstetrics and Gynecologists and the International Confederation of Midwives. Specific criteria for admission to the course were also suggested. The jury felt that licensing should be granted through a written examination and that midwives should be protected by malpractice insurance. It also saw a need for establishing birthing centres and standard equipment for all midwives. The conclusion of the jury was that the need for midwifery has been voiced by the public and that government legislation must respond to that need.

Under the current law in Canada, midwifery is neither legal nor illegal. This ambiguous status is further complicated by the acceptance and need for midwives who practise in remote areas of Canada. This is especially true in rural Newfoundland, the Northwest Territories, and northern Alberta.

The position of the Canadian Medical Association (CMA) was outlined in an article in *Health Care*: "While the CMA has no formal policy on midwives—they are tolerated so long as they are under the supervision of a medical doctor—the practice of planned home delivery is not sanctioned. As recently as August 1985, the association's general council adopted Resolution 85-39 which condemned home births. The resolution is as follows: Be it resolved that the Canadian Medical Association is opposed to home deliveries by midwives and doctors except where hospital based care is impossible and states that it considers any such step which would expose neonates and mothers to unnecessary high risk to be retrogressive and irresponsible."

While there are many contrasting opinions regarding midwifery, there are undeniable changes occurring in our health-care system. Advocates of legalizing the practice draw attention to these changes. Women today cannot expect the complete care from their family physician that women of the previous generation experienced. Today, because of the declining role of the general practitioner in urban hospitals, specialists are handling an increasing number of deliveries. The role of nurses is also changing, and they now are involved to a greater degree in health-care decision making. The situation of the low-risk pregnancy woman, however, is not changing. Her need to be involved in the decision-making process has not been addressed by our current system.

Studies have also shown that those countries with the highest proportion of midwives have the lowest perinatal mortality rates. A recent U.S. study, in examining 2.8 million births, found that the midwives were as competent as the doctors. In fact, they actually showed greater expertise in ''out of hospital'' deliveries.

In 1985 it was reported that the Quebec government planned to introduce legislation in the fall of 1985 that would establish the role of midwives as well as determine their required training. As of July 1986, action had not yet been taken.

The most current development in legislation for midwifery in Ontario was made by the Minister of Health in January 1986. He stated that midwifery will be legalized in the province and established a task force to recommend a framework for how it should be practised and the type of educational program best suited to training midwives. The task force consists of two lawyers, a family physician, and a nursing professor. While the Ontario Association of Midwives felt that the task force was composed of distinguished and worthy members, they were disappointed that a practising midwife and an informed consumer were not included in the group. The task force is examining midwifery in relation to training, scope, standards of practice, governance of the profession, location of practice, patient access, hospital status, and the nature of the service (independent or organized group).

Artificial Insemination

During the last decade, the legislation governing artificial insemination has been rigorously developed, examined, and revised. Amendments and additions to legislation have been made in many provinces.

In 1975, the British Columbia Royal Commission on Family and Children's Law published a report on artificial insemination. The intent of the commission was to protect all parties involved without making any value judgment on the issue itself. It recommended that, when conceived in marriage, the child should receive all of the legal protections and legal status of a child normally conceived, provided that consent to artificial insemination by donor (AID) had been granted by both the mother and her husband. The donor should remain anonymous and not be liable for financial support.

In order to ensure confidentiality of the child's origins, the commission recommended that the donor possess similar blood characteristics to those of the father and that the child's origins not be published on the birth registration or in the records of the Division of Vital Statistics. The commission also suggested that sperm banks should screen their participants in the program and that these banks should be run by "critical academic and professional authorities."

The Alberta Institute of Law Research and Reform published its "Status of Children" report in 1978. Because cases of artificial insemination had revealed fewer birth defects than had been expected, and because AID had not caused emotional upheavals in the participating families, the report stated that, "artificial insemination is a socially acceptable and beneficial medical procedure." The report outlined guidelines for AID centres. It also suggested that no legal relationship exists between the donor and the child and that children born through AID should be considered legitimate.

In 1981, the Law Reform Commission of Saskatchewan addressed the role of the physician in artificial insemination cases, stating that the physician should be considered liable if the child suffers injuries "en ventre sa mere" as a result of the physician's negligence. The commission clearly stated that if the husband does not consent to AID, the child's legal status would be illegitimate. Great emphasis was still placed on confidentiality.

Ontario's first test-tube-baby clinic was opened in February 1983. Canada's first in vitro fertilization (IVF) baby was born on Christmas day in 1983 out of Vancouver's Shaughnessy Hospital clinic. By 1985, IVF programs existed in four Ontario hospitals: Toronto East General, Toronto General, Chedoke-McMaster, Hamilton, and University Hospital, London. There are also clinics in Vancouver, Calgary, and Montreal. Canadian clinics are allowed to set their own rules, and the great cost of AID has come under criticism for contradicting the equal-accessibility principle of socialized medicine. Medical costs as well as lab-research costs are only partly covered by provincial health-insurance plans.

Outside of Canada, confidentiality is being re-examined. A law proposed in Michigan requires that the name and medical history of the sperm donor, the egg donor, the embryo donor, or the surrogate mother be made available to the child at the age of eighteen.

The law in Sweden states that it is illegal to preserve anonymity of the sperm donor. It is the right of the child to know his or her father, and doctors must therefore keep their records for seventy years.

Ontario lawmakers are now recognizing that perhaps the child should have the right to know his or her natural father. The long struggle to protect confidentiality may be abandoned. It cannot be denied that, whatever is decided, we have made significant progress from the 1921 legislation that regarded artificial insemination by donor as adultery.

Surrogate Motherhood

In 1982, a Florida woman was employed by a couple in Scarborough, Ontario, for the purpose of bearing them a child. The procedure seemed quite simple: the woman was impregnated by injection of sperm in a gynecologist's office, delivered the child in a Scarborough hospital, signed the release forms, and returned home.

Many legal problems resulted from this "simple" procedure. First, under the *Child Welfare Act*, the exchange of money related to obtaining a child for adoption (except legal fees) was prohibited. In addition, the Ontario *Vital Statistics Act* assumed that, legally, the Florida woman's husband was the child's father. Because the surrogate mother had legally abandoned the child, the Catholic Children's Aid Society subsequently took custody.

Problems arose in this case over setting a precedent. Ontario does not want to condone the marketing of babies. These particular parents may have been very fit, but questions were raised regarding other potential parents. Many legal quandaries became apparent. For example: Who is liable for birth defects? Is it ethical for doctors to be involved with surrogate mothers? What is the legal status of the child?

Following the assumption of custody by the Catholic Children's Aid Society, a Family Court judge awarded the Scarborough couple temporary custody of the child. The final outcome was in the parents' favour.

Three years later, an Ontario Law Reform Commission report addressed the issue of surrogate motherhood. The same problems still concerned the commission. As long as contract motherhood is illegal the surrogate mother can reclaim the child. She can also sue for support or refuse to give up the child even after having signed a contract. It has been suggested that regulation is necessary to bring together couples wanting children and women who want to serve as surrogate mothers. The Ontario Law Reform Commission affirmed that guidelines and regulations to do this are essential. Ignoring the issue may promote a "black market" in babies.

The Law Reform Commission came up with a complicated system of legal procedures to govern such issues as payment, suitability, blood tests, and consent. These factors were to be decided in a court designed for this purpose. The same court would deal with such problems as birth defects. While the Ontario Law Reform Commission has made preliminary recommendations for legislation in this area, surrogate motherhood may never be legalized in Ontario.

The other provinces are grappling with the same problems as Ontario. All have legislation prohibiting payment for a child. Some have very substantial penalties. For example, in British Columbia a judge can impose a fine of up to $10,000. Many statutes give the judge the discretion to impose a prison term. In all provinces, the natural father would not be presumed to be the father of the child. These legal difficulties deter most infertile couples from pursuing surrogate motherhood as an alternative.

Abortion

The name Morgentaler is synonomous with the legal battle in Canada over the issue of abortion. This controversy has existed for more than a decade, but it has become more explosive in the last five years, even though a majority of Canadians agree that the decision to have an abortion should rest with the woman.

Section 251 of Canada's *Criminal Code* prohibits the procuring of a miscarriage. An abortion is legal where an accredited hospital committee certifies that the continuation of the pregnancy would endanger the life or health of the pregnant woman. Dr. Henry Morgentaler has worked to set up clinics independent from hospitals in a number of provinces. In Quebec, in the mid-1970s, Dr. Morgentaler was charged with unlawfully procuring the miscarriage of a female person. Dr. Morgentaler was acquitted on three occasions by juries and, after protracted legal battles, the stated policy of the Parti Québécois attorney general for Quebec was not to prosecute physicians in that province for performing abortions without approval of an accredited hospital. As a result, it is estimated that almost half of Quebec abortions take place in doctors' offices and privately or publicly funded health clinics without any approval from a hospital committee. (Whether this situation will continue under succeeding governments is not certain, however.)

The need for such clinics throughout the rest of Canada is obvious. In February 1986, the doctors at the Sarnia General Hospital in Ontario refused to sit on the therapeutic abortion committee or to perform abortions. It was part of their protest against actions by the provincial government to restrict extra billing. The Canadian Abortion Rights Action League (CARAL) responded to their action by stating that it demonstrated a "callous disregard for women." According to CARAL, the Canadian Medical Association has been calling for the removal of all references to a therapeutic abortion committee from the *Criminal Code* since 1971. CARAL argues that there is no need for abortions to occur only in hospitals. In the United States, where abortion is legal, 80 percent of the operations are performed in clinics or physicians' offices. Since legalization, there has been a dramatic decline in complications, and there have been no delays as a result of increased accessibility.

A recent Canadian report found that the most active abortion committees were in hospitals in large urban areas. There was great regional disparity, with northern and eastern Canada having little or no access to legal abortions. As of August 1986, Newfoundland became the second province in Canada without an accredited hospital that would perform abortions. In June 1986, the only hospital in Prince Edward Island performing abortions disbanded its therapeutic abortion committee. The provincial and federal governments have taken the position that they cannot dictate to doctors or to hospitals on the volume or scheduling of medical and surgical procedures.

Despite the demonstrated need for independent clinics, the attorneys general in provinces other than Quebec continue to prosecute Dr. Morgentaler. There are outstanding charges in Manitoba, and several charges have been laid in Ontario against Dr. Morgentaler and his colleagues.

There have been a number of attempts to use the civil courts to restrict women's access to abortion. In 1979, an Ontario lawyer brought an action to prohibit further therapeutic abortions from being performed in the Ottawa Civic Hospital and the Riverside Hospital. The application was brought "as representative of those unborn persons whose lives may be terminated by abortion in the defendant hospitals." The Ontario Supreme Court denied standing. However, the Court of Appeal while upholding the decision of the Supreme Court, also dealt with the plaintiff's contention that the court should restrict abortions because "the unborn are human beings from the moment of conception."

The question of when human life begins is one which has perplexed the sages down the corridors of time. In my respectful view, even if the theological, philosophical, medical, and jurisprudential issues involved in it could be answered in a courtroom, the answer would be beside the point in so far as this lawsuit is concerned. Accepting as fact the conclusion the plaintiff seeks to establish by testimony at trial, that is, that a foetus is a human being from conception, the legal result obtained remains the same. The foetus is not recognized in law as a person in the full legal sense. The plaintiff has cited no case that holds a foetus is within the concept of a legal person entitled to the rights asserted in this action. The cases here and elsewhere demonstrate that the law has selected birth as the point at which the foetus becomes a person with full and independent rights.

In enacting a code establishing the circumstances in which legal abortions may be performed, Parliament has balanced, in a manner it thought proper, a concern for foetal life on the one hand and for life and health of an expectant mother on the other. Whether the right to terminate a pregnancy should be eliminated, as the plaintiff argues, or broadened, as others would argue, is not a matter for the Court. The Court is not entitled, as the plaintiff suggests, to substitute its judgment on the wisdom, policy or values underlying the legislation for that of Parliament. Nor viewing the law as I do, is it now open for a Court to circumvent or nullify the abortion legislation enacted by Parliament within its constitutional mandate by postulating the existence at any stage of gestation of a new person in law. The Arguments as to abortion urged by the plaintiff, in my opinion, are non-justiciable or reserved to the Legislature. The Court is not the appropriate forum for their resolution.[1]

In Saskatchewan, Joseph Borowski sought to argue that the abortion provisions of the *Criminal Code* violated the Canadian *Bill of Rights*. He was allowed standing but was ultimately unsuccessful. In Ontario, in 1984, a man sought to stop his estranged wife from obtaining an abortion. He was unsuccessful in the Ontario courts. The League for Life in Manitoba Inc. brought an action to restrain Dr. Morgentaler from performing abortions in a clinic. The league was denied standing.

In 1985, two members of a hospital society in British Columbia sought standing to argue that the courts should restrict the definition of ''health.'' They were unsuccessful in obtaining standing. In 1985, the Saskatchewan legislature considered Bill 53, *Freedom of Informed Choice (Abortion) Act*. Bill 53 would have made it an offence to perform, cause, or approve an abortion without the written consent of the prospective mother and her husband (if married) or if unmarried and a minor, her parents or guardians. The Court of Appeal held that the bill overreached the power of the provincial legislature, and that it dealt with matters within federal jurisdiction.

In every province except Quebec, women still do not have access to free-standing clinics. Dr. Morgentaler and other sympathetic doctors have been prosecuted in the criminal courts. Appellate judges have repeatedly overturned jury acquittals. However, the courts have also been reluctant to take any action to restrict access to abortion under section 251 of the *Criminal Code*.

---

1. Dehler *v.* Ottawa Civic Hospital et al. 25 O.R. (2d) 748, 14 C.P.C. 4 (H.C.J.), affd. 29 O.R. (2d) 677.

CHAPTER 5

FINANCIAL PLANNING

Debora H. Zatzman

Debora Zatzman is a partner in the firm of Anderson, Huestis and Jones, of Dartmouth, Nova Scotia, where she practises mainly in the areas of corporate, commercial, and tax law. She studied at Dalhousie and Carleton universities and was called to the Bar of Nova Scotia in 1980. She has taught at Dalhousie Law School and is a lecturer for the Nova Scotia Bar Admission course in corporate and tax law.

WOMEN TODAY HAVE more money of their own than ever before. More women are now holding jobs outside the home, and equal opportunities for women are steadily becoming more accepted in principle and practice. Provincial matrimonial laws automatically confer an interest in family property on both spouses, subject to an adjustment by the courts depending on the facts of each case. As a result, all women, whatever their financial circumstances, need proper financial planning in order to survive in contemporary Canadian society.

At the same time, society is becoming ever more complex and sophisticated. The Canadian economy is suffering from the effects of long-term inflation, high unemployment, and a rising cost of living. The financial picture in Canada also reflects the instability of the international economy, and there seem to be as many different theories about its operation as there are theoreticians.

Considering the above factors, no one can afford the luxury of being fiscally unaware or irresponsible. We must all attempt to understand our financial situations and to plan for and control our financial futures to the greatest extent possible.

This chapter deals with four aspects of financial planning:

1. *The Canadian income-tax system.* It is difficult to understand the income-tax system and to keep pace with annual changes in tax laws. However, income taxation affects all Canadians in some aspect or another, whether as employees, business people, or the elderly receiving government pension cheques. The more you know about tax, the better able you will be to control your own financial future.

2. *Tax planning.* Tax planning by the family unit through the use of income splitting and incorporation is emphasized.

3. *Retirement planning and pensions.* The goal in such planning is to ensure that you will have sufficient cash flow in your retirement years to maintain the standard of living to which you are accustomed. Although some of you may believe you are too young to consider plans for retirement, in fact the sooner such plans are begun the more beneficial they may be. This chapter explains how life insurance and the family business, in addition to registered deferred income plans and government and private pension schemes, can be used as vehicles of retirement planning.

4. *Investment.* No attempt is made here to offer investment advice. However, some of the investment questions to consider and the various options that are available are pointed out. The importance of obtaining appropriate professional advice is stressed.

The laws governing your financial situation are constantly changing. This chapter deals with the laws in force in July 1986.

INCOME TAXATION

It is essential to financial planning that you understand your own income-tax situation and the basic concepts and principles that underlie the Canadian tax system.

First, income tax is payable by all people who are resident in Canada and who earn certain levels and types of income anywhere in the world. For tax purposes, individuals, trusts, estates, corporations, and societies are people who may have to pay taxes. Residence generally means permanent residence in Canada or physical presence in Canada in the year for a total of 183 days or more.

Non-residents are also liable to pay Canadian income tax on income earned in Canada.

Tax payable by individuals is calculated on progressive rates, so that increasing levels of income attract progressively higher rates of tax. Corporations pay taxes computed on a fixed rate, subject to credits, rebates, surtaxes, and other adjustments.

Second, different types of income receive different treatment under the *Income Tax Act* of Canada. A key distinction is made between income and capital gains. In general, a capital gain or loss is produced by disposing of property. For example, if you sell a piece of land for a higher price than you originally paid for it, you have experienced a capital gain. Amounts earned other than as capital gain are taxed as income, unless specifically exempt from tax under the *Income Tax Act*.

In simplified terms, a capital gain equals the profit you make if you sell something for more than you originally paid for it. Only one-half of your profit or capital gain is taxed, unlike other income, which is fully taxable. During your lifetime you may earn a maximum of $500,000 of capital gains that is exempt from taxation if properly documented and reported to Revenue Canada. This capital-gains exemption is being phased in over six years. The exemption limit in 1985 was $20,000 and in 1986, $50,000. For 1987 the limit is $100,000; for 1988, $200,000; for 1989, $300,000, and for 1990 and subsequent years, $500,000.

Third, income from different sources receives distinctive treatment. The three main sources of income are employment, business, and property. A person earning employment income (such as, salary or wages, and related benefits) may take very limited deductions in calculating taxable income. Income from property means revenue produced from any property you own that is not part of an active business. Examples of property income are interest on investments, dividends received on shares, rents, and royalties. Business income generally means the profit from a business, including a profession, a trade, or a commercial undertaking. On income from business or property you may take much broader deductions in calculating your taxable income than on income from employment and may thereby reduce the amount of tax you must pay.

Taxable Income

Some of the most common types of income and their treatment under the Canadian tax system are described below.

Interest

Amounts received or receivable in the year as interest are taxable income and must be declared on your tax return. Up to $1,000 a year of interest and dividend income is deductible from income, by an individual or by a trust under a will after personal exemptions have been deducted. You must report accrued interest on "investment contracts" every third calendar year after purchase, unless you choose to report interest annually. "Investment contract" includes any debt instrument, except one under which accrued interest is reported more frequently than three years, and except income bonds and debentures, small business development bonds, or small business bonds. Mortgages, demand debentures, and promissory notes may be examples of investment contracts.

Dividends

As of January 1, 1987, the full amount of all dividends plus one-third of such dividend received by a shareholder must be included in the shareholder's income and, two-thirds of such increase constitutes a federal tax credit for that shareholder. For example, if A Holdings Limited pays you a $100 dividend, you must pay federal income tax on ($100 + $33.33 =) $133.33, but you enjoy a federal tax credit of ($\frac{2}{3} \times$ $33.33 =) $22.22.

Life-Insurance Proceeds

Amounts received from an "exempt policy" (that is, one not governed by the December 1982 tax amendments) are tax-free receipts. Ask your insurance agent to identify whether your policy is exempt. Note that if the life-insurance policy is not exempt, the insured person must pay tax, on every third anniversary of the policy, on interest accruing but not actually received.

Gifts

The recipient of a gift does not pay income tax on it. But the person making the gift is treated as having sold it for its fair market value and generally must pay taxes on any capital gains, unless the gift was made to a spouse (and is subject to the capital-gains exemption discussed later in this chapter).

Inheritances

Inheritances are treated in the same way as gifts made during the giver's lifetime, in that the recipient is not taxed. However, the donor is considered to have sold the property for its fair market value, and the estate must pay taxes on any capital gains. Gifts made to a spouse by will allow the capital gains to be deferred until the spouse in turn sells the property.

Lottery Winnings

In the same category as gifts, lottery winnings are not taxable income.

Scholarships, Bursaries, Prizes

The amount of a scholarship, bursary, or prize for achievement in excess of $500 in an area in which you are ordinarily involved is taxable income. A prize of less than $500 is not subject to income tax.

Damages

Damages recovered in a personal-injury lawsuit are not taxable income. Damages awarded for breach of contract are taxable either as income or capital gain just as if the contract had been performed without court enforcement and amounts received by parties to the contract were reported in tax returns.

Pensions

Any amount received in a year as a pension benefit or superannuation is taxable income, unless the specific pension plan is exempt from tax.

Proceeds from the Sale of Your Home

Amounts received upon the sale of your home are generally not taxable, provided your house was your principal residence rather than rented throughout the period you owned the house.

Maintenance and Alimony

Generally speaking, maintenance and alimony payments made periodically and received by a spouse are deductible by the payer and taxable income to the recipient in the year of payment provided conditions specified in the *Income Tax Act* are satisfied.

Alimony and maintenance payments by common-law spouses are subject to the same treatment, if the payments are made pursuant to a court order and if the recipient resides in a province listed in regulations under the *Income Tax Act*. At present only if the recipient resides in Ontario may common-law partners meet the requirements entitling them to deduct or include the payments for tax purposes.

Deductions

The *Income Tax Act* not only determines what is taxable income but also restricts which amounts may be deducted from income for tax purposes. The following are a few of the permitted deductions.

Expenses to Earn Income

Expenses made for the purpose of earning income from business or property are deductible. For example, interest payments on a bank operating loan used to carry on business, the cost of ordinary office supplies, and reasonable employees' salaries are all deducted from income.

Capital-Cost Allowance

The worth of certain property diminishes over its lifetime. The *Income Tax Act* allows a fixed percentage of the cost of such property to be deducted during each year of its useful life. For example, if your business owns its office building, the cost of the building may be deducted at a rate of either 5 percent or 10 percent each year, depending on the material with which it is constructed.

Tuition Fees

A student enrolled at a specified educational institution in Canada may deduct tuition fees in excess of $100. There is also provision to deduct tuition fees paid to a university outside Canada, where a taxpayer was a full-time student enrolled in a degree course.

Child-Care Expenses

As a parent, you may deduct child-care expenses in relation to a child you supported, to a maximum of the lesser of $8,000 in total or $2,000 per supported child, or two-thirds of your earned income for the year. "Child-care expenses" include the cost of baby sitters, day care, and board and lodging at boarding school or camp incurred to enable the parent to work or pursue training or research.

Pension-Income Deduction

If you are age sixty-five or over, you may deduct up to $1,000 of certain pension income received in the year in calculating your taxable income. Pension income that qualifies for the deduction includes receipts from a pension plan, an RRSP, an RRIF, and a DPSP. Payments under the *Canada Pension Plan* and the *Old Age Security Act* are not eligible for the deduction.

Overriding the right to make deductions is a general prohibition from deducting any amount except to the extent that is reasonable in the circumstances. For example, if a salary of $250 a week is found to be unreasonable in a particular situation, and only $150 a week would have been a reasonable payment to that employee then the employer may deduct only $150 a week.

The *Income Tax Act* also specifies certain deductions that are not allowed. Of general interest is the disallowance of deductions for personal or living expenses, except travelling expenses while away from home on business. Thus, such costs as clothing, furniture, or a car used for personal rather than business purposes may not be deducted in computing income.

The preceding discussion of income taxation is in very general terms. It is intended to convey a basic understanding of how certain amounts received are treated for tax purposes and of how the system may affect you as a taxpayer. You are urged to consult a professional adviser regarding specific problems or concerns you may have.

Attribution

It is common for families to attempt "income splitting" by redistributing property among family members to enable children and a spouse earning little or no income to pay a lower marginal rate of tax on income earned in their hands. The *Income Tax Act* imposes "attribution" to minimize income splitting.

Assume for example that an individual paying taxes at the highest marginal rate gives $5,000 to a spouse paying taxes at the lowest marginal rate. The spouse then invests the money and earns annual interest income of $500. The effect of attribution is that Revenue Canada considers the donor to have earned the $500 interest and to owe taxes on it.

By virtue of the attribution rules, upon transfer or loan of property to a spouse or spouse trust, income or loss and capital gain or capital loss from the transferred property are attributed back to the transferring spouse for tax purposes. Similar rules attribute back income or loss on property transferred or loaned to a person under eighteen years of age.

The attribution rules have a direct effect on family financial and tax planning. A brief outline follows of some methods of family tax planning available under the present income-tax system notwithstanding the attribution rules.

TAX PLANNING

As a taxpayer you should be familiar with some of the common methods of reducing taxes. Minimizing your tax liability merits long-term planning, which may result in substantial savings.

Income Splitting

The *Income Tax Act* of Canada treats each individual as a separate taxpayer, requiring you to file your own tax return separate from other family members. But the *Income Tax Act* to some extent acknowledges the family as a financial unit, giving preferential treatment as follows:

1. Spouses may transfer between themselves certain deductions in computing taxable income. It is advisable for a low-income spouse to transfer deductions to the high-income spouse, to minimize the taxes payable.
2. Spouses may transfer tax refunds between themselves. Thus if your husband is entitled to a refund of $1000 and you owe taxes

in the amount of $1000, by authorizing transfer of the refund you may avoid sending money to Revenue Canada. This is particularly advantageous because taxes must be paid by an individual on or before April 30, whereas a refund may not be received until much later than April 30.

3. Property may be transferred from one spouse to the other without producing immediate tax consequences. This deferral applies to a transfer during the lifetime or upon the death of the transferring spouse. For example, by his will your husband leaves you an apartment building. Upon his death, your husband's estate will owe no income taxes in relation to transferring the apartment building, whereas tax would have been payable had he or his estate sold it to anyone other than you. Because of the deferral, no income taxes will be payable until you (or your estate) dispose of the apartment building.

4. An individual who is not contributing the maximum allowable to an RRSP may contribute to a spouse's RRSP and may deduct the contribution from taxable income.

5. Until the end of 1987, a taxpayer may transfer the shares of an incorporated small business to his or her child or grandchild without payment of capital-gains tax. Up to $200,000 of capital gains on which the taxpayer would have had to pay taxes may be deferred until the eventual sale of the shares by the child or grandchild. Because this $200,000 deferral is in addition to the $500,000 capital-gains exemption, it is advisable to do this share transfer before it expires in 1988.

6. A number of tax-deferred transfers of property are available to farmers. During a taxpayer's lifetime or upon death, farm land, certain farming property, shares in a family farm company, or an interest in a family farm partnership may be transferred to his or her child without immediate tax consequences.

7. In addition to the preceding methods of income splitting using existing vehicles under the *Income Tax Act*, other methods of family tax planning are available. For example, where practical you may wish to employ family members in your business. By paying a salary that is reasonable in relation to services rendered, income may be legitimately distributed among spouses and children without attracting attribution.

8. Another example of income splitting is the transfer of long-term investments to children over fifteen years of age. Because of the three-year interest-accrual rule, tax on accrued interest will be payable only when a child is eighteen or over. Income is not attributed back to the transferring parent once a child attains age eighteen, so that the income will be taxable in the child's hands, presumably at a lower tax rate. Moreover, there is no capital-gains attribution from child to parent, meaning that capital gains produced by selling investments will be taxable in the child's hands.

Incorporation

Another basic instrument of tax-planning is the limited liability company. If you as an individual earn enough income that you pay taxes at a high marginal rate, you may wish to incorporate your business (if this is legally permissible). Although both your company and you, as a shareholder of the company, will be subject to taxes on income earned, there may be advantages offered by incorporation.

First, taxes may be deferred. If the company earns more income than you need to maintain your standard of living, excess income may be retained in the company rather than paid to you. On such excess income, tax is paid at the corporate rate, which may be lower, and is deferred in your hands until paid out of the company.

Second, if you are a shareholder employed by a company, you may receive income partly as salary and partly as dividends. Salary is fully taxable income, whereas dividends, as mentioned earlier, receive a different tax treatment. The appropriate mix of salary and dividend income will result in lower taxes. A professional adviser will be able to specify the mix of payments most advantageous to you.

Another somewhat more complex approach to tax planning is the "estate freeze." An estate freeze is a plan for an intergenerational transfer of business or properties in order to minimize tax conse-quences on the death of the transferor and to provide continuity in family involvement. Many estate plans require incorporation of new companies to hold shares in existing operational companies, and depend on the distribution of shares of the operational and holding companies to various family members. You should consult a professional adviser for a more detailed explanation of an estate freeze and whether such a plan would be beneficial to you.

RETIREMENT PLANNING AND PENSIONS

Statutory Deferred Income Plans

Registered Retirement Savings Plans
A registered retirement savings plan (RRSP) is an arrangement registered with Revenue Canada whereby a portion of your earned income is paid into a trust and invested by the trustee. Interest accumulates tax free in the trust and is only taxable when you withdraw funds from the plan.

RRSP contributions are tax deductible for the year they are made, so long as they are within specified limits. In 1986, an individual who has only RRSPs may deduct a maximum contribution of $7,500, subject to an overall limit of 20 percent of earned income.

RRSP contribution limits are gradually increasing, starting in 1988 with annual raises until 1991. Employees who save only through RRSPs may contribute up to 18 percent of their earned income for the year, deducting a maximum of $9,500 in 1988, $11,500 in 1989, $13,500 in 1990, and $15,500 in 1991. Unused RRSP contributions may be carried forward for a period of seven years.

If you contribute to both RRSPs and to other registered employment pension plans, you should consult advisers to determine your maximum annual contribution limits.

An RRSP is a desirable means of retirement planning for any employee, both because contributions are a deduction from net income and because income accumulates tax free in the plan until it matures. A taxpayer also may contribute to a spousal RRSP. These contributions are tax deductible subject to the same limits specified above.

Registered Retirement Income Funds
When you cash in your RRSP, the money you receive is taxable. You may have to pay out a relatively large amount of tax, which a registered retirement income fund (RRIF) allows you to defer.

Transfer of the RRSP payment into an RRIF will give you annual payments at a selected rate of interest during the term of the plan either until your death or until you or your spouse become ninety years of age. This way you are taxable on (lower) payments received each year from the RRIF rather than on one (larger) lump sum received from the RRSP.

For RRIFs set up or amended after February 1986, you may withdraw any amount from the RRIF each year, so long as you receive the minimum payout required by the *Income Tax Act*. In this way, an RRIF provides the flexibility needed to meet your particular financial circumstances in any year (for example if you require additional funds for an emergency).

Under an RRIF, you may designate your spouse to receive annual payments from the plan during its term after your death. If the surviving spouse is younger than the deceased planholder, then the term of years over which payments were to be made may be extended by the difference in their ages.

If you die before receiving all of the payments out of the RRIF, and there is no surviving spouse or your designated beneficiary is someone other than a spouse, the remaining amount of the fund must be generally included in your taxable income in the year of death. Thus, if your personal circumstances permit, it is financially advantageous for RRIF payments to be continued in favour of a surviving spouse.

Payments received from an RRIF qualify for the annual $1000 pension income exemption under the *Income Tax Act*.

Deferred Profit-Sharing Plans

A deferred profit-sharing plan (DPSP) must be accepted for registration by the Minister of National Revenue in order to offer the qualities described below. It is a program available only to employees.

Under a DPSP, your employer makes payments to a trustee for the benefit of its employees who are participating in the plan. Such contributions are calculated by reference to the profits of the business, and are deductible by the employer subject to certain limits. As an employee, you may contribute to the plan, but your contributions are not deductible for tax purposes.

Contribution limits to DPSPs are increasing starting in 1988. In

1990 the limit will be $7,750, subject to the overall ceiling of 18 percent of earned income. In 1986 the maximum tax-deductible contribution to a DPSP for an employer was $3,500, subject to the overriding limit of 20 percent of earned income.

Payments received by an employee from a DPSP are taxable income, but tax liability may be delayed if you transfer these payments into another qualifying DPSP or into an RRSP.

All amounts that you are entitled to receive must become payable within ninety days after the earliest of:
– your death;
– termination of your employment;
– your seventy-first birthday;
– termination of the DPSP.

Life Insurance*

One customary reason for buying life insurance is to provide supplementary retirement income. There are many different kinds of insurance policies available. It is essential to understand your purpose for buying insurance to allow you to arrange for the type of policy appropriate to your particular situation.

Term insurance provides coverage for a fixed period, such as ten years, with premiums payable during that time. A specified amount is paid upon your death provided you die within that period. Premiums increase as you get older, because it becomes more likely that you will die during the insured period.

Whole life insurance offers permanent protection during your entire lifetime as long as the premiums continue to be paid. The amount of insurance that is paid at death has traditionally been the difference between the face value of the policy and savings at any time accumulated under the insurance contract (namely premiums plus accrued interest). Premiums remain the same throughout the policy period.

Recent developments have brought many options to traditional plans, such as variable premiums, the possibility of prepaying for lifetime insurance coverage, and the feature of having the savings

* The author wishes to thank Sheldon Lipkus, Manager of the Halifax office of North American Life Assurance Co., for providing background information and helpful suggestions in the area of life insurance.

added to the face amount of the policy as a death benefit (which has interesting tax advantages).

Joint life insurance covers two people, usually spouses. Under such a policy, the benefits are payable to the survivor when the other insured person dies. The other extreme is last-survivor insurance, whereby the amount is payable on the death of the last insured to die. Where a husband leaves his estate to his wife (or vice versa), there are no taxes payable until the death of the last surviving spouse. Thus, last-survivor insurance is available to meet tax liabilities when they arise, as well as to provide an inheritance to the next generation.

Many hybrid forms of policy are available to meet the particular needs of each insured. For example, a last-survivor policy may provide for payment of a fixed amount on the death of the first to die should the survivor require a certain amount of cash. The balance of the amount in the policy is paid at the death of the last survivor.

Another kind of coverage available is disability insurance, which provides regular payments when long-term disability prevents the insured person from earning income. Payments generally are made only until the disabled person becomes sixty-five. The definition of disability may vary among policies offered by different insurance companies and should be carefully reviewed and understood before you commit to a particular policy.

Adequate insurance coverage will assist a surviving spouse to cope upon the disability or death of an income-producing spouse. It is essential that a dependent spouse be named as beneficiary of any such insurance policy, and any dependent spouse should ensure that he or she is named.

Premiums paid on life and disability insurance policies are not tax deductible, unless a lender specifically requires such insurance as collateral security for a loan.

Insurance was dramatically affected by 1982 amendments to the *Income Tax Act* of Canada. It is advantageous to enter into an insurance contract exempt from the 1982 amendments (namely, an "exempt policy"). Non-exempt policies attract detrimental tax consequences, including the obligation of the insured to pay tax every third year on accrued income not actually received. Be sure your agent or broker specifies whether your policy is exempt or non-exempt, explains the tax consequences of your insurance arrangements, and reviews the exempt status of your policy annually.

For exempt policies, life-insurance proceeds received upon the death of the insured are not taxable. Similarly, where disability-insurance premiums were paid by the insured person, disability-insurance proceeds are not taxable income.

The Family Business

If you or your spouse own a successful business, you may choose to direct all your finances and efforts to that business (rather than to pay premiums to an insurance company or to contribute to a registered deferred income plan) and to rely entirely on the business to support you in retirement. For example, upon retirement you may sell the shares of your incorporated family business and live off the income produced by investing the proceeds of sale.

This option will be available only where a family business is sufficiently valuable that its sale would produce enough money to maintain an acceptable lifestyle after retirement. It is often not possible to predict the worth of a business several decades in the future. In the worst circumstances, receivership, bankruptcy, poor market conditions, or tight competition may eliminate the retirement fund. It is clear that there is a degree of risk in relying on the family business to the exclusion of statutory pension plans and insurance policies.

Moreover, a registered deferred income plan offers substantial tax advantages, allowing accumulation of tax-sheltered income over the life of the plan.

These factors should be weighed by owners of businesses before they decide how best to develop a retirement fund.

Government Pensions

A critical aspect of retirement planning in Canada is the system of public pensions. All pension programs are administered by Health and Welfare Canada and at present are universally available to Canadian residents who satisfy the pension requirements. To receive pension benefits it is necessary to file an application with the Income Security Programs Office of Health and Welfare Canada.

The basic *old age security pension* is a monthly pension available to any person sixty-five years of age and over who is a Canadian citizen, landed immigrant, or has a visitor's permit, and who meets certain residence requirements. The amount of pension received is taxable income.

The *guaranteed income supplement* is paid to any applicant receiving the old age security pension whose other income is below specified levels. Effective January 1986, for married couples of whom both members receive the old age security pension, the highest combined yearly income that would nonetheless entitle them to receive a monthly supplement is $10,607.99.

The *spouse's allowance* is payable to a Canadian citizen, landed immigrant, or person who has a visitor's permit and is between the ages of sixty and sixty-five, meets certain residence requirements, and whose spouse receives the old age security pension and the guaranteed income supplement. Separation of spouses disqualifies them from receiving the spouse's allowance. The amount of allowance depends on combined yearly incomes other than pension and supplement.

The spouse's allowance program has recently been extended to widows and widowers between sixty and sixty-five years of age, regardless of whether their spouses were receiving the old age pension. Amounts of monthly allowance payments are calculated in proportion to other income received by a widow or widower. Such payments cease on death, on attaining age sixty-five, or on remarriage.

Basic pension, supplement, and spouse's allowance are indexed in proportion to inflation to help recipients keep pace with the rising cost of living. The basic old age security pension is subject to income tax, but the guaranteed income supplement and the spouse's allowance are not taxable.

The *Canada Pension Plan* is funded by mandatory employer and employee contributions of equal amounts. From each payment an employer must withhold 1.8 percent of the salary of each employee and remit it to Revenue Canada and also must contribute the same amount. Self-employed individuals must (as both employer and employee) contribute 3.6 percent of salary. Payments received from the plan are taxable income.

It is proposed by new federal legislation that, as of January 1,

1987, employer and employee contributions will increase. In 1987, a total of 3.8 percent of earnings must be remitted, being 1.9 percent by each of employer and employee. Contribution levels will gradually increase, so that by 2011 the total contribution will be 7.6 percent of earnings.

Canada Pension Plan contributions may entitle you to receive three types of benefits: retirement pension, disability benefits, and death and survivor benefits. Retirement pension payments may be received one month after a pensioner's sixty-fifth birthday, continuing until death. After the new legislation comes into effect, contributors may start to receive retirement pension payments at any age between sixty and seventy. The older the contributor when payments begin, the larger the payments will be.

You are eligible for disability benefits if you have contributed to the Canada Pension Plan, are under the age of sixty-five, and sustain a severe and prolonged mental or physical disability. If you qualify, you will receive monthly disability payments until your disability ends, your death occurs, or you become sixty-five, whichever occurs earliest. If you are receiving disability benefits when you reach sixty-five, such payments are automatically converted to retirement pension payments. Bill C-116 proposes starting in 1987 to increase the level of monthly disability benefit payments.

Death and survivor benefits are available to a person whose parent or spouse contributed to the Canada Pension Plan and is deceased. A lump-sum death benefit is payable to help with funeral expenses; as well, survivor benefits are payable monthly.

Residents of the Province of Quebec participate in the *Quebec Pension Plan*, Quebec's equivalent to the Canada Pension Plan. Canadians who have lived in Quebec and in other parts of Canada and contributed to both plans may be "dual contributors." Upon satisfying residence and age qualifications, such people may receive payments from both plans.

Private Group Insurance

Private group insurance offered by insurance companies is a retirement vehicle in addition to government pension schemes. An employer may enter into an arrangement with an insurance company for the benefit of all employees and their families.

Group insurance may be financed by combined employer and employee contributions. Employer contributions do not constitute (in the year they are made) taxable income to an employee, but they may reduce an employee's RRSP maximum contribution limit.

Customary benefits available under a group insurance plan are pension benefits, health, disability, and dental coverage, and life insurance. Under the group pension plan, employer and employee contributions will provide for pension payments upon the employee's retirement or upon death (should that occur before the normal retirement date). The amounts of employee contributions are relatively low. They are generally required to be payroll-deducted and, within limits, are deductible from taxable income. After retirement or death, pension payments are taxable income in the hands of the recipient.

Health and dental coverage offers reimbursement to member employees for the cost of prescribed drugs, certain hospital expenses, specific drug expenses, and other medical costs specified in the plan. Disability benefits are payable to defer lost income in the event of an employee's long-term disability through accident or illness. The payments cover a fixed percentage of the disabled employee's salary, up to a maximum amount.

Insurance coverage, as with an individual policy, provides money to the surviving family of a deceased employee or other named beneficiary.

Private group insurance may be part of an attractive compensation package, which should be kept in mind when job-hunting or considering a job offer. Check with your employer or prospective employer about the availability of group coverage to you and your family.

The federal budget of May 23, 1985, proposed improvement of minimum standards for group pension plans operating under the *Pension Benefits Standards Act* of Canada. This act governs such federally regulated industries as banking, radio and television broadcasting, and federal Crown corporations.

As a result of these changes, pensions will be more readily transferable when employees change jobs. Eligibility for pension benefits will be extended to certain part-time workers and to some employees who decide to retire early. If you leave your job before you have a right to receive your pension, your contributions to the pension plan must be returned with interest at a reasonable rate. Pensions payable to surviving spouses will no longer automatically cease upon remarriage of the survivor. Benefits will be provided to surviving spouses of plan members who are already retired when they die. Upon divorce, separation, or dissolution of a common-law relationship, the value of pension credits and pensions already being paid will be divided equally between spouses according to the applicable provincial matrimonial property laws.

These will be some of the basic amendments, of particular assistance to women, to pensions under the *Pension Benefits Standards Act*. Note that similar changes have been proposed to comparable provincial legislation and to the *Canada Pension Plan* to enhance pension uniformity for Canadians.

INVESTMENT

Getting Financial Advice

Let us assume that you want to earn money through investment but have little or no business experience. It is prudent to obtain good advice before making any financial commitments, considering the vast numbers of investment options open to you.

Common sources of financial advice are bankers, lawyers, accountants, insurance agents, and stock brokers. It is not possible to elaborate here on the services provided by each type of professional. In general terms, the profession you select depends on the type of information sought and your purpose in seeking advice. For example, you will want to consider the following questions:

- Do you have funds available to invest, or do you require a loan?
- Do you want to start a business or to make a passive investment?
- Do you know what business and investment opportunities are available?
- Are you hoping to develop a ''nest egg'' to provide security upon your retirement, or are you interested in immediate monetary returns?
- Do you intend to hold the investments in your own name, or

would you prefer to put them into a trust for your children's benefit?
• Are you in financial trouble?

Different advisers will assist you in making an investment, according to your particular needs and help you select the most appropriate professional advisers in other areas of business.

At the outset of any relationship with a professional, you as a client should establish certain matters to your satisfaction:

1. Be comfortable with your adviser in the sense that you feel confident in relying on the advice you will receive. The relationship you will establish with a professional is known as a "fiduciary" relationship, meaning one of trust or confidence. As your adviser, a fiduciary has a duty to act in the utmost good faith for your benefit and not to derive benefit from the relationship unless expressly agreed between you.

   Fiduciary duties arising out of this special trust relationship between you and your professional adviser should be strictly enforced by the relevant professional societies (barristers' societies, institutes of chartered accountants, and so on) as well as by the courts. Categories of people who bear a fiduciary duty include lawyers, brokers, agents, partners, directors of companies, guardians, executors, and trustees.

2. Identify in writing precisely what you expect your adviser to do for you. Without a clear understanding of your goals, you may not be satisfied with the advice you receive. Moreover your professional may perform less efficiently and perhaps at greater expense to you.

3. Agree on a time-table for work to be performed. A lawyer or insurance agent who is very busy may not be able to provide you with an opinion or a proposal within the week. If your adviser cannot meet your schedule, you may wish to consult with someone else. Such details should be discussed during a first meeting between professional and client.

4. Agree on a fee for services to be provided where applicable. Ask whether your professional charges by commission per transaction, hourly rate, or fixed fee. Inquire what percentage commission or how many dollars per hour are charged and how many hours you can expect the file will demand, or what is the cus-

tomary fixed fee for the type of work to be performed. Neither you nor your adviser should be embarrassed by a frank discussion of fees; it will eliminate haggling over the invoice after work has been completed.

Insurance

Insurance should be understood as a long-term investment that may be made for a variety of reasons.

First, and perhaps most commonly, an insurance policy is purchased to make funds available to a family upon disability or death of the breadwinning spouse. If the insured has an "exempt policy," premiums are paid annually and accumulate sheltered from many adverse tax consequences. The total of these premiums accumulated over the years, which is known as the "cash surrender value," has provided supplementary retirement income for many individuals and couples.

Second, insurance may be an integral part of estate planning by the owner of a successful business. Upon the death of the owner, or (if the will transfers the business to the surviving spouse) upon the death of the owner's spouse, tax payable on capital gains and recaptured depreciation may be substantial. Unless alternate plans have been made, it may be necessary for the estate to mortgage or even sell many business assets to meet the tax burden. Joint life or last-survivor insurance will provide cash to pay such taxes, and will thereby allow a smooth transfer of the business intact to the next generation.

Third, a business may buy "key person" insurance on the life of its owner or important employees whose involvement is essential to the success of the business. Lenders sometimes require such insurance as protection against the financial loss expected at the death of a key person. Such a policy will help to minimize disruption to the business until replacement of the key person, and may also pay death benefits to the family of the deceased owner or key employee.

Fourth, insurance may finance the purchase of shares of a private company, pursuant to a buy-sell agreement. Shareholders frequently sign agreements among themselves, requiring the remaining shareholders, or the company, to buy a person's shares in the event of death, disability, or forced or voluntary retirement. However, many shareholders and companies do not have available at any given time enough cash to buy at market value the interest of one of the owners of the business. Insurance on the lives of the shareholders, owned by the shareholders or the company, provides the necessary funds without impairing the financial situation of the surviving shareholders or the company's ability to carry on business.

If you are considering investment in an insurance policy, consult an experienced insurance broker or agent about the policies available that will best meet your particular personal and business needs. A *broker* represents a number of different insurance companies and will be able to quote premiums on a competitive basis. On the other hand, an insurance *agent* acts on behalf of only one insurance company, and should be very familiar with the policies offered by that particular insurer. As with other advisers, the personal competence and integrity of the individual will be important factors in your choice.

Investing in Public Companies

Stock exchanges and financial institutions offer another method of investment. Shares, equity mutual funds, interest-bearing securities, bonds, commodities, futures, government treasury bills, term deposits, and guaranteed investment certificates are only a few examples of possible investments.

As with any other investment process, you must decide on your goals at the outset. Are you hoping to earn high income quickly regardless of a degree of risk, or are you more concerned to minimize risk and realize slower long-term growth? Or is your priority to shelter your earnings from income tax? Answers to such questions as these will assist you in selecting your particular investments.

You should consult a stock broker with whom you feel comfortable dealing on a regular basis. Your broker will explain the different kinds of investments available and will give you an opinion on their earning prospects. If you have made your goals clear, your broker will be able to propose a package of investments tailored to your particular financial needs and to advise you of improvements or down-swings in the fortunes of public companies in which you are interested.

It is essential that you formulate your own theories about how different investments will perform. No broker can guarantee the outcome of particular investments. However, by asking a broker questions about matters you do not fully understand, ensuring that your broker gives you regular updates and evaluations of your portfolio, and checking interest rates and reading stock-exchange reports, you will be able to make informed investment decisions.

Note that Revenue Canada may treat you differently depending on how often you buy and sell shares and other investments. If you hold your investments for a long period of time, only occasionally selling them and buying new ones, profits received on such sales will generally be taxed as capital gains, so that only half of your profit is taxable. But if you frequently buy and sell shares, selling them to make a profit rather than holding them to earn income, you may be considered to be in the business of trading securities, and the full amount of your profits will be taxable.

Investing in a Private Company

An alternative form of investment you may wish to make is to lend money to or buy shares in a family company or other private company. Although you may be investing in a family business and dealing with your friends or relatives, this method of investment must be approached carefully and its merits evaluated.

The following are some of the basic questions to address:

1. What is the financial viability of the business? You must determine whether it is a good investment or if it will lose money.
2. If you proceed by loan (rather than buying shares), is your loan adequately protected or "secured" in case the company defaults in its payments to you? For example, the company could make a mortgage in your favour, charging certain of its assets, or the principals of the company could give you their personal guarantee of payment.
3. If you invest money by purchasing shares, what rights do those shares confer on you? Do the shares entitle you to vote at meetings of shareholders, or to receive a dividend? What is the rate of return on such dividends? What are your rights to return of your capital investment if the company is being wound up? Can you force the company to buy back your shares should you wish to have your funds returned?
4. If you proceed by purchasing shares, is there a "shareholders'

agreement'' among all of the shareholders governing their respective rights? At the start of a business relationship you may
be optimistic that all of the shareholders can resolve any differences in a fair and friendly manner. However, once a problem
arises and the shareholders are defensive and upset, it is often
too late to have reasonable discussions about financial rights and
obligations. It is generally prudent to agree on shareholders'
rights at the outset, and to have all parties sign a comprehensive
shareholders' agreement.

Such topics as organization and management of the business,
financial commitments by shareholders, decision-making authority
of the board of directors, and restrictions on issue and sale of shares
are typically covered in a shareholders' agreement.

By a provision of the May 1985 federal budget it is possible for
a registered retirement savings plan to buy shares in certain Canadian
companies. If you have a self-administered RRSP, up to one half
of its funds may be used to buy the shares in a qualifying company.
If $25,000 or less is invested through an RRSP, a maximum of 50
percent of the company's voting shares may be acquired. For an
investment of more than $25,000, the rules impose a maximum of
10 percent of the company's voting shares.

The major advantage of investment by means of an RRSP is that
contributions to an RRSP are tax deductible within limits.

PART TWO

Women and the Family—
Your Rights in Domestic
Relationships

CHAPTER 6

MARRIAGE AND COHABITATION

Peggy Hales

Peggy Hales is a lawyer in Vancouver, B.C. She has been active in the field of public legal education, notably with the People's Law School, for many years. She is a member of the Bar of British Columbia.

HISTORICALLY, THE FAMILY has been considered to be of pivotal importance to the well-being and survival of society. Even today, the family unit is a basic element in our economy and social system. As such, society has a vested interest in the security and continuance of the family. It is not surprising, then, that the bonds of wedlock cement not just a social institution but a complex legal institution as well.

When people marry, they acquire certain rights and responsibilities and are given recognition as married persons by the law. They belong to a class of persons upon whom the law confers a special status.

Lawful matrimony confers mutual conjugal rights and imposes mutual support obligations. In addition, legal spouses are entitled to a variety of benefits not granted to other persons: for example, the right to share in the estate of a deceased spouse and the right to share in the property of the marriage.

Marriage is essentially a contract in which numerous laws must be complied with in order to make the contract valid. However, it is a special contract with unique requirements. Unlike other contracts, marriage cannot be ended by the simple consent of the parties. Legal procedures set out in the *Divorce Act* are required in order to terminate the marriage. From its celebration to its dissolution a large number of laws affect marriage.

In order to marry you must have the capacity to marry and you must comply with the formalities of the marriage ceremony. The law with respect to the capacity and formalities of marriage has various origins. As discussed in more detail in Chapter 20, our laws in Canada come from several sources: the Constitution, federal statutes, provincial statutes, and the common law. The Constitution grants to the federal Parliament exclusive authority to legislate regarding the capacity to marry and divorce. These laws apply across Canada and are the same in all jurisdictions. The provinces and territories have authority to legislate regarding the solemnization of marriage (that is, all the formalities leading up to the marriage ceremony). The provinces may also make laws about all other aspects of marriage breakdown (such as property division) except divorce. This is why the law relating to those issues varies so widely across Canada.

In this chapter, you will learn about your rights in respect of engagement, marriage, and annulment. You will learn who can and who cannot marry, and how to protect yourself by a marriage contract. Common-law marriages, lesbian relationships, and second marriages are also discussed.

THE ENGAGEMENT

At common law, a promise to marry another person is a legally binding contract, assuming that there is an intention to enter into a legal relationship at the time. The general law of contracts governs all such agreements.

The engagement ring is considered at common law to be a conditional gift, given on condition that the wedding takes place. If you mutually agree to break off the engagement, you are obliged to return the ring; if your fiancé calls off the engagement without a valid reason, you are free to keep the ring. Gifts to the couple from friends are considered to be given on condition that the wedding takes place, and these must be returned if it does not.

While the courts cannot compel a man to marry you, you can sue in court for damages for the breach of the contract. The breach must be something definite, such as a refusal to marry or marriage to another.

The kinds of damages for which you can sue include damage to your pride and feelings and loss of money in preparing for the wedding ceremony. If special damages were incurred, they can be specially pleaded. While a legal action for breach of promise to marry is not common, it is still recognized by our courts.

The Legal Requirements of Marriage

The legal definition of marriage has remained unchanged through the ages. In 1866, marriage was defined as follows by Lord Penzance in the English case of *Hyde* v. *Hyde*: "Marriage is the voluntary union for life of one man and one woman to the exclusion of all others." This definition is still the legal definition of marriage in Canada today.

In order for a marriage to be valid, several requirements must be met. These concerns relate to

- age
- mental competence
- consent
- consanguinity/affinity
- monogamy

Age

The federal government has authority to legislate on the topic of marital capacity, but it has not generally done so. That being the case, it is the common law as modified by any relevant statutes that governs.

While at common law, the minimum age for marriage of a male was fourteen and a female was twelve—these being the ages at which the sexes were considered capable of reproduction—today the age at which you can marry has been raised by virtue of the provinces' and territories' enactment of statutes requiring parental consent to marriage below a certain age. Under these statutes, the age of majority is the age at which you are free to marry without parental consent. This age limit, which varies across Canada, may be as low as twelve or as high as nineteen (see the section below on "The Marriage Ceremony" for specific details).

If you are below the age of majority and wish to marry, it is necessary to obtain your parents' consent. If they will not consent, all provinces and territories provide a mechanism whereby you can appeal the parental decision to a court.

Mental Competence

At the time of the marriage ceremony, both parties to the marriage must have the basic ability to understand the nature of the marriage ceremony and of their rights and duties under the marriage contract. Both parties must essentially understand that they are to live together, to remain sexually faithful to one another, and to provide for one another.

If your judgment is impaired by alcohol or narcotics, you cannot legally marry, as you are not able to form the necessary legal intent to marry.

If, at the time of the marriage ceremony, one of the parties lacked the requisite mental competence, then the marriage is void "*ab initio*"; that is, it never existed in the eyes of the law, and a decree of nullity—an annulment—may be issued.

Consent

In order for a marriage to be valid, both parties to it must enter into the marriage of their own free will. If either party marries under duress, the marriage may be declared void. Note that duress does not include self-created fear or anxiety. Neither is it reluctance to embarrass yourself or your family by backing out of the wedding. Rather, duress or coercion must be such force as to elicit substantial fear and to prevent you from being a free agent.

Consanguinity and Affinity

Marriages between close relatives are prohibited. This prohibition dates back to biblical times. Affinity means people who are related by marriage. Consanguinity means people who are related by common blood. If you are related within these classes, you cannot legally marry in Canada. If you marry within these prohibited degrees, the marriage is void as if it never existed at law. The prohibited degrees of affinity and consanguinity for a woman are these; you cannot marry your:

- grandfather
- grandmother's husband
- husband's grandfather
- uncle
- aunt's husband
- husband's uncle
- father
- stepfather
- husband's father
- son
- husband's son
- daughter's husband
- brother
- grandson
- granddaughter's husband
- husband's grandson
- nephew
- niece's husband
- husband's nephew
- husband's brother

Even if these relationships are through half blood or illegitimacy, you still cannot legally marry. Furthermore, sexual intercourse between certain close relatives, such as parents and their children, constitutes incest under the *Criminal Code* of Canada and is a serious criminal offence.

Monogamy

You must be free to marry. You must not be already married to another man. If your prior marriage has not been dissolved by death, divorce, or annulment, then the second marriage is not only void but you may also be guilty of bigamy.

These are the essential capacity requirements necessary to a valid marriage. If any of these essential requirements is lacking, the marriage is void and can be annulled.

ANNULMENT

An annulment is not a divorce. A divorce terminates an existing and valid marriage. A legal annulment, a nullity decree, declares that a marriage did not exist in law, that it was null and void from the very beginning. If either party lacked the essential capacity to enter the marriage contract, the marriage can be annulled. So, if you were not of sufficient age, lacked the necessary mental competence, did not freely consent, were too closely related through affinity or consanguinity, were already married, or didn't comply with the formalities of the marriage ceremony, then grounds for an annulment exist. This is not to be confused with the annulment granted by some churches to allow their members to remarry within the church. An annulment decreed by a religious institution is not binding on the state, although it may be binding on the conscience of the partners.

Mistake

In addition, if you did not understand the nature of the marriage ceremony or were mistaken as to the identity of the person you married, then the marriage is void. A mistake about the superficial characteristics of the other person is not sufficient in law to void a marriage. It would have to be a substantial mistake (for example, marrying the wrong twin) to annul the marriage. If you had recently arrived in Canada and did not understand that you were participating in a marriage ceremony, then a nullity action will be available to you.

Sexual Capacity

Conjugal rights are part of the marriage contract. If either party is incapable of having sex with the spouse such that the marriage cannot be consummated, then the marriage is voidable. A voidable marriage is one that is valid until annulled by the courts. The sexual incapacity must have existed at the time of the marriage ceremony and must have continued for some time. Note that intercourse prior to marriage does not constitute consummation. Simple refusal to consummate the marriage is not sexual incapacity. Neither is sterility. Annulment of the marriage is not possible because one of the spouses is incapable of reproduction. Also, if the sexual incapacity occurs after the marriage has been consummated, the marriage may not be annulled.

THE MARRIAGE CEREMONY

In addition to the essential capacity requirements for marriage set down by the federal government, there are the formalities leading up to the marriage ceremony that must be observed if the marriage is to be valid. The provinces and territories, under their constitutional authority to legislate for the solemnization of marriage, have enacted statutes called ''marriage acts'' or ''ordinances.'' These statutes govern the steps and procedures leading up to the marriage ceremony. There is considerable uniformity across Canada in the formalities that must be observed to celebrate a legal marriage.

Prior to the marriage ceremony it is necessary to obtain a marriage licence or to have your banns published. In Alberta, Nova Scotia, and Prince Edward Island you must obtain a marriage licence. In all other jurisdictions you have the option of having banns published in your place of worship or obtaining a licence. Publishing banns means that your clergyman will announce for a period of successive weeks your intention to marry.

It is also necessary to establish that you are free to marry—that no impediment exists to your marriage. If you had a prior marriage, it will be necessary to prove the death of your prior spouse, or the dissolution of the marriage through divorce or annulment.

You will also have to establish proof of age. All provinces and territories have established minimum ages below which you may not marry without your parents' consent. The age at which you may marry without your parents' consent is sixteen in Newfoundland; eighteen in Alberta, Manitoba, Ontario, Prince Edward Island, Saskatchewan, and New Brunswick; nineteen in Nova Scotia, British Columbia, the Northwest Territories, and the Yukon Territory. In Quebec, a girl may marry at twelve, and a boy at fourteen.

If you are below these ages and your parents have withheld their consent, you may be able to apply to the court for an order dispensing with their consent.

Licences and banns are valid for specific periods of time. Upon completion of the waiting period, you are free to have the marriage ceremony. There are generally few restrictions on the actual ceremony itself. All of the provincial and territorial statutes provide for either a religious or a civil ceremony and authorize civil or religious officials to conduct the actual ceremony. In some jurisdictions it is necessary to present a medical certificate prior to obtaining a marriage licence. The ceremony requires two witnesses. There are few restrictions on where or when a marriage ceremony may take place. However, you must get the consent of the person authorized by law to conduct the ceremony to hold the ceremony in such unusual circumstances as underwater at Expo or in the Concorde within Canadian territorial jurisdiction.

RIGHTS AND OBLIGATIONS IN MARRIAGE

Debts

You and your spouse are each liable for your own debts. You are liable for your husband's debts only if you have co-signed for them. If you guarantee your husband's business or personal debts, your liability to repay them will survive the dissolution of the marriage. In seeking to recover payment of the debt, the lender is not obligated to seek payment first from your spouse. If you are not in a position to repay the debts, you could be forced into petitioning for personal bankruptcy. It is imperative that you seek independent legal advice prior to signing loan documents to determine the nature and extent of your obligations. (This is discussed more fully in Chapter 1.) Remember also that married women in particular have special reason to ensure an independent credit rating.

Name

Upon marriage, many women elect to use their husband's surname. In the absence of statute, there is no compulsion to do so. You may choose to retain your maiden name or hyphenate your surname and your husband's.

If you have remarried you may elect to keep your maiden name, or your first husband's name or your second husband's name or a combination of your old and new names.

If you wish to change your name, the process is usually one of establishing residence and of advertising your change of name and filing the necessary documentation.

Authority to legislate name changes rests with the provinces.

Property

Up until the latter part of the nineteenth century, married women could not own property in their own names. If they brought property into the marriage, it reverted to their husband. However, for some time now, married women have been legally able to hold property in their own right. During marriage, you and your husband may each have your own separate property and may not steal the property of the other.

Upon marriage breakdown, however, different rules apply. Today most provinces have enacted statutes that codify the belief that marriage is an equal partnership entitling both partners to an equal share of the marital assets upon the triggering of specific events signalling marriage breakdown, such as separation. Some jurisdictions limit marital property to those assets used for family purposes. Others do not. Many of these statutory provisions may be avoided by marriage contracts drawn in compliance with statutory requirements. Upon separation, divorce, or annulment you are entitled to an equal share of marital assets subject to what the marriage contract stipulates.

Wills

Your marriage will have an immediate impact upon any will you have made. Marriage revokes any will made prior to the marriage unless the will was expressly made in contemplation of marriage. This is discussed more fully in Chapter 10, "Death in the Family."

One of the valuable protections afforded to married women by the law is their entitlement to share in the estate left by a deceased spouse. If the spouse has left a will, it is still possible under wills-variations statutes to contest the will on the basis that insufficient support was given to the wife by the testator.

If there is no will, under the laws of intestacy, the wife and children are given priority.

Sex

Conjugal rights have always been one of the legal elements of marriage. As we have seen, sexual intercourse must take place in order for a marriage to be legally consummated. Sex is also an ongoing part of marriage. For example, divorces have been granted in Canada on the grounds of cruelty because one spouse refused to have sex for more than a year.

Although sex is recognized as one of the rights of marriage, you may not be forced to have sex against your will. Recent changes to the *Criminal Code* of Canada allow a husband to be charged if he rapes or sexually assaults his wife. This is discussed more fully in Chapter 9, "Violence in the Family."

Income Tax

As we saw in Chapter 5, "Financial Planning," the tax treatment given to married couples differs in some significant respects from that given to individuals. If both you and your spouse have income, you must each file separate tax returns, although you may be entitled to transfer certain deductions between yourselves in order to obtain the best tax deal possible. You are also allowed to make certain inter-spousal transfers of property, both during your lifetime and by will, in which you can defer the payment of tax.

THE MARRIAGE CONTRACT

A marriage contract is a contract between couples who are about to be or are married. The purpose of the contract is to set out the arrangements the parties have agreed upon to govern their marriage relationship and to provide, with some degree of certainty, what will happen upon the breakdown of the marriage. Marriage contracts are especially important for those couples residing in jurisdictions with family statutes that provide for an equal division of assets upon the occurrence of an event that signals the breakdown of the marriage. In those jurisdictions, in the absence of a valid marriage contract, there is an equal sharing of marital property.

In order to be a valid contract, the document must comply with the formalities required by the relevant statute. Most require that the contract be in writing, and be witnessed and signed and/or sealed after each party has obtained independent legal advice.

Typically, a marriage contract addresses the terms and conditions of the marriage, in particular the division of domestic duties, support provisions during marriage and upon separation, custody and guardianship of children, and division of property upon separation. In fact, you may incorporate into the marriage contract whatever terms and conditions you and your spouse consider important, although you may not contract out of any of the legally implied terms and conditions of the marriage contract. Furthermore, there is a limit to what the courts will enforce. Terms and conditions that would undermine the special character of the marital relationship, such as a covenant not to consummate the marriage, would not be enforced by the courts as these would offend against public policy. Covenants relating to personal services, such as who is responsible for domestic chores, would also not be enforceable, as the courts do not enforce contracts for personal services. Further, a term in the contract providing for custody of the children of the marriage would be reviewable by the courts under the inherent jurisdiction of the court to ensure the best interests of the child.

Like all contracts, a marriage contract is subject to being defeated if it is obtained through duress, undue influence, or misrepresentation, or if it was unconscionable.

It is important that the marriage contract be reviewed with a lawyer of your choice prior to signing. Your legal counsel can advise you what, if any, legal rights you may be giving up of which you are not aware and whether the contract complies with the formalities of the statute. If you fail to comply with the appropriate formalities required by your jurisdiction, you run the risk that the contract will not be enforceable and that, upon marriage breakdown, the statutory provisions and not the agreement of you and your spouse will govern the disposition of your marital property.

COMMON-LAW MARRIAGES

Contrary to popular opinion, mere cohabitation is not sufficient to constitute a common-law marriage. Neither does continued cohabitation make you a common-law spouse after seven years. Unless a specific statute provides otherwise, there must be a mutual agreement between a man and a woman to live together as man and wife to the exclusion of all others for the duration of their lives, and the essential capacity requirements for marriage must be met: the parties must freely consent, be of sufficient age, have the requisite mental capacity, not be too closely related through affinity or consanguinity, and be free to enter into the marriage (there must be no valid and subsisting marriage); the marriage must be consummated, and there must be continued cohabitation or holding out to the public of a marital relationship.

While often all that is lacking is the formal marriage ceremony, the law does not confer any automatic rights upon common-law spouses as it does to legal spouses. In fact, you are strangers in the eyes of the law. Your rights as a common-law spouse do not arise from implication of the law as in a legal marriage. They are infinitely more complex and arise out of statute and legal concepts that date back to the Middle Ages. Your rights, if any, will depend upon the definition of common-law spouse and such other requirements as are set out in the statute, such as the duration of the relationship.

Selected federal statutes, for example, confer benefits upon those common-law spouses who qualify under their specifications: the Canada Pension Plan may grant benefits to a common-law spouse who has cohabited for a period of time; dependent children may be claimed as exemptions for income-tax purposes, and income may often be advantageously split between common-law spouses; un-employment-insurance claimants may be allowed to have a common-law spouse qualify as a dependant.

Provincial statutes may make allowance for common-law spouses to obtain benefits from workers' compensation and support upon separation, or to share in the spouse's estate upon intestacy. How-ever, there are no automatic property rights granted to common-law spouses either during the relationship or upon its termination or the death of a spouse. Property rights for common-law spouses arise from equitable principles, such as constructive and resulting trusts. In a very general sense, these principles state that if you assisted your spouse in money or money's worth to obtain, maintain, or enhance the value of matrimonial property, the courts will consider your application to share in the division of that matrimonial property. The courts will look to determine if there was an enrichment of your spouse and a corresponding deprivation to you and no sufficient legal justification for the enrichment.

Because the rights of common-law spouses are so few at law, many couples today choose to enter into a cohabitation agreement. A cohabitation agreement is an agreement between a man and a woman who are living together or intend to live together but are not married. Couples who live together may use a contract to set out their respective rights and obligations during the period of co-habitation, on ceasing to cohabit, or upon death.

These contracts usually address the same considerations as mar-riage contracts. If, after entering into a cohabitation agreement, you marry, it automatically becomes a marriage contract.

Again, the contract should be in writing and should be reviewed before signing with a lawyer of your choice who can advise you what, if any, your rights are under statute and what, if any, rights you may be giving up.

Whether all or part of a cohabitation agreement will be enforceable depends upon the jurisdiction in which you reside.

SECOND MARRIAGES

Legally, you may marry as many times as you wish, provided you are able to meet all of the requirements of a valid marriage. In the case of second or subsequent marriages, you must, of course, be able to prove that any prior marriage has been dissolved or legally annulled. A final certificate of divorce is required as proof of the dissolution.

The rights and obligations of men and women in second marriages are exactly the same as those in first marriages, although they may be complicated by the contractual arrangements made in respect of any earlier marriage.

If you remarry, you must continue to make any support payments that you were ordered to pay to your first spouse as a result of the original separation agreement or court order; if you are receiving support and you remarry, your first spouse must continue to make the payments, unless the court orders a variation or your agreement specifies otherwise.

These obligations also may continue beyond your death, so that the second spouse is left with the burden of supporting the first spouse. In addition, if you have children from the first marriage, you should ensure that your will provides for them adequately. In all cases of a second marriage, it is advisable, therefore, to seek legal advice as to how you can best protect yourself and your estate from certain undesirable consequences otherwise decreed by the law.

GAY AND LESBIAN RELATIONSHIPS

Because the legal definition of marriage refers to the union of one man and one woman, people of the same sex are precluded from attaining legal status as married spouses in Canada. Even if the definition were changed, persons of the same sex would still be unable legally to consummate a marriage, as the act of sexual intercourse is required for consummation. However, there is nothing to prevent the use of a ''marriage contract'' in such a relationship, to set out the financial and property arrangements that the parties agree upon, both for the duration of the cohabitation and upon breakdown of the relationship. The use of a cohabitation agreement may be especially important in these circumstances, since the definition of common-law spouses in provincial legislation does not generally extend to persons of the same sex, and the law therefore recognizes no special support or property rights for gay or lesbian marriages.

CHAPTER 7

SEPARATION AND DIVORCE

Nancy Morrison

Nancy Morrison practises law in Vancouver in the area of civil litigation with an emphasis on family law. She also acts as an independent arbitrator in labour matters.

Prior to returning to the private practice of law, she was a provincial court judge in British Columbia, vice-chairman of the Labour Relations Board of B.C., and an assistant city prosecutor in Vancouver. She also practised law for several years in Saskatchewan with her father and in Niagara Falls with Judy LaMarsh. She has also taught law and lectures frequently on the topics of law reform, minority rights, and education.

Nancy Morrison is a former director of the Canadian Institute for Public Affairs, the Children's Aid Society, and the Vancouver Crisis Centre, and is currently a director of Telefilm Canada. In 1984, she was a Liberal candidate in the federal election. She was formerly a member of the Bars of Ontario and Saskatchewan, and is currently a member of the Bar in British Columbia.

IN THIS CHAPTER you will be taken through the legal proceedings that usually occur from the time you and your husband decide to separate up to a final divorce decree.

There are never any easy separations or divorces, especially where children or assets are involved. Everyone feels the trauma. But some separations and divorces are more civilized than others. These can occur when competent professionals assist and when expectations are realistic and not punitive.

SEEK LEGAL ADVICE

Before the separation occurs, go to a lawyer, one specializing in family law, and seek advice with regard to your rights on child custody and access, division of family assets, maintenance for yourself and the children, grounds for divorce, legal fees and court costs, and all other matters that are bound to arise once a decision to separate and/or divorce is made. Remember that the lawyer who put the transfer through on the house you and your husband bought ten years ago is not necessarily the lawyer qualified to give you advice on family law matters. And within the group of lawyers who specialize in family law, make sure that you choose a lawyer with whom you feel comfortable.

The solicitor-client relationship is a two-way street. The lawyer gives advice to the client, and the client then gives instructions to the lawyer. There should not be blind obedience on either side, but rather a sharing of information, a respect for one another's instincts and expertise, and a method of communicating that lessens the opportunities for misunderstanding. If a lawyer quotes a certain fee or price structure, it should be confirmed by way of a written letter or a contract signed between lawyer and client. There should be no misunderstanding right from the start, and remember, at all times when you are in the lawyer's office or communicating by letter or telephone, the meter is ticking. Be businesslike; be prepared.

If you have reached a decision that a separation is inevitable, or your husband has left and the separation is a fact, you can save time and legal fees by going to that first interview with the following information already prepared and legible, either written or typed.

1. *An information sheet* about yourself, your husband, and your children giving full names, including your maiden name and any divorced surnames, dates of birth of yourself, your husband, and your children, the date and place of the marriage, business and home addresses and phone numbers, your date of entry to Canada if you have immigrated, and the date your residence in the province commenced. Add to this occupations and anything else that you think might be pertinent.

2. *A statement of your estimated monthly expenses*, assuming that you and the children are living on your own or soon will be

living on your own. This should include *everything* that is spent over the course of a year, estimated out on a monthly basis, including allowances for vacation, legal fees, accounting fees, car depreciation, and replacement of furnishings, as well as the more mundane and obvious day-to-day expenses of housing, food, clothing, allowances for the children, sporting and extra-curricular activities, club memberships, pet supplies, and so on. This will eventually become a document that will be very crucial in an application or negotiation for monthly maintenance for yourself and the children, so it is important that nothing be forgotten and that there be an estimate for everything. Your lawyer will no doubt have a form available for you to fill out but, by anticipating this and keeping track of your expenses, you are assisting your own case and hastening things along.

3. *A statement of assets.* This should include assets in your name, in your husband's name, and/or in your names jointly. It should include any assets that either of you own, whether they are in your names or not, and any asset in which either of you has a beneficial interest. There should also be a market value of what those assets are. There will be many cases in which you simply cannot know the values, such as for the shares of a family company, until the asset is appraised by an expert. There are other assets whose values are easily ascertained. For an automobile, for example, telephone dealers or look in newspapers for sales of comparable autos; for real estate check with your local realtors; for furniture, estimate low, as if everything had to go to a garage sale tomorrow.

Generally speaking, all assets are valued for their sale price today. Do not give the original cost value, and do not consider the insured value or the replacement value. It is the actual value of an asset today that is relevant to determine the financial worth of you and your husband as of the date of separation.

4. *A statement of debts,* including those of yourself, those of your husband (to the best of your knowledge), and any joint debts. This will include any mortgages on the property, credit-card debts, and loans outstanding from parents.

5. *A statement of your earnings* for the current year and photocopies of your income-tax returns for the previous three years.

6. If there are *allegations of physical and/or mental cruelty* on which you wish to base a claim for marriage breakdown in divorce or a claim for custody of the children, you should write out a complete, chronological history of that cruelty, commencing with any events that occurred prior to the marriage. This is a painful document to produce. It is important to do it chronologically. Do not worry about editing. Let your lawyer edit it. If there has been a great deal of cruelty over the years, the material may easily fill a child's school scribbler. Do not worry about the length. Let your lawyer know the full extent of your allegations.

7. If you or your husband are involved in any kind of business, then of course any *financial statements, annual reports, income-tax returns for corporations, appraisals*, and anything else that you can lay your hands on will be very useful for your lawyer. If there are items in a joint safety deposit box, and you fear that your husband may clean them out, at least take the precaution of photocopying any documents that are in the safety deposit box. But seek legal advice before removing any or all of the contents of a safety deposit box or joint bank account. This can often be a hasty and ill-thought-out step that provokes World War III, when only a minor skirmish might otherwise be indicated.

OTHER PROFESSIONAL ADVICE

Your lawyer is not your family counsellor, nor your psychiatrist, nor your best friend. A time of separation is traumatic for both spouses, and for the children as well, and after you have picked your lawyer, your next immediate step should be to make sure that you have a competent *family counsellor*, someone who can assist you through the difficult months to come and help you deal with the problems that arise with regard to the children, and with your own feelings of anger, betrayal, guilt, and so on.

You may prefer to go to a psychiatrist, which is usually financed through medicare if you are referred by your family doctor. Or you may choose counselling from a psychologist, for which the fee varies. Family counsellors can be located through the family coun-selling services of your local ministry of Human Resources or its equivalent. There are also experienced senior social workers who have established their own private counselling services. As with a lawyer, it is important to find a family counsellor who is suitable for your needs. This is not meant to be someone who will try and reconcile you and your husband. It is assumed in this chapter that you have already made a decision—or had the decision forced on you—that the separation is a reality.

At the same time as you seek out the appropriate lawyer and family counsellor, you should also make sure that the *family doctor* who looks after your general health is tuned in to what is going on in your life. If you do not have a good family doctor, make all the necessary inquiries to find one. If possible, look for someone who does not believe in sedating through tranquillizers, who will make sure that your physical health is everything that it should be, and who can assist you in dealing with the stress and tensions that separation inevitably bring. Do not hesitate to take the assistance offered by friends and family members who wish to help you through a difficult period of time. Remember that you would want to help others in the same way. Often the help of people who have been through a similar experience is the most valuable. With your support network in place, you can treat your lawyer as a lawyer only, not a friend or a psychiatrist, and keep your legal fees down as much as possible.

A word of caution when dealing with psychologists. There are different certifications in different provinces, and if you intend to use the services of a psychologist or social worker, check out this person's qualifications with the relevant professional association in your province.

If you and your husband both decide to go for counselling to help you deal with the trauma of the separation and work out any problems with the children, it is often wise to let the spouse who is most vulnerable, the spouse who trusts counselling the least, make the first contact. This helps to avoid a situation in which one spouse distrusts the counsellor and refuses to continue going.

An *accountant* is essential if the assets involved are substantial or complex. You should have your own accountant, not your husband's. Make sure this is someone whose advice you understand, who will explain and assist, and who will guide you to make your own decisions.

SEPARATION

While no change in legal status flows from a separation, certain legal rights do. It is prudent, therefore, to have a separation agreement written up and signed by both parties—if the parties can agree on what should go in the agreement. If not, you may have to apply to the court, commencing with an action to deal with problems of custody, access, division of family assets, and maintenance.

Interim exclusive occupancy of the family home, interim maintenance for yourself and the children, and interim custody of the children may be dealt with by way of an application to the court seeking an interim order before there is a final resolution of all matters in the ultimate trial.

Bear in mind that, if there is a physical separation only—that is, if one party moves out of the home and there is no written agreement or court order to evidence the terms of that separation—some unhappy events may occur. For example, if the husband has moved out, he may decide to move back in, and there is nothing to stop him from doing so. It is still his home, his residence. There has been no determination with regard to who gets custody of the children, so he can still assert his authority, which may be at odds with yours.

If the parties have signed a simple agreement establishing their respective rights, they should have immediate recourse to the police and to the courts to enforce the agreement if one of them attempts to breach it.

Drafting a Separation Agreement

There is no law that says you may not draw up your own separation agreement, but it is always wise to have it checked by your own lawyer. It is also advisable to have an agreement checked *before* you sign anything, rather than after. Whether you draw up the agreement yourselves, or whether you have a lawyer draw it up for you, remember that the agreement must be in language that can be understood, especially by you. If it is not, have it redrafted. Never sign what you cannot understand. Never sign what you have not read, word for word, preferably out loud, and preferably with a lawyer present who specializes in family law.

And *never* be shy about saying, ''I don't understand that''; or, ''What does that mean?'' If an agreement cannot be understood on a first careful reading, it is probably badly drafted. Do not be overawed by the mystique of so-called legal language.

Do not get rushed into signing or making an agreement that you do not understand or cannot live with. Take the draft agreement home; read it over carefully; sleep on it. Make notes about questions and about possible changes, additions, and deletions.

Do not be intimidated by any lawyer. A competent lawyer welcomes your comments and should encourage them. However, your lawyer may well (and properly) dissuade you from adding the sentences that sum up the total lack of parenting, care, and sensitivity you feel your husband has shown over the years. The agreement will not be enhanced by vicious (if accurate) phrases about your husband's rotten behaviour. You might feel better for getting it off your chest and seeing it in ''a legal document.'' However, that is ultimately self-indulgent and of no use to anyone. Also, your husband will not sign such a paper, and there goes your agreement. See you in court, many moons and dollars later.

Go to your family counsellor to get the rage out of your system, and keep the agreement simple and neutral, written in non-threatening language, and drafted so that both you and your husband can live with it.

What Is in a Separation Agreement?

Whatever the parties can agree upon. The following are some of the items that you may wish to establish in an interim or a permanent separation agreement:

1. Custody of the children is to go to the wife, with the husband having reasonable access. Alternatively, joint custody of the children may go to both parents, with an agreement worked out as to which days or weeks the children will reside in which home.

2. The wife is to have exclusive occupancy of the matrimonial home until there has been a decree absolute of divorce, or alternatively, until the occurrence of some other event or time agreed upon between the parties (e.g., the youngest child reaches eighteen years of age, etc.).

3. Each spouse is to respect the privacy of the other's residence and neither is to enter the other's residence unless expressly invited to do so by that spouse.
4. Interim maintenance of $____ per month is to be paid to the wife until further agreement or an order of the court.
5. Interim maintenance of $____ per month per child is to be payable to the wife on behalf of the children, until further agreement or an order of the court.
6. The parties agree not to interfere with, molest, or annoy each other in any way, leaving each other free to live as if they were single persons.
7. The parties agree not to sell, transfer, or dispose of any property under the control and management of either of them without prior written consent by the other party.
8. The parties agree that the wife will declare the maintenance received by her on behalf of herself and the children as income and that the husband will deduct the said maintenance for purposes of income tax.

There may be other items that could be included in an interim agreement, but often the parties can agree on some short-term items such as immediate custody, access, and interim maintenance just to allow the separation to begin working and to give them time to get the rest of their financial matters straightened out and consult further with their lawyers.

If there are assets of any size, determining the value of those assets will often be difficult and time consuming. If there is real estate involved, there will probably have to be an appraisal or appraisals done. If there are companies involved, accountants will have to be brought in, one to represent each spouse, to give advice on proper valuations of the companies and their shares.

Sometimes, as an interim or short-term measure, the only thing a husband and a wife can agree upon may be the amount of monthly maintenance for the children for a short period—say, three or six months. Establishing a short-term agreement may be an advantage. It buys time and peace, and it is the first step in re-establishing trust between the parties; that is essential, especially if children are involved, as the co-parenting must go on regardless of the type of custody arrangements made.

Once any kind of written agreement dealing with maintenance is signed by both parties, if that maintenance is payable to the wife, and if it is payable on a periodic basis, the wife must declare that money as income for tax purposes and pay tax on the money received.

Often the husband will pay maintenance only if he has the guarantee of a written agreement or a court order confirming the amount. This is because Revenue Canada, bless them, require evidence in writing, by means of either a separation agreement or a court order, confirming that maintenance is being paid for a spouse and/or children in periodic payments.

There are no set rules on any of the items to be considered in the Separation Agreement. Everything is open for negotiation.

Am I "Legally Separated"?

The existence of a separation agreement, or of a court order declaring the terms of custody and maintenance and confirming that the parties are living separate and apart, does not create any special legal status. The parties are still married. Separation somewhat resembles limbo. It is a period of madness and recovery, if you like, but there is no special status in law except as evidence of marriage breakdown as grounds for divorce. The length of time of the separation is important. If the parties have been separated for one year, grounds of marriage breakdown exist for a divorce.

There are only two ways to get unmarried: death or divorce. For those parties who wish to know if they are "legally separated," the only answer is that there are no "illegal separations." Clients often ask if they are now free to date. They are free to date whether they are married or not, or living with their husbands or not. Whether they date is simply a matter of their own conscience and their own moral code. It has nothing to do with the law. There is some exception to this: there is sometimes a risk that a third party may be sued for causing the breakup of a marriage by deliberately engaging in adultery with a married person and thus standing in the way of any possible reconciliation attempts.

Breaking or Varying a Separation Agreement

The courts generally take the view that once two adults have made an agreement, they should be bound by that agreement, regardless of what may occur at a later date. The reasoning is that the parties should be able to plan ahead and should be able to rely upon the sanctity of the contract. The courts bring the sanctity of the contract from the marketplace into the breakup of a marriage and try and apply the same rules. However, those rules are not always equally applicable to the marketplace and the family domain. Generally, there may be four reasons for attempting to break, nullify, or vary an agreement that has been made. They are as follows:

1. Lack of independent legal advice for either party. If you have been forced or encouraged to sign without seeking independent legal advice, or have seen your husband's lawyer rather than your own, you may have grounds for attacking the agreement.

2. Failure to disclose certain financial information. This would have to be withholding information of a fairly significant nature; but if, say, your husband held back information about his assets, and you later found out about these assets, you might well have grounds for attacking the agreement.

   In this regard, it is often recommended that statutory declarations be sworn under oath by both parties and that they be attached to and form part of any final separation agreement. The declarations are statements of property disclosing all the assets of each party, including any asset in your own names, plus any and all assets in which you may have a beneficial interest. For example, your husband's mother, brother, or girl-friend may be holding something in trust. If so, this must be declared in the statutory declaration or perjury has been committed.

3. Duress, coercion, or fraud. If a party is induced to sign a contract when any of these elements are present, the contract's validity could be questioned.

4. Unfairness. This may not apply in all provinces, but in British Columbia, for example, a number of agreements have been attacked because the end result of the agreement was extremely unfair to one party. In such cases the contract has not been allowed to stand, or has been altered.

Generally, however, once you sign an agreement, you should assume that you are going to be stuck with that agreement. Hence, care should be taken at each stage.

DIVORCE

When marriage partners split, they mainly fight about two things: children and money. The divorce itself is seldom the cause for much disagreement. But it is often used as a negotiating point, when one party has grounds and the other does not, as in the case of adultery.

Described below are the various legal issues in a divorce action.

Residence

You do not have to be married in Canada to be divorced in Canada. But you must be a resident of one province for at least a year before bringing the petition for divorce in that province.

Your residence is a place where you may live from time to time. You may have a number of residences. Your home residence may be in Toronto, your cottage in the Laurentians, and your villa in Switzerland. Those are three residences, but your principal or ordinary residence must be in the province in which you bring your divorce petition.

This is simply a rule under the *Divorce Act* to prevent Canada from being another jurisdiction for quickie divorces.

Grounds

Historically, in Canada, until the 1968 *Divorce Act*, one could divorce only on the grounds of adultery. The exception was Nova Scotia, where cruelty had also been grounds for divorce even prior to Confederation.

In 1968, the federal government brought in some major reforms to the *Divorce Act*, allowing grounds, in addition to adultery, of mental and physical cruelty and/or marriage breakdown based on a three- or a five-year separation, depending on the so-called guilt or innocence of the party leaving and the party who was left. Also included (though seldom cited) were such grounds as gross addiction to alcohol or other drugs, sodomy, and bestiality.

In June 1986, in an attempt to move closer to no-fault divorce, revisions to our present *Divorce Act* came into effect stating that marriage breakdown would be the grounds for divorce. Marriage breakdown could be based on a one-year separation, on adultery, or on mental or physical cruelty.

This means that today in Canada, provided the necessary residence requirement has been met, a spouse can bring a divorce action against the other spouse if a one-year separation can be proved, regardless of who left whom, or of adultery or physical or mental cruelty.

Age and Disability

Two intriguing paragraphs on the divorce petition deal with the legal capacity of both spouses. They require the petitioner (the person bringing the divorce action) to certify that neither party to the petition is under the age of majority in that particular province. There is a further assertion that "no party . . . is under any other legal disability . . . ."

These two requirements can be explained by a quick look back into history. Historically, three classes of people in British common law were judged not to have the requisite legal capacity to bring an action on their own behalf, to defend an action, or to own land in their own name or manage their own affairs. Those three classes of persons were children, "lunatics," and women.

Women have now emerged from this protected classification, although that emergence has been fairly recent. However, children (those under the age of majority), are still excluded, as are individuals suffering from a mental disability so extreme that they would not be able to appreciate the nature of proceedings brought either on their behalf or against them.

Children

Under the *Divorce Act*, children are referred to as "children of the marriage" and are defined as children under the age of sixteen years or children sixteen years and over who are still under the charge of a parent or parents and are unable, by reason of illness, disability, or other cause, to withdraw from the charge of the parent and provide themselves with the necessaries of life. In other words, if a child is still living at home with one or both parents and attending school on a full-time basis, and is thus unable to provide the necessaries of life for himself or herself, that child is legally defined as a child of the marriage and is subject both to an order for custody and access under the *Divorce Act* and to an order for maintenance.

Children who have left home and become independent, regardless of age, are not to be included in a divorce petition, since they do not qualify as children of the marriage under the act.

In spite of some intensive lobbying by certain groups within Canada, the new *Divorce Act* did not bring in any provisions that would encourage the courts to push for joint custody. The argument whether sole custody or joint custody is preferable once a separation occurs is still raging. In the new act, however, there are some signs of movement towards treating the spouses more equally, whether in relation to maintenance, self-sufficiency, or custody and access.

The new act refers to maintenance orders that will "cause the spouses to share any economic consequences." It also states that any order for maintenance should recognize the economic advantages and disadvantages to the spouses that have arisen out of the marriage and those arising from the breakdown. The new *Divorce Act* also, for the first time, refers to "economic self-sufficiency" for both spouses, within a reasonable time of the making of any order for maintenance. In a further attempt to move away from misconduct towards no-fault, the new *Divorce Act* provides that maintenance will be ordered regardless of spousal misconduct.

As far as sections directly affecting children, the new *Divorce Act* states that the spouses have a financial obligation to maintain the children of the marriage, and that those obligations, as far as practicable, will be apportioned between the spouses according to their relative abilities to contribute, taking into account the means and needs of the spouses and the children.

The consolation prize for those who were advocating joint custody is the provision in the new *Divorce Act* that states: "the children of the marriage ought to have as much access to each of the spouses as the circumstances permit." The act goes on to provide that where in the opinion of the court it is required for the interest of the children, a lawyer or advocate should be appointed to represent the children independently. The court has the power to order such an appointment.

It is still common practice in most custody cases where there is no suggestion of child abuse for the court to refuse joint custody and to award sole custody to the mother. This may appear to be a win for the mother, but economically it is often far from that. She is then responsible for most of the burden of parenting for 365 days of the year, with little chance to improve her career and earning abilities and often a fight to collect the maintenance that may have been agreed upon or ordered by the court.

Collusion, Condonation, and Connivance

In the divorce petition, the petitioner is obligated to confirm to the court that there has been no collusion in relation to the petition; that is, that there has been no agreement or conspiracy to which the husband or the wife, directly or indirectly, has been a party, to subvert the administration of justice. Further, they must state that there has been no agreement or understanding to fabricate or suppress evidence in order to obtain the divorce and to deceive the court.

In a case where the grounds for divorce based on marriage breakdown include adultery or physical or mental cruelty, the petitioner must confirm that there has been no condonation or forgiveness by the petitioner, and no connivance; that is, that the petitioner has not encouraged the spouse to commit the act of adultery or cruelty. Prior to 1968, when adultery was the only grounds for divorce in all provinces but Nova Scotia, many divorces were obtained by manufacturing false grounds of adultery. This involved employing photographers, renting motel rooms, and hiring private investigators and sundry other bit players. The court still needs reassurance that these bit players have been retired, and no longer play their roles.

With the recent amendments to the *Divorce Act*, many people believe that the problems of divorce have been made much simpler. Strictly speaking, that is correct. The divorce itself can be obtained without the necessity of a court appearance by either party; it can now be done by paperwork alone.

However, if the parties cannot agree on the two crucial questions of children and money, the new *Divorce Act* makes little difference. The quarrels over custody of and access to children, distribution of family assets, and the payment of spouse and child maintenance can still be prolonged for months or years in court, depending on the perseverance of the parties, and their means to sustain a court action. The court action to resolve the financial and custody issues may be included in a divorce petition, or it may be commenced separately from the divorce petition, under the relevant provincial statute. In either case, the agonies associated with divorce problems do not lie with the actual divorce itself, but rather with those issues involving children and money.

REMEDIES

What kind of action do you begin? It depends on what remedies you are seeking. To sum up, they may include the following:

1. A decree of divorce.
2. A declaration that reconciliation is impossible, or that the parties are deemed to be judicially separated.
3. Interim custody of the children, either sole or joint.
4. Permanent custody of the children, either sole or joint.
5. Interim maintenance for the children, pending the final decree of divorce or the final outcome of any custody and property actions.
6. Permanent maintenance on behalf of the children.
7. Interim maintenance for the wife.
8. Permanent maintenance for the wife, involving either lump-sum or periodic payments.
9. A declaration from the court as to what assets are family assets and what assets are not.
10. A division of family assets, either on a fifty-fifty basis, or on some other percentage, depending on the circumstances, the contributions made by the parties, and so on.
11. A *lis pendens* against the property or properties in the name of or controlled by the other spouse that are affected by the matrimonial dispute. The *lis pendens* certifies that legal title to the property in question could change as an outcome of the matrimonial proceedings that have been commenced.

    The filing of a certificate of *lis pendens* against the property in the land registry office of the relevant province acts as a caution to any third party attempting to deal with the property. For example, if the third party attempts to put a mortgage on that property or to purchase it, that party is warned that there is an action pending and that the spouse placing the *lis pendens* on the title may well have a claim to all or a portion of that property.

12. An order restraining the spouse from selling, transferring, mortgaging, or dealing in any way with any property, pending resolution of the matters in question. This type of restraining order, or freezing of assets, is meant to preserve the assets pending their division by the court or by agreement. This is an extreme remedy that should only be asked for when there is serious concern about the dissipation of assets. Seeking this remedy where major assets may involve active stocks being traded can cause serious problems. An order freezing such assets may be tempered to allow the spouse to continue to trade under strict supervision and reporting conditions.

    If you think there is a real danger that your husband is going to cause a flow of funds and assets to either a Swiss bank account or an account in Grand Cayman or the Isle of Man, then the sooner you obtain an order freezing assets the better. This is an order that would be claimed in the original petition or the original writ of summons, but it would usually be made the subject of an interim order prior to trial if your concern is sufficient.

    Here again is where you should trust your own instincts and make sure that your lawyer is aware of your instincts. If you have been living with a spouse for twenty years, you know that person well. If your instinct says that money is being spirited out of the country, it frequently is.

13. In the case of physical abuse, a restraining order that the husband shall have no contact directly or indirectly with the wife.

14. An order giving one spouse conduct of the sale of the matrimonial home, to ensure co-operation with the realtor with regard to open houses, make sure that the house is clean and presentable for viewing, and prevent sabotaging of the listing. The latter has been known to happen.

This is not a comprehensive list, nor is it meant to be. It is a brush with reality, to help guide you to the appropriate professionals and to help you bring all the relevant information that you must to your lawyer.

Family Assets

The *Divorce Act* is a federal law, the same across Canada. Do not confuse it with provincial laws that settle property rights between parties. When you are dealing with the division of family assets, you are dealing with property rights, and this is a matter that comes within provincial jurisdiction. Therefore, each province has a somewhat different act dealing with how family assets should be determined and divided between the parties. You may combine with your divorce action an action to settle the family assets, by including your relief sought under the provincial statute as well. Under the provincial statute, you are asking the court to decide what is a family asset and who gets what share of those assets.

Your provincial family property laws may limit you to division of what are termed "family assets" only. In that case you should work to have everything judged a family asset, based on your contributions, monetary or otherwise.

Within the last twenty years, family laws as they relate to division of assets acquired by marital partners have changed dramatically in Canada. The economic and emotional contribution that women make in the home is now recognized in most provinces. Also, in most provinces it does not matter in whose name the asset may be; both parties are deemed to have an interest in that asset, whether it be a pension plan, an RRSP, a matrimonial home, or a vacation cottage. It is probably fair to say that the laws involving the division of family assets between marital spouses provide the most litigation in matrimonial disputes.

Maintenance

Maintenance has now become an area in which growing equality between the sexes is making some interesting changes. Traditionally, women have stayed home and husbands have been the breadwinners; in the event of a separation, the husband would continue to pay maintenance to the wife for her own support, in addition to maintenance for the children.

Cases in which the woman is the one working outside the home or the one with the substantial assets because of inheritance or other factors are now becoming more common. In such cases, a husband who is unable to find work or who cannot work because of illness or disability is entitled to maintenance from the wife.

For the purposes of this chapter, however, we will assume that we are dealing with the wife who has remained at home to fulfil the role of wife and mother, and who, upon separation, finds not only that she has not developed a career outside the home but that she is still expected by both her husband and the courts to become economically "self-sufficient."

The courts are now more than willing to ensure that maintenance for the wife is provided for a period of time, to allow her time to "rehabilitate." The term "rehabilitation" is somewhat offensive, because it has presumably been introduced into matrimonial law from the criminal law field. As the dictionary defines it, to rehabilitate means to restore to a former capacity of position, or "to re-establish in the esteem of others." The implication is clear: this woman needs to shape up and get out into the work world, to re-establish herself in the world's esteem. This seems to suggest that, in the home where she has been working full time with no pay, she has *not* been in the work world and not held in esteem.

It is not easy to be booted off the pedestal at the time of a separation, told that the old rules no longer apply: "No wife of mine will ever work"; "I want my wife home where she belongs, looking after me and raising my children"; "Being a wife and mother is the greatest and only career my wife needs." Come the separation and divorce proceedings, and a wife, provided she is still young enough, must become self-sufficient.

Increasingly, a wife may now, if she wishes, return to school to complete her high school or college or university education. The argument is that the best investment the husband can make with regard to his soon-to-be-ex-wife is to educate her so that she will indeed be self-sufficient. Having two parents who are economically self-sufficient also offers double protection for the children, in case something happens to one parent.

If the separation occurs after a lengthy marriage and the wife is not young enough or in poor health which would preclude her working outside the home, it is assumed that maintenance will continue for her despite any separation or divorce.

It is also important, where maintenance is provided, that the estate of the husband be bound by the terms of the separation agreement or divorce decree. Alternatively, some parties agree that rather than have the husband's estate bound, which can often leave the second wife under the unhappy obligation to pay maintenance to the first wife, an insurance policy sufficient to provide equivalent maintenance payments after the husband's death can be provided and kept up by the husband.

It should be noted that the terms "alimony" and "maintenance" are not precisely interchangeable. Alimony is often referred to as the money paid during a period of separation, before the divorce becomes final. Maintenance, a more comprehensive term, refers to maintenance or support payments paid for a spouse and children both before and after the divorce decree.

The Divorce Certificate

There used to be two decrees issued in a divorce proceeding. There was a Decree Nisi, a provisional decree, which means, "a divorce unless" issued after the trial. It sets out the terms of the court order. There was then a three-month wait after the issuing of the Decree Nisi before a Decree Absolute could be issued. Once the Decree Absolute was issued, the period was over for either party to launch an appeal, and the decree became final. Under the revised Divorce Act, procedures and waiting periods have been shortened.

In place of a Decree Nisi, there is now simply an Order of the Court. This is followed by a thirty-one day waiting period, and a Certificate of Divorce is issued, in place of the former Decree Absolute. Parties may then remarry, once they have a certified copy of the Divorce in hand.

CHAPTER 8

CHILDREN AND THE LAW

Marie Irvine
Susan Chernin
Ivonna Danbergs

Marie Irvine is a member of the Ontario Bar and is executive director of Justice for Children. Her experience in children's law includes policy development, law reform, public legal education, and direct legal representation of children, young persons, and their parents.

Susan Chernin is a member of the Ontario Bar and practises as a legal advocate with the Advocacy Centre for the Elderly. She is on the Board of Directors of Justice for Children and has had experience in children's issues both in private practice and as counsel to the Children's Aid Society of the Municipality of York.

Ivonna Danbergs is a social worker with Justice for Children. She is an Australian-trained lawyer and social worker, with experience in counselling, advocacy, and legal representation of children and young persons.

TO UNDERSTAND THE LAW AS it relates to children, it is important to recognize that concern for and interest in the legal treatment and rights of children is a relatively modern phenomenon. This ''new'' approach, coupled with the fact that the legal system is increasingly called on to address questions of equality and discrimination, means that the whole area of children's law is in a state of flux.

The very definition of a child is evolving moreover, the law is

144

inconsistent in its treatment of young people, considering them adults for some purposes and children for others.

Historically, the child in western society has been under the total control of the family. In the early Middle Ages, parents freely contracted marriages and indentures for apprenticeships for even very young children. For other purposes, however, the period of childhood had ended, and seven- and eight-year-olds shared in the income-generating work of the family.

By the sixteenth century, the period of childhood was extended. This reflected the length of time required for children to be educated to assume the more complex responsibilities of an increasingly industrialized society. With industrialization came greater hardship for the child labourer; but it was not until the nineteenth century, with the advent of charitable societies, that pressure was brought to bear to afford children at least the same protections that had been established for animals.

In the twentieth century, with the development of psychological and educational theories, the recognition of childhood as an important growth stage emerged. The assumed criminal liability of children was questioned, and special juvenile court systems were implemented to deal with the social and emotional factors behind criminal behaviour. At the same time, greater recognition was given to the neglected and the physically and emotionally abused child.

Today, the state is expected to provide the legislative and social-service systems that prevent abuse of children. Moreover, parents are demanding more accountability from the professionals who care for their children. Thus society is slowly recognizing that children are not the chattels of either their parents or the state. The concept of children's rights has emerged, and its acceptance is growing.

This chapter informs parents, professionals, and young people of the current laws applicable to children. It is not meant to offer a definitive legal analysis of any of the issues presented. If you need legal assistance or a legal opinion on any matter addressed, you should consult a lawyer.

The focus of much of this chapter is based on Ontario legislation, but the issues facing young people are the same throughout the country, and many provinces have adopted or are currently considering adopting similar legislation to that which is discussed below.

Table 8:1   Summary of Age Limitations Relating to Children and the Law

Jurisdiction / Legal age for...	New-found-land	Prince Edward Island	Nova Scotia	New Bruns-wick	Quebec	Ontario	Manitoba	Sas-katch-ewan	Alberta	British Columbia	Yukon and North-west Terri-tories
Starting and leaving school	6–15	8–15	6–16	7–16	6–15	6–16	7–15	7–15	6–15	7–15	6–16
Marrying	16	18	19	18	Girls 12 Boys 14	18	18	18	18	19	19
Reaching age of majority	Each province sets own age (usually 18 or 19). The age of majority under federal legislation is 18.										
Obtaining driver's licence	Each province sets own age (usually 16).										
Drinking	Each province sets own age (usually 18 or 19).										

Leaving home	Each province sets own age (usually 16).
Receiving social assistance	Each province sets own age (usually 16).
Renting premises	No general rule.
Obtaining medical treatment without parental permission	No general rule. For surgery or treatment in hospital, usually 16.
Giving evidence in criminal court	Usually 14
Being tried in adult criminal court	Age 18

WHO IS A CHILD?

What Is the Age of Majority?

Each province sets its own age of majority, usually eighteen or nineteen years. In addition, the federal government may prescribe the age of majority for situations involving federal law: for example, it has provided eighteen as the upper limit to which the *Young Offenders' Act* applies, and the age at which persons may vote in federal elections.

When May a Young Person Drive a Car?

Each province sets its own age. Usually a person must be sixteen years of age to obtain a driver's licence or drive a motor-assisted vehicle or snow vehicle on a highway.

When May a Young Person Drink or Smoke?

Each province sets its own age for these matters, usually eighteen or nineteen. Generally, it is against the law for anyone under this age to buy, try to drink, or drink liquor or beer, or for anyone to sell or give liquor or beer to such a young person. A young person may, however, be given liquor or beer by a parent or guardian if this occurs in a private residence.

A young person who smokes does not commit an offence. It is against the law, however, for any person to sell or give a young person under the age of eighteen any tobacco, including cigarettes.

Does a Young Person Have to Go to School?

Each province establishes a ''compulsory education'' rule, prescribing the minimum and maximum ages between which a child must attend school. In Alberta, Newfoundland, and Quebec, a young person must attend school from the age of 6 to 15 years. In British Columbia, Manitoba, and Saskatchewan the ages are 7 to 15. In New Brunswick, it is 7 to 16, and in Prince Edward Island, 8 to 15. In Nova Scotia, the Yukon and Northwest Territories, and Ontario, a young person must attend school from the age of 6 to 16 years.

Each province sets out limited exceptions to the ''compulsory education'' rule. For example, in Ontario, with the exceptions listed below, a young person must attend school until his or her sixteenth birthday. Although the law regarding school attendance is under review at this time, it is likely that children will continue to be required to attend school. At present, where a young person does not attend school on a regular basis, a school attendance counsellor may speak to the young person and his or her parents. If the parents refuse or do not make reasonable attempts to ensure their child's attendance, they may be charged under the *Education Act* and fined. The pupil may also be charged.

Young persons may be absent from school if they are ill or, in some cases, if they are receiving a proper education at home. As the rules concerning home education are rather technical, parents who wish to remove their child from the public system should seek legal advice before doing so. A parent may apply on behalf of his or her fourteen- or fifteen-year-old child for acceptance into a program known as supervised alternative learning (early school leave). If accepted into such a program, a pupil is permitted to work full or part time at a place approved by the school, and may be required to attend school part time.

When May a Young Person Legally Leave Home?
Generally, a young person has the right to leave home at the age of sixteen years.

When May a Young Person Get Married?
Each province determines the age at which a person may independently enter a contract of marriage. In British Columbia, the Territories, and Nova Scotia, it is nineteen; in Newfoundland it is sixteen years, while in the other provinces (with the exception of Quebec), it is eighteen years. In Quebec, a girl may marry at twelve, and a boy at fourteen.

Most provinces allow a young person who is sixteen years of age to marry with parental consent. In Ontario, in special circumstances, a young person of this age may apply to a court to marry without this consent. As well, a young person aged fourteen or fifteen may apply to the Minister of Consumer and Corporate Relations for permission to marry.

May a Person Under Eighteen Receive Social Assistance?

Each province sets its own rules concerning the receipt of social assistance. In Ontario, a young person who is sixteen may receive social assistance. Special rules exist with respect to sixteen- and seventeen-year-old persons, however; they generally have to convince administrators that their parents are not willing to let them live at home, or that it is not in their best interests to remain living at home. Administrators may require young persons to sue their parents for support (see below). As well, young persons requiring social assistance in order to complete their education will generally need a letter from the school stating that it is desirable for them to continue with their education. Non-students must be actively seeking employment.

An unmarried parent aged sixteen or seventeen may be able to receive social assistance for the child. This is possible whether or not the young person is living in the parental home. Unmarried parents not living at home may be able to receive welfare for themselves as well.

In some cases it is possible to appeal a caseworker's decision to refuse social assistance.

What If a Landlord Refuses to Rent Premises to a Person Under Eighteen?

Generally, the provincial human rights codes do not provide redress to a young person who has been rejected as a tenant because he or she is under eighteen years of age. The *Charter of Rights and Freedoms* may provide a remedy in these circumstances, but the success of such a challenge has not yet been tested in the courts.

What If a Child Is in Need of Medical Treatment?

Parents have a duty to ensure that their children receive necessary medical treatment. Where parents refuse to provide their child with needed treatment, the local children's aid society or an advocate for the child may invoke the court process to intervene on the child's behalf. In an emergency, a doctor may always treat a young person in order to save his or her life or a part of the body.

May a Doctor Treat a Young Person Without a Parent's Consent?

Other than in an emergency, at common law a doctor may give medical treatment to a young person without a parent's consent if the doctor decides that the young person fully understands what the treatment involves and how it may affect him or her. With one exception, there is no general rule that a young person must be at least sixteen (or eighteen) years of age in order to get medical treatment at his or her own request. This exception involves treatment in a hospital.

May a Doctor Perform Surgery on a Young Person without a Parent's Consent?

Generally, surgery in a hospital will be performed on a young person under the age of sixteen only with a parent's written consent. If you are sixteen or seventeen years old, parent's consent is not required if you understand what the surgery involves and how it will affect you. These special rules about hospital treatment apply to abortions. As well, in order for anyone (regardless of age) to get an abortion anywhere in Canada, a doctor must get the approval of a special committee in a hospital.

Is a Child Eligible for Counselling without a Parent's Consent?

Under provincial legislation, some counselling services may be given to a young person without parental consent at the age of twelve. For other counselling services, the law is somewhat unclear, and those seeking assistance should determine the policies of the particular agency.

CHILD-PROTECTION LEGISLATION

When May the State Intervene to Protect a Child?

Child welfare falls within the domain of provincial governments. To address protection concerns and to ensure the least amount of intervention in the life of the family appropriate in the circumstances, each province has enacted legislation that attempts to balance the rights and responsibilities of the particular parties involved. At the same time, a minimum level of child care below which the state may find itself justifiably intervening in the best interests of the child must be established. The onus (or primary responsibility) is also on the state to show that such intervention is warranted. Except in those situations where voluntary arrangements or agreements are entered into by the parties, the court process will be invoked by the local children's aid society, most commonly by a protection application. This application is filed with the court and served on all the parties, including a child who is twelve years of age or older. Where the child's safety is at imminent risk, the child may be apprehended from the care-giver.

Who Is a Child in Need of Protection?

As mentioned earlier, many provinces have adopted or are considering legislation similar to that in effect in Ontario. In Ontario, the *Child and Family Services Act* establishes twelve categories within which children must fall before they can be found to be in need of protection. The most common categories are: physical harm, or its risk; sexual molestation, exploitation, or its risk; required medical attention where the parent refuses to consent, or for some reason is unable to consent; emotional harm demonstrated by anxiety, depression, withdrawal, self-destructive or aggressive behaviour, or the risk of such conditions developing; and situations where a child suffers from a mental, emotional, or developmental condition and the parent does not or cannot attempt to remedy the situation. The act also addresses situations where a child is abandoned or where the child under twelve has committed a very serious offence or two or more offences against a person or property. As well, where a parent acknowledges an inability to care for a child, the child may be brought before the court if both the parent and the child over twelve years consent to this action.

The following is a list of children who are all similar in at least one respect:
• a twelve-year-old girl who has reported to her teacher that she has had intercourse with her father;
• a three-year-old child who has been repeatedly admitted to the hospital with broken bones;

- a fifteen-year-old girl who wishes to have an abortion and whose parents have refused consent to the operation;
- a nine-year-old boy who has been involved in a series of fire settings.

The common factor is that each may be a child in need of protection.

How Does the Court Process Work?

Once the matter is before the court, a two-stage process is put into effect. The first stage requires the court to make a finding that the child falls within one or more of the categories set out in the act and therefore is in fact "a child in need of protection." Only after such a finding has been made can the court consider what action would be in the child's best interests.

Various options are available to the court. These include: an order for the child to remain with or be returned to the custodial parent or other appropriate person, subject to supervision by the local children's aid society; an order for the child to remain in the care and custody of the children's aid society for a temporary period and, where appropriate, a direction that the child return home under supervision at the expiry of a specific period of time; an order that the child be made a Crown (permanent) ward of the province and committed to the care and custody of the children's aid society. Finally, the court may determine that no order need be made. This last option may occur if the child's family has addressed the protection concerns of the local children's aid society through the voluntary involvement of the children's aid society itself, of independent professionals, or of other community supports. Before any of the above dispositions may be made, the children's aid society must prepare a plan of care for the court that not only sets out the reasons for its involvement or continuing involvement but also satisfies the court that the least intrusive form of intervention appropriate under the circumstances has been recommended and specifies what efforts have been made to meet the needs of the child in the family setting.

Is There Any Review or Appeal?

In those cases where a supervision order or a temporary wardship order has been made, an automatic review will take place at the expiry of a specific period of time. This "status-review application" will be initiated by the children's aid society that has jurisdiction in the matter. As well, the children's aid society may bring a status-review application at an earlier date if a change in circumstances warrants it. While other parties to the proceedings have a similar option, it is not available until six months have passed from the making of the order (subject to abridgment of this requirement by a Provincial Court judge in the best interests of the child).

The six-month rule also applies to those cases where a child has been made a Crown ward. Once the child has been placed for adoption, however, this application is barred.

Besides the status-review process, a party who is dissatisfied with either the finding or the disposition of the provincial court judge may appeal the decision to a higher court.

Who Must Report Child Abuse?

Anyone who believes that a child is in need of protection must report this to a children's aid society. This is a general provision that applies to the community at large. There are also categories of professionals, including health-care professionals, teachers, clergy, youth and recreation workers, peace officers, service providers and their employees, and lawyers (except in the context of a solicitor/client relationship), who must report any child they suspect is a victim of abuse; failure to do so may result in a fine. It is important to note that volunteers do not come within this professional reporting duty.

Does a Child in Care Have Any Rights?

Generally, a child in care has the following rights:
- the right not to be detained in locked premises;
- the right not to be subjected to corporal punishment;
- the right to regular visits with family;
- the right of access to counsel;
- the right to privacy of mail communications;
- the right to reasonable privacy and possession of personal property;
- the right to freedom of religious practices;
- the right to a plan of care;
- the right to receive appropriate and well-balanced meals;

- the right to be provided with appropriate and good-quality clothing;
- the right to receive medical and dental care at regular intervals;
- the right to receive an education that corresponds to the child's aptitude and abilities;
- the right to participate in recreational and athletic activities;
- the right to participate in significant decisions affecting him or her;
- the right to be informed of internal complaint provisions;
- the right to be informed of and to have access to the Office of Child and Family Services Advocacy;
- the right of the child aged twelve to a review of his or her placement;
- the right to be informed of the rules governing the residence in which he or she is placed.

THE CHILD VICTIM OF SEXUAL ABUSE

In addition to the protection given to children by provincial child-protection legislation, a person who sexually abuses a child commits a criminal offence under the federal *Criminal Code*, and may be prosecuted in criminal court.

How Old Must a Child Be to Give Evidence in Criminal Court?

Generally, a child aged fourteen or over may be allowed to give evidence in court on the same basis as an adult. For the child under the age of fourteen, special rules apply. In this case, the judge must be convinced that the child understands the nature of an oath. The child need not understand any spiritual consequences, but must understand that the oath involves a moral obligation to tell the truth.

What If a Child Does Not Understand the Nature of an Oath?

The judge may still hear the evidence of the child, if the judge is satisfied that the child is possessed of sufficient intelligence to justify the reception of the evidence and understands the duty of speaking the truth. This is called "unsworn evidence."

May an Adult Be Convicted on the Basis of the Unsworn Evidence of a Child Alone?

No. Where a child under fourteen gives unsworn evidence, that evidence must be corroborated by some other material evidence. This is called "corroborating evidence."

What Is Corroborating Evidence?

Corroborating evidence is evidence tending to support the truth of the other evidence presented. In sexual abuse cases, it could be, for example, the findings of a medical examination.

The law of evidence as it applies to children is being reviewed at the present time, and may be revised to make it easier for a child to be heard in court.

What Can Be Done to Prepare a Child for the Court Experience?

Most witnesses suffer anxiety prior to testifying in court. For children, confusion about the court process may create additional stress. The child is expected to relate the story in a calm, rational manner, using adult interpretations and understandings of the event and recalling events that could have taken place many years prior to the court hearing and that are painful to subject to judicial scrutiny. Care should be taken not to interfere with the child's evidence, but these anxieties should be acknowledged and dealt with, where possible, by a competent professional.

As a practical matter, the following steps may alleviate some of the child's anxiety: arranging a meeting with the Crown attorney prior to the court date; taking the child for a tour of the courtroom and giving him or her an opportunity to speak from the stand; demonstrating basic court procedures (for example, who stands where in court and when witnesses must leave the courtroom); providing counselling and support for the child; and bringing activities for the child to do while waiting to testify.

Is Financial Compensation Available for Victims (Including Victims of Sexual Abuse)?

Yes. In Ontario, for example, whether or not a conviction has been obtained in a sexual-abuse trial, an application may be made on a child's behalf for compensation from the Criminal Injuries Compensation Board. Although an application must generally be brought within twelve months from the date of the offence, in many cases this rule will be dispensed with. The Official Guardian's office should be contacted for further information.

THE CHILD AND THE CRIMINAL LAW

What Law Applies to Young Persons in Conflict with the Law?

Young persons between the ages of twelve and seventeen who break the criminal law are dealt with under the federal *Young Offenders' Act*. Those under the age of twelve may be dealt with in accordance with provincial child-protection law (see above).

What Approach Does the *Young Offenders' Act* Take to Young People?

The act sets out its approach in the Declaration of Principle. Basically the following principles apply:

- A young person who breaks the criminal law will bear responsibility for his or her actions.
- Young offenders will not always be held as responsible or suffer the same punishment as adult offenders.
- The public should be protected, as needed, from criminal acts by young persons.
- While young offenders need control and discipline, they also have special needs and require assistance.
- Rather than taking a young offender to court, the police should consider some other action or no action if the public will still be protected.
- Young persons have rights and freedoms, which include those in the Canadian *Charter of Rights and Freedoms* and the right to participate and be heard when decisions are made about them.
- Young persons should have special guarantees of their rights and freedoms.
- Young persons have the right to be told about all their rights and freedoms in the criminal-justice system.

- Young persons have the right to the least possible intervention with their freedom as long as the public is protected and the needs of the young persons and the interests of their families are considered.
- Parents should look after and guide their children, and young persons should not be taken away from their parents' control, partly or entirely, unless nothing else suitable can be done.

Do Young Persons Have Special Rights When Dealing with the Police?

Yes. The police must inform any young person whom they arrest of the following rights:
- the right to know the reason for the arrest;
- the right to remain silent;
- the right of access to a lawyer;
- the right to talk to a lawyer or adult, usually a parent, before telling the police anything or answering any questions;
- the right to have a lawyer or a parent present if the young person decides to talk to the police.

Do Young Persons Have the Right to a Lawyer?

Young persons have the right to be provided with a lawyer when they appear in court on a criminal charge.

Will Young Persons Be Told of the Right to a Lawyer?

Yes. The police and (where a young person does not have a lawyer at any hearing, trial, or review) the judge must tell young persons of this right and give them a chance to contact a lawyer.

May a Young Person's Name Be Published or Broadcast in the Media?

Except where publication of the name of a young person who is charged with a serious crime and is considered dangerous is necessary to assist in apprehending the young person, no one may publish or broadcast a young person's name or any other identifying information in connection with a criminal charge.

What Kinds of Sentences May a Young Person Be Given?

Depending on the circumstances, the sentences available to the judge may include the following:

- an absolute discharge (this means the young person will not be punished);
- a fine of not more than $1,000;
- a compensation order;
- a restitution order;
- a personal-services order;
- a community-services order;
- an order that the young person be detained for treatment (this order may only be made if the young person, the parents, and the treatment facility agree to it);
- a probation order;
- a custody order.

THE CHILD AND THE FAMILY

Do Parents Have to Support Their Children?

Parents have the duty to ensure that their children have food, clothes, and a place to live, or enough money to get these things for themselves. Generally, parents must support their children up until age eighteen, unless a sixteen- or seventeen-year-old child leaves home voluntarily. However, if a young person leaves home because the parents have forced this withdrawal, or were abusive, the parents may still have the obligation to support that child. As well, in the context of a divorce, an application for support may be made under federal law, the *Divorce Act*, and the *Divorce and Corollary Relief Act*. In certain circumstances, support of a child of the marriage may be extended beyond the age of eighteen.

EDUCATION

The laws regarding obligatory school attendance are discussed earlier in this chapter.

How May a Pupil Be Disciplined?

Regulations regarding strapping or other forms of physical punishment vary from one school board to another. Whatever method is used, it is restricted to that kind which a kind, firm, and fair parent would administer, and it must be reasonable in the circumstances. Some school boards do not permit the use of the strap in their schools.

A principal may be given the authority to suspend a pupil from school for damaging school property, swearing, not attending school, or not doing what the pupil is told. The principal must tell the student and the parents in writing of the suspension. Parents may appeal the suspension to the school board if they disagree with the reasons given.

A student may be expelled from school if the student's behaviour is dangerous to other students. The pupil and the parents must be informed in writing of any recommendation to expel a pupil. The parents have the right to make representations on behalf of their child at a hearing conducted by the school board.

Are School Records Kept?

A student record is kept at a pupil's school. It contains information about the pupil's achievement and progress in school. It may also contain other information that school personnel feel is important for improving the pupil's education.

May this Information Be Seen or Changed by a Parent or Pupil?

The pupil and the pupil's parents have the right to see the student record and to ask to have any information in it changed if that information is false or not connected with the improvement of the pupil's education.

Do Exceptional Children Have the Right to Go to School?

All students have the right to an appropriate education that meets their needs, their disabilities notwithstanding. Where a regular school class is not appropriate for a student because of a disability or special problem, that pupil has the right to a special class or services better suited to his or her needs. Only the pupil's parents or the principal, however, can ask for a meeting of the school board to consider the pupil's needs. Parents should obtain a copy of the school board's guide to special education if they think their child is having problems in school.

Who Decides If a Pupil Is in Need of Special Education?
A committee of the school board will decide whether a pupil is in need of special education and what placement is best.

May This Decision Be Appealed?
Parents who do not agree with the decision of the committee may appeal it further. Parents wishing to appeal are advised that they should seek legal advice, as the appeal process is complicated.

ADOPTION

Who May Place a Child for Adoption?
Adoption is a provincial matter. Usually, a child under sixteen may be placed for adoption only by a children's aid society or an adoption licensee (i.e., a holder of a licence issued by the Ministry of Community and Social Services), unless the child is being adopted by a relative (including a grandparent, great-uncle or -aunt, aunt or uncle, whether by blood, marriage, or adoption), a parent, or a spouse of a parent.

To What Information or Services Are Prospective Adoptive Parents Entitled?
The person or agency placing the child with a prospective adoptive parent has the responsibility to share medical and social histories in writing. Follow-up visits are essential, and the licensees must have access to the professional services of a physician, a psychiatrist, a registered psychologist, and a lawyer, as well as an approved social worker. A home study must be completed before any placement can be made.

May a Child Be Placed for Adoption Outside the Province or Canada?

The above provisions apply to a placement in another part of Canada. However, if the child is placed by an adoption licensee, the Ministry of Community and Social Services must give its approval unless there is an exemption.

Additional criteria are taken into consideration when a child is placed outside of Canada. At least one of the proposed adoptive parents should be a Canadian citizen, and at least one should be related to the child by blood, marriage, or adoption, unless the placement is for the preservation of the child's cultural or linguistic background.

Who May Bring a Child into Canada for Adoption Placement?

With the exception of a relative (as defined above), a parent, or the spouse of a parent, these placements may only be made by a children's aid society or a specified adoption licensee.

What Protections Do the Child and Prospective Adoptive Parents Have Pending Finalization of the Adoption?

Usually these are set out in the applicable provincial legislation. The following safeguards, for example, are set out in the *Child and Family Services Act* of Ontario:

- Interference with the child is prohibited.
- Visiting or communicating with the child for the purpose of interfering with the child is prohibited.
- The prospective adoptive parents have the right to presumed continuity of the adoption placement.
- The prospective adoptive parents have the right to a review by the ministry directory if the adoption licensee or children's aid society decides to remove the child from his or her adoption placement.
- The director has the power to confirm the child's placement pending finalization of the adoption.
- The court file concerning the application for an adoption order is open only to the court and its authorized employees, the parties

to the adoption (adoptive applicants, their solicitors and agents), a ministry director, and a children's aid society local director.

• If the adoption has not been completed within a year of placement or within a year of the signing of the consents (whichever is earlier), a mandatory review of the situation is effected by the Ministry of Community and Social Services.

Does a Natural Parent Have any Rights?

Other than in those cases where a child becomes a permanent ward of the province, a parent (as defined by the legislation) must give consent before the child may be placed for adoption. No consent may be given before a child is seven days old, and the parent has the right to withdraw the consent within twenty-one days. Withdrawal of consent must be done in writing. If the parent has custody of the child immediately before giving consent, the child must be returned once the consent is withdrawn. Furthermore, the parent has the right to be informed, upon request, whether the child has been adopted (i.e., an adoption order has been made).

It is important to note that where a child is a Native person, thirty days' written notice must be given to the child's band before the child may be placed for adoption.

Is Adoption Private for all Purposes?

This area of the law is under review. At present, certain "non-identifying" information may be obtained from a children's aid society by an adopted person or an adoptive parent. Identifying information may be obtained under exceptional circumstances only, generally for medical purposes. No access order may be made in favour of the child's biological family after adoption.

In Ontario, an adult (eighteen-year-old) adopted person or a biological parent may register with the Adoption Disclosure Registry. No disclosure will take place unless the biological parent(s), the adoptive parent(s), and the adult adoptee all consent. If present proposals are accepted the consent of the adoptive parents will no longer be required.

CHAPTER 9

VIOLENCE IN THE FAMILY

Kay Vanstone Marshall

Kay Vanstone Marshall is a graduate of the University of Manitoba and Carleton University and obtained her law degree from the University of Ottawa. She practises law in Ottawa where she is active in many organizations working for women. She has written a number of briefs on law reform and is a regular legal contributor to a community newspaper. In addition she has taught courses in law and done extensive public speaking on the topic of family law and family violence.

HOME CAN BE a dangerous place. Those closest to us are capable of rousing our deepest feelings. The chances are greater that you will be murdered by a spouse or lover than by a stranger. You are safer on the streets than at home. This violence is usually directed at the most vulnerable members of our society—women, children, and the elderly—but the most common victim is the abused wife.

WIFE ABUSE

What Advice Would We Give an Abused Wife?

1. *Don't put up with it!* No one has the right to assault (hit or threaten) another person. Verbal violence leads to physical violence, which becomes increasingly severe and occurs at more frequent intervals. It can result in your death and in permanent damage to your children. Your son becomes an abuser and your daughter looks for an abusive mate.
2. *It is not your fault.* The National Advisory Council on the Status

of Women reports that one in every ten women is living with an abusive partner. You are not alone. Many women report that abuse goes in a cycle. First they feel the tension building. Then there is violence, which can be triggered by almost anything, followed by pleading for forgiveness by a contrite, ashamed husband who promises never to be violent again. The cycle then repeats itself.

3. *You can change your life.* You are not a punching bag! Something has to happen to make the abusive partner want to change. Many times the husband promises to take counselling sessions. On that basis, the family reunites, and the husband then neglects to follow through on the counselling. You must put the onus on the abuser. Let him prove he can change before you consider reconciliation.

4. *There is too much privacy in the home.* The old adage "A man's home is his castle" gave a man licence to abuse his wife and children, and the authorities were reluctant to interfere. If you are abused, *you* have nothing to be ashamed of. It is the person who resorts to violence who must take responsibility for it, not the victim.

Violence can take many forms. There may be a great deal of verbal violence or "threatening" without actual physical assault. Sometimes a husband will take a wife's car keys or her wallet so that she is unable to leave; this is theft, and the police may be called. Threatening violence is also an assault. What starts as a slap or a threat often, over time, becomes a severe beating.

Assault is usually defined as the intentional application of force to a person without the consent of that person; it includes situations in which the application of force is threatened or attempted. In cases of sexual assault, the force is directed at those parts of the body associated with sexual activity.

Physical assault includes slapping, punching, kicking, shoving, choking, and pinching. Sexual assault often starts with the demeaning of women through jokes and name-calling and then proceeds to unwanted touching and forced sexual activity. The offence of rape no longer appears in the *Criminal Code*. It has been replaced with different degrees of sexual assault and applies equally to men and women, including spouses. Psychological abuse differs from emotional or verbal abuse in that there is greater power to induce fear by threats and thus wear the victim down. Destruction of property is psychological abuse in that it is a direct message to the wife of what will happen to her. Any of these can end in murder.

Have You Been Abused?

What to Do Immediately
1. *Call the police.* It is wise to keep the phone number of the police near the telephone. In fact, paste it right on the phone, as this may save precious seconds. Give your address to the police and be sure to tell the dispatcher your life is in danger—because it is. It will make a difference as to whether the officers answer a robbery call first or come immediately. If the police have been to your home several times before, however, they may not respond as quickly.
2. *Should I leave without calling the police?* If you can leave, even without telephoning, do so. Many women believe if they leave the home, even while being beaten, they give up rights to their children. This is not so. It is called "constructive desertion." That means that one party drives the other out. If you do leave without the children you must return at your first opportunity, usually the next morning, to collect them. If you wait too long to collect them, you risk losing custody, and you are leaving them in danger. It is best to leave the premises immediately and call the police as soon as possible.
3. *What happens when the police arrive?* There are nearly always two officers: one to talk to your husband and the other to talk to you. Give them all the information you can, show them the torn clothing, broken dishes, and any other evidence of the fight. Any bruises you have will not be visible until the next day. It is important that you are rational with and respectful to the police. Domestic disputes have resulted in many police deaths; they need your help just as you do theirs. Be sure to tell the police whether you fear that your husband will beat you again after they leave.
4. *What can the police do?* Their job is to assess the seriousness of the assault and to "keep the peace." Since November 1984, police in Ontario have been directed by the provincial govern-

ment to lay charges against the abuser if they have evidence to conclude that an offence has been committed. There are several charges that may be laid, and these are listed in the Appendix at the end of this chapter.

a) "Assault" and "assault causing bodily harm" are the charges most commonly laid by the police if your husband has threatened you with violence or behaved violently towards you (for example, by making you do something against your will). It is important to note that "threatening violence" is an offence.

b) If the police have witnessed the violence or have reasonable grounds to believe your husband will assault you after they leave, they can lay a charge of "breach of the peace."

Get the policemen's names. You may need to call them later.

5. *Will the police arrest my husband?* In some instances they may, but in most cases they do not. Usually they simply make a report and, if the decision is to charge your husband, he will receive a summons to appear in court. This usually takes three weeks. If the police do arrest your husband, he will likely be released an hour later or the next morning. The police may try to convince one of you to leave the house for the night, but no one is compelled to leave. If you decide to leave, ask the police to stay while you pack your suitcase. Take the children with you. Depriving them of a few hours' sleep cannot compare with leaving them in danger and perhaps losing custody of them later.

6. *What if the police don't lay a charge?* You may lay a charge yourself by going to Provincial Court, either the Family or the Criminal Division. You should telephone ahead, because sometimes all "domestic" matters are referred to the Family Division, and in most cases you will need an appointment. If you must wait more than a day for an appointment, consult a lawyer. A lawyer can speed things up. The appointment will be with a justice of the peace who will take your information under oath, formulate the charge, and issue a summons for your husband to appear in court, usually in about three weeks. Provincial Court (Criminal Division) takes a more serious attitude to as-

saults; it deals with all kinds of assault on a regular basis. If you lay the charge yourself, the Crown attorney may continue the prosecution. It is best to consult a lawyer to guide you through this process and to help you decide the charge or charges to be laid.

7. *What is a peace bond?* The charge most commonly laid by the woman herself is a "fearing" charge under the *Criminal Code* (see the Appendix to this chapter). You swear before a justice of the peace that you fear another person will harm yourself, your family, or your property, and your husband will receive a summons to appear in court. If the court finds that there are reasonable grounds for your fears, the court will order the abuser to enter into a "recognizance" by signing a promise to "keep the peace" and be of good behaviour for one year. The abuser may be ordered not to go near your home or place of employment or contact you by telephone. The court may also order sureties. This means that your husband must put up a sum of money to be forfeited if he does not "keep the peace." A recognizance can be a good deterrent against violence. It results in a criminal record only if it is broken, so that whether to face criminal proceedings becomes the offender's decision, not the victim's.

8. *What may I take with me?* You may take those items that are clearly yours, such as clothing, personal effects, and, most important, all your personal papers. The police will assist by "keeping the peace" while you gather your things.

    If you, like many battered women, are afraid to live in the family home because your spouse knows how to get in, you will need furniture to live elsewhere. It is wise to return at the earliest possible time to retrieve your furniture. Generally, you are entitled to half the furniture, plus the children's if you have custody of them. It is best to take what you need and readjust later if necessary. You are also entitled to one-half of any joint bank accounts or term deposits. If in doubt, withdraw the amount you consider you are entitled to and readjust later.

9. *Where should I go?* The police will have the telephone number and address of the closest shelter for battered women, and you

might ask them to take you there. In most metropolitan areas there are shelters. Many women have reported how important it was to meet women in the same situation, to know they were not alone, to find a sympathetic ear, and to find a sense of safety and security. The staff will have information on social agencies, lawyers, and physicians that you will need. Seeking shelter with friends or relatives is helpful if they have been through a similar crisis. Otherwise, although they may be supportive, they may also feel uneasy, and your husband may threaten them.

10. *Must I leave?* Many women say they don't want to leave but just want the violence to stop. Although it *should* be possible to continue living together, if you are realistic, you will know it is not. Whether the police lay the charge or you do, it will be three weeks before your husband has to appear in court, and it may be six months before the charge is heard. In the meantime, more severe beatings may take place, and the police may not respond as quickly to repeated calls at the same address. If your husband is convicted, and he repeats the assault, the judge and police may not be particularly sympathetic to someone who has not taken steps to remove themselves from the violent situation. In some cases, however, police may ''red flag'' an address and give calls top priority.

11. *Can my husband be ordered to leave the home?* If there has been physical violence, your lawyer may make an application for "exclusive possession" of the matrimonial family home which may be a house or apartment that you own or rent. Your lawyer must show that there is not other suitable accommodation for you and that it is best for the children to remain in their home.

What to Do the Next Day

1. *Consult your doctor.* Ask for a medical report of your injuries. If there are bruises, have a colour photo taken.

2. *Consult a lawyer.* A lawyer can advise you—whether you plan to stay in the marriage or to separate—about your legal rights and about how you can protect what you have. If charges have

been laid by the police, your lawyer can guide you. Without a lawyer, you take a chance of losing everything if your husband commences legal proceedings against you.

3. *How do I find a lawyer?* Personal referral is the best way. Find someone who has been through a similar crisis and ask for a recommendation. If that lawyer can't help you, ask for a referral to someone else. Women's centres and shelters for battered women often know the names of lawyers who have dealt with similar cases.

What Can my Lawyer Do?

Your lawyer can tell you how your property would be divided, who would have custody of the children, and how much support, if any, is normally awarded in the courts in such circumstances. Every woman should know her rights. Most men seem to know their rights, but that is not always the case with women.

If you stay with your partner you will be better prepared, should the violence recur, if you have a clear understanding of your legal position.

If you decide to leave your partner it is critical that you seek legal advice at the earliest possible moment. Your lawyer may be able to get court orders for exclusive possession of the home or apartment for you and for custody of the children, plus an order restraining your spouse from harassing, molesting, or annoying you and the children, but this must be done quickly. If you have left the children at home, your lawyer will likely tell you to return for them so that they will be with you at the time of the court hearing. Judges don't like to move children. The orders listed above would be on a temporary basis only, until your husband could appear and argue why they should not be permanent.

The non-harassment order is a civil order under provincial family property legislation and is enforced by the sheriff, who unfortunately is available only from 9:00 to 5:00, Monday to Friday. This order is not as effective as a conviction under the *Criminal Code* (see the Appendix to this chapter), but it does provide some immediate protection. If the civil order also states that the police are to assist in its enforcement, the police will help. If your husband does not obey the civil order, he will be held ''in contempt of court''; how-

ever, the courts are reluctant to impose fines or committal to jail in
such cases.

1. *Do I have to divorce?* No. You may ask the court for a division
   of property and for custody and financial support (maintenance)
   without asking for a divorce. When the other issues have been
   settled, either party may apply for a divorce at a later time.

2. *Do I have to go to court?* Your lawyer will make an application
   immediately for custody, support, and so on, but it will be on
   an "interim" or temporary basis—that is, until the parties can
   give evidence before a judge at trial. However, once an "interim" order is obtained, the lawyers usually negotiate to reach
   a settlement. If negotiations fail, then you and your husband
   go with your lawyers to a "pretrial" hearing. The purpose of
   the hearing is to get the opinion of the judge or commissioner
   on how the case will be decided if it goes to trial. This opinion
   is based on a long experience of how similar cases have been
   dealt with at trial. Once the opinion of the judge or commissioner is obtained, most cases are settled, and very few go on
   to trial.

3. *What is mediation?* Mediation is similar to attending a pretrial
   hearing, but without the lawyer. A third party—the mediator—
   tries to resolve the issues. Ideally, the spouses should see their
   respective lawyers to have their rights explained before going
   to a mediator. The parties themselves select a mediator and
   share the cost. Legal rights may be mediated only by a lawyer,
   but non-lawyers may mediate custody and access—often the
   most difficult issues. If mediation does not work, you are back
   in the courts, and a judge will make a decision for you.

   Mediation presupposes that the parties are able to discuss
   their problems rationally and are of equal strength. In many
   marriages, however, the wife has assumed the submissive role,
   and this puts her at a disadvantage. When the spouses have
   reached an agreement, they must return to their respective lawyers, who draft the agreement and advise them on it. Mediation
   is useful if it helps to sever the emotional ties. Only lawyers
   can sever the legal ties.

4. *Will I have custody of my children?* The court usually awards
   custody on a temporary basis to whoever has the children when

the application is made. The court considers "the best interests of the children," and that usually means moving them as little as possible. Whoever has interim custody will likely be given permanent custody if the matter goes to trial.

In disputed custody cases, the court always wants the opinion of a third party (for example, a psychologist). The parties select the psychologist and share the cost of the assessment. To obtain custody, you must show that you are better able to look after the children than your husband. In addition, if the children are ten years of age or over, the court may ask their opinion.

If you are awarded custody of the children, your husband will be awarded visiting rights (access).

5. *What if my husband uses his access rights to harass me?* Ask your lawyer for a non-harassment order stipulating that your husband is not to attend at your residence or at your place of employment. Make sure that you insist that your husband respect the order. If your husband attempts to enter your residence, call the police or the sheriff. Always carry a copy of your order in your purse and have a "certified true copy" (obtained at the court house for $7-$10) in a safe place to show the police if they ask for it. If your children are very young, you may make arrangements for a third party to supervise your husband's visits with the children. You place yourself in a vulnerable position if you try to "supervise."

6. *What if my husband refuses to return the children?* Call the police immediately. When they arrive show them the court order or separation agreement giving you custody. The police will go with you if you know where the children are and may lay a charge of abduction against your husband. If there is no custody order, but the children normally reside with you, you may still call the police, although they may not be able to assist you. For this reason, it is best to have a custody order as soon as you separate.

7. *Will I receive support for myself?* Generally, you are expected to support yourself. If you can show you can't support yourself because the children are very young, or you need retraining to update your skills, or you are unable to work because of illness, the court will order support for you if your husband has the

financial means to pay. The support awarded is generally inadequate and is given for a year or two at most. Women over fifty are usually not expected to support themselves if they have been homemakers all their lives. Your husband's conduct, no matter how terrible it has been, will not affect the amount of support awarded. In most provinces support can be paid directly to the Family Court, but the court will hold it for thirty days before sending it to you.

8. *Who will pay to support the children?* In almost all cases, your husband will be ordered to pay some support for the children, if you have custody. If your husband has custody, you will be expected to contribute to their support. Joint custody, which must be consented to by you and your husband, is becoming more popular, and if both parties are similarly employed, then neither pays support. Joint custody could mean that you do the looking after of the children and he makes the decisions. Be sure you understand what is involved.

9. *Can the amount of support be changed?* Support can always be changed as circumstances change. If you lose your job, you may apply to increase the support; or it may end if your husband loses his job.

10. *What if my husband refuses to pay?* In all provinces except Manitoba the responsibility is on the recipient (i.e., you) to collect the support. In all provinces except Manitoba, 85 percent of support orders are not complied with. Manitoba has put in place a system of enforcement that has resulted in 85 percent of orders being paid. In most provinces there is a penalty of jail for "contempt of court" (that is, for not paying as the court has ordered), but most judges are reluctant to enforce this. Enforcement of support orders is done through Provincial Court (Family Division), but the success rate is poor.

11. *What if my husband sells everything before we reach a settlement?* Sometimes a spouse will sell or dispose of all assets in his name so that he will not have the financial means to pay support. If you think your spouse may do this, ask your lawyer to apply for an order that no assets are to be dissipated or sold before trial. This is one of the reasons you want to see your lawyer as soon as possible after you separate.

12. *Do I have grounds for divorce?* You may get a divorce right away if you can show that your husband treated you with sufficient physical and mental cruelty to make living together impossible. You will have to have witnesses and evidence from your doctors to back this up, although a conviction for assault under the *Criminal Code* is sufficient.

If you cannot prove "fault" (adultery, cruelty, etc.) then you must wait until you have been separated for one year.

How Can I Protect Myself if I Am Not Ready to Leave?

1. Consult a lawyer; know your rights.
2. Put the phone number of the police on the telephone. Know where you would go in an emergency if you have to leave.
3. Keep extra car keys, money, and clothes in a hidden place or at a friend's. Keep twenty dollars pinned to your clothing.
4. Alert your neighbours to call the police if they hear a fight.
5. Keep your friends and neighbours informed of the violence or threats. Their evidence may later be useful.
6. Save money for an emergency in a separate bank account.
7. Keep a diary; notes may later be used in court.
8. Familiarize yourself with the family finances.
9. Preserve evidence such as written notes of apology, bank statements, and other documents.
10. Prepare to support yourself by taking courses or re-entering the work force.
11. Find out about resources and self-help groups in your community that can help you (for example, Alanon, for the spouses of alcoholics) and make use of them.
12. Find a counsellor who will build up your self-confidence and give you strength to change your situation from being a victim to having control of your life.
13. Lay a charge of assault and leave home briefly while it is heard.
14. Try to predict when the violence might occur and simply leave or send for help.

CHILD ABUSE

It is generally accepted that the family structure best meets the needs of the developing child, yet there must be protection for the child if parents are unable to meet those needs. For some, childhood is a prison sentence of sixteen or more years. In response to the growing incidence of child abuse, in 1986 the federal government introduced amendments to the *Criminal Code* of Canada to include a wider range of offences. At the same time the provinces have been encouraged to amend their child-protection laws to provide a wider range of support and social services. Both levels of government must work together to provide adequate protection for our children. The *Criminal Code* is the same for all Canadians, but you must check with your local child-protection agency to understand the law in your province.

Who Is a Child?

Generally, anyone who is or appears to be under the age of sixteen.

What Is Abuse?

1. *Physical abuse* includes assault—for example, hitting or punching enough to cause injuries; or physical neglect—for example, not providing proper nutrition, clothing, or supervision.
2. *Psychological abuse* includes habitual humiliation or emotional neglect, such as lack of holding, cuddling, or nurturing, that injures the child's mental health so as to cause permanent damage.
3. *Sexual abuse* includes intercourse, molestation, exhibitionism, or exploitation.

My Child Is Being Abused. What Can I Do?

You must report it immediately to a child-protection agency. As a parent you are obliged to protect your child not only from yourself but from anyone else. It is neglect if you know and do not report. Call the police.

Most child-protection agencies provide twenty-four hour service, and there is usually a child-abuse telephone number at the front of your telephone book. There is a strict responsibility for professionals (for example, teachers, doctors, social workers, dentists) to report if they suspect a child is being abused.

How Can I Protect My Child Immediately?

Leave and take your child or children with you. If the abuser is your spouse, your lawyer should apply immediately to the court for an order giving you temporary custody of your child and an order that the abuser is not to molest, annoy, or harass either you or the children in your custody.

Will the Police Lay Charges?

Charges may be laid under the *Criminal Code* for assault, sexual assault, or incest (see the Appendix to this chapter) depending on the nature of the abuse. The criminal process is slow (six months at least) and results in a criminal record for the abuser. However, a conviction shows the abuser that the community will not tolerate the abuse and holds the abuser responsible. The police work in close co-operation with the child-protection agencies to reduce the number of times the child has to relate the events and to enable child-protection workers to protect the child throughout the process. The present law requires evidence to support the word of the child, but the proposed amendments to the *Criminal Code* would relax this requirement.

May the Child-Protection Agency Lay Charges?

The child-protection agency, when notified, will begin an investigation. Usually a worker will visit the home within forty-eight hours. Ideally, the child will be interviewed by a team composed of a child-protection worker and a police officer. The child-protection worker's function is to protect the child, while the police officer's function is to collect evidence for use at trial.

If the child-protection worker believes the child to be in immediate danger, a warrant may be obtained for immediate removal of the child, and a summons will be issued for the parents to appear in court the following day.

If there is a finding of no abuse or neglect, the child-protection worker must so report within forty-eight hours. If the abuse has been confirmed, however, and the child is not in immediate danger of repeated abuse, the worker will ask the family to co-operate in a program of volunteer counselling. If the parents refuse, the child-protection agency will ask the court to intervene to protect the child.

What Can the Court do?

The issue in "protection proceedings" is the "best interests of the child," but it is also whether you as parents are adequately protecting your child. If the answer is no, the court makes an order in the "best interests of the child." The order may be one of the following:

1. The child is returned to one or both parents or another person, subject to the supervision of the child-protection agency for a specified period of three to twelve months.
2. The child is made a ward of the child-protection agency and placed in its care and custody for a period up to twelve months.
3. The child is made a ward of the Crown.

For you to retain custody of your child, your lawyer must convince the court that you can care for your child or will be able to do so in the future. Your child is also represented by a lawyer.

May the Child Be Removed from the Home?

Only in the most severe cases will the child be removed from the home, and usually only after other methods of assistance have failed. A child that is removed is placed in a foster home, group home, or residential care, with a review after six months. Parental contact is maintained, because the goal is the eventual return of the child to the family.

What Is a Supervision Order?

You retain custody of your child but under the supervision of the child-protection agency. The supervision order provides some leverage to enforce counselling or treatment of the family. The court may also order an assessment of the child and the family and access or supervised access by the abuser to the victim. This will assist the non-abusing parent. In many cases abuse involves most members of the family.

Will I Be Protected if I Report Abuse and None is Found?

Yes, you must report and in good faith. Only if you are acting maliciously may you be prosecuted.

Will the Child Have to Appear in Court?

Generally a child under twelve does not appear in court unless the court is satisfied that the child can understand the hearing and will not suffer emotional harm.

There will also be a ban on publication if requested. Laws of evidence requiring witnesses and corroboration have also been relaxed.

What Can I Do if I Suspect My Child Is Being Abused But I Am Not Sure?

1. Contact the child-protection agency. Child abuse takes many forms, some of which are very difficult to detect. If spotted early enough, however, serious problems may be prevented.
2. Always believe what a child tells you. Show real concern, but avoid alarm or anger.
3. See your lawyer and know your rights.
4. Keep a diary; notes may be useful in court later.

What Is Sexual Abuse?

Perhaps the most alarming form of abuse is sexual abuse. It is the exploitation of the power of an adult over a child to involve the child in acts for a sexual purpose. It is damaging because the abuser is often the same adult the child looks to for comfort and support. Sexual abuse ranges from exhibitionism and fondling to rape and incest.

Who Are the Most Likely Victims of Sexual Abuse?

It is reported that the most vulnerable children are those aged two to four (the trusting age) and those aged twelve to fourteen (the peak of puberty).

Who Are the Abusers?

The abusers are most often a parent, a relative, or an older friend or neighbour, rather than a stranger.

Is Sexual Abuse Usually a Single Incident?

No. Because the child is often persuaded to keep the activity a secret, it can continue undetected over a number of years. The general unwillingness to disclose is complicated by the child's feelings of guilt and complicity. Adolescent children are quicker to disclose sexual abuse than younger children, perhaps because they are more independent.

What Is Incest?

Incest is a criminal offence and is narrowly defined. It is the act of having sexual intercourse with a blood relative, such as one's parent, child, brother, sister, grandparent, or grandchild.

What May the Abuser Be Charged With?

Currently under the *Criminal Code* the abuser may be charged with sexual assault, indecent acts, nudity, or seduction, depending on the offence. It is only during the past three years that child sexual abuse has begun to be examined and that the limitations in the present law have become apparent. The proposed amendments to the *Criminal Code* create three new offences: sexual interference; sexual exploitation; and invitation to sexual touching; as well as simplifying the existing offences (see the Appendix to this chapter).

What Can the Child-Protection Agency Do?

A finding by the court that a child has been sexually abused and is "in need of protection" changes the balance of power from the abuser to the child-protection agency. The agency's role is to protect and support the child, who is under enormous pressure to deny the abuse. This protection extends to before, during, and after court proceedings, whether criminal, civil, or both.

How Will the Child Testify in Court?

The proposed amendments to the *Criminal Code* relax the laws of evidence requiring witnesses and other evidence to back up a child's story. The amendments will also make it possible in cases of sexual abuse to show in court a videotape of the victim describing the abuse and to have this admitted as evidence if it is reaffirmed by the victim in the course of testifying.

If My Child Tells Me about Sexual Abuse What Should I Do?

1. Leave the scene of the abuse and take your children with you.
2. Always believe your child; try to understand the nature of the offence and do not show alarm or anger.

3. Reassure your child that he or she is not responsible for what happened.
4. Reassure your child that you will do everything possible to prevent future abuse.
5. Contact the child-protection agency immediately.
6. Call your doctor or go directly to the hospital if your child is injured.
7. Call the police.
8. See your lawyer.

What Can I Do to Protect My Children?

Tell your child never to keep a secret about touching. Inquire about programs to "street-proof" children. A child who is properly informed about sexual abuse is less likely to become a victim than an uninformed child.

ELDER ABUSE

Elder abuse is hidden. It resembles child abuse in that the victims are often totally defenceless and dependent on relatives for their care and well being. Elder abuse, however, is not as easily discovered. While children go to school, elders often remain behind closed doors with almost no outside contact.

Canada's aging population and the increasing tendency to keep the elderly at home rather than in institutions suggest that the problem of elder abuse will continue to grow.

Who Are the Elderly?

Generally, anyone over sixty-five years of age is considered elderly. The "old" are sixty-five to seventy-four, the "very old" are seventy-five to eighty-four, and the "old, old" are over eighty-five. There are more elderly women than elderly men. Women make up 55 percent of the "old" category, 60 percent of the "very old," and 70 percent of the "old, old." According to Statistics Canada, in 1901 5 percent of the population was over sixty-five years of age; in 1981 the figure was 10 percent; by 2001 it is expected to have increased to 12 percent. The proportion of elders within this group who are over eighty is expected to increase from 19 percent in 1981 to 24 percent in 2001.

What Is Elder Abuse?

1. *Physical abuse* includes assault, rough handling causing physical injuries or discomfort, neglect, avoidance of needs for assistance, and the withholding of such physical necessities as food, personal and hygienic care, or medical care.
2. *Psychological abuse* includes confinement, isolation, inadequate attention in terms of time, concern for, and understanding of needs, the removal from active participation in one's own life, humiliation, intimidation, derogation, infantilization, or any treatment diminishing identity, dignity, or self-worth.
3. *Financial abuse* includes the withholding of finances, trickery, fraud, theft, misappropriation or misuse of funds or property, and withholding of the means for daily living.

Who Would Abuse an Elderly Person?

The answer may be, "We would." Statistics in Canada are scarce, but the Manitoba Council on Aging commissioned a study in 1982 showing that the most likely victim is a woman over seventy-five who is confused and physically dependent, and who has resided with the family for ten or more years. The abusers were family members (75 percent), and the most likely abuser was the son (60 percent), followed closely by the daughter.

A large number of abusers were themselves over sixty years of age, which suggests that adding the responsibility of caring for a dependent elder to the care-giver's other difficulties—retirement, fixed income, increased health problems—tends to produce a breaking point and a situation conducive to abuse.

Is There a Requirement to Report Abuse?

Only three provinces in Canada have laws to protect the elderly: Newfoundland, Nova Scotia, and New Brunswick. In these provinces, there is a requirement to report any elder abuse, neglect, or exploitation to the nearest family-service agency. There is protection for the informant. There are also procedures available to protect the elderly by supervision and even removal of the abuser if necessary.

In the rest of Canada, however, those who have knowledge of the abuse (for example, neighbours or doctors) may be seen as interfering by the family and as invading privacy by the elder.

Should I Call the Police?

In cases of assault, theft, or fraud, criminal charges may be laid, but this is not a practical alternative unless the elderly person is prepared to live elsewhere. Many elderly people fear removal to an institution where they may be worse off. In the provinces where laws exist to protect the elderly, the criminal charges may be used together with the provincial laws to improve the situation for the victim.

Who Can Help?

Caring for an elderly relative can create severe difficulty in the home. Care-givers may not be prepared for the rage and frustration involved in caring for an ill, helpless, and confused person. Adult children can be overwhelmed by the constant supervision required, by the cost, and by the lack of support services.

Counselling may be provided to help the family, but more help should be given to families before they take in an aging relative. There is a double dilemma for women in that most of us will spend some time as care-givers and later as elderly persons, capable of making decisions but not able to carry out our wishes unassisted. What is needed is education about the "aging process," so that we know what to expect both for ourselves and for our parents.

What Is Needed?

1. Laws to protect the elderly: systematic reporting, a central register of abusers, and the means to intervene to protect the victim.
2. A protocol for hospitals and social agencies to help them detect and monitor abuse.
3. Temporary shelters.
4. Support services in the community (for example, in-home services, day-care facilities, home care, meals on wheels, stroke clubs, and other self-help groups).
5. An intervention team composed of the police and representatives

of the family-service centre that can intervene where necessary and follow up with help for the victim and the family.

6. Public education and awareness of the problem.

APPENDIX A

WIFE ABUSE

The most commonly laid charges under the *Criminal Code* of Canada are:

1. *Fearing*, s. 745

   Anyone who fears that another person will cause injury to themselves or to members of their family or damage to their property may lay an information and ask for a peace bond or recognizance.

2. *Assault*, s. 245

   There are three levels and they apply to all forms of assault, including sexual assault:

   a) attempted or *threatened* assault by act or gesture, for the purpose of applying force to another person without that person's consent;

   b) assault with a weapon or causing bodily harm, which usually means bleeding or broken bones;

   c) aggravated assault where the victim is wounded, maimed, or disfigured, or has her life endangered.

The following offences apply under rare circumstances:

1. *Wounding*, s. 228

   Anyone who injures you or discharges a firearm, pistol, or air gun intending to endanger your life or to wound, disfigure, or maim you may be charged with this offence.

2. *Administering a noxious thing*, s. 229

   It is a criminal offence to poison or make anyone take a noxious or destructive thing, whether the intent is simply to annoy the person or to injure him or her seriously.

3. *Pointing a firearm*, s. 84

It is a criminal offence to point a firearm at someone without lawful excuse (for example, self-defence) even if the gun is unloaded. It is also unlawful to handle a firearm carelessly.

4. *Possession of a weapon*, s. 85

It is a criminal offence to carry or use a weapon in a way that is dangerous to the public peace, or for an unlawful purpose, such as assaulting someone. The definition of ''weapon'' is very broad. For example, a beer bottle thrown at you is considered to be a weapon.

5. *Intimidation*, s. 381

Intimidation includes use of threats, violence, or tactics such as following you about, watching your house, or hiding your property for the purpose of getting you to do something or not to do something.

6. *Extortion*, s. 305

Anyone who uses threats or violence to try to make you do something for his own gain may be charged with this offence. For example, your partner may be charged with extortion if he threatens to beat you unless you turn over your paycheque to him.

7. *Threatening letters and phone calls*, s. 331

If your partner writes or phones you or sends any message that is intended to threaten you, your property, or even your pet with death or harm, he may be charged with this offence.

8. *Mischief*, s. 387

Mischief can be committed in many ways. The most common is by destroying, damaging, or interfering with the use of property.

9. *Attempted murder*, s. 212 and s. 24

Anyone who tries to kill you or harms you in a way that he knows is likely to cause death and is reckless about whether you might die may be charged with attempted murder.

PRESENT CRIMINAL CODE PROVISIONS, SEXUAL ABUSE OF CHILDREN: A SUMMARY

1. *Sexual assault*, s. 246.1, 246.2, and 246.3

These relate to three levels of assault directed at those parts of the body normally associated with sexual activity (see "Assault," s. 245, above).

2. *Sexual intercourse* with a female:
a)   under fourteen years, s. 146(1);
b)   between fourteen and sixteen of previously chaste character, s. 146(2);
c)   who is a step-daughter, foster daughter, female ward, or female employee under twenty-one years, s. 153(1).

3. *Incest*, s. 150
Sexual intercourse with a blood relative.

4. *Seduction* of a female:
a)   between sixteen and eighteen years of previously chaste character, s. 151;
b)   under twenty-one years, of previously chaste character, and under promise of marriage, s. 152;
c)   who is a passenger on a vessel, s. 154.

5. *Corruption* of persons under eighteen in their home, s. 168.

6. *Indecent Acts*, s. 169;
Nudity, s. 170;
Buggery or *bestiality*, s. 155;
Acts of gross indecency, s. 157;
Necrophilia, s. 178(b).

PROPOSED CRIMINAL CODE AMENDMENTS, SEXUAL ABUSE OF CHILDREN: A SUMMARY

1. *Sexual assault* (three levels of assault).
2. *Sexual interference* (touching any person under fourteen for a sexual purpose or urging another person to do so).
3. *Invitation to sexual* touching.*
4. *Sexual exploitation* (touching any person aged fourteen years but under eighteen years for a sexual purpose by a person in a position of trust or authority).*
5. *Indecent acts* and indecent exposure (exposure of genitals to any person under fourteen for a sexual purpose).
6. *Incest* (unchanged).
7. *Buggery*.
8. *Bestiality* and associated offences.

9. Parent or guardian *procuring sexual activity*.
10. Householder *permitting sexual activity*.

---

* Asterisk indicates entirely new offences.

CHAPTER 10

DEATH IN THE FAMILY

Julia Turnbull

Julia Turnbull is a lawyer in private practice in Calgary. She studied at McMaster University in Hamilton and obtained her law degree from Osgoode Hall Law School. She has chaired several committees in the Alberta branch of the Canadian Bar Association and is active in a number of community organizations in Calgary. Julia Turnbull is a member of the Bar of the Province of Alberta.

IT IS VERY DIFFICULT to face one's mortality. It is a subject that we are loathe to discuss even though we are all aware of life's inevitable end. To minimize the trauma of the event for your survivors it is wise to prepare and plan for it. Such preparation requires an ongoing review as the circumstances of your life alter. As your age, assets, marital status, and dependents all change, so should your plans for your estate. This chapter will briefly summarize most of the major aspects of wills and estates and will provide you with a general overview of the area.

You would be wise to obtain specific legal advice for your individual concerns. Like so many areas of law, estate planning involves the interplay of continually evolving federal and provincial legislation.

WHAT HAPPENS IF I DIE WITHOUT A WILL?

If you die without a will, the legislation relating to intestacy of the province in which you last resided will govern how your estate is distributed.

Generally, your surviving spouse will receive a preferential share,

187

and the balance of your estate will be divided between your spouse and your children. This division is dependent upon the number of children you have. For example, in Alberta the first $40,000 of the net value of your estate will go to your surviving spouse. The balance will be divided equally between your spouse and your child. If you have more than one child, one-third of the balance will go to your surviving spouse, with the remaining two-thirds being divided equally among your children. If your children have predeceased you but have left children of their own, those children will inherit their parent's share of your estate. If you have no children or grand-children, your surviving spouse inherits everything. If you have no surviving spouse, children, or grandchildren, your estate goes to your parents, or the survivor of them. If your parents have prede-ceased you, it is divided equally among your surviving brothers and sisters. If you have no surviving brothers or sisters, it will be divided among your nieces and nephews. If there are no nieces or nephews, your next of kin will inherit. If you wish to avoid this rigid distri-bution, you should prepare a will.

WHAT IS A WILL?

A will is a written document, signed by you, that disposes of your property on death. A will may also deal with choosing an executrix, disposing of personal and real property, appointing a guardian for your children, and disposing of your remains. It is not necessary to hire a lawyer to prepare a will for you, although it is generally advisable.

Legal Capacity to Make a Will

Most provinces require you to be over the age of eighteen to make a valid will, unless you are married or actively serving in the Ca-nadian Armed Forces. In British Columbia and New Brunswick you must be nineteen years of age. In Nova Scotia you must be the age of majority or married. Newfoundland requires you to be seventeen years of age. In Quebec, only persons over the age of eighteen may make a valid will.

Types of Wills

There are many different types of wills. They may be categorized as follows:

Conventional Wills

A simple will is a basic document that merely appoints an executrix, names guardians of your children, and disposes of your estate. It does not include complex tax schemes or set up elaborate trusts.

Printed wills are forms that are usually obtained from a stationery store. You are simply required to fill in the blanks with pertinent information, such your name and the disposition of your estate.

A complex will is one that disposes of a complicated estate. For example, you may own a family farm or business that you wish to transfer to your spouse or children to avoid capital-gains tax. You may wish to set up a life estate for your spouse (for example, a capital fund from which your spouse can live, with the balance remaining divided among certain persons after your spouse's death). Generally, a complex will involves a large estate consisting of many diverse assets and involving a large number of beneficiaries, both existing and potential. There may be tax consequences to consider as well as the conflicting needs of the various beneficiaries. Such an estate demands individualized legal attention and is not well-suited to the simplicity of a holograph or printed will.

All conventional wills must be signed by you in the presence of two witnesses. Both witnesses must then sign in the presence of each other. It is prudent to date the will. Both witnesses and you should initial each page of the will and all corrections. This will ensure that there are no changes or substitutions after execution.

The witnesses to the will cannot be beneficiaries or spouses of beneficiaries under the will. If either witness is a beneficiary or a spouse of a beneficiary the will is not invalidated, but in some provinces that beneficiary's bequest is voided so that the beneficiary does not receive it. In such a case the bequest forms part of the residue of the estate. In other provinces (Ontario, for example), it is necessary to prove to the court that there was no undue influence in order to validate the bequest.

Holograph Wills

A holograph will is a handwritten one. It must be completely in your own handwriting. No witnesses are required, but it must bear your signature at the end. Holograph wills are, by their very nature, not prepared by lawyers. They are often written by individuals on their deathbed. People who wish to dispose of their estate in a simple, uncomplicated, and inexpensive way often choose to prepare a holograph will. One cautionary note—sometimes the lay person makes errors in this type of will that are not discovered until after death. Unfortunately, those errors can not be corrected at that late date. Therefore, a holograph will can be recommended only in the simplest or most urgent of circumstances.

A holograph will is acceptable in Alberta, Manitoba, Quebec, Saskatchewan, Ontario, the Yukon, and Newfoundland. Certain provinces do *not* recognize holograph wills as valid except in certain circumstances. For example, British Columbia and Prince Edward Island allow them only for members of the Canadian Armed Forces, mariners, and seamen. It would be prudent to seek independent legal advice prior to the preparation of a holograph will.

Notarial Wills

Notarial wills are allowed only in Quebec. Simply put, the witnessing requirements vary such that the will must be executed by you, one notary, and two witnesses *or* you and two notaries. The date and place of its execution must be stated in the will. The witnesses must be named and described in the will. The original will must remain with the notary.

Challenging the Validity of a Will

It is possible for your heirs to challenge the validity of your will after your death. The most common challenges include fraud, duress, undue influence, and lack of testamentary capacity.

Fraud involves situations in which your signature on the will was forged or the contents of the document were misrepresented to you in order to obtain your signature or were changed after you signed the will.

If someone is forcing you to make certain provisions when you make a will you are said to be under "undue influence" or "duress."

A will made in these circumstances can be contested by other parties after your death. Usually the only parties who would contest it are those who otherwise would have been entitled to share in your estate. An example commonly seen is that involving a second spouse and children from a prior marriage. If your will left all of your estate to your second husband and nothing to your children, your children might contest the will after your death and say that you were unduly influenced or forced by your new husband to give him all of your estate.

You must be mentally capable in order to make a valid will. If you have become senile and have no or a very vague recollection of events, you are most likely without the testamentary capacity to make a will. This test relates strictly to mental not physical capacity. If you are under a physical incapacity, such as blindness, you have the right to make a will as long as it mentions your disability and shows that you understood and approved the contents. You do not have to be physically capable of signing the will in order for the will to be effective. If a lawyer prepares your will for you, your lawyer must be satisfied that you have the testamentary capacity to make it.

Testamentary capacity may be proven after death by obtaining the evidence regarding your mental capacity at the making of the will from the witnesses to the will, the lawyer who prepared it, your physician, and any friends or relatives.

Your will is still valid should you become senile or lose mental capacity at any time after you have signed it. Testamentary capacity relates to your capacity during the preparation and execution of the will.

WHAT PROVISIONS SHOULD I INCLUDE IN MY WILL?

A will not only disposes of assets; it may also deal with many other things that you wish to occur after your death. A will allows you the luxury of specifying your wishes with respect to the transfer of your property on death, the appointment of your executrix, and the choice of a guardian for your children, as well as of making any specific bequests.

Choice of Executrix

First, you should appoint an executrix of your estate. An executrix becomes the trustee of all your assets on your death and carries out the wishes contained in your will. You should also name an alternate executrix in the event that your first choice predeceases you or is unable or unwilling to act. It is wise to consult with your executrix prior to your death. Your choice should not come as a surprise.

You should choose someone who resides in the same province, and preferably in the same city. Your executrix will be required to perform many tasks and execute a number of documents on behalf of your estate. The fewer miles she must travel, the easier and less expensive it will be for her and your estate.

In addition, if your executrix resides out of the province of your residence, the court may require her to post a bond as security for your estate. This bond is commonly equal to twice the value of your estate. The posting of a bond is a financial burden that can be avoided by choosing an executrix who resides in the same province as you.

An executrix is entitled to charge a fee for services. This fee is established by the court or agreed to by the beneficiaries once your estate has been completely administered. In general, the maximum fee an executrix would be entitled to is 5 percent of the estate. A number of factors enter into the court's mind when setting the fee, including the size and complexity of the estate and the nature of the tasks performed. Your executrix is also entitled to be reimbursed for all expenditures and payments made on behalf of the estate.

Types of Executrices

You may wish to consider choosing joint or corporate executrices. Joint executrices are often appointed where the person making the will has concerns about the ability of the sole executrix to exercise discretion fairly. If you have such concerns, you may, for example, choose two of your five adult children to administer your estate jointly rather than choosing one alone.

Corporate executrices are often chosen to administer a large, complex estate. In cases where the beneficiaries are not considered competent or willing to handle the decisions arising in the administration of an estate, a corporate executrix may be chosen to save them the time involved in estate administration.

An executrix should keep records of the time expended and the duties performed on behalf of the estate to assist the court when approving the accounts of the estate.

Specific Bequests

A will may also provide for the disposition of specific gifts to specific persons. For example, you may wish to leave your jewellery to your daughter and your motor vehicle to your son. A specific bequest is one that deals with a certain item, be it cash, personal, or real property.

Residuary Clause

Every will should contain a clause that disposes of the residue of your estate. The residue of your estate is comprised of the portion remaining after payment of all funeral expenses, taxes, liabilities, and specific bequests. It is virtually impossible to estimate the exact value of your estate prior to your death, so it is wise to provide for the disposition of any residue in your will.

Choice of Guardian for Persons and Estates of Infant Children

If you have infant children, your will should definitely contain your wishes as to who should be the guardian of those children. There are two aspects of guardianship—the person and the estate—and you should provide for both in your will.

Guardianship of the person involves a designation of the person you wish to have physical custody of your child. If you wish to have your married sister as guardian of the person of your child, you would be wise to specify only her in your will. In these times of frequent divorce it would be most unfortunate if you specified both your sister and brother-in-law and the courts had to choose which one of them should in fact be the guardian. You should also name an alternate guardian to act if your first choice is unable or unwilling to act. Once again, you should discuss this with the potential guardian prior to naming her in your will.

Guardianship of the estate involves the choice of the person whom you wish to handle the financial resources or monies of your child. Quite often the guardian of the person and estate are identical.

However, in some cases you may be satisfied that a certain person would take the best physical care of your child but have qualms about her ability to handle financial matters. That type of situation warrants the appointment of separate guardians for the person and the estate of your child. Other situations may also warrant such a decision. You would be wise to examine critically your choice of guardian in terms of physical care and financial capabilities and make the decision appropriate to your case.

It is important for you to realize that the court is not bound by the choice of guardian contained in your will. There may well be competing applications for the guardianship of your child after your death, and the court is generally governed by the principle of determining what is in the best interests of the child. Nevertheless, a guardianship clause in your will is evidence of your intention and would be a factor taken into account by the court. If there were no competing interests or court applications, your choice of guardian would most likely prevail.

Survivorship

Your will should also include a provision specifying how your estate will be divided in the event that you and another person who is a beneficiary die in circumstances rendering it impossible to determine which of you survived the other. Each province has legislation dealing with this problem. In Quebec, you are deemed to have died simultaneously. Generally, however, the legislation in most provinces deems that the younger person survived the older one. To illustrate this problem, consider the following case:

You are older than your husband and your will specifies that everything you own should go to him or, if he is dead, to your parents. Both of you die in an automobile accident, and no one knows who died first.

In this case your entire estate will go to your husband and then be distributed in accordance with the wishes contained in his will. This result becomes of critical importance if you have children from a previous marriage or if your wishes and bequests are not the same as your spouse's. To prevent such a problem, it is prudent to have a provision in your will specifying that in the event of your death in such circumstances you wish your estate to be distributed as if that person had predeceased you. If your will contains such a clause, your estate will be distributed in accordance with the instructions contained in your will regardless of your age or the event of a common disaster.

It is not necessary to have such a clause in your will if you reside in Ontario or Manitoba. In both of those provinces the legislation specifies that your property will be distributed in such a case as if the other person had predeceased you.

WHAT ASSETS SHOULD I INCLUDE IN MY WILL?

Many of the items you own may never become estate assets. For example, if you own real property in joint tenancy with another person (usually your spouse), your interest in that property automatically passes to the surviving owner and is not a part of your estate that can be distributed by your will. The same holds true for joint bank accounts, which have a right of survivorship.

There are certain assets for which you may designate a named beneficiary. Once a beneficiary is specified, this asset does not form part of your estate. For example, you may designate your spouse as the beneficiary of your life-insurance policy. If this is done, those proceeds will not form part of your estate unless your spouse predeceases you.

The sole exception to the foregoing is found in Ontario under the new *Family Law Reform Act*. The surviving spouse may elect to be paid half the difference between the value of his property and the deceased spouse's property. Alternatively, a surviving spouse may elect to go along with the terms of the deceased's will. A surviving spouse has six months to decide whether to accept the equalization payment or the terms of the will. If he accepts the equalization payment, he will not receive the proceeds of any life-insurance policy, even if he is the named beneficiary, unless the insurance policy contains a declaration that the proceeds are intended to be in addition to any equalization payment under the act.

Canada Savings Bonds
If your Canada Savings Bonds are held jointly with another person and if they specify that the survivor shall receive the bonds on the

death of the other, the bonds will not form a part of your estate. In the event of your death, the bonds would be transferred by right of survivorship to the survivor. An original death certificate must be provided to effect such a transfer.

With respect to Canada Savings Bonds held in your name alone, up to $40,000 worth may be transferred on your death to your beneficiaries without the requirement of a grant of probate or letters of administration if you die without a will. If you have more than $40,000 worth of Canada Savings Bonds in your own name, a grant of probate or letters of administration will be required to effect the transfer to your beneficiaries.

Registered Retirement Savings Plans (RRSP)
This type of plan has undergone a number of changes as a result of recent amendments to the federal *Income Tax Act*. Therefore, you are urged to obtain the advice of an accountant before redeeming or transferring the proceeds of the plan. Normally, the financial institution administering the RRSP will be in a position to explain the various options available.

It is possible to designate a beneficiary of your RRSP and avoid tax consequences if that beneficiary is your spouse or an informed dependent and elects to roll over the proceeds into his own RRSP. In addition, if you have dependent children or grandchildren and no spouse at the time of your death, $5,000 per year for each year that the child is under twenty-six may be rolled into a new RRSP in favour of each child.

Jewellery and Personal Effects
You may include these personal items in your will if you wish to have them go to certain persons. Or, to simplify matters, you may wish to insert a clause in your will to indicate that you have attached a list to it outlining your bequests regarding these items. If you have no specific wishes with respect to these items it is not necessary to list them in your will, and they will simply form a part of the residue of your estate.

How Do I Amend My Present Will?

If you wish to make minor changes to your present will you may make them on the original, provided you and both of the original witnesses initial all corrections.

Another way of amending your existing will is to prepare a "codicil." A codicil is a page or pages attached to your will specifying the deletions and additions you wish to make to the original. It must be signed by you and witnessed by two witnesses. You are not required to use your original witnesses, although the execution requirements for a codicil are identical to those of a will.

When Do I Make a New Will?

You should review your will periodically. It is a good idea to do so every two years or if your marital status changes, you adopt or give birth to a child, there is a material change in the value of your estate, or one of your beneficiaries dies.

Change in Marital Status

If you marry after making a will, most provincial legislation deems that the will is invalid. Therefore, if you marry after making a will, you should prepare a new one. If a will is made in contemplation of marriage and specifically states so in the body of the will, it will not be invalidated by your marriage. This is an exception, however, and you should therefore assume that the golden rule is that marriage after the making and execution of a will revokes it.

The same does not apply to your will in the event of a divorce. A divorce does not invalidate an existing will. Therefore, if your will leaves everything to a former spouse, that spouse will inherit even if you were divorced at the time of your death. However, Ontario, British Columbia, and Saskatchewan have enacted legislation providing that a certificate of divorce or a declaration that the marriage is a nullity revokes a testamentary gift to a spouse unless a contrary intention is contained in the will.

If you have remarried after your divorce, your original will would be invalid, and your estate would be distributed in accordance with the relevant provincial legislation governing intestacy.

Generally, if you die without leaving a will and prior to getting your certificate of divorce, your spouse is still your spouse in the eyes of the law, even if you have been living separate and apart. As a result, your spouse would inherit in accordance with the relevant provincial legislation with respect to intestacy.

Birth or Adoption of a Child
You should make a new will in the event of the birth or adoption of another child if your will refers to your children by name. Generally wills are drafted so that a reference is simply made to "children." In that case it is not necessary to change your will when you increase your family. Please note that the term "children" usually includes illegitimate children.

Material Change in the Value of an Estate
If your estate increases or decreases substantially, it may be wise to consider changes to your will to accommodate the change in value.

DUTIES OF THE EXECUTRIX

First and foremost, the executrix should assist with the funeral arrangements for the deceased, if necessary. Within a reasonable time after the funeral, the executrix should obtain, review, and carry out the instructions of the will.

The first step in carrying out the instructions of a will involves gathering the assets of the estate, valuing them, and assessing the outstanding liabilities. For example, a typical estate might include a matrimonial home, a Registered Retirement Savings Plan, Canada Savings Bonds, a pension, cash in the bank, and personal belongings. If the matrimonial home is not jointly owned, it will be necessary to obtain an appraisal of the fair market value of that home. With respect to the RRSP, the executrix should write to the institution holding it to determine its cash value. The value of the Canada Savings Bonds and the accrued interest, if any, must be determined also. With respect to the pension, the executrix should write to your employer to determine its value and transferability. At the same time the employer should be asked if there are any employee benefits (for example, life insurance, death benefits, or survivor's benefits).

The executrix should immediately write to all of your banking institutions to determine the amount of money you had in each account including accrued interest, if any. In some cases fair market appraisal of your personal belongings may be advisable. The safety-deposit box should be opened and its contents reviewed and listed.

In addition to valuing the assets, the executrix must make all efforts to preserve them. For example, if the matrimonial home is now vacant, it is the executrix's responsibility to contact the insurance company to make sure that there is proper insurance coverage on the home and its contents. In the event that the home is destroyed and not covered by insurance as a result of vacancy, the executrix may be held personally responsible to your estate and its beneficiaries for negligence.

The executrix should check the amounts owing with respect to Revenue Canada taxation, provincial taxing authorities, funeral expenses, credit cards, or any loans; she should review any life-insurance policies, make inquiries as to the amount of money to be paid, and determine who is the named beneficiary of the proceeds. The Government of Canada should be advised of your death. The executrix should review various government programs, including Canada Pension Plan or Quebec Pension Plan, for such benefits as survivor's benefits, orphan's benefits, disability benefits, and widow's pension, to ascertain if the estate or any of the dependants are eligible for monies from any of these programs.

The executrix should advertise for creditors and claimants. Each province has different requirements with respect to advertising. If the estate is a small one, it is generally necessary to advertise on only one occasion in the local newspaper. However, if the estate is larger, it is usually necessary to advertise two or more times on successive weeks. A solicitor in your province should be contacted to determine the actual requirements with respect to advertising for creditors and claimants. In the event that all of the assets of the estate are paid out and creditors or claimants come forward whose claims can no longer be satisfied, the executrix will be held liable for the deficiencies unless she can prove that there was proper advertisement for creditors and claimants. An affidavit of publication, with the actual advertisement attached as evidence, should be obtained from the newspaper.

At some point in this process the executrix must make a decision as to whether the estate should be probated (legally authenticated by the court). If the bulk of the assets were jointly held or payable to name beneficiaries, (as, for example, with the proceeds of life-insurance policies), it may not be necessary to probate the estate. Quite often banks will transfer account balances to pay funeral expenses or transfer funds to a beneficiary upon receiving a copy of the will. (As was mentioned earlier, for example, Canada Savings Bonds to a maximum value of $40,000 may be transferred without a grant of probate or letters of administration.) Whether probate is required is a discretionary matter. In the case of a complex estate with a number of beneficiaries, it is wise to probate the estate. In smaller estates with only one or two beneficiaries, probate may not be necessary.

Once all of the assets and liabilities have been determined, and provision has been made for the payment of any debts and taxes owed, the executrix must pay out specific bequests. These are bequests that transfer specific assets or sums of money to beneficiaries. For example, you may have left your jewellery to one person and the sum of $5,000 to another. These bequests should be attended to prior to distribution of the residue of the estate.

The executrix should then establish trusts, if any, as provided in the will. For example, you may have directed a trust fund to be set up for any children under the age of twenty-one with the interest income and as much of the capital as may be required to flow to the trustee of the children's estate for their maintenance, education, or benefit. The trust should be set up immediately so that interest begins to accrue.

Once the specific bequests have been paid, trusts have been established as provided in the will, all tax requirements have been satisfied, and clearance certificates have been obtained, the executrix is in a position to pay out the residue of the estate to the beneficiary or beneficiaries named in your will.

A release should be obtained from each beneficiary at the same time as the beneficiary receives the bequest as specified in the will. This release will then protect the executrix from any future liability arising with respect to that beneficiary.

Potential Liability of the Executrix

Essentially the position of the executrix is one of trust. You have entrusted this person with the estate monies and with your directions about the disposition of these monies subject to the laws in your province. If this trust is breached, the executrix may be liable. For example, if the executrix does not exercise proper discretion in the preservation of assets, she may well be liable for the consequences. If the executrix neglects to give notice to the parties required under the relevant provincial family-relief and matrimonial-property legislation, she may be held personally liable in the event that the estate is distributed before any claims of these parties have been satisfied.

It is important for an executrix to obtain legal advice to avoid any personal liability.

Applying for Letters of Administration or Application for Probate

"Letters of administration" are required when the deceased dies without a will or someone other than the named executrix is administering the estate. If there is a will and the named or alternate executrix is administering the estate, an application for probate is filed.

Considerable documentation is required for either of these applications. It is possible to file letters of administration or an application for probate without requiring the services of a lawyer, although the many technical requirements would make it somewhat difficult to complete this documentation properly without specialized knowledge.

This documentation must be filed with the Surrogate or Probate Court of the jurisdiction in which the deceased resided and must meet all of the court's formal requirements. If there is a will, the original will must be attached to the application, and an affidavit of one of the subscribing witnesses to that will is also required. An affidavit must also be executed by the executrix giving information about the deceased and the estate and including an inventory of the estate assets and liabilities and a schedule of beneficiaries.

Public Trustee

Generally there is a Public Trustee in each province. The Public Trustee must be contacted where there are beneficiaries or potential beneficiaries under the age of majority or mentally or physically disabled and dependent for their support on the deceased. The Public Trustee must be notified whenever minors or missing beneficiaries are involved. The role of the Public Trustee is to represent and protect the interests of those people who are not able to protect themselves. In some cases, the Public Trustee will be actively involved in negotiating a settlement for a dependant, locating a missing beneficiary, or applying for letters of administration.

Tax Consequences

Revenue Canada has numerous requirements with respect to the filing of tax returns on the death of a taxpayer. First, your executrix should determine if there are any outstanding tax returns for the years prior to the year of your death. Then, a T-1 terminal tax return must be filed for the "stub period" (from the beginning of the fiscal year until the date of death). This return must be filed by April 30 or within six months of the date of your death, whichever comes later.

In the event that your estate has any income, a T-3 trust return must be filed. This return must be filed on an annual basis until the estate is finally distributed. Prior to distributing any estate, your executrix should obtain clearance certificates from Revenue Canada certifying that all taxes payable by you, the deceased (to the date of death), or by the estate, have been paid. Once the clearance certificates are obtained and the taxes are paid, the balance of the estate may safely be distributed to the beneficiaries.

An executrix who fails to file the necessary returns, pay any tax owing, or obtain clearance certificates may be personally responsible for payment of any tax owing by you or the estate.

It is possible to minimize the tax burden payable by the estate. The executrix should meet with an accountant and obtain professional advice both with respect to minimizing that tax burden and fulfilling the requirements of the *Income Tax Act*. Also note that certain financial penalties may be imposed if tax returns are not filed on time.

Rights of One Spouse to Property Owned by the Other

Dower and Curtesy

One quite commonly hears the phrase "dower rights." Essentially, traditional dower rights provide the wife with a life interest in one-third of all the real property held by the husband, except for land that he held in trust.

In Canada, dower rights have evolved over time. Generally, such rights require that any disposition of the homestead (residence of the spouses) owned solely by one spouse must have the written consent of the other unless the judge orders otherwise. Alberta, British Columbia, Manitoba, and the Northwest Territories also give a surviving spouse a life interest in the homestead after the death of the owner. A life interest means that you may have the beneficial use of the homestead until your death. You do not have the benefits of ownership. For example, if your spouse bequeathed the homestead, which he owned in his name alone, to his mistress, you would by virtue of your dower rights, be entitled to live on that homestead until your death. After your death, the mistress would have the use, benefit, and ownership of the homestead. In British Columbia and Saskatchewan these rights are given only to wives. After you obtain a certificate of divorce you no longer have any rights under these acts.

Dower rights have been abolished in New Brunswick, Nova Scotia, Ontario, and Prince Edward Island. Newfoundland and the Yukon do not have specific legislation regarding dower rights.

Family Relief Legislation

Every province except Quebec has legislation allowing a spouse, or a minor or a mentally or physically disabled child over the age of majority who has been left out of a will or received a minimal portion to apply to the court for a share or larger share of the estate. This legislation also applies to those persons who receive a minimal share of the estate on an intestacy. The spouse, minor child, or disabled child over the age of majority must show financial dependency on the deceased and possible impoverishment if a more generous provision is not made from the deceased's estate. Ontario, Manitoba, and Prince Edward Island allow common-law spouses to make application within the provisions of their respective acts. Ontario and Prince Edward Island each have a broader definition of the term "dependant" that includes such extended family members as dependent parents and grandparents.

Each province requires the executrix to give notice to potential dependants of their rights and remedies under the relevant family-relief legislation prior to distributing the estate to the named beneficiaries. Those persons interested in making an application under the applicable provincial family-relief legislation must commence it within six months of the grant of probate or letters of administration, unless a judge orders otherwise.

The executrix must not distribute the estate until six months after obtaining the grant of probate or letters of administration unless all persons entitled to apply for family relief consent to the distribution or the court so authorizes.

Matrimonial Property Legislation

Most provinces now have legislation specifying what proportion of the matrimonial property separated or divorced spouses should receive. Although this legislation is not specifically directed to estates, some provinces require the executrix to notify your surviving spouse of his matrimonial property rights in those cases where he does not receive the entire estate. In Alberta, for example, the executrix may be held responsible if the estate is distributed prior to giving six months' notice to the surviving spouse of his rights under the *Matrimonial Property Act*, unless he consents or the court authorizes the distribution.

Gift Tax and Succession Duty

Quebec is the only province in Canada to have gift tax or succession duty. Essentially, gift tax involves the taxation of gifts made during your lifetime. Succession duties are payable by your beneficiary on the taxable value of any property received from your estate. There are numerous exemptions from payment of gift tax or succession duties in Quebec, and you would be wise to seek legal advice about your specific situation.

PART THREE

Women at Work—
Your Rights
in the Workplace

CHAPTER 11

EQUALITY IN EMPLOYMENT

Suzanne P. Boivin

Suzanne P. Boivin is a partner in the firm of Melançon, Marceau, Grenier & Sciortino, of Montreal, Quebec. She has taught employment law at a Montreal law school. Prior to her admission to the Bar, she served as a human rights investigator for the Nova Scotia Human Rights Commission as well as for the Canadian Human Rights Commission. She is also a former steering committee member of the National Association of Women and the Law.

THIS CHAPTER DEALS with legislative provisions enacted by the federal, provincial, and territorial jurisdictions to guarantee equality in the workplace. Only those provisions of special interest to women are discussed. Four separate topics are addressed: anti-discrimination legislation, equal pay, sexual harassment, and affirmative action.

In addition to setting out the applicable law, special attention is given to the practical aspects of seeking redress for violation of equality rights.

The very notion of equality is "a living tree"—that is, a developing concept. What has become apparent in recent discussions is that equality no longer means the *same* treatment for all. In some circumstances, special measures and the accommodation of differences are required. The concept of equality rather than sameness has evolved partly because we now recognize that what used to be considered an ideal general rule applicable to all was often a norm suited to white middle-class males. Take, for instance, height and weight requirements, which allowed many Caucasian men to compete for jobs as police officers and firefighters but systematically excluded women and most men of Asian origin. Such requirements have been successfully challenged when employers failed to prove them essential to the performance of the job.

For women, another key factor has been wider acceptance of their right to work and have families, regardless of whether they are the sole supporters of their family. This has meant recognition of the needs of working women as child-bearers, leading to maternity-leave provisions and protection from hazards to pregnancy. Special measures for women and other disadvantaged groups are part of the right to equality in the workplace.

A word of caution: this chapter deals only with the non-constitutional statutes that offer the means of bringing complaints against employers. A separate chapter of this book deals with equality rights guaranteed in that part of the Canadian constitution called the *Charter of Rights and Freedoms*. The constitutional charter should not be confused with the various human rights laws or with the Quebec *Charter of Human Rights and Freedoms*.

ANTI-DISCRIMINATION LEGISLATION

Every Canadian province and territory and the federal government have enacted legislation that prohibits discrimination against women in the workplace. Generally, laws that deal with discrimination are called human rights acts or codes; in the territories, the term "fair practices" is used. Quebec is the only jurisdiction in which the anti-discrimination provisions are included in a law bearing the title of "charter." Most of the acts include a preamble that sets out the fundamental nature of the rights and freedoms protected as a matter of public policy, thus giving an overriding character to human rights statutes over other types of laws.

These statutes prohibit discrimination on the basis of sex, which, of course, applies to men as well as women. In some jurisdictions, sex discrimination has been interpreted as including actions related to pregnancy. Federally and in Alberta, the statutes provide specifically that, where a complaint of discrimination is based on pregnancy (the federal statute adds "or childbirth"), the discrimination shall be deemed to be based on the ground of sex. The Quebec charter adds pregnancy as a separate ground. Only Quebec, Ontario and the Northwest Territories protect victims of discrimination on the basis of sexual orientation.

Typically, human rights statutes prohibit employers from discriminating against women in hiring, promotions, and any other terms and conditions of employment. As well, employers are barred from using application forms and advertisements that directly or indirectly create gender-based limitations or preferences in recruitment. In some jurisdictions, the statute goes so far as to prohibit employers from requiring applicants to furnish information as to their gender.

Exceptions to the No-Discrimination Rule

The most important exception to the no-discrimination rule is that employers are allowed to refuse to employ women or treat them differently from men if the employer establishes a ''bona fide'' occupational requirement justifying the different treatment. Only a few jurisdictions have given a definition of what is deemed to be such a ''bona fide'' (or good faith) requirement. For example, the Bona Fide Occupational Requirement Guidelines adopted under the federal statute stipulate that certain justifications (for example, a requirement based on co-worker or customer preference not related to an individual's ability to perform the job) do not qualify as ''bona fide'' requirements.

Another exception found in most human rights statutes relates to legitimate pension and insurance plans. It is generally allowed that the use of actuarial tables that differentiate on the basis of gender is *non*-discriminatory. Sometimes such tables work to the benefit of women (for example, with respect to automobile-insurance premiums), while in other situations they work to the detriment of women (for example, in determining the terms and conditions of long-term disability insurance). Whether pension and insurance plans will continue to be exempt from the non-discrimination rule is a matter of conjecture. Already, law suits have been brought to challenge the validity of clauses creating this type of exception on the grounds that they infringe the right to equality guaranteed by the Canadian constitution.

The duty not to discriminate against women also extends to unions and to employer organizations both with respect to the right of women to join and participate in the activities of such organizations and with respect to the negotiation of employment contracts, including collective agreements.

Filing a Human Rights Complaint

In all jurisdictions, enforcement of human rights legislation has been entrusted to a government agency. Most are called "human rights commissions." In British Columbia, the commission was recently replaced by a Human Rights Council, while a single commissioner is named for the Northwest Territories and the Yukon. The duties of human rights agencies include providing the public with information about equality and non-discrimination.

Initial contact with the human rights agency need not be formal, but eventually a written complaint is required for further investigation. It is usually part of the agency's mandate to help you draft your complaint. Once a formal complaint is filed, it is assigned to an officer for investigation. Unfortunately, backlogs are a common occurrence, and actual investigation may not commence for some time. Investigators' powers give them access to your employer's records as well as the right to interview any witnesses. The employer is advised that a complaint has been filed and is given an opportunity to tell the other side of the story. At any stage where it appears that the complaint does not fall within the agency's jurisdiction or where it appears frivolous or without merit, the complaint must be dismissed. Where the investigator concludes that a complaint is substantiated, a more-or-less-formal attempt at settlement will be made by the agency.

Up to this point, the legislation is standard throughout the country, except for Quebec, where the rules of practice provide for two types of investigation. One type follows the pattern above and involves a fact-finding process similar to a police investigation. The other is more formal and involves a proceeding more akin to a commission of inquiry. In the latter type of investigation, the investigator subpoenas witnesses and expects the parties to lead evidence. Often, the parties are represented by counsel even at the investigation stage.

If you and the employer are unable to agree on a settlement, most statutes provide for a formal inquiry by a board or tribunal to arrive at a finding based on the evidence heard. Usually, the human rights agency will plead your case, but retain independent counsel. Some statutes provide for an appeal of the board's decision, while others stipulate that the decision is final.

It should be noted that time limits are specified in some statutes with respect to the filing of a complaint. Inquiries should be made as soon as possible to the human rights agency to determine whether such a time limit is specified in your jurisdiction.

In addition to the complaints procedure, most legislation on human rights states that contravention of the duties prescribed by the statute constitutes an offence. Thus, employers may also be ordered to pay a fine. Penal proceedings may only be instituted with the consent either of the minister, the commission, or the attorney general.

The decision to file a complaint, especially when you are still an employee of the respondent, is not to be taken lightly. You will not be popular with your employer. Ironically, even some of those who may ultimately benefit from your complaint may resent you. It is important to be prepared for this reaction. Where possible, allies should be found to give you support throughout what may be a lengthy process. Conversely, you may gain concrete results and the added satisfaction that other women will benefit from your willingness to stand up for your rights.

Proving Discrimination

A woman who alleges that she has been a victim of discrimination must prove her case. This is not always easy, especially if the discrimination is indirect.

Direct discrimination may occur, for example, where the hiring policy is that only men will be hired as labourers and only women as receptionists. Where you are turned down for the job of labourer, you will have to show that you applied, that you were qualified for the job, and that you were turned down. Usually, by the time the case is heard, you will be able to indicate who was hired in your place.

The refusal to hire may result from a line foreman's prejudice against women working in this type of position. If this is the case, he may have made some reference to your physical frame, or to the fact that he wouldn't want his daughter doing this type of work, or to his fear that his male employees will resent you or feel the need to cover for you. He may require you to submit to a test of physical strength—such as lifting an object with one hand—that male applicants are not asked to take and that tests abilities that would never be needed in the job. These are examples of direct discrimination. Another would be a personnel office's practice of systematically, and without consultation with individual applicants, placing applications from men in one file and from women in another.

The refusal to hire may, on the other hand, be based on indirect or systemic discrimination. In this type of case, the apparently neutral workings of the system have the effect of limiting the employment opportunities of women.

Let's again consider a case in which you, a woman, apply for a labourer's job. Often, the employer's defence in this type of case will rest on the fact that the male applicant was more qualified than you. This defence triggers consideration of whether the man's extra qualifications are really material to the job. Since the job of labourer is generally an unskilled position, the fact that the man has a welding course becomes immaterial. Many employers argue, however, that they have the right to select even an over-qualified person who will be more likely to fit into the job-progression pattern later.

In response, women's groups point to the dismal under-representation of women in blue-collar positions. They add that, given patterns of discrimination in schooling, vocational training programs, and the like, and given the current unemployment situation, to allow employers to hire over-qualified men rather than qualified women will ensure that women will never have access even to entry-level jobs in the blue-collar sphere.

It is impossible to give a comprehensive list of all practices that constitute systemic discrimination. Identifying such practices in your workplace involves the following questions: *Are there jobs that show a strong imbalance between male and female representation? What are the likely reasons for the imbalance? Are women being overlooked for promotions? Do the job postings reflect actual job content? Is there a reason why you are reluctant to apply for a particular job? Do men and women have access to equivalent training opportunities?* You should not be afraid to question even time-honoured rules. It is surprising how we have come to accept as unchangeable rules that have become outdated and illegal.

All anti-discrimination statutes prohibit direct discrimination. Deliberate *intent* to discriminate is not required. A mistaken belief that one's actions are legitimate does not constitute a defence to a complaint of discrimination. The only impact of such a defence will be on the complainant's right to special damages, as discussed in the next section.

Systemic discrimination, however, is not covered by all statutes. According to judicial interpretation, the law must be worded so that the prohibition against discrimination extends to practices that have the effect of creating a distinction or preference. In those jurisdictions where the wording is more narrow (in Quebec, for example), it is important to lobby for an amendment to extend coverage to systemic discrimination.

Remedying Discrimination

What can be gained by filing a complaint? If you were fired, will you be reinstated? What about lost earnings?

Where a complaint is upheld, an employer may be ordered to cease a discriminatory practice and to make available to the victim the rights and opportunities that were denied as a result of the practice. This includes the right to reinstatement. As well, orders for compensation to the victim for lost wages and expenses may be made. Special moral damages for injury to feelings and self-respect may also be ordered, but some statutes stipulate that such damages apply only where it is shown that the discriminatory practice was engaged in wilfully or recklessly. The federal and Saskatchewan statutes set a maximum of $5,000 for moral damages, while the British Columbia statute refers to a special order to a maximum of $2,000.

Finally, some statutes specify a maximum period, usually two years prior to the complaint, for which compensation for lost wages may be ordered.

It is difficult to give a comprehensive assessment of the outcome of human rights complaints, since most complaints are settled out of court, with many respondents specifying that the terms of settlement are not to be divulged. Also, until recently, access to tribunal decisions was restricted because very few decisions were published. The situation has improved with the increasing number of legal reporting services specializing in human rights.

From the reported case law, it appears that, generally, monetary awards under human rights statutes tend to be low. This reflects the historical pattern in human rights enforcement wherein emphasis has been placed on education rather than coercion to achieve the aims of the legislation. Thus, efforts have been directed at convincing people to set aside their prejudices rather than punishing offenders through large financial awards to complainants.

As well, tribunals have shown some reluctance to exercise their powers fully. For example, they have hesitated to order a successful complainant to be hired if this would mean the lay-off of an unsuspecting applicant who was given the job in violation of the complainant's rights. This is in keeping with the traditional feeling that human rights should not be promoted at the expense of innocent third parties.

It should be remembered that the duty to mediate is still an entrenched part of the approach taken by human rights agencies. You may have to insist, if you feel that the mediated settlement is not to your satisfaction.

EQUAL PAY

One of the major disadvantages facing women in the work force is that they are paid less than men. Studies have shown various factors that contribute to the wage differential. It is recognized, for example, that more women work part time than men. Women are also clustered in a few job categories, mainly in service and clerical or secretarial positions, that are low on the pay scale. But even where all other factors are weighed—including age, education, and job experience—women still earn less than their male counterparts.

The purpose of equal-pay provisions is to address the part of the wage gap that is caused by sex discrimination. When such provisions began to appear in the 1960s, it was common to find, within the same classification, different wage columns with such headings as "female" and "male" (or the equivalent). Invariably, the wage set for the female worker was lower. More recently, such distinctions have become exceptional if not extinct. What is still frequent, however, is the establishment of different categories within a job classification that replace the "female/male" headings with "category A/category B" headings.

The more typical situation however is that the jobs occupied by women are called something totally different from those occupied by men. Sometimes this may occur when the job content is quite similar, if not identical. (The example that recurs most often in equal-pay cases is that of nurses' aides and orderlies.)

The situations described above were the main target of early equal-pay legislation, which stipulated a duty for employers to pay equal wages for equal work. In order to bring a claim of unequal treatment under such a statute, it was necessary for women to show that they performed identical tasks to those performed by men and that the men were receiving higher pay.

As the years passed, however, it became apparent that the equal-pay-for-equal-work standard had done little to close the wage gap between men and women. Studies in the 1970s pointed rather to an increase in the wage gap. It became clear that the most significant factor contributing to the wage differential is job segregation—that is, the concentration of women in lower-paid occupations. Thus, additional emphasis was put on employers' classification systems in order to determine whether the jobs occupied by women are undervalued in comparison to the jobs occupied by men. Obviously, this problem could not be addressed by the criterion of equal pay for equal work, which has now been expanded in various ways by different jurisdictions.

Currently, all Canadian jurisdictions have specific equal-pay provisions, except for New Brunswick, which can nevertheless address an equal-pay complaint under the prohibition against discrimination on the basis of sex found in its *Human Rights Code*. Equal-pay provisions are contained either in human rights statutes (federally and in Alberta, British Columbia, Newfoundland, the Northwest Territories, Prince Edward Island, and Quebec) or in labour-standards laws, sometimes called employment-standards acts or codes (in Manitoba, Nova Scotia, Ontario, Saskatchewan, and the Yukon Territory).

The actual wording of equal-pay provisions in Canadian law is diverse. Most statutes refer, with slight variations, to a requirement of equal pay for similar work or for substantially the same work. The federal statute refers to "equal pay for work of equal value," while Quebec uses the term "equivalent" work. All statutes except that of Quebec add to the basic criterion a list of additional factors on which to base the job comparison. Most refer to the concept of skill, effort, and responsibility, which, in effect, creates a standard of comparison based on the value of the job performed rather than on the actual nature and quantity of the tasks. An added requirement contained in these statutes however (with the exception of British Columbia and the federal statute), is for the work to be performed under similar working conditions. A more restrictive standard is found in the provisions of Alberta, Manitoba, and the Northwest Territories, which refer to a similarity in the job, duties, or services the employees are called on to perform. Finally, most statutes require that the female and male employees being compared work at the same establishment.

Exceptions to the Equal-Pay Rule

All statutes provide for exceptions to the equal-pay rule. Some statutes frame the exceptions in general terms, providing that a wage differential between male and female employees as a result of factors that normally or reasonably justify such a differential will be deemed not to violate the equal-pay provision. Under the federal and Manitoba statutes, the duty to determine which factors fall under the general exception lies with the enforcement agency, respectively the Canadian Human Rights Commission and the Wage Board. A list of the factors prescribed by the federal commission as "reasonable factors" appears in the *Equal Wages Guidelines.*

Other statutes refer to specific factors that are deemed to justify wage disparity. The most common are a seniority system, a merit system, or a system based on quantity or quality of production. It is implied or expressly provided that such factors must be applied without discrimination. It should be noted that the courts have decided that the fact that wages have been arrived at through the history of collective bargaining while male and female employees were members of different bargaining units does not itself constitute a justification of unequal pay.

Means of Redress

Where the equal-pay provision appears in a human rights statute, the regular complaints procedure applies. Under labour-standards legislation, investigative powers are given to officers or inspectors, and a claim for unpaid wages may be made by employees. In addition, most statutes provide for the possibility of instituting penal proceedings that could result in a fine to employers who violate the equal-pay provision. However, such proceedings may not be instituted by the employees themselves, though some jurisdictions specify that an aggrieved employee may commence a court action based on a violation of the equal-pay provision. Finally, one must be aware of the time limits that govern the right of redress. These may be determined by the general legal rules applicable in each jurisdiction or by the specific statute. For example, in Alberta, an employee who chooses to bring a lawsuit must commence the action within twelve months from the date the discrimination occurred and the claim for recovery is restricted to the twelve-month period immediately preceding the commencement of the action.

Proving Unequal Pay

Enforcement of equal-pay provisions necessarily implies a comparison process between employees of the same employer and within the same establishment. In addition, you must find an employee of the opposite sex who earns more and whose job fits the comparison standard set by the legislation. Although this may seem easy at first several problems may arise.

First, employees are not encouraged to divulge their salaries to one another. This makes it difficult to know whether a wage differential actually exists. It is not surprising that equal-pay complaints tend to involve employees in a unionized setting, where wage scales are set in collective agreements, or in the public sector, where job postings include salary ranges.

Second, finding a suitable counterpart for the comparison process can be difficult. Often an individual equal-pay complaint will arise where a woman is aware that a particular male colleague is earning more than she is and the comparison process will be on a one-to-one basis. However, one or several women may complain that their job category is undervalued, in which case the complainant(s) will have to establish that the job category in question is female-dominated, and that a male-dominated job category is better paid. If jobs in the former category are done totally by women and in the latter totally by men, a basis of comparison based on sex will be possible: however, the same would not automatically occur if the job categories have been somewhat mixed, so that, for example, the former is 75 percent female staffed, and the latter 60 percent male staffed. This is not to say that comparison then becomes impossible, but rather that Canadian law is not settled on this point.

Third, the concepts of employer and establishment are not clearly defined, and this can create difficulties in today's corporate society.

Remedying Unequal Pay

In principle, an equal-pay complaint should bring a readjustment of the wage scale as well as an order for back pay. It should be noted that employers are prohibited from trying to adjust the differential by lowering the men's wages.

Where equal-pay complaints involve a comparison of job categories, the ensuing order may involve sizable awards. Some federal cases have generated much publicity, largely on account of the size of the monetary award. Of course, compensation is distributed among all the complainants named in the complaint. In this respect, it is important to remember that if only one woman files a formal complaint, the remedy will not necessarily be applied to all other women in her job category.

It is useful, therefore, to include as many complainants as possible in the complaint. Some statutes allow for third-party complaints with or without the consent of individual complainants. On this basis, unions may file complaints on behalf of aggrieved members. This is so even though the wage scale has been achieved through collective bargaining.

An interesting development in this area has occurred in Manitoba, where the *Pay Equity Act* calls on employers and bargaining agents to meet and discuss implementation of pay equity. The act has applied to the civil service since October 1985, and its application will extend to Crown entities and to the province's universities and health-care facilities as of October 1986. The act also provides for the establishment of a pay equity bureau within the Department of Labour to serve as an adviser to both the public and the private sectors on the implementation of pay equity.

SEXUAL HARASSMENT IN THE WORKPLACE

Although most women today have heard the expression "sexual harassment," many would have difficulty explaining what it means. This is not surprising since the expression is new, although it refers to a phenomenon that has existed for a long, long time. It is only recently, however, that women have raised public and legal consciousness of the problem by airing their complaints about the behaviour of their male bosses or colleagues. Recent legislation, as well as a burgeoning case law, have helped to give a legal definition to sexual harassment.

What Is Sexual Harassment?

The federal government and the provinces of Newfoundland, Ontario, and Quebec have included provisions prohibiting sexual harassment in employment in their human rights statutes. These jurisdictions (excepting Ontario) also prohibit harassment of employees on the other grounds of discrimination mentioned in the statute. The Newfoundland statute further provides that no person who is in a position to confer, grant, or deny a benefit or advancement to another person shall engage in sexual solicitation or make a sexual advance to that person where the person making the solicitation or advance knows or ought reasonably to know that it is unwelcome. A similar provision is found in Ontario. Other jurisdictions have held that a prohibition of engaging in sexual harassment is included in the general prohibition relating to sex discrimination.

Increasingly, as well, protection from sexual harassment is one of the guarantees specified in collective agreements.

According to the case law, the concept of sexual harassment may cover two types of situations. The first involves the solicitation of sexual favours in exchange for rewards or under the threat of punishment. The second relates to the creation of an atmosphere "poisoned" by sexual innuendo or gender-based conduct, without necessarily involving a direct tie-in with the provision of sexual favours.

The dual nature of sexual harassment is recognized in the definition adopted in the *Canada Labour Code*, which states that sexual harassment means any conduct, comment, gesture, or contact of a sexual nature:

a)   That is likely to cause offense or humiliation to any employee; or

b)   that might, on reasonable grounds, be perceived by that employee as placing a condition of a sexual nature on employment or on any opportunity for training or promotion.

Thus, although your employer may not go so far as to say, ''Sleep with me or else,'' if he engages in repeated attempts to ask you out, regardless of your negative response, or if he constantly subjects you to sexist remarks or insists on massaging your neck or patting your bum, in spite of protests or even an unspoken attitude of withdrawal, a complaint of sexual harassment could be upheld under the ''poisoned condition of work rule.'' This is so even if you have not been dismissed or demoted or have not suffered financially in any way. In the absence of a concrete measure taken against you by the harasser, you are expected to show that you suffered through loss of health benefits or withdrawal from your work situation leading to lost enjoyment and resulting failure to take advantage of opportunities. Some cases deal with complainants who resigned rather than put up with sexual harassment.

In deciding whether a particular situation fits the definition, adjudicators will take into account several factors. The repetitive nature of the offending conduct is likely to weigh in your favour. As well, adjudicators do not rely on the subjective evaluation of the facts by either the harasser or the victim. Rather, an objective test will be applied to determine whether the facts complained of constitute sexual harassment. This is so because it is recognized that men and women may have different perceptions of the nature of a given form of behaviour. Many women may be offended by conduct that many men perceive as mere flirtation. On the other hand, a recurring statement is that the purpose of the legislation is not to eliminate all social contact in the work place.

Who Is Sexually Harassed?

Men, like women, can be sexually harassed, although few reported cases deal with men as victims.

This is not surprising, since it is mostly women who find themselves in low-level, powerless occupations. Women have less economic power and less sexual power than men and are vulnerable to both economic and sexual exploitation by men. This vulnerability is enhanced in the several occupations where women act as assistants to men and where there is interaction, whether voluntary or imposed, of work-related services and help with personal and family matters. Thus, many reported cases involve women who worked as secretaries or waitresses.

These cases show that some men feel that sexual services are an implicit part of their female assistant's job description and will not hesitate to badger the woman and, ultimately, to replace a reluctant woman with a more responsive one. Men who go this far feel secure that their authority will not be challenged in the workplace and, thus, that their word about "unsatisfactory" work performance by the dismissed woman will automatically prevail over any claim she could make that the real issue is sexual harassment.

Other cases involve women who have just crossed the threshold into male-dominated blue- or white-collar occupations. In addition to incidents of grabbing and touching, these cases show examples of gender-based insults and offensive remarks that attest to the reluctance of supervisors and even co-workers to accept women in their ranks.

Studies show that these are not isolated cases. Indeed, sexual harassment appears to be an alarmingly widespread phenomenon. A 1976 study conducted in the United States by *Redbook* magazine revealed that 88 percent of the nine thousand women who answered had been sexually harassed on the job. A study later conducted in the American federal civil service showed that 42 percent of the 10,648 women responding had been recently sexually harassed. Studies in Canada show similar results. A survey conducted in Quebec in September 1981 indicated that of the 2,465 women responding, 64 percent had been sexually harassed in their workplace.

Who Is Responsible for Sexual Harassment?

Where legislation specifically deals with sexual harassment, it is clear that a complaint may be brought against the harasser himself, whether he is a co-worker or a supervisor. On the other hand, where a complaint rests on a provision dealing generally with sex discrimination, the wording of human rights statutes makes it necessary for the complaint to be directed against the employer.

In all cases, however, it is preferable to include the employer as a party to the proceedings in order to ensure future compliance with the legislation. How can an employer, often an impersonal corporate entity, be held liable for sexual harassment? In the same way that he can be held liable for other damages caused by his employees. Human rights decisions have applied general-liability rules that hold an employer responsible for actions of his employees of which he has knowledge or should have knowledge. Where the actions were taken by senior management, the legal concept of vicarious liability entails a presumption of knowledge by the employer.

It has been decided that in order for an employer to escape liability under the above rules, he must take appropriate steps to ensure that his employees benefit from a work environment free from sexual harassment. According to this case law, an employer who stands idly by will be precluded from denying responsibility on the basis that he did not actively participate in sexual harassment.

However, a recent decision of the federal Court of Appeal has taken issue with this case law. In the case of *Brennan* v. *The Queen*, the court held that nothing in the wording of the *Canadian Human Rights Act* imposes on employers an obligation to prevent, or take effective measures to prevent, employees from engaging in discriminatory practices. The case is now before the Supreme Court of Canada.

Ultimately, an employer will be required to have demonstrably adopted a clear policy relating to sexual harassment. Such a requirement is now a legal obligation for employers who come under the jurisdiction of the *Canada Labour Code*. This includes banks, airlines, railway companies, and broadcasting corporations. After stating that every employee is entitled to employment free of sexual harassment the code creates a general duty for employers to make every reasonable effort to ensure that no employee is subject to sexual harassment. One component of this duty is specifically to issue a policy statement concerning sexual harassment. The policy must contain the following:

a) a definition of sexual harassment that is substantially the same as the definition in the code;

b) a statement to the effect that every employee is entitled to employment free of sexual harassment;

c) a statement to the effect that the employer will make every reasonable effort to ensure that no employee is subjected to sexual harassment;

d) a statement to the effect that the employer will take such disciplinary measures as the employer deems appropriate against any person under his/her direction who subjects any employee to sexual harassment;

e) a statement explaining how complaints of sexual harassment may be brought to the attention of the employer;

f) a statement to the effect that the employer will not disclose the name of a complainant or the circumstances related to the complaint to any person except where disclosure is necessary for the purposes of investigating the complaint or taking disciplinary measures in relation thereto; and

g) a statement informing employees of the discriminatory-practices provisions of the *Canadian Human Rights Act* that pertain to rights of persons to seek redress under that act in respect of sexual harassment.

The employer, after consulting with the employees or their representatives, may add other elements to the policy statement as long as these are not inconsistent with the provisions of the code.

What to Do About Sexual Harassment in Your Workplace

The best first step to dealing with most situations is communication. Women must tell each other about incidents that make them uncomfortable. When sexual harassment is covert, women sometimes find it difficult to pinpoint why they are uneasy. The best way to cope with this type of unease is to exchange information with other employees. Unfortunately, some women still react negatively to another woman's claim of sexual harassment. It is important for all to recognize that such claims deserve attention and serious consideration. We are entitled to different levels of tolerance of such conduct as sexist remarks, for example. If one woman feels that such remarks are offensive while others are ready to take them in jest, she is nevertheless entitled to respect for her point of view.

Women must also talk to men about such situations. Not all men will concede that a particular set of facts constitutes sexual harassment. However, not all men will condone the actions of other male co-workers and supervisors.

Dealing with sexual harassment is like dealing with any other type of affront to one's dignity. Mixed feelings of outrage and guilt arise. Women, even though they are victims of another's actions, will often look to themselves as the cause, asking themselves such questions as: Is it how I dress? Have I been too friendly? It is not easy to accuse someone of sexual harassment. Women will try to explain away the harasser's behaviour, attributing it, for example, to his temporary family problems. If the offending conduct persists, the woman may fear that she will be exposing herself to ridicule or retaliation if she reveals the situation. Her initial lack of response may work against her, and she may be faced with disbelief. How could she have endured that for so long without complaining? she may be asked. Again, finding someone to confide in will help.

Most important of all, perhaps, is learning to express your feelings frankly. Both for the purposes of clearing up ambiguous situations and providing the basis for a formal complaint if necessary, you should tell the harasser that his remarks, invitations, leers, caresses, and so on, are unwelcome and insulting. There is no simple approach that applies to all cases, but bear in mind that it is always helpful to have a witness, if not of the harassment itself, at least of your warning.

Women who are unionized should consult their union representative. Most collective agreements contain a provision against sex discrimination and/or sexual harassment, the existence of which gives you access to the grievance procedure. Similarly, an unwarranted dismissal, demotion, or refusal of a promotion may be addressed through the grievance procedure, where evidence as to the illicit cause could be adduced. Whether a grievance is preferable to a complaint to a human rights commission depends on the circumstances of the case. Also, one recourse does not necessarily preclude the other. Wherever possible, you should try to gain the support of your union, regardless of which route you eventually choose. Many unions have set up status-of-women committees that can be particularly helpful.

Even in an unorganized workplace, a policy on sexual harassment may exist. We have already seen that federally regulated employers are legally bound to have such a policy. Often, some forum for a complaint is provided. This should be considered as an avenue for a complaint. You are usually not required to act alone. You may call on a co-worker for assistance or on someone outside the establishment, for example, a representative of an organization specializing in assistance to victims of sexual harassment, or even a lawyer.

A complaint to the appropriate human rights agency is the main recourse if your employer has no policy or if sexual harassment was the cause of your not being hired. The normal complaints procedure applies.

The courts may also provide a remedy for damages resulting from sexual harassment. At least one decision has held an employer liable for damages based on the wrongdoing of a manager who has dismissed a female employee allegedly on the grounds that her emotional problems made her unable to function within the department. The woman had filed and won a grievance against her dismissal. Notwithstanding her reinstatement, she argued successfully that she was entitled to moral damages arising not out of the collective agreement but out of the legal duty of the employer to provide her with a workplace free from sexual harassment. She was awarded $3,000 for humiliation and psychological trauma.

In any of the above forums, it is necessary to prove that you have been a victim of sexual harassment. The main source of proof is your own testimony about what happened. Legally, this evidence is sufficient. However, it is likely that the employer will deny the events or give them an entirely different interpretation. Where the decision depends on two contradictory testimonies, the rules about the credibility of each version will apply. If one is as credible as the other, then you will lose, since you have the burden of establishing sexual harassment on a balance of probabilities.

It is useful, therefore, to provide additional evidence. The three main sources of additional evidence are: an eyewitness, a confidante, or someone who experienced similar conduct from the harasser. The confidante may be a friend at work, or even your husband or boyfriend or someone else from your family. A witness about similar facts will usually be a co-worker or a former employee.

Evidence of emotional damage may be proved through your own testimony supplemented, where available, by oral or written testimony from your doctor. As for loss of employment opportunities, the evidence required will vary from case to case.

If sexual harassment is not a problem at your workplace, it may nevertheless be helpful to discuss the topic in general with a view to raising consciousness about the seriousness of the issue and to requiring that your employer adopt a policy, just in case.

AFFIRMATIVE ACTION

More and more we are hearing of special employment programs for women and for other disadvantaged groups. Different labels are given to such programs; sometimes they are called employment-opportunities programs or affirmative-action programs. The current term is ''employment equity,'' which was favoured in the *Report of the Commission on Equality in Employment*, chaired by Judge Rosalie Abella and commonly referred to as the Abella Report.

The common goal of these programs is to eliminate workplace barriers that may not be the result of intentional discrimination but that nevertheless operate to limit the employment opportunities of designated groups or individuals. The various labels reflect differences in the actual process set up by the program to deal with the barriers. In the United States, the term ''affirmative action'' has become synonymous with quotas. It was largely to allay negative reaction to quotas in Canada that Judge Abella opted for the concept of employment equity, with goals and timetables. Affirmative action and employment-equity programs share a common strategy to counter systemic barriers. The steps are described as follows in the Abella Report:

a)   a clear statement of executive support, the appointment of senior management accountable for implementing an employment equity program, the establishment of an implementation structure, the assignment of appropriate resources, and the development of a suitable labour-management consultative process;

b) the design and implementation of an organizational plan to include:
   i) the identification and removal of discriminatory barriers in a company's hiring, training, promotion, and income policies;
   ii) alternative, corrective systems;
   iii) special remedial measures designed to remove the effects of previous discrimination;
   iv) quantifiable goals with an appropriate monitoring and assessment system to ensure that women and minorities are equitably represented and remunerated at all levels within the organization.

Why Affirmative Action?

Opponents of affirmative-action programs claim that the data-collection requirements are cumbersome, and that the under-representation of women and others is the result of their lack of qualifications, so that employers will be bound to hire and promote unqualified persons. Employees who could benefit from such programs may also express a reluctance based on their unwillingness to be selected ''just because they are women.''

Supporters of affirmative-action programs point to the failure of anti-discrimination legislation to correct historical imbalance. They add that the free market does not provide equality of opportunity but serves rather to perpetuate the systemic barriers that created the imbalance in the first place. They also argue that lack of qualifications is often the result of lack of opportunity to obtain adequate training, whether on the job or in educational institutions. Finally, the claim that affirmative action makes good business sense has been buttressed by a recent article in *Fortune* magazine, in which managers of American corporations were quoted as saying they were in favour of retaining affirmative-action goals and timetables.

Voluntary versus Mandatory Programs

Insofar as affirmative-action programs create any distinction, exclusion, or preference based on sex and other prohibited grounds of discrimination, they are open to attack under anti-discrimination legislation, which prohibits such distinction, exclusion, or preference. However, Canadian lawmakers have recognized that special measures are necessary to correct years of exclusion of women and other disadvantaged groups from full participation in all aspects of employment. In most jurisdictions therefore, human rights statutes permit employers to set up voluntary affirmative-action programs subject, in some cases, to prior approval by a human rights commission.

Voluntary programs have been set up in the federal public service and in many major companies—banks and Crown corporations, for example. Few, however, include all the steps referred to in Judge Abella's report. Often, implementation of the plan is assigned to a person within the human resources department whose level of authority is insufficient to guarantee success. As well, it appears that the focus of integration of women is placed more readily on management rather than on blue-collar classifications.

Mandatory programs differ from voluntary programs in that employers are required to set up a program and the progress achieved by the program is monitored by some outside agency. The federal statutes and those of Quebec and Saskatchewan provide a means of ordering an employer to implement an affirmative-action program where investigation of a case confirms the existence of discrimination. In a well-publicized case, a human rights tribunal appointed under the *Canadian Human Rights Act* ordered the CNR to adopt certain measures to promote the recruitment of women in blue-collar positions.

The Abella Report recommended that the federal government adopt a law requiring all federally regulated employers—including Crown corporations, government departments and agencies, and businesses and corporations in the federally regulated private sector—to implement employment equity. It added that the legislation should include three major components:
- a requirement that federally regulated employers take steps to eliminate discriminatory employment practices;
- a requirement that federally regulated employers collect and file

annually data on the participation rates, occupational distribution, and income levels of employees in their work forces, by designated group; and
• an enforcement mechanism.

With respect to the enforcement mechanism, the report presented four alternative mechanisms, all based on the monitoring of employers by an independent agency.

Employment Equity

The federal government's response to the Abella Report has led to the enactment of the *Employment Equity Act*. Perhaps the most important part of the act is its statement of purpose, which recognizes the evolution of the concept of equality or equity as follows:

Purpose

2. The purpose of this Act is to achieve equality in the work place so that no person shall be denied employment opportunities or benefits for reasons unrelated to ability and, in the fulfilment of that goal, to correct the conditions of disadvantage in employment experienced by women, aboriginal peoples, persons with disabilities and persons who are, because of their race or colour, in a visible minority in Canada by giving effect to the principle that employment equity means more than treating persons in the same way but also requires special measures and the accommodation of differences.

The *Employment Equity Act* requires that employers under federal jurisdiction who employ at least one hundred employees implement employment equity by identifying practices that result in employment barriers to women and other designated groups. The employer must then eliminate such practices and institute positive policies and practices, and must make a reasonable accommodation so that the number of female employees in each position will be at least proportionate to the number of women in the work force or in identified segments of the work force. In taking these measures, the employer must consult with designated representatives of the employees or, where applicable, with the bargaining agent.

An employer must prepare a plan for each year, with goals and timetables, and must keep the plan on file for a designated period. The only monitoring provided is that, beginning June 1, 1988, employers are directed to file with the minister of Manpower and Immigration a yearly report containing statistical information as to the composition of their work force under the various headings stipulated in the act or in subsequent regulations. Failure to report renders the employer liable to a fine not exceeding fifty thousand dollars. Copies of the report will be available from the minister's office.

The minister's task will then be twofold. First, a copy of each report is to be sent to the Canadian Human Rights Commission. Second, the minister will be responsible for tabling before Parliament each year a consolidation and analysis of the reports.

The legislation introduced by the Honourable Flora MacDonald has drawn some criticism, from representatives of the groups designated in the act, that a mere reporting obligation does not correspond to the recommendations of the Abella Report. Specifically, it is felt that without a proper enforcement mechanism, it will be impossible to monitor those employers who lack commitment to employment equity. The minister defended her bill by expressing confidence in the ability of the Canadian Human Rights Commission to detect offenders and institute proceedings under the *Canadian Human Rights Act*. Only time will tell whether the minister's choice will be vindicated. However, a means of periodically reviewing the effectiveness of the mechanism has been worked into the act.

Contract Compliance

Another component of a commitment by government to affirmative action is called contract compliance. This refers to a requirement that where government awards contracts to the private sector, an explicit or implicit term of the contract is that an employer should abide by the human rights legislation or even make a commitment to affirmative action. Whereas the first may seem redundant, since the obligations in human rights statutes apply to all employees regardless of any actual contract, a contract-compliance requirement does impose a further penalty of loss of government contracts on an employer who is found to have engaged in discriminatory practices.

Nevertheless, a direct commitment to affirmative action coupled with a duty to show representation of women and other disadvantaged groups is much more conducive to actual results. After all, why should contractors who benefit from tax dollars not have to prove that they are model employers?

CHAPTER 12

EMPLOYMENT RIGHTS: THE MINIMUM AND HOW TO GET MORE

Elizabeth J. Shilton Lennon

Elizabeth J. Shilton Lennon, B.A., M.A. (University of Toronto), LL.B (Dalhousie University), and LL.M. (Harvard), is a partner with the Toronto firm of Cavalluzzo, Hayes & Lennon, where she specializes in the representation of trade unions and employees in matters connected with labour and employment relations.

MOST OF THE ISSUES dealt with in this chapter fall under provincial jurisdiction. This means that they are governed by provincial law rather than federal law. All provinces have laws in these areas that with very few exceptions are alike in their general structure. There are, however, significant differences in the detail, and no attempt is made here to provide an exhaustive analysis of all the relevant legislation. This chapter will give you sufficient guidance about the sources of rights and the types of rights so that you will know what to look for and where to find answers to specific questions, regardless of your province of residence.

In addition to provincial laws governing the area of employment rights, there are situations in which you would look at federal laws as well. Some enterprises are under federal jurisdiction; common examples of these include banks, companies in the business of interprovincial transportation and communications (for example, CP Air and Bell Canada), and federal Crown corporations. Almost all the laws governing women in these industries will be federal laws. In addition, some federal laws deal with employment rights that apply to all Canadians, whether they work under provincial or federal jurisdiction. These laws include unemployment-insurance laws and income-tax laws.

Some important employment rights are derived from no legislation at all, but from the common law. The common law is a body of judge-made law developed in Anglo-Canadian courts over hundreds of years. It can be superseded by legislation, and in the employment area it largely has been. The old judge-made rules were slanted so heavily in favour of employers that they have not stood the test of modern conditions and have been largely replaced. The common law still maintains vitality in the area of employment rights, however, in the doctrine of wrongful dismissal.

EMPLOYMENT-STANDARDS LEGISLATION

Every province has employment-standards legislation, although the legislation has different names in different provinces. In Nova Scotia, for example, it is called the *Labour Standards Code*, and in Prince Edward Island simply the *Labour Act*. Employees in federal jurisdiction find their "employment standards" in Part III of the *Canada Labour Code*. Women attempting to determine what their rights are in any given jurisdiction should be careful to check the regulations as well as the statutes.

The first questions to ask in examining the legislation are, Who is covered? and Who isn't? The exemptions from employment standards are often hidden in the regulations.[1] In Ontario, for example, the *Employment Standards Act* appears to apply to anyone who performs work for monetary compensation. The regulations, however, provide for a complicated series of exemptions from the general provisions of the act and from specific employment standards. Many of the provisions of the act do not apply to professionals, students in training for professions (such as articling students), teachers, agricultural workers, and domestic servants. Certain other provisions do not apply to trainees, to management employees, or to firefighters. There are some separate regulations covering certain

---

1. Complete sets of statutes and regulations are available in law libraries, and sometimes in public libraries as well. It may be simpler, however, to purchase paperback editions of particular statutes known as "office consolidations." These are available at government bookstores, and include the regulations.

kinds of domestic workers, agricultural workers, and residential-care workers. With a great deal of patience and perseverance, workers *can* find their way through this maze, but not without the suspicion that there is a great deal the legislature does not want us to know!

Hours of Work and Overtime

The acts contain basic minimum provisions for how many hours employees can be required to work, and under what circumstances they must be paid overtime. In Ontario, the basic rule is that employees may not be required to work more than forty-eight hours in a week, or more than eight hours in a day. A cynic might suggest, however, that the general rule is written into the act only to mislead employees, since all these rules may be broken with the approval of the Director of Employment Standards. Under the Ontario act, however, even in those situations where employers have been authorized to work excessive amounts of overtime in their plants, employees are not *required* to work more than eight hours in a day or forty-eight hours in a week. They do not have to work this overtime unless they or their union consent. (Watch out for ''concerted refusals,'' however; if a group of employees gets together and makes a joint decision not to agree to work excessive overtime, it may be called an ''illegal strike''!)

Although employers may require work days of from eight to twelve hours, the act requires that they provide eating periods of at least one half hour every five hours. Predictably, this half-hour break, too, may be shortened with the approval of the Director of Employment Standards.

Vacations and Vacation Pay

The acts also deal with minimum vacation entitlement and vacation pay. In Ontario, every employee who has been employed at least twelve months with the same employer is entitled to a paid vacation of at least two weeks. The minimum pay for this vacation is 4 percent of wages in the previous twelve-month period. This means that although you must be given a minimum of two weeks' vacation provided you have been employed for at least twelve months, if you have been absent from work for any significant period of time

in the last twelve months, you may end up with less than two weeks'
pay. The act provides that your employer has the right to tell you
when to take your vacation, and may split it into two one-week
periods or require you to take it in one chunk. The only limitation
on the employer's right to schedule is that you must be given your
vacation not later than ten months after the end of the twelve-month
period for which the vacation was given. Some employees, therefore, may work as much as twenty-two months in a new job without
a vacation. If you leave a job before you have worked for twelve
months, or before you have taken your earned vacation, your employer must pay you 4 percent of wages earned for which you have
not already been given vacation credit.

Statutory Holidays

In addition to paid vacations, the *Employment Standards Act* provides for what is known as "statutory holidays." In Ontario, statutory holidays are New Year's Day, Good Friday, Victoria Day,
Canada Day, Labour Day, Thanksgiving Day, and Christmas Day.
Only certain employees qualify for statutory holidays. You must
have worked at least three months with the same employer, have
been paid wages for at least twelve out of the twenty-eight work
days immediately preceding the holiday, and report for work on the
work day immediately before and the work day immediately after
the holiday. If you meet these qualifications, you are entitled to a
paid day off. If the public holiday falls on a day in which you are
not scheduled to work, you must be given another working day off,
or if you agree, you may be paid an extra days' pay. In certain
kinds of enterprises that operate twenty-four hours a day, seven days
a week (for example, hotels, hospitals, and factories that must run
continuously), employees may be required to work on statutory
holidays without extra compensation provided that they are given
another day off. Except in these special kinds of enterprises, employees who work on statutory holidays are entitled to be paid, *in
addition to* their holiday pay, wages at the rate of time-and-one-
half for the time worked on the holiday.

As Canadian provinces go, Ontario is rather stingy with its statutory holidays; other provinces, for example, may recognize Re-
membrance Day, Heritage Day, and a holiday in August.

Minimum Wage

All provinces have minimum-wage provisions. Many provinces establish different classes of employees for purposes of payment of minimum wages. In Ontario, for example, the basic minimum wage is $4.35 an hour. In Saskatchewan it is $4.50 an hour. Lower minimum wages are recognized, however, for students working part time or during the school vacation period, and for employees classified as "learners." Construction workers have a slightly higher minimum wage in recognition of their seasonal employment. For purposes of determining whether the minimum wage has been paid, the regulations provide for standard deductions for room and board. For example, an employer who provides room and board is currently credited with a payment of $51.00 a week.

Recent amendments to the regulations under the Ontario act provide for the first time for minimum wages for domestics and nannies. The minimum rate is $4.00 an hour. There is also provision for daily, weekly, and monthly rates, which turn out to be an exceptionally good deal for employers. The only limitation on hours of work for domestics and nannies is that they must be given one free period of thirty-six consecutive hours and one free period of twelve consecutive hours in any week without deduction from pay. If the employee agrees to work during this free period, she must be given "lieu time" at a rate of time-and-one-half (i.e., 1 1/2 hours for each hour) or be paid $6.00 an hour in addition to regular wages. (If the nanny lives out, she is entitled to a minimum wage of $6.00 an hour for hours worked in excess of forty-four a week.) As long as an employer complies with these provisions, the live-in nanny may be required to work twenty-four hours a day. Under these conditions, a minimum wage of $32.00 a day seems remarkably ungenerous.

Methods of Payment and Allowance Deductions

The acts not only provide a basis of calculation for the wages of employees; they also attempt to ensure that employees *receive* the money to which they are entitled. To this end, the Ontario act provides that wages must be paid in cash or by cheque, at the workplace or at any other place mutually agreed upon, and on the regular payday. Your employer is required to provide you with a statement with each pay cheque telling you the period of time for which you are being paid, the rate of wages, the amount of wages, the amount of each deduction from wages and the purpose for the deduction, any living allowances, and the net amount of money being paid. When you leave a job, you must be paid all monies owing within seven days of termination.

The act also limits the deductions that may be made from an employee's paycheque. The employer, of course, must make the deductions required by law, including deductions for income tax, deductions for unemployment insurance, and deductions for Canada Pension Plan. No other deductions may be made unless the employer is ordered by a court to make them (as a result of a garnishment order, for example), or the employee agrees to them. There are many situations in which you may "agree" to deductions because you feel you have no choice. The act gives some limited protection against such coercion by providing that employees are not *permitted* to agree to accept deductions for faulty workmanship, cash shortages, or missing equipment or other property of the employer where somebody other than the employee also has access to the cash or property.

Enforcement

Most provinces provide an administrative agency to enforce the provisions of employment-standards legislation. In most cases, if you feel that you are not getting what you are legally entitled to, you should contact your local employment-standards branch and make a complaint. There may be time limits on making a complaint, so do not delay! Employment-standards officers familiar with the legislation are available to advise you, and you should not require a lawyer to make a complaint about a breach of employment standards. These administrative agencies have extensive powers to enter employment premises, examine employers' records, and gather information. You may not be fired, disciplined, or punished in any way for making a complaint about employment standards, provided that you make your complaint directly to the enforcement agency. In many jurisdictions, your identity may be kept confidential.

Job Security

Under the common law and before any legislation was passed in this area, the judge-made rule was that unless there was a specific agreement to the contrary any employer might dismiss any employee (judges viewed such dismissals as simply a termination of the employment contract) provided that reasonable notice was given. If you had a written employment contract providing for a period of notice, or employing you for a specific period of time, "reasonable notice" would be determined by the specific provisions of your contract. If you did not have a written employment contract, your employment was considered indefinite, and "reasonable notice" would vary from case to case. Judges would consider factors like your length of service, the type of job you were doing, your level of salary, the level of skill involved, and your general employability in the job market. Periods of reasonable notice might vary from as little as one day to as much as thirty-three months. If your employer actually gave you this notice (that is, if you were told your employment would terminate two years from now and you were kept on and paid for that period), you would not be entitled to any termination pay. If, however, you were terminated immediately, the law required that you be given pay in lieu of notice in an amount equal to the salary and benefits you would have earned over that period of time.

One major problem with this remedy for terminated employees was that it did not get their jobs back. A second major problem was that it had to be enforced in court, a cumbersome and expensive procedure that was therefore available only to relatively high-income earners. To fill the gap for low-wage earners, especially those who are not unionized, legislatures have provided a variety of remedies for different types of dismissals. Let us examine some of them.

Notice

In almost all provinces, there are minimum notice periods provided for all employees. These minimum notice periods do not *replace* common-law notice periods; you may still sue for wrongful dismissal if you choose. The statutory notice periods are, however, much easier and cheaper to enforce. In Ontario, for example, these provisions are found in the *Employment Standards Act* and apply to all employees who have been employed for at least three months. The period of notice ranges from one week for an employee of less than two years' service to eight weeks for an employee of ten years' service or more. If you are not given notice, your employer must pay termination pay equivalent to the wages and benefits you would have received during the period of notice.

Plant Closures

The economic recession of recent years resulted in a large number of highly publicized plant closures, with resulting loss of jobs and substantial economic dislocation in the communities affected. In order to alleviate these problems, the legislature in Ontario passed amendments to the *Employment Standards Act* providing for particular rules to be followed where the employer intends to terminate the employment of fifty or more employees in any period of four weeks or less. If the work force affected by the termination is less than two hundred people, eight weeks' notice is required. If the work force is more than two hundred and less than five hundred, twelve weeks' notice is required. If more than five hundred people are to be affected, sixteen weeks' notice is required.[2] These termination provisions do not apply if an employee is hired for a specific period of time that has expired, or if the employee refuses a reassignment.

In addition to the right to lengthy periods of notice, the Ontario act also provides for severance pay for employees whose workplace is being shutdown and who are part of a group of fifty or more who have their employment terminated over a six-month period. If they have been employed for five years or more, they are entitled to one week's pay for each year employed, to a maximum of twenty-six.

Layoffs and Wrongful Dismissal

The provisions discussed above assume that employees are being terminated because work has been permanently discontinued and they are "redundant." They do not apply if an employee is temporarily laid off (the Ontario regulations define "temporary layoff" as a layoff of fewer than thirteen weeks). They also do not apply if your employer dismisses you for "cause." Cause is defined in

2. These numbers apply only to employees "in an establishment." Dominion Stores, for example, terminated more than fifty employees over a period of four weeks, but at a number of different stores. Is Dominion Stores "an establishment," making employees eligible for lengthy periods of notice, or is each store "an establishment"? The issue has not yet been decided.

the Ontario *Employment Standards Act* as "wilful misconduct or disobedience or wilful neglect of duty that has not been condoned by the employer."

In Ontario, if you don't have a union, your employer claims to have discharged you for cause, and you disagree, you may make a complaint to the Employment Standards Branch, which then determines whether you are entitled to termination pay. If you are lucky enough to work in the federal jurisdiction (and in some provinces as well) you may actually seek to have that dismissal reversed. As with all these provisions, there are detailed qualifying conditions but, if you meet these conditions, you have a right to make a complaint to the federal Department of Labour, which will then appoint an arbitrator to decide whether you have been dismissed unjustly. If an arbitrator finds that the discharge was unjust, you may be reinstated in your employment with full back pay. In Ontario, if you feel that the minimum period of notice provided under the *Employment Standards Act* is insufficient, you may challenge a wrongful dismissal only by going to the courts.

PARENTAL RIGHTS IN THE WORKPLACE

Maternity leave is the right to an unpaid leave of absence from employment for childbirth and child care. Leave for fathers and for adoptive parents, however, is less readily available in Canada. Once again, the rights of workers vary from province to province, and between provincial and federal jurisdictions. The general pattern, however, is similar.

Maternity Leave

Maternity leave for natural mothers of at least seventeen weeks is the legal minimum in most of Canada. The leave is not, however, available to all women workers. In order to be eligible for maternity leave in Ontario, for example, a woman must have been employed by the same employer for at least twelve months and eleven weeks immediately preceding the estimated date of delivery (governments have peculiar ideas about the period of normal human gestation!). The pregnant worker has the choice of when to take her seventeen weeks' leave, as long as it begins some time during the period of eleven weeks immediately prior to the estimated date of delivery.

Normally, the leave must extend to at least six weeks following delivery, unless you provide specific medical evidence that you are fit to resume work earlier than that date.

In order to ensure that you are eligible for at least the statutory minimum periods of maternity leave in your jurisdiction, be careful to follow the rules for making application for leave. In Ontario, you must give at least two weeks' notice of the day on which you intend to begin your leave of absence; the notice must be in writing and accompanied by a medical certificate certifying the pregnancy and giving an estimated date of delivery. If the baby arrives unexpectedly early and you have not yet applied for maternity leave, or if you become sick as a result of your pregnancy and are forced to leave work before you have an opportunity to apply for maternity leave, there is a special provision providing for retroactive application.[3] Provided you comply with these simple rules, your seniority and benefits are protected, and you have a right to return to your job or another position of a comparable nature. The only exception to this occurs when the employer has ceased to operate during the period of maternity leave.

As provisions for maternity leave under Canadian law go, Ontario is somewhat backward. Women under federal jurisdiction are much better off. In addition to the seventeen weeks' basic maternity leave, they are also entitled to a further period of twenty-four weeks' leave for child care. Furthermore, the federal government takes a more realistic approach to eligibility requirements; a pregnant woman need have been employed for only six months in order to be eligible. Not only are seniority and benefits frozen at the point of leave; under federal jurisdiction seniority continues to accumulate and the employer is required to continue to make benefit payments on behalf of the employee during the entire period of leave, always provided that the employee continues to contribute her share.

Paternity and Adoption Leave

Ontario and several other provinces have no provision for leave for adoptive parents or natural fathers. Under federal jurisdiction, adoptive parents of both sexes have the same rights as natural mothers:

---

3. If you become sick earlier than eleven weeks before your expected date of delivery, you may be in trouble, since you have no right to maternity leave prior to that time. Many employers' sick-leave plans would apply at this stage.

the right to seventeen weeks' initial leave and a further twenty-four weeks of child-care leave. A peculiar feature of the legislation is that there is no similar right for natural fathers. This anomaly has been noted and commented on by the Boyer Commission, which is studying federal legislation from the point of view of whether it complies with the Canadian *Charter of Rights and Freedoms*. The anomaly is likely to be corrected soon.

Paid Benefits

The previous discussion relates only to the circumstances under which employees are entitled to a leave of absence and to a job to which they may return. There is no legislation in Canada requiring employers to *pay* employees for periods of parental leave. There is, however, a provision in the *Unemployment Insurance Act*, a federal statute that applies to all employees in Canada, for fifteen weeks of paid benefits for mothers and for adoptive mothers or fathers. The anomalous exclusion of natural fathers that appears in the *Canada Labour Code* is reflected in this legislation as well. These benefits are available to claimants in these categories who have experienced an interruption in earnings as a result of maternity or adoption regardless of whether they are eligible for leave from their employers or are officially on leave from their employers. Even if you have been fired or quit on account of your pregnancy or parenthood, you are entitled to this minimum benefit. The only qualification is that you be a "major attachment claimant." The definition of major attachment claimant varies from time to time; currently it requires that an employee have twenty weeks of insured employment in the last fifty-two. Benefit levels are the same as those for any recipient of unemployment insurance. Some employers do provide "paid maternity leave"; this usually means that the employer "tops up" the UIC benefits to a level of 95 percent of regular wages. There is no legal requirement for an employer to do this, however.

Can I Be Fired for Being Pregnant?

Not all pregnant employees will be eligible for maternity leave. For those who are not, it has been generally assumed that unless they or their unions have been able to negotiate protection, they may be fired simply on the grounds that they are pregnant. This conclusion is vigorously disputed by many human rights advocates, who take the not unreasonable view that discrimination on the grounds of pregnancy is a form of sex discrimination. Unfortunately, the Supreme Court of Canada does not appear to agree with this view. Nevertheless, many provincial human rights commissions will accept and attempt to mediate complaints filed by employees who have been discriminated against on the grounds of pregnancy. If you are in this situation, it's at least worth a try! In addition to women who are not eligible for maternity leave because they have not worked long enough with the same employer, employees run into serious problems if they become sick as a result of pregnancy prior to the time when they are eligible to begin maternity leave. Such individuals have no specific statutory protection. Pregnancy-related illness is, or should be, regarded in the same way as any other illness. The general rights of sick employees will be discussed below.

Day Care in the Workplace
Although the vast majority of Canadian workers are parents, and well over 50 percent of mothers of children under five work at least part time, neither the state nor the majority of employers recognizes any obligation to provide adequate and regulated day care, either in the workplace or outside it. An increasing number of employers have begun to recognize the value of workplace day care in attracting and keeping skilled employees. Workplace day care is convenient and allows parents to spend free time with their children. Many advocates of occupational health and safety, however, take the view that, as a matter of social policy, trends towards workplace day care should be resisted. Many women, indeed many workers of both sexes, are forced by economic pressures to work under conditions that are immediately hazardous, or with equipment and materials of which the long-term effects are still unknown. They feel that young children should not be exposed to such hazards or potential hazards.

Although there is no assurance that Canadian women will be able to find adequate day care for their children while they work, there are two sources of government financial assistance if women are lucky enough to find day-care space. One is the day-care subsidy, which is available in most municipalities for extremely low-income earners and students who are preparing themselves to enter the work force. The second is the child-care tax deduction. This deduction may be taken by single parents or by the lowest wage earner in a two-parent family. The deduction is currently a maximum of $2,000 per child, a figure that does not begin to reflect the actual cost of good day care. Subsidies are available only for placement in provincially or municipally licenced day-care facilities. The child-care tax deduction is available for any child-care expenses incurred to enable a person to earn income or undertake training or research, and may include amounts paid to a baby sitter, a nanny, or even a private school or summer camp.

PART-TIME WORK

There are more than a million and a half part-time workers in Canada. Almost three-quarters of these are women. There is no recognized legal definition of "part time," and these women may be working as little as one hour a week, or as much as thirty-nine hours a week. The term "part time" may even include women who are working full-time hours, but on a "casual" or temporary basis. The only common denominator is that part-time workers are viewed as a secondary work force. They are, by and large, paid less for the same work and given fewer or no benefits, and they have less job security.

In most provinces, part-time workers are, at least theoretically, entitled to the same minimum standards and other employment rights as full-time employees. A careful analysis of the conditions of eligibility for those rights, however, makes it clear that part-time workers are less likely to be able to take advantage of those rights. For example, part-time workers will be much less likely to meet the conditions of eligibility for statutory holidays, since they will be less likely to have worked the minimum required number of days prior to the holiday. There are also provinces (New Brunswick, Nova Scotia, and Prince Edward Island, for example) in which part-time workers are not eligible for vacation. Part-time workers may find that their employment does not make them eligible for unemployment insurance, since for a week of employment to qualify as a week of "insurable" employment, an employee must have worked a minimum of fifteen hours in that week.[4]

Because of the nature of the occupations in which they are concentrated, part-time workers are much more likely than full-time workers to be excluded from employment-standards legislation. For example, domestic work and student work are both categories dominated by part-time workers.

Statistics on wages and benefits for part-time workers lead inevitably to the conclusion that part-time work is one of the many traps laid for women in the workplace. This is unfortunate, since part-time work has the potential to liberate workers of both sexes. It can increase employment opportunities in general by providing opportunities for job sharing. It can also increase the amount of work-free time available for leisure, for community activities, and, perhaps most important of all, for parenting. It's an issue that is worth some attention.

BENEFITS

Most of what we call "benefits" are not available to Canadian employees as a matter of right. With some insignificant exceptions, such benefits as dental plans, drug plans, and sickness and disability benefits must be negotiated with the employer, who has no legal obligation to provide them. Many large employers provide such benefits to all their employees. Never forget, however, that these benefits are part of your wage package; you've *earned* them!

There are, however, certain minimum statutory benefits to which all employees are entitled. These include unemployment insurance and the Canadian Pension Plan (except in Quebec, where employees are covered by the Quebec Pension Plan).

Unemployment Insurance

The details of the Unemployment Insurance Plan are constantly changing; even unemployment-insurance counsellors may be unaware of the most recent changes. The general outline of the in-

---

4. You may be able to count a week with fewer than fifteen hours if your hourly rate is high enough; the week will count if you earn at least $99.00, even if you did not work fifteen hours.

surance program, however, has not changed since it was first instituted. Employers and employed workers jointly contribute to a fund that is then available to provide a reduced but guaranteed level of income at least for a period of time, to workers who become unemployed. Unemployment-insurance benefits are available only to workers who have *been* employed for the minimum periods of time; the benefits are designed to ensure against temporary unemployment only. Once your benefits expire, you may make a new claim only after you have been employed for the minimum period of time again. The length of time during which you may collect benefits will depend on the unemployment rate in the particular region and on whether you are a "major attachment claimant" (currently a worker with at least twenty weeks' insured earnings in the last fifty-two) or a "minor attachment claimant" (currently a worker with at least fourteen weeks insured earnings in the last fifty-two). These eligibility periods need not be consecutive, so even if you didn't work this long in your most recent job, you may find that a combination of jobs in the past year may make you eligible to claim. The level of benefit is currently 60 percent of insured earnings to a maximum of $297.00 a week.

The *Unemployment Insurance Act,* and the regulations passed under it, constitute a thick document; the rules are very technical, and there are many pitfalls. Almost any money earned while collecting benefits will be deducted on a dollar-for-dollar basis from benefits. Certain "lump-sum" amounts received by an employee at the time of termination will be characterized as earnings, and benefits will not commence until these amounts are used up. Currently, these include severance pay and vacation pay. Pension benefits are also characterized as earnings. The rationale for considering amounts like these as regular earnings is not always clear, and the rules regarding them have changed a number of times since the Unemployment Insurance Plan was first put into place. The plan is a very expensive one, and the government of the day is constantly chiselling away at it. The counsel of caution for all claimants would be to report any amounts received from the employer as earnings, since it can be expensive to have to repay benefits that the government subsequently decides you are not entitled to.

In order to claim unemployment insurance, you need to get from your employer a document called a "Separation Certificate," which contains the reason for termination and lists your weeks of insurable employment. Your employer is required to give you this. If you have been laid off for lack of work, or terminated for some other reason the government regards as acceptable, your benefits will begin after a two-week waiting period. If you are viewed as being responsible, or partially responsible, for your termination, a penalty of up to six weeks may be imposed. You have a right to appeal a denial of benefit or the imposition of a penalty.

Canada Pension Plan

As with the Unemployment Insurance Plan, both employers and employees are required to contribute to the Canada Pension Plan (or, in Quebec, to the Quebec Pension Plan). The features of the two plans are essentially the same.

Premiums for the Canada Pension Plan "click in" once earnings in every calendar year rise above a certain minimum. There is also a maximum contribution, which most full-time employees reach prior to the end of the calendar year.

Because this is a government-administered plan, it travels with the worker from job to job. When you retire, the pension you receive is calculated on the basis of 25 percent of "average *lifetime* yearly earnings." All years of potential employment are calculated in, and not just years of actual employment. Therefore, if you have taken time away from the work force in order to raise a family, you will be substantially penalized. There is a maximum benefit per month, which is protected against inflation.

Private Pension Plans

In addition to the pension benefits provided under the Canada Pension Plan, some employers (a minority) provide private pension plans for their employees. There are many types of such plans, providing a wide variety of levels and types of benefits. Private pension plans have been severely criticized over the years for their lack of stability and their lack of "portability" from job to job. There is now legislation in many provinces providing some measure of regulation over private pension plans in order to ensure that benefits to which employees contribute during their working lives are actually available at the time of their retirement. This legislation also regulates the extent to which employees and employers may withdraw contributions made to pension plans. With respect to your own contributions, the general rule is that they become "locked in" or "vested" after you have been contributing for ten years or after you reach the age of forty-five, whichever is later. Prior to that time, you may withdraw your contributions on termination of employment without penalty, but you forfeit the contributions the employer has made on your behalf up to that time. Since these employer contributions are also part of the wage package and are therefore "earned," this is a substantial disincentive to employees to withdraw their contributions.

Sick Benefits

Employees who are sick have little statutory protection in Canada. In Ontario, unless you or your union have negotiated superior benefits, you need not be paid. If you are so sick that you cannot perform your duties and there is no reasonable prospect of improvement, you may be discharged without recourse. The theory of the common law is that the employer and employee have made a contract in which the employee agrees to provide services and the employer agrees to provide wages. If you do not provide the services, even if your failure is for reasons beyond your control, then you have not fulfilled your part of the contract, and the employer is entitled to terminate your contract. This rule applies even if you are unable to report for work because you were injured or made sick by your work and are collecting workers' compensation. If you are only partially disabled, however, you may wish to pursue the possibility of a human rights complaint; in some jurisdictions an employer is required to make "reasonable accommodation" for a disabled employee.

Once again, employees under federal jurisdiction are more fortunate. The *Canada Labour Code* prohibits employers from terminating employees who are sick for less than thirteen weeks, and also prohibits them from terminating employees on workers' compensation at any time as long as the employee is receiving rehabilitation services from the workers' compensation authority.

Even where you are *not* discharged from your employment because of illness, you have no assurance of a continued income. Employers provide a variety of types of "sick-leave" plans. Many of these plans provide for reduced levels of income when an employee is sick; some of them provide for no income at all. You may, of course, purchase your own disability plans from insurance companies, and many self-employed professionals do this.

If you are unable to earn income for substantial periods of time and your employer has no paid sick-leave plan, you may be eligible to collect sick benefits under the *Unemployment Insurance Act*. These benefits are available on terms similar to the "maternity benefit" discussed above: you must be a "major attachment claimant," and you must be unable to earn income as a result of your illness. You may be eligible for this benefit even if you are not employed at the time, if you are unable to seek work on account of illness and you have enough weeks of eligibility. The federal government also provides for a longer-term disability benefit under the Canada Pension Plan. This benefit is normally available only to people who are totally disabled and do not anticipate ever returning to the work force.

COLLECTIVE BARGAINING

You will recall that in our discussion of general employment-standards legislation, we referred to the benefits provided by that legislation as "minimum standards." These rights are the legislative rock bottom, and in some cases these minimum standards are very minimal indeed. The question for most working women is: How can I get more?

You may, of course, simply go in and ask for more. But unless you have more bargaining power than 99.9999 percent of your working sisters, you know what the answer will be. But what if you all went in and confronted your boss together? The real solution to your problem, or at least a concrete step towards that solution, may be a union.

Current figures show that approximately 30 percent of women workers are already unionized; the figure for men workers is 40 percent. Women tend to be concentrated in the least heavily unionized areas of the economy: the service industries, for example, and the financial sector. Almost all women workers, however, would be eligible to unionize. Unionization, like labour standards, is under provincial jurisdiction, and most workers would look to the legislation of the province in which they reside in order to determine their eligibility for unionization. The exception, as with employment standards, would be women employed in industries under federal jurisdiction, such as banking.

Who May Organize?

Collective-bargaining legislation (the general term for legislation relating to unionization) encompasses a fairly wide range of statutes. If you are a teacher, for example, or a police constable, a firefighter or a civil servant, you may find that there is a special act of your provincial legislature governing your bargaining rights. For the vast majority of women, however, answers about unionization will be found in their provincial labour relations act. That act will tell you who is eligible to unionize and who isn't, and will set out the rules according to which union representation will be legally recognized.

Employees interested in union representation have two basic choices. They may decide to form their own union, or they may contact and join an established labour organization. The second course of action is certainly the simplest and, in most situations, the most effective. Large labour organizations have knowledge and expertise and the financial resources with which to back up bargaining demands. There are established labour organizations available to represent employees in almost all sectors of the economy. Such an organization will give you advice in the initial organizing stages, support (both financial and legal) if your organizing campaign should run into difficulties, and strike funds to back you at the bargaining table.

There may be some special situations, however, in which you may not feel that joining an established labour organization is appropriate. Your bargaining unit may be very small (the legal minimum is two people), and you may have difficulty attracting the interest of an established labour organization. You may feel that your needs are too specialized to be adequately represented by a larger organization, or you may simply feel that founding your own employee association will reduce the level of confrontation. If you decide you want collective bargaining rights but want to ''go it alone,'' you will need to get some professional advice right from the beginning, because there are technical legal requirements involved in establishing an organization that complies with the definition of ''trade union'' under a labour relations act and meets the requirements of majority support. I strongly recommend that you get your hands on the book *Getting Organized*, a detailed ''how-to'' manual written by a labour lawyer and a union organizer (see under Further Reading in the Resource Guide at the end of this book). It will tell you things as basic as how to draft a union constitution, what a union membership card looks like, and the address of the Ontario Labour Relations Board. Although it is written with the Ontario *Labour Relations Act* in mind, the similarities among labour relations acts across Canada make it useful far beyond the boundaries of Ontario. Your provincial labour relations board will also be able to provide you with information on the requirements under your specific legislation.

In addition to those categories of employees outlined above who are covered by their own special collective bargaining legislation, there are (fortunately only a few) categories of employees who are not eligible for collective bargaining at all. These categories vary from province to province; in Ontario, the most obvious examples are agricultural and domestic workers. Most modern commentators feel that these exclusions are of dubious social utility and of questionable legality now that the *Charter of Rights and Freedoms* guarantees equal protection of the law to all Canadians. There may soon be challenges to these exclusions.

Benefits of Organizing

What are the benefits of unionization? If your workplace is unionized, your employer is legally obliged to bargain with the union about all ''terms of conditions of employment.'' This expression is so broad that there is virtually no employment-related issue that cannot be placed on the bargaining table. The crucial word, of course, is ''bargaining.'' Your employer is obliged by law to *discuss* all these issues with your union; he is not obliged by law to *agree* with your union's position on any of these issues. This is where bargaining power comes in. It is only common sense to suggest that an employer will be more likely to agree to the collective demands of all his workers than he will be to agree to the individual demands of any one worker. After all, if the individual worker doesn't like her working conditions, her only recourse is to quit. If every employee quit or went out on strike, however, the employer would be severely handicapped in continuing to run his business. This common-sense position is backed by statistics. The most recent figures available show that both men and women earned more in unionized jobs than in non-unionized jobs. Surprisingly, however, the effect of unionization is even more beneficial for women than it is for men. Unionized men earned $0.60 an hour more than non-unionized men in 1981; unionized women earned $0.65 more than non-unionized women in the same year. Unionization will almost certainly improve your job-security rights, as well. In most union contracts, there is protection against discharge without "just cause," and "seniority" (length of service) usually becomes a factor in layoffs and promotions.

Women now comprise almost 30 percent of union members. Union leadership positions and union staff positions are still, however, heavily dominated by men. Not all unions have been receptive to dealing with women's issues, either at the bargaining table or in their own internal policies. But change is coming to the trade-union movement, as it is to society as a whole. Most women activists feel that fighting sexism within the trade-union movement is the better choice and is far more likely to produce benefits for women in the workplace than remaining aloof from collective action.

CHAPTER 13

HEALTH IN THE WORKPLACE

Mary Cornish
Susan Bazilli

Mary Cornish practises in the area of employment and labour law on behalf of employees and unions. She also teaches employment law and is the Director of the Ontario Bar Admission Course section on employment law. She has served on a number of legal committees on labour relations, unemployment insurance, and legal aid and is the co-author of Getting Organized: Building a Union *(The Women's Press, 1980). Mary Cornish is a founding member of the Charter of Rights Educational Fund and the Equal Pay Coalition. She is also a frequent speaker to community groups and other organizations.*

Susan Bazilli holds a B.A. from Queen's University, an M.A. from the University of Toronto and a law degree from Osgoode Hall Law School. She has hosted a community television show on the law and is a member of the National Association of Women and the Law and the Law Union of Ontario.

A WORKER DIES on the job in Canada every six hours. One out of ten workers is injured annually. Many workers are suffering from slowly evolving occupational diseases. As more Canadian women work outside the home their exposure to workplace hazards to health and safety has also increased. Women are still occupationally segregated, and the types of dangers they face are related to the type of work they do. While both men and women usually face similar risks when exposed to the same hazard on the job, the predominance of women in certain sectors means that specific hazards will affect women more than men.

There is a myth that ''women's work'' is safe: a myth that is finally being exposed in areas heavily staffed by women, such as the health-care, sales, teaching, clerical, and industrial fields, and inside the home.

Many workers have suffered health complaints in silence, believing that their work environment is safe or that they alone are suffering. Women have tended to blame themselves for symptoms, or have been blamed for excessive complaining or absenteeism.

Employers are usually reluctant not only to inform workers of the hazards in the workplace but to act to remove the hazards. The cost of cleaning up the work environment is often balanced against the number of jobs provided and the amount of profit made.

While not all hazards can be eliminated, you have the right to work in a safe place. Your employers have an obligation to make reasonable provisions for the health and safety of their employees.

This chapter will show you how to recognize hazards in your workplace and tell you what your rights are. Once you have a general idea of the special problem in your workplace, you need to know what your legal rights are, how you can enforce them, where you may go for help, and what strategies to use to realize better working conditions.

You will need to refer to the acts and regulations for a complete picture of coverage, qualifications, and exemptions. These statutes may be either provincial or federal. In most cases, where you work (in which industry or province) will determine which jurisdiction you fall under. Most workers would be covered by a provincial statute governing occupational health and safety. However, if you work in a federal sector (for example, in a bank or for a railroad), you would have to use the provisions of the *Canada Labour Code*.

Your right to a safe working environment is a legal right. Women represent half of the labour force in Canada, and employers and legislators must recognize and act on the health and safety concerns of women workers.

How Do You Recognize the Problems?

Do you leave work every day with a headache or feeling tense? Have you been breathing in dust or chemical fumes all day? Did you injure your back by lifting too many heavy patients? Are you thinking about getting pregnant and wondering what the radiation from your video-display terminal (VDT) will do to the baby?

The first step to eliminating the health hazards in your workplace is to recognize them. If you or someone you work with feels ill and you want to know if the illness is related to your job, it is helpful to look for patterns. Does everyone in your department feel sick? Do people feel better on the weekends or holidays? Have your co-workers had more health problems since they came to work?

What Are the Health Hazards at Work?
Some hazards, such as noise or excessive temperatures or faulty machinery or visible dust, are obvious. But hidden hazards, such as toxic substances or everyday office equipment may be harder to see as a cause of your health problem. The following is a brief review of some of the more common health hazards.

Stress
Stress is the single most common occupational hazard. Not only is it considered the most significant mental-health problem, but stress can lead to heart disease, strokes, cancer, ulcers, kidney disease, and high blood pressure. There are a variety of stressors found in the workplace: job dissatisfaction; lack of control over the work process; shift work; concern over job security; overload or underload of one's tasks; sexual harassment; such physical irritants as noise, poor ventilation, vibration, and so on.

Studies on job-related stress have tended to focus on male workers. But researchers have found that women with the highest risk of heart problems were in clerical and sales occupations, married, with several children, working for non-supportive bosses, and feeling a definite lack of control over their lives. Nurses, child-care workers, flight attendants, waitresses, clerical workers, telephone operators, bus drivers, and mothers: all suffer from the same condition.

Consider the effect of the enormous stress and fatigue that the "double day" causes for women who have paid work outside the home and family responsibilities. And consider the effects that stress at work can have on your family.

While not all job-related stress can be avoided, employers who expose you to unreasonable stress may be forced to change their practice and to compensate you for your stress-related illness.

VDTs

Video-display terminals (VDTs), or cathode-ray tubes, are the television-type screens that display information in computers and word processors.

VDT users may experience visual impairment, eyestrain, musculo-skeletal discomfort, headaches, dizziness, tendonitis, tenosynovitis, carpal tunnel syndrome, and psychosocial stress symptoms. No standards have been set in any legislation related to occupational health and safety for permissible levels of exposure or the amount of time that a worker should spend at a VDT.

A VDT emits low levels of various kinds of electromagnetic radiation: x-rays, ultra-violet light, infrared light, microwaves, static electricity. Research has shown that exposure to these types of radiation may have serious effects on health. The research is contradictory and not conclusive. There is also controversy over the impact of VDT use by pregnant women and the effect on foetal development. A 1983 Health and Welfare Canada report on VDT use stated that there was no cause for concern about VDTs. However, other studies indicate a contrary view. If you become pregnant and are using a VDT, you should know about the different studies and what rights you might have.

If you work with VDTs, discuss all ill effects with your co-workers. Guidelines should be established in your workplace to provide for the regular testing of the equipment, shielding of terminals with high levels of radiation, scheduled rest breaks, anti-glare screens, fully adjustable chairs and desks, lighting levels, annual eye examinations, and so on.

Loss of Privacy

Another serious by-product of the new technology is the ability of the employer to monitor the performance of workers. Computer monitoring can create a constant source of stress through surveillance and loss of privacy. A major source of stress is the constant fear of job loss.

Radiation

VDTs are not the only source of radiation in the workplace. Radiation is also emitted by x-rays and copying machines. Government and industry have claimed that their standards for radiation exposure are "acceptable" levels. This has not withstood scientific investigation. While the most extreme exposure to radiation that causes cancer and other fatal diseases is that experienced by workers in the nuclear-energy field, all workers should be aware of the recent research on the sources and standards of radiation. What you can't see, *can* hurt you.

Hazards in the Health-Care Field

The majority of hospital and health-care workers are women. While hospitals can make the sick healthy, they can also make the healthy sick. Hospitals are filled with communicable diseases, hazardous devices, radium, x-rays, dangerous gases, drugs, and infected biological specimens. Health-care work is physically and emotionally demanding. Injuries are common: one of the highest rates of work-related back problems is that of hospital workers. In an eight-hour day, an aide giving twenty baths a day could lift about 3,000 pounds; this is more lifting than that required of a man in an auto-assembly plant.

Infection from direct patient contact is only one way that contagious diseases are spread. Handling, analysing, and disposing of biological specimens (for example, blood samples) are prime methods of contagion. Puncture wounds and burns lead to particularly dangerous risks of infection.

Radiation from x-rays can cause cancer and create reproductive hazards. Ozone can damage the lungs. Chemical hazards from anesthetics create birth defects and liver damage. This applies not just to hospitals, but to doctors' offices, laboratories, and dental offices.

One of the most severe hazards suffered by health-care workers is stress. It is well documented that shift work creates stress, fatigue, marital problems, irregular eating, the use of stimulants, ulcers, high blood pressure, and heart conditions. Hospitals are always understaffed, and scheduling problems exacerbate the shift-work stress. Burn-out can result from patient care, not just from caring for patients, but also from caring about them.

Lighting

A major cause of work-related complaints suffered by office workers concerns one of the most important physical aspects of the work environment: lighting. Lighting affects not only your ability to see but also your comfort, safety, efficiency, and mood. Proper illumination is necessary in order to work without undue strain, and different tasks require different levels of illumination. Visual fatigue results from the physical exertion of seeing, and not only the eyes are affected by the general weariness.

If you experience fatigue or eyestrain at work, whether you use a VDT or not, the lighting in your office could be affecting you. Measurements can be taken and office lighting design plans and studies consulted to see where improvements might be made.

Fluorescent lights are widely used in offices because they generate four times as much light as regular incandescent bulbs and make less heat. Fluorescent lights are known to give off low-level ultraviolet radiation, and office workers have complained of skin rashes and other problems.

Ventilation

Headaches, sore eyes, dry skin, dry noses, and fatigue can all result from the phenomenon known as ''sealed-office syndrome,'' ''office workers' disease,'' or ''building illness.''

The World Health Organization has declared indoor air to be increasingly damaging to health, because a well-insulated, energy-efficient office building in combination with an inadequate ventilation system may produce air that contains a wide variety of toxic substances.

The absence of fresh air and the presence of such chemicals as ozone, formaldehyde, carbon monoxide, carbon dioxide, cleansing solvents, photocopier fumes, and cigarette smoke create serious environmental pollutants. The used air is recirculated over and over, ensuring epidemics of such common diseases as colds and flu, along with many other irritating complaints and serious allergic reactions. Ducting and insulation in office buildings may also contain asbestos, a known deadly contaminant, which is rarely monitored or tested for in office buildings.

It may take a long time to realize that your health problems are caused by the air you breathe at work. But with the co-operation of your union and/or your co-workers, you can find out. For example, Les Terrasses de la Chaudière is a complex of three federal government office towers in Hull, Quebec. Employees complained about health and environmental problems associated with their work in these offices. Finally an investigation was undertaken that included measurements of ventilation, temperature, and humidity regulation, air-borne particulates, and organic vapours. Noise and lighting were also subjects of complaints of ill health. It was discovered that between 1977 and 1983, 25 percent of the workers attributed absences from work to these symptoms.

Toxic Substances

Over 50,000 chemicals are commonly used in our workplaces. New substances are introduced, untested, at the rate of 1,000 per year. Very little is known about these potential poisons. Standards for allowable exposure barely exist.

Questions about the use, storage, and disposal of chemical hazards in the workplace cannot be divorced from questions about toxins in our water, pollutants in the air we breathe, and poisons in our food. Workers must put the chemicals into the spray, spray the crops with poison, transport the poisonous waste, live beside the storage tanks, and eat the toxin-sprayed food.

Substances that have direct toxic effects on the body may take the form of gases, dusts, and metals and may enter your body through inhalation, absorption, or ingestion.

Immediate effects of chemical exposure are often difficult to recognize.

Exposure may result in immediate or long-term effects. Chronic effects of chemical damage may build up over twenty to thirty years before you realize that your health has been affected. A latency period may allow you to be exposed to hazards for ten to forty years before the occupational disease shows up as cancer or asbestosis or emphysema.

Obtaining access to information is difficult. There are few legal requirements that impose an explicit duty on employers to test your workplace, or even to share the results of any tests with you and your co-workers. Ineffective laws protect the producers of the chemicals while workers' health is threatened. The choice must *not* be between dying on the job or having a job at all.

Smoking

It is now a well-known fact that cigarette smoke contaminates and pollutes the air, creating a health hazard to smokers and non-smokers alike. Second-hand smoke has been linked to cancer and other debilitating conditions, from allergies to asthma.

What can you do if you are bothered by smoke at work? Some health and safety statutes leave room to include cigarette smoke with traditionally recognized workplace hazards. A recent decision found that a clerk in a federal government office was "exposed to a dangerous substance because some of his co-workers smoked," and ordered the federal government to confine smokers to separately ventilated areas in the workplace.

More and more people are demanding the right to smoke-free air at work. With so many employees addicted to smoking, employers should make arrangements to assist employees in ending the smoking habit.

Sexual Harassment

Sexual harassment is an occupational hazard for women that affects their health and safety. Some studies have shown that nine out of ten women are subject to harassment in their places of work. Many women who are victims either lose their jobs or are forced to quit. The psychological effects vary from depression and poor self-esteem to insomnia and severe stress-related health problems.

Various laws are supposed to provide redress to women in such situations: human rights legislation, collective agreements, *Labour Code* amendments, and so on. But laws to date have not prevented sexual harassment, so other channels should be used as well: laws related to occupational health and safety and to workers' compensation; criminal law and tort law. Perhaps the most effective source of help, however, is your union or other employee organization.

If you ever experience sexual harassment in your workplace, you must document the harasser's actions and decide whether to confront him directly and when and how to approach the supervisor and file a complaint or grievance. Talk to other women in your workplace for corroboration. Careful consideration of the problem in consultation with groups and lawyers with experience in this area will provide you with the right course of legal action. Your legal rights in dealing with sexual harassment on the job are discussed more fully in Chapter 11, "Equality in Employment."

Reproductive Hazards

The issue of reproduction and the workplace raises several major questions. How do substances in the workplace affect you or your partner's reproductive ability? How do they affect the foetus? Do you have the right to do other work or to be compensated if you cannot or should not do your job while pregnant? Should women be excluded from certain jobs to be protected from hazards? What can you do if your sterility or miscarriage or baby's birth defects have been caused by your work environment?

Reproductive hazards are found in a multitude of workplaces. They are usually invisible, and their effects may not be documented for years. In office buildings, textile factories, chemical plants, laundries, smelters, hospitals, etc., workers are confronted daily by hazards that can have an adverse effect on reproductive ability. Exposure to toxic chemicals, dangerous substances, and other adverse conditions can result in sterility, miscarriage, birth defects, and impaired sexual functioning.

The effect of reproductive hazards depends on such things as the type of hazard, the duration, level, and mode of exposure, the health and genetic make-up of the individual, and the way in which hazardous substances interact with other substances in the worker's environment. A reproductive health hazard is any agent that has a harmful effect on the adult male or female reproductive system or the developing foetus or child. The agent may be chemical (pesticides), physical (x-rays), or work-related (shift work). Exposure to workplace hazards can adversely affect the reproductive process at any stage: prior to conception, during conception, during pregnancy, and after childbirth.

There are many examples of inadequate protection for women from workplace hazards. In 1985, women working in the reservation offices of CP Air in Toronto were told that the office was to be painted. Several pregnant workers were concerned about exposure and were advised by their doctors to avoid the paint fumes. The women discovered that the paint contained aromatic hydrocarbons. They refused to go in to work during the painting, and the employer refused to pay them. They have filed a grievance under their collective agreement (BRAC) objecting to the violation of health and safety provisions and are seeking paid leave for time lost.

In the first lawsuit of its kind in Canada, an Ontario woman has filed a $7-million claim against her employer for reproductive hazards. In the very early stages of her pregnancy, the woman worked in an unventilated plastics factory. Her son was born blind and seriously disabled. The toxic substances present—styrene and polyvinyl chloride—have been linked to birth defects.

Many forms of legal remedies are now being pursued for reproductive damages. Workers'-compensation claims have been filed for miscarriages; wrongful-dismissal claims have arisen where pregnant women were refused transfers to safer jobs without exposure to pesticides; human rights cases have been instigated where employers attempted to exclude all women of childbearing age from specific work.

Quebec is the only province that gives pregnant workers the right to preventive leave if working conditions are hazardous. This "right to reassignment" should be enshrined in all statutes governing occupational health and safety, as well as in all collective agreements. In some instances, redress may be attempted under human rights legislation, the *Charter of Rights and Freedoms*, union grievance procedures, and complaints under occupational health and safety statutes.

When analysing the need for legislative reforms and the content of collective-bargaining positions, issues such as foetal damage, selective hiring policies, discrimination in the work environment, workers'-compensation claims, and "right to know" legislation should be examined in the context of the right of all workers to safe and healthy working conditions.

How Can You Find Out if Your Workplace Is Safe?

Do you have a right to know what the hazards are that you work with, either before or after you suffer ill effects? Does the paint contain toluene? Do the solvents have vinyl chloride in them? Are you handling PCBs? In order effectively to enforce your rights to a safe workplace, you must have access to information about what hazards are present in your workplace. Employers have an advantage because they generally know what the hazards are, whereas most employees don't. Employers have historically refused to give employees information that would potentially identify for them that they are working in a hazardous situation. For years, the asbestos industry exposed workers to high levels of asbestos, causing thousands of workers to die from asbestosis, without informing those employees of the known danger.

Most workers in Canada do not have an enforceable "right to know." But, after years of lobbying, some legislatures have finally started to recognize the right of employees to be given information by their employer concerning dangerous situations and hazardous materials in their workplace. For example, Ontario has recently introduced legislation that would make it mandatory for employers to prepare inventories of hazardous materials and physical agents and to make the information available to workers.

In addition, Ontario's *Occupational Health and Safety Act* also imposes a duty on supervisors to "advise a worker of the existence of any potential or actual danger to the health or safety of the worker of which the supervisor is aware." While this section goes far beyond the requirements of any other province, employees must still prove that the supervisor was aware of the danger. Most jurisdictions also require you as an employee to inform your employer of any hazards that come to your attention.

Generally governments provide educational or informational services to employees on health and safety issues. Check with your local occupational health and safety branch of the Ministry of Labour to determine what information is available. The Canadian Centre for Occupational Health and Safety in Hamilton, Ontario, is also an important resource for employees. It was established by the federal government to serve as a central clearing house for occupational health and safety resource materials.

Workers' Compensation boards across the country also distribute health and safety information. Ontario however is the only jurisdiction that allows you to request from the Workers' Compensation Board a statement on the accident and disease performances of your employer from the previous year.

WHAT OPTIONS ARE AVAILABLE TO YOU: WHAT CAN YOU DO?

If you think you have a problem with health and safety at your workplace, there are a variety of options available to you in trying to resolve the problem.

Co-workers

Check with co-workers to see if they are experiencing similar problems. For example, often employees who are working with video-display terminals have been experiencing headaches, eyestrain, or fatigue but have not associated their problems with their workplace conditions until they have shared this information with co-workers. Your employer will likely be more responsive to your concerns if the problem appears to be widespread and not just peculiar to yourself.

Health-and-Safety Committees

Look to see if your workplace has or should have a joint health-and-safety committee to monitor and resolve health-and-safety concerns. Nearly all Canadian jurisdictions have legislation requiring employers to set up such bodies. Committees are usually composed of equal numbers of management and employee representatives.

Some jurisdictions also make provision for a health-and-safety representative to be chosen by the employer to act as the employees' "watch dog."

Even in provinces with legislation requiring the establishment of health-and-safety committees, not all workplaces are required to have such committees. Most of the workplaces where women traditionally predominate are excluded from the requirement to have such committees. For example, in Ontario, workplaces with less than twenty employees as well as all offices, shops, restaurants, and hotels are exempt.

Generally the purpose of these committees is to meet regularly to discuss complaints, develop and monitor health-and-safety programs, and educate and inform both the employer and the employees. However, these committees do not have the power to force an employer to resolve a complaint, though they may recommend a solution. Their restriction to an advisory role and the fact that employee representatives are sometimes management-dominated have seriously limited the committees' effectiveness, although they do still play an important role.

Unions

It is very important in matters of health and safety to act collectively in dealings with your employer. Part of the battle is already won if you have a union in the workplace. You may then take your complaint to the union, usually through the local steward or union representative. Many unions are very experienced in handling health-and-safety issues and are knowledgable about workplace hazards.

The collective agreement between the employer and the union may also contain provisions that cover your situation. For example, if you are pregnant and operating a video-display terminal, the collective agreement may give you a right to transfer to another job with no loss of pay. If your employer has violated the collective agreement, you may then file a grievance and the union may take your complaint to an arbitration board with the power to resolve the matter.

Other Organizational Assistance

Other organizations in your province may be willing to give assistance to employees who have health-and-safety problems. For example, the Non-Smokers' Rights Association, in appropriate circumstances, has given advice and assistance to employees who wish to require their employer to have a smoke-free workplace. Other organizations (e.g., the Ontario Workers' Health Centre) exist to provide information and advocacy assistance to employees. The

National Action Committee on the Status of Women, community legal aid clinics, community health centres, environmental lobby groups, and so on, are all groups that could provide you with information and expertise.

MAY YOU REFUSE TO WORK IF YOUR WORKPLACE IS UNSAFE?

If your complaint has not been dealt with satisfactorily or is too urgent to wait for the complaint process, you may wish to refuse to continue to work until the matter is dealt with. Your right to refuse to do work that you believe is unsafe or hazardous may be found in rights arising out of legislation, the common law, or collective agreements. This right will vary depending on what law applies or what kind of work you do.

Generally an employer is not entitled to discipline an employee for refusal to do work if the performance of the job could imperil the health or safety of the worker. However, jurisdictions differ both on what degree of danger there must be to an employee before the employee is entitled to refuse to work, and on what to do if the employee cannot later prove there was any danger. You must be able to prove that you were genuinely and seriously concerned about the problem.

Be aware of the proof problems in your case. For example, some statutes require the presence of "imminent danger" for a worker to refuse to work. However, the risk of exposure to a substance or hazard from which the damage may not show up until years later is not always considered "imminent," even if the exposure itself is immediate.

This raises particular problems for women, because the majority of women work in situations in which occupational health hazards may result in illness, disease, or physical disability that has gestated over a long period of time.

Not all jurisdictions will spell out the precise steps to follow in the process to refuse work, but most do. In any event, the procedure is basically the same everywhere, whether the law prescribes the steps or not.

The procedure involved is as follows:

1. You report the situation to your supervisor.
2. The employer or health-and-safety committee then investigates.
3. If there is insufficient resolution, you may report the matter to an inspector at the Ministry of Labour.
4. The inspector either orders improvement or requires you to return to work.

One of the problems with the present "right-to-refuse" laws is that the worker must rely on the opinion of a government inspector as to whether the work is safe.

Even if your statutory right to refuse work is uncertain, you may have a right if you are covered by a collective agreement.

Apart from legislation and collective agreements, the common-law principles governing employer-employee relationships may offer some small protection to you. There is not much practical help, though, when you can only seek redress by suing for wrongful dismissal.

MAY YOUR EMPLOYER BE PROSECUTED FOR FAILING TO PROVIDE A SAFE WORKPLACE?

In recent years there has been an increase in the use of the criminal law to pursue employers who have taken unnecessarily high risks either with their workers' health or with the health of society at large (through environmental pollution, for example). Society seems to be taking a tentative step towards recognizing that employers will only move to eliminate unsafe conditions when they realize that the government will use its criminal sanctions to enforce the law.

What May Your Employer Be Prosecuted For?
It is usually a criminal offence for an employer to violate any of the provisions of health-and-safety legislation (such as failing to set up a health-and-safety committee where required). In these circumstances, you may commence a prosecution whereby your employer is brought before a judge to be tried. If found guilty, the employer may be fined or even jailed.

In Ontario an employer who violates the *Occupational Health and Safety Act* or refuses to follow an inspector's order may be fined up to $25,000 and imprisoned for up to twelve months, or both.

In addition to violating health-and-safety legislation, your employer may also have committed an offence under the federal *Criminal Code*, which covers all jurisdictions throughout Canada. Employers commit criminal negligence when they do something or fail to do something that it is their duty to do and thereby show wanton or reckless disregard for the lives or safety of their employees.

Some commentators have looked at ways in which the criminal sanctions against negligence, assault, conspiracy, and murder could be used to prosecute violations of health-and-safety laws.

One of the problems with pursuing prosecution as a remedy is that normally the court does not have any power to order the employer to reinstate a worker or to compensate the worker for damages that have been suffered. In addition, the acquittal rate on prosecutions is fairly high. In criminal prosecutions, the Crown must prove that the employer intended to cause the harm, and judges have been reluctant to find this intention.

However, recently the prosecution tool has been used by health-and-safety advocates with greater success, and judges are now becoming more familiar with the serious health risks facing employees in the workplace.

What Do You Do if Your Employer Retaliates When You Complain?

Unfortunately most employers are not grateful when an employee points out that the employer may be acting in an unsafe manner. Many employers resent any interference in the operation of their business and also fear the cost of remedying the problem. However, generally an employer is not entitled to penalize an employee for seeking to remedy a health-and-safety concern. Many provinces' legislation on health and safety specifically prohibits any reprisals. Even if you are in a province without such legislation, if you were dismissed, you would have good grounds to sue for wrongful dismissal at common law if the reason for the dismissal was such retaliation. However, a suit for wrongful dismissal will provide you only with compensation for a period of reasonable notice and will not reinstate you in your job. Nor can the common law easily be used to correct a retaliatory appraisal or reinstate a promotion that was unfairly denied to you.

If you are unionized, most collective agreements provide that you can't be discharged or disciplined without just cause, and any employer reprisals would be considered unjust. Collective agreements also usually provide a mechanism for challenging a bad appraisal or unfair denial of a promotion.

It is, however, often difficult for employees to prove that the employer action was in fact a reprisal for the health-and-safety initiative. For example, if you express a concern about health and safety and later receive a bad appraisal, the employer will likely argue that your prior poor work performance justified the appraisal. However, if you can show that other employees who did not complain also had poor work performances but did not get a poor appraisal or were not disciplined, an adjudicator would likely decide that the real reason was your complaint about health and safety.

COMPENSATION FOR INJURY

What can you do to get compensated if your health has been adversely affected by workplace conditions?

Workers' Compensation

Workers' compensation is a system of social insurance. Coverage is usually compulsory, and assessments are levied on employers and compiled into a common fund out of which benefits are paid to workers disabled as a result of their employment. Administration and adjudication are carried out by a statutory corporation known in most jurisdictions as the Workers' Compensation Board.

Workers' compensation acts are provincial legislation. Federal government employees are covered by a federal statute, but the administration is carried out by provincial boards.

Workers are compensated for work-related loss of earning capacity without regard to the fault of the worker or employer. As a trade-off, workers and their dependants who are covered by compensation laws lose the right to sue their employer.

Between 70 percent and 95 percent of workers in Canada are covered by this statutory scheme. However, there are some occupational categories that are not covered under Canadian statutes—housewives, home workers, piece workers, casual workers, and self-employed persons, among others. Women are usually in the majority in these categories: low-paid, immigrant, non-union, non-English speaking. You should check with your employer, your union, or the Workers' Compensation Board to see whether you are covered. If you are not covered, you may want to approach your employer to make an application for coverage. If you are unionized, you could ask your union to make the request. You may also write directly to the Workers' Compensation Board to request coverage for your particular employment, or for your occupational category as a whole. Some jurisdictions allow optional coverage for certain categories.

The workers' compensation acts prescribe some of the basic principles, but generally the legislation gives the provincial boards broad powers to make regulations. The same discretion usually applies to appeal procedures. Check your provincial board to find out what type of appeal is available.

Most of the effective law comes from rules, orders, directives, and decisions of the boards themselves. There are some court decisions on workers'-compensation matters from an appeal or a review of a Workers' Compensation Board decision. However, even where these exist, boards are not bound to follow court decisions.

When Are You Eligible for Compensation?

Usually to be eligible for compensation benefits you must:
a)   have coverage under the act;
b)   suffer from a disability or loss that is compensable under the act;
c)   have had your disability or loss resulting from, and in the course of, your employment.

The criteria for determining eligibility from compensation will often depend on whether you are making a claim for an injury resulting from an ''accident'' or for a disability resulting from an occupational and industrial ''disease.''

In most jurisdictions, the rules relating to injury from an accident are different from those relating to injury from a disease. There may not be any exclusive definitions in the particular statute or board procedure in your province or territory, but it is generally necessary to clarify whether a disability results from accidental injury or from disease.

Injury: Accident

You must first establish that there was an accident. Usually the term "accident" is defined in the statute; the injury must have been caused "by reason of" the accident; and have arisen "out of and in the course of employment." The most common disabilities classified as accidental injuries would be physiological changes induced by trauma (e.g., wounds, fractures, burns, strains). One of the most common types of accidental injury suffered by workers is low-back strain and injury. However, only recently have some of women workers' most common complaints been seen as compensable injuries. In Ontario, a woman clerical worker was awarded benefits for pain and numbness in her hands as a result of an increased workload at a VDT. She required drug therapy and three operations to correct her symptoms of back and neck pain and her hand/wrist injuries.

Injury: Disease

For a medical condition to be recognized as a (compensable) industrial or occupational "disease," the condition must be recognized by the Workers' Compensation Board. Some jurisdictions include "disease" in the definition of "injury" or "accident." Often a particular disease may result from trauma resulting from an accident.

The burden of proving that a disease resulted from an employee's employment is always on the worker.

Because many diseases result from exposure over many years to a toxic substance, it is often difficult to establish the connection between a worker's exposure and a disease. This difficulty has been exacerbated by the general reluctance of workers' compensation boards to recognize such factors. Boards have developed "schedules of industrial diseases" that are a partial attempt to link a specific disease with particular types of employment. These are usually industrial, and pertain to such diseases as silicosis, asbestosis, and tuberculosis.

If a disease is not mentioned in the schedule as being work-related, then the board may have to decide the case on an individual basis.

This has important repercussions for women workers. Women are exposed to a myriad of chemically and biologically hazardous substances in their work, and there is very little information available on the long-term health effects. Ozone from copying machines, solvents such as toluene in glues, cleaners, and disinfectants, cathode rays from VDTs, chemicals commonly found where beauticians work: all have been overlooked as causes of serious disabling diseases.

What Benefits Are Available?

Compensation benefits or monetary payments differ in each jurisdiction according to set schedules, but they have one thing in common: they are all woefully inadequate. They also don't compensate for pain and suffering.

You are initially entitled to any short-term wage losses. The rate of benefit allowable is calculated according to a set percentage of earnings depending on the classification (anywhere between 70 and 90 percent). Classifications in most jurisdictions distinguish between "temporary total disability," "temporary partial disability," "permanent total disability," and "permanent partial disability." Special rules may modify what appear on the surface to be straightforward benefits. For example, pension benefits for permanent disabilities are generally awarded according to the "meat-chart" system. A worker gets a percentage of income loss based on what part of her body has been disabled. Not only does this result in totally inadequate monetary amounts, but it does not take into account the different occupational categories that are predominantly staffed by women.

In addition to short-term wage losses, an injured worker is entitled to receive, free of charge, any medical aid that is necessary as a result of a work-related injury. Medical aid usually means doctors, treatment, drugs, and hospital charges. However, it also covers anything considered by the board to be necessary, such as prosthetic devices, wheelchairs, special clothing, and so on.

Physical and vocational rehabilitation may be possible in jurisdictions where boards have appropriate facilities and resources.

How Do You Make a Claim?

It is of the utmost importance when making a claim to the Workers' Compensation Board to be able to substantiate your claim. You must inform the proper people (employer, doctor, co-worker) of your accident, including all disabilities, known or suspected diseases, and known or suspected dangerous conditions. A simple accident claim, when properly reported, should enable the worker to obtain compensation without undue difficulty. However, board procedures are often complicated, bureaucratic, and liable to involve delay and enormous frustration. Most boards have various appeal levels. Clear records should be kept, documenting the progress of symptoms, as well as all the actions you have undertaken. You will have a better chance of achieving results if your claim can be substantiated early on. Appeal procedures are time-consuming and generally require a legal representative.

Where Do You Get Help?

Very few lawyers have expertise in workers' compensation. The best resource for help would be your local legal-aid clinic, especially student-staffed legal-aid clinics at law schools. Some communities have specialty clinics that deal only with workers' compensation. Trade-union representatives often know their way around the system. Where your Ministry of Labour maintains workers' advisory staff, they can explain the system to you. Members of provincial legislatures often have staff who are trained in dealing with workers'-compensation procedures.

Finally, always remember to seek outside help from one of these resources. Do not rely solely on your employer's submission of your claim, or on the Workers' Compensation Board.

What if You Are Fired Because You Are Disabled?

Generally, human rights legislation prohibits employers from discriminating against workers who are suffering from disabilities. If your workplace has made you disabled in some way, your employer has a duty to make reasonable accommodation for you. At common law, your employer cannot dismiss you for being ill unless there is no likelihood that you will be able to return to work within a reasonable period of time.

WHAT IF YOU ARE NOT COVERED BY WORKERS' COMPENSATION?

The only workers who have the right to sue their employer in civil courts are those who are not covered by workers'-compensation schemes. Quebec is the only exception: there you may sue your employer if an injury was caused by an act that was a violation of the law. The costs of civil litigation are high, and the risk is substantial. But in some instances monetary awards have been made by the courts where employers have breached their implied contractual obligations to provide a safe workplace.

An argument could also be made that the normal prohibitions against suing an employer covered by workers' compensation are not applicable where the employer has been criminally negligent.

In some cases, you may be entitled to some minimal compensation from the Criminal Injuries Compensation Board. The most frequent claimants are police officers, prison guards, taxi drivers, and barroom staff who have been assaulted. This route may be expensive for the claimant, but you stand a better chance of succeeding if you have also had criminal-negligence charges laid.

Even if you otherwise cannot sue your employer, it may be possible to sue the manufacturer of the product that injured you. This tactic is used much more in the United States, where suits against suppliers for injury and disease caused by defective safety equipment and untested and unsafe chemicals have been brought. You should consult a lawyer experienced in this area of the law as soon as possible after your injury occurred or your disease was diagnosed.

WHAT IF YOU ARE EXCLUDED FROM A JOB BECAUSE OF REPRODUCTIVE HAZARDS?

Many employers who fear that women and their foetuses may be endangered by a workplace hazard decide to handle the situation by refusing to allow women of child-bearing years to do certain jobs unless they are sterilized. Instead of ensuring that the workplace does not endanger the reproductive capacity of *all* workers, these employers try to eliminate women from the workplace. Policy discussions of this issue are confused by attitudes about women's "proper role." Some protective legislation historically contributes to the exclusion of women from a significant part of the labour market, justifying relegating women to occupationally segregated, poorly paid, *and* often more or equally hazardous work.

The law is not clear on whether employers can be prevented from taking this position. Many argue that such selective employment policies are discriminatory because women, but not men, are forced to choose between having a job and having children. Some women who badly need their jobs have been forced to undergo sterilization in order to keep them.

Against this problem of discrimination must be weighed the responsibility to protect the foetus and the necessity of ensuring a safe workplace for all.

Some commentators have argued that the employer's action will be discriminatory unless the employer can prove that the exclusion of women only from these workplace opportunities is the only reasonable solution to the problem. For example, women employed by the Atomic Energy Control Board complained to the federal Human Rights Commission about their employer's policy of excluding women as nuclear operators. The complaint was finally resolved when the employer changed its mind and decided that the dose limit of radiation for men and women should be the same, subject to a lower dose limit for pregnant women. Furthermore, in the interests of the employees' right to privacy, the employer agreed that the women would be responsible for ensuring that their exposure remained within the limit, and the employer would be responsible for advising the female workers of the proper limit. This was a compromise between the individual right of women to decide such issues and the employer's purported interest in protecting the foetus.

The *Charter of Rights and Freedoms*, as well as human rights laws, may also be used to challenge such exclusionary policies where they exist.

It was pointed out earlier, in the section entitled "Reproductive Hazards," that protective leave or reassignment should be a right for all women workers. The issue must be seen as not simply the "protection of unborn children," but the protection of all workers from reproductive and other health hazards. Employers refuse to recognize that the male reproductive capacity is also at risk under most of the same conditions. Generally, male workers work unhindered *and* unprotected. Exposures that would be harmful to a foetus often harm adult men and women as well. Employers must make the workplace safe, not just exclude women from certain jobs.

We must ensure that all women have access to sufficient information and reasonable alternatives in employment to permit them to make their own individual decisions about where and when they will work while pregnant.

OTHER STRATEGIES

There are tactics, other than purely legal ones, with which to exert pressure on your employer to make your workplace safe. Lobby your legislature and Parliament; organize public-education forums; set up health-and-safety programs in your workplace. Make strategic use of the media. Community health-and-safety centres, legal-aid clinics, environmental groups, women's organizations, public hearings, and unions of injured workers may be able to provide resources and assistance.

The collective strategy, however, is probably the most effective. Even if you, or you and your legal representative, have been able to remedy your situation through available legal channels, generally workers are more likely to have safe working conditions if the workplace is unionized. Women share with all workers a desire for better and healthier working conditions, and the best guarantee of achieving that goal is a strong collective agreement.

CHAPTER 14

ORGANIZING YOUR BUSINESS
Joan Garson

*Joan Garson is a partner in the Toronto law firm of Bla-
ney, McMurtry, Stapells, Aarons & Watson where she
practises in the area of corporate and commercial law.
She is a graduate of Dalhousie University in Halifax and
the University of Toronto Law School.*

BEFORE YOU MAKE the exciting decision to start your own business,
you will have spent many hours planning. You will have developed
an idea that you hope will be profitable. You will have undertaken
formal or informal market studies and will likely have made com-
parisons of your plans with the activities of other, similar businesses.
You will certainly have held heart-to-heart talks with your accountant and bank manager. This is also the time to think about how to
structure your business to give expression to your idea most effectively.

WHY WORRY ABOUT STRUCTURE?

The selection of a business structure may seem to be a dry detail.
However, you may be surprised by the consequences, both direct
and indirect, of a decision about the appropriate structure for your
business.

An appropriate form of organization will help you to maximize
your return and reduce costs. If you think you will want to attract
new investors or partners, you may need to know that some business
structures lend themselves more easily than others to the introduction
of such new participants. Banks and other lenders may be prepared
to lend to some types of businesses and not to others. The ability
of your business to grow will be affected by its structure.

From your point of view, the business structure will have a major impact on your ability to undertake tax planning. Both your status as a spouse, former spouse, or parent and the status of your partners or co-owners may dictate structure or require additional planning, as discussed in Chapter 5, "Financial Planning." Particular structures may also reduce the personal financial risks you may run as an entrepreneur.

Clearly, while the manner in which you organize your business is just a tool to give expression to your idea, it is a key tool. Unfortunately, as a new entrepreneur you may lack the knowledge to choose from the available range of alternatives the structure best suited to your needs. The aim of this chapter is to introduce you to the options open to you, so that you may then explore on your own those that may warrant further examination. The discussion will also assist you in evaluating the advice given to you by the experts you will be consulting. Since in many cases an expert will be skilled in only some aspects of establishing a business, it is important that you keep in mind the broad range of issues that will affect your decision.

You should be aware that certain kinds of businesses may require a particular business structure. For example, doctors are not entitled to incorporate in some provinces, while engineers may do so. This chapter will not address these particular kinds of constraints. You should in every case attempt to contact a trade association or licensing board in the business you propose to engage in to determine the nature of any such restrictions. As well, trade associations often provide useful free sources of expertise, advice, and support from people more experienced in the field.

KINDS OF BUSINESS STRUCTURES

There are three principle ways in which to structure a business: sole proprietorship, partnership, and corporation. Additional options such as joint ventures or limited partnerships are useful in particular situations but generally are appropriate for more sophisticated requirements than you will encounter when starting up.

Each province has its own laws governing sole proprietorships, partnerships, and corporations, and the federal government has laws for corporations. Accordingly, the information contained in this chapter is very general; you should obtain advice about the laws of your particular province from your provincial department of corporate affairs before starting up your business.

Each of the three main structures has advantages and disadvantages. These are briefly summarized below.

Sole Proprietorship

Sole proprietorship is the form of business carried on by an individual directly. It has the advantage of direct control by its owner. A sole proprietorship is inexpensive to establish and maintain, and is subject to few formal requirements. The freedom from regulation that sole proprietorships enjoy means they are very flexible.

Balanced against these advantages are various disadvantages. The most significant is that you as owner will have unlimited personal liability for all losses of the business. Any amount the business loses or earns is the personal loss or gain of the proprietor. This includes not only earnings or losses in the ordinary course of the conduct of the business, but also losses arising from extraordinary events, such as lawsuits, to the extent that the business does not carry insurance against the particular risk. If you enter into a lease and then decide to cease carrying on business, you will be personally responsible for the remainder of the lease. All personal and business assets of the owner are ultimately liable to seizure in fulfilment of these business obligations.

A sole proprietorship is simply the business carried on by the entrepreneur. As a result, except by way of a loan to the owner personally, no one can invest in a sole proprietorship. This means that a sole proprietorship offers no possibility of long-term tax or estate planning, although the establishment of a business will have tax consequences for its owner.

There is a total absence of any continuity in a sole proprietorship. If you die or cease to carry on business, the business will end with you. Of course, the assets used in carrying on the business, including the name and the goodwill, may be sold.

Partnership

A partnership is a business carried on by two or more people together. Partnerships are easy to start up. Like a sole proprietorship, the business is carried on directly by its owners. Simply by carrying on business together with a view to profit, you and your partners will have created a partnership, and will be subject to its advantages and disadvantages.

Because new partners may be added to a partnership at will, this type of structure provides more flexibility and continuity than a sole proprietorship. A partnership is inexpensive to start up and to maintain. The partnership structure and the relationship between partners are constrained by few formal and/or legislative requirements. Risk is generally shared equally among all partners as between themselves, although a person with whom the partnership does business is usually entitled to recover all amounts owing by the partnership from a single partner.

There are several disadvantages attached to a partnership. So-called passive investment in a partnership is somewhat complex to structure. As noted above, partners, as well as all of their business and non-business assets, are at risk for losses of the partnership. Since by definition partnership entails the right of one partner to bind another, partners must trust each other absolutely. Occasionally, partners may encounter difficulty in separating their business from their personal liabilities, with disastrous consequences for the other partners who become liable for unexpected losses. The tax- and estate-planning options provided by a partnership are limited. Continuity is provided only by the partners' lives: the partnership has no existence independent of its partners.

Finally, the equal right of each partner to participate in partnership decisions may make decision making difficult. An agreement prior to start-up among the partners about such major matters as are likely to arise during the course of the business may help to avoid some problems. The relationship of partners is very close; it is often likened to a marriage—and it lacks some of the obvious advantages of that arrangement!

Corporation

A corporation is a form of business organization created by the laws of a province or the federal government. It exists only to the extent permitted by law and is completely governed by appropriate legislation. When you are a sole proprietor, you directly own the assets of the business. In contrast, when a business is conducted by a corporation, its owners own only an interest—a "share" in the corporation; the corporation owns the assets of the business. So long as you understand the framework within which a corporation operates, it has several advantages.

Since the corporation exists as an entity separate from the individuals who own it at a particular time, the liability of each of its owners or "shareholders" is limited to the amount the shareholder has invested: there will generally be no personal liability as owner beyond that amount. The maximum amount that you as a shareholder can lose is the amount that you have invested. If a corporation fails to pay on its lease, you cannot be sued; only the corporation is responsible.

The corporate structure permits long-term and estate planning, to the advantage of its shareholders. It is ideally suited to structuring passive investment and to adding active investors, that is, persons who will not only provide capital but will also participate in the management of the corporation.

The business community knows and is comfortable with the corporate structure; using a corporation may therefore add credibility to your business.

The existence of a corporation as a separate legal entity provides continuity. The death of a shareholder does not affect the existence of the corporation. Ownership of the shares of the corporation as well as of its assets may be transferred, permitting further flexibility.

First among the disadvantages of the corporate form is the need for expert assistance in establishing and maintaining the corporation. Establishing and maintaining a corporation is relatively costly, both because of the need to pay experts (lawyers, for example) and because governments charge fees for creating a corporation and then for permitting you to amend the documents that establish it. Even a name change costs money.

The tax system in force in Canada currently imposes some penalties on the use of the corporate form of business organization. Governments require more extensive record-keeping for the corporate entity than for a sole proprietorship or partnership.

Keeping in mind the considerations listed above, you should discuss the choice of structure with your financial adviser or lawyer before reaching a decision. The particular kind of business you wish to establish and your own financial and other circumstances will affect the weight that should be given to these factors.

CREATING THE BUSINESS STRUCTURE

The mechanics for establishing and maintaining any of these business forms are set out briefly below.

Sole Proprietorship

If you are carrying on a sole proprietorship under a name other than your own, or have added such words as "and Company" to your name, you are required, in most jurisdictions, to file a name declaration under the appropriate legislation. This is to ensure that persons doing business with the sole proprietorship can determine the individual with whom they are actually dealing. This registration must be updated from time to time.

In Canada, a person is not permitted to confuse the public as to the person with whom it is dealing, or to benefit without payment for the privilege from the goodwill created by another business. Accordingly, before you choose the name under which you will be carrying on business, you should search the telephone book and other sources of information to ensure that no business with a similar name exists, particularly in a field related to your proposed activities. This investigation also benefits you, since you will be spending time and effort to develop goodwill for your name, and you will not want any other business to benefit from your work.

Many provinces have a registry of all business names used in the province. This is an important source of information which you can search for a nominal fee.

As there is no agreement necessary to structure a sole proprietorship (no one is involved as its owner but you) and no government consent or other filing is required except as noted above, no other formalities are needed to "create" a sole proprietorship: it comes into existence when you decide to begin carrying on business.

There are generally no annual requirements to be observed to maintain a proprietorship, except those arising from laws of general application, such as tax laws.

Partnership

A partnership is generally required by legislation to register its name, together with certain information about its partners, so the public can determine with whom it is dealing. A declaration in proper form must be filed at the appropriate government registry office. Any subsequent changes in the membership of the partnership must be filed. This registration generally must also be renewed periodically. Selecting the name of the partnership requires the same type of investigation as that described above for a sole proprietorship.

Even if you and your partners take no steps to enter into a partnership agreement, legislation exists that will give a structure to your partnership. You may well wish to enter into an agreement with your partners both to avoid certain provisions of the legislation and to cover additional matters. The agreement should address such topics as the name of the partnership, the business to be conducted by it, the procedure for adding new partners, the manner in which decisions are to be made, the procedure for buying out a dissenting partner, and the terms for ending the partnership. You should agree upon the person who will keep the financial records of the partnership.

You and your partners will have to decide on the goals for the partnership. Will profits be taken out of the business and divided among the partners or applied to the growth of the business? This is often a contentious area, since the financial requirements of the partners may differ and/or may change over time.

Your lawyer can be of great assistance to you in advising you about what should be included in the partnership agreement, and then in drafting the agreement.

Except as noted above, there are generally no annual filing requirements for maintaining the existence of a partnership, other than those arising from laws of general application, such as tax laws.

Corporation

To understand the requirements for creating and maintaining a corporation, it is helpful to keep in mind that incorporation creates a "person" that, for legal purposes, may be separate from its shareholders, officers, and directors from time to time.

Jurisdiction

Before establishing a corporation, you must select the appropriate jurisdiction in which to incorporate. Each province has legislation to permit the incorporation of a corporation; the federal government also has such legislation. The law is different from jurisdiction to jurisdiction.

You will have to choose between the law of the province in which you are intending to carry on business and federal law to select the better incorporating jurisdiction for your business. If you will be carrying on business in only one province, you may decide to choose provincial jurisdiction, particularly in provinces that do not require annual filings, since a federal incorporation imposes such a requirement. However, many provinces have not significantly revised their corporation statute for many years, whereas the federal law is quite recent and relatively flexible. If you will be carrying on business in more than one province, the federal form offers an advantage, in that it will protect the name of your corporation across the country. Every province has legislation permitting a corporation created elsewhere to carry on business in that province upon compliance with certain formalities.

Name

The selection of a name for a corporation requires not only that you satisfy yourself that the name is not confusingly similar to that of another business or to an existing trademark, but that you meet any standards for names set out in the corporate statute; in some jurisdictions you must also satisfy the government department responsible for incorporations that this standard has been met.

The search for an appropriate name is done in many jurisdictions through a computerized name search. There is a charge for this service. There are other regulations restricting the names that can be used; for example, the selection of a name suggesting the practice of certain professions or a connection with the Crown may be prohibited. You will require expert advice and assistance in choosing the name for your corporation.

A possible alternative may be to incorporate under a number rather than a name, avoiding the formal name-selection process, and then to carry on business under a business name. Appropriate filing of this business name is required in most provinces. You will want to make sure the general principles with respect to a business name outlined above are met by this name.

Incorporation
The documents required for incorporating a corporation are set out by each corporate statute. Incorporation requires filing of the appropriate forms in the appropriate government office, and the payment of a fee. This is generally done by a lawyer.

Constitution
Once the corporation has been incorporated, a "constitution" for the operation of the corporation is then adopted, and in some cases also filed with the government. This document will be in a standard form used by your lawyer, with some individual variations. The constitution, together with the incorporating documents, will set out the basic framework under which the corporation will operate.

Shares
Ownership of the corporation, as noted above, is evidenced by possession of "shares," for which shareholders may pay a nominal or a substantial amount, depending on how much they wish to invest in the corporation. Shareholders elect directors, who oversee the management of the corporation. Directors elect such officers as a president and a secretary, who manage the corporation from day to day. The corporation can only act through its directors and officers. Although the liability of shareholders of a corporation is restricted, the corporate statutes have created a new area of personal liability for directors who do not comply with statutory standards and requirements.

Shareholders' Agreement
It is often wise, when starting a corporation with others, to enter into a shareholders' agreement with all shareholders. This agreement will cover such matters as who will be directors and officers of the corporation, requirements for unanimity among shareholders for the taking of various actions by the corporation, rights to buy out other shareholders in the event of a dispute, and generally all matters that

may arise in the course of the business conducted by the corporation. Tax and family law considerations will be very important in structuring the shareholders' agreement, and all shareholders will require expert advice.

Maintaining the Corporation

The corporation's day-to-day activities then proceed, generally without further special requirements. Major actions are approved at meetings of directors and shareholders, or by having these individuals sign evidence of their approval (called "resolutions"). Applicable corporate statutes, the corporation's own constitution, or a shareholders' agreement may require formalities for particular actions. The advice of a lawyer as to which are the appropriate formalities will be useful, at least initially.

Corporate statutes impose annual requirements for approval of financial statements, election of directors and officers, and other matters. In addition, many jurisdictions require annual filings to be made by the corporation and, in some cases, payment of a fee. Other provinces require merely that the information on file concerning the corporation be kept up to date. Again, your lawyer will advise you.

WHAT ELSE DO YOU NEED?

After you have selected a format for your business, there may still be a number of formal steps required to start business. A few of the areas in which such legal requirements must be met are set out below.

Location

The location of the business will be dictated first of all by the zoning requirements of the particular area in which you choose to locate. You must ensure that the operation of your proposed business is permitted under the zoning by-laws. The choice of location will also be affected by the cost of space and by the taxes imposed on your business, which may vary widely even between neighbouring municipalities. You will either buy or rent space; if you rent, you will require a lease. Once again, expert advice will be important to ensure you get what you want as far as possible. If you wish to undertake any building or renovation, a municipal building permit is likely required.

Licences, Permits, and Special Regulations

Businesses require various kinds of licences and permits. A business licence is usually required by a municipality, and a fee will be payable. In addition, special licence requirements may be imposed by the province or the municipality, depending on the industry. For example, a liquor licence is required in the operation of a business involving the sale of liquor.

Special regulatory provisions will apply to particular business activities. Real-estate agents in Ontario, for example, are governed by the *Real Estate and Business Brokers' Act* of Ontario. The *Travel Industry Act* governs all persons in that business in Ontario. Once again, you should contact the trade association or licensing board in your industry for advice and assistance in this area.

Taxes

Your business will be subject to federal and provincial taxes on income. Sales taxes and other taxes such as customs duties may also apply. You may need to register with various taxing authorities. An accountant with some experience in your industry will be of great assistance to you.

Employees

If you will be hiring employees, you will need to consider a wide range of matters, including labour standards and safety legislation, registration with the appropriate workers'-compensation program, and payroll deductions for income taxes. Many industries are largely unionized, and this involves additional legal concerns. In a corporation, directors may be held personally liable for failure to remit payroll deductions to the federal government.

Insurance

Before you start up your business, you should consider whether insurance for you and the business is appropriate. A very wide range of insurance is available. A reputable insurance broker will assist you in selecting the appropriate kinds and amounts of insurance for your business, bearing in mind the amount you can afford to spend on this aspect of the business. If you are leasing premises, your lease may well impose insurance requirements. You should review these with your broker.

Financing

All of this sounds expensive. That's why you must prepare yourself well for dealing with your bank or other source of financing. It is especially important at this initial stage to be extremely professional with your lenders. They will want to see a business plan that fairly assesses the risks as well as the possible gains in your business. You should consider whether the assistance of a financial adviser might be justified at this time. Lenders will want to see a source for repayment of any loan, as well as security they can sell if necessary to pay themselves back if your forecast turns out to be unduly optimistic. The best advice for dealing with a lender may be to keep him or her fully informed concerning your business at all times. A constant flow of information can soothe many an anxious banker.

Many lenders will require that you, and sometimes also a financially stable other person, guarantee the loan being made to you. A request for a spousal guarantee is not necessarily a sign of discrimination against you as a woman entrepreneur, but may reflect family-law concerns. Giving a guarantee means that you, or any other guarantor, will be personally liable to the lender for the debts of the business, even if you have used a corporation to limit such liability.

You should also explore additional sources for financing. Do not forget the many government plans and programs available. As well, there is a burgeoning venture-capital industry in Canada that will invest in rather than lend money to your business. Bear in mind, however, that the amounts a venture capitalist may want to invest may be too large for your needs, at least initially.

General Requirements

General legislation concerning the manner in which businesses must conduct themselves also exists. These statutes impose duties generally to practise business fairly, including protecting consumers and avoiding misleading advertising. Your lawyer should inform you of which statutes apply to your business.

Trademarks

If a particular word, group of words, or design used in your name or in connection with your business is the key to your advertising and promotion, you might consider attempting to obtain for it the protection of a trademark registration. This requires an application under the federal *Trade Marks Act*. You should consult a lawyer who specializes in this area for expert advice.

Consequences of Failure

The alternative to success will not be far from your mind during the early stages of your business. Apart from your bank or other lender, who will likely hold security in your assets or those of your corporation, most of your creditors will not hold security. Accordingly, if they are not paid, their primary remedies will be either to sue you (or in the case of a corporation, your corporation) for the amount owed, and then to seize and sell assets to recover this debt, or to put you or your corporation into bankruptcy. You should be aware that in the event of a financial disaster, there are statutory provisions governing the rights of you and your creditors. If you are concerned about your ability to repay your debts, you would do well to consult a professional adviser.

An alternative to the difficulties of starting your own business may be the purchase of an existing business. The groundwork for establishing the business will have been laid and the initial risks taken by someone else. The success of the scheme will be apparent. However, you should again ensure that you have adequate professional advice. There are usually extensive legal formalities to be observed in the purchase of a business. A careful financial analysis to determine the manner in which you should acquire the business and the price you eventually pay for it, with professional assistance as required, is an absolute prerequisite to an acquisition.

CHAPTER 15

IMMIGRATION AND EMPLOYMENT

Barbara Jackman

*Barbara Jackman is a lawyer in private practice in To-
ronto. She is on the executive of the Canadian Bar Association's Immigration Section and teaches Ontario Bar
Admission courses on immigration, the Charter, and administrative law. She has participated in giving a number
of seminars for lawyers and is presently co-authoring a
book on immigration law.*

SINCE 1978 CANADA's immigration law has had as one of its principal
objectives the prohibition of discrimination, on grounds of race,
national or ethnic origin, colour, religion, or sex, against anyone
seeking to come into Canada. Women are not directly discriminated
against in the application of the immigration laws, regulations, or
policies. However, by virtue of their economic and social position
within our country and other countries, they are often disadvantaged
in seeking admission to Canada or in seeking the admission of their
close family members. This is because the cornerstone of immigration policy is the potential for successful establishment of persons
seeking to enter Canada, either by their own efforts or through the
efforts of their family members in Canada. Women as a group tend
to lag behind men in acquiring the occupational skills that would
permit them to meet the criteria for selection as independent immigrants to Canada. As well, because they often lack such skills,
those resident here who wish to bring their close family members
into the country may fail to meet the economic standards required
to sponsor their relatives. This is not to say that women cannot and
do not immigrate to Canada. It is only to say that women on average
have more problems in meeting the immigration criteria for inde-

pendent admission and for family reunification. This should be kept in mind when reviewing the following summary of immigration law.

For the purpose of the chapter, it is assumed that the applicant for entry to Canada is a woman.

OVERVIEW

Only Canadian citizens have a constitutional right to enter and remain in Canada. Non-citizens must meet the requirements of Canada's immigration laws. These laws are designed to protect our country from unwanted aliens and to assist in our economic, social, and cultural development. Within this framework, the law provides for a procedure whereby individuals may be allowed into Canada as visitors or immigrants. There are three main classes of persons permitted to enter Canada on a temporary basis: (i) tourists, (ii) students, and (iii) temporary workers. There are three main classes of persons permitted to come into or to remain in Canada as immigrants: (i) close family members, (ii) refugees, and (iii) independent persons with needed occupational skills or the business expertise and capital to set up business in Canada. As well, the law provides for the exclusion or removal of such prohibited classes of persons as criminals or terrorists or those found to be medically inadmissible. Prohibitions may be overcome where there exist strong humanitarian or public-policy reasons for making exception to the normal rules.

The rules regarding admission and removal of non-Canadian citizens are set out in the *Immigration Act*, and regulations passed by the federal cabinet pursuant to this act. In addition, the Immigration Commission publishes a policy manual with instructions on how immigration officers are to implement the laws and regulations. Although certain parts of this manual are not public, those volumes that are can be found at local Canada Immigration centres.

ADMISSION TO CANADA

All persons who are not Canadian citizens or permanent residents must apply for a visa at a visa office in a Canadian embassy or consulate before coming to Canada, unless there is a regulation exempting that person or class of persons from this requirement or a policy that permits a person or class of persons to obtain an exemption from the visa requirement while in Canada. Persons seeking to immigrate as permanent residents normally must obtain a visa beforehand. Temporary visitors are more often exempt from the visa requirement.

Visitors

Students, workers, or tourists coming to Canada for a temporary purpose fall within a class of persons defined as "visitors" in the *Immigration Act*. A visitor is a person lawfully in Canada or seeking to come into Canada for a temporary purpose, who is not a Canadian citizen, a permanent resident, an immigrant entering Canada temporarily for an examination, or a holder of a "Minister's Permit."

When a person applies at a Canadian visa office for a visa, or arrives at the Canadian border, she must satisfy the immigration officer that her stay in Canada is intended to be temporary. It cannot be a visit of indefinite duration; the person must ask for a specific period of time to stay in Canada. Once she is in Canada, the visa may be extended. For example, if a woman is coming to visit her children living in Canada, she may ask to stay for three months. If she decides to stay longer, she may go into an immigration centre before the three months expires, and ask for an extension of the visa for another three months. The length of time a person may stay temporarily in Canada varies. For example, a student may extend her student's authorization from year to year for six or seven years, while a tourist may stay a day, a month, or a year, depending on why she is visiting in Canada. Any person seeking to stay in Canada longer than three months needs written permission from an immigration officer and normally is required to have a medical examination approved by Canada Immigration Medical Services. Visitors must also satisfy an immigration officer that they have the means to support themselves while visiting in Canada or that a relative or friend in Canada has the means and is willing to support them while they are visiting.

Students

Persons coming to study in Canada must normally obtain authorization from a visa office outside of Canada before entering the country. Students are visitors and, as such, must satisfy an immigration officer that they will leave Canada once the course of study is completed. As most students will stay in Canada longer than three months, medical approval is required.

Students must show evidence of admission to a university, college, or other institution for a course of at least six-months' duration and at least twenty-four hours of instruction per week, or must show evidence of admission at a federally or provincially licensed institution for a skills or language-upgrading program. Students must also prove that they have sufficient resources to pay for their tuition, to support themselves while studying, either by their own means or through relatives or friends able and willing to help, and to pay for their departure from Canada when their course is completed. Once a student has entered Canada on a student authorization, this may be extended from within Canada. Students must stay at the institution and in the course of study set out in the student authorization. If they wish to change schools or their course of study they must apply for this at an immigration office in Canada before making the change.

Certain classes of persons do not need to apply for the student authorization at a Canadian visa office before coming to Canada. For example, spouses or children of diplomats, armed forces personnel, clergy, or foreign news company personnel stationed in Canada may obtain the student authorization while in Canada. If one adult in a family is in Canada on a student or work authorization, the spouse or children may also obtain a student authorization while in Canada. As well, persons in Canada for some other reason may obtain from within Canada a student authorization for part-time studies, where the course is incidental or secondary to the person's main purpose for being in Canada. For example, a teenager coming to visit relatives for the summer may enrol in a course in English as a second language and obtain a student authorization while in Canada. Similarly, a person working temporarily in Canada may take part-time courses.

Temporary Workers

Persons coming to work temporarily in Canada must normally obtain authorization from a visa office outside Canada before coming. Workers who will stay in Canada longer than three months, or who are employed in an occupation where the protection of public health is essential, require medical approval.

Usually, a worker cannot obtain an employment authorization unless the person's prospective employer has obtained approval from the Canada Employment Commission. This approval will not be given unless the employer can satisfy the employment counsellor that there are no Canadians or permanent residents available to take the job offered. The employer is usually required to post the job with a Canada Employment centre and to advertise it in newspapers and professional or trade magazines in order to see if there are Canadians or permanent residents available to take the job. If the job is approved, notice of this will be sent to the Canadian visa office where the worker intends to apply for the employment authorization.

There are certain classes of persons who may obtain an employment authorization without having had the job approved by the Canada Employment Commission. These include, for example, a person working for a charitable or religious organization without pay; a person whose employment will create or maintain significant employment benefits or opportunities for Canadians or permanent residents; and other special categories, as permitted by the regulations.

There are also classes of persons who are not required to obtain the employment authorization outside of Canada. This includes the spouse and children of diplomats, armed forces personnel, clergy, foreign news company personnel, and others.

Finally, there are classes of persons who may work without an employment authorization in the job for which they have come to Canada. These include diplomats, members of the armed forces of other countries, foreign news company personnel, clergy, and others as specified in the regulations.

Permanent Residents

Most persons wishing to live permanently in Canada, as noted above, are required to apply for and obtain an immigrant visa before coming to Canada. Exceptions to this are dealt with below. An immigrant visa will be given to a person if the person satisfies the requirements of the *Immigration Act* and regulations. There are selection criteria in the regulations, which set out different categories of persons who may qualify for admission to Canada as an immigrant. In addition to fitting within one of the immigrant categories, all immigrants must be admissible on criminal, medical, and security grounds. A prospective immigrant is required to undergo a medical examination to ensure that she is not afflicted with a disease, disability, or disorder that would endanger the public health or safety in Canada or impose an excessive demand on our health or social services. As well, an immigrant must provide a police clearance certificate in order to verify that she has had no serious criminal conviction. At the present time the Department of External Affairs arranges for a security check to be done on all prospective immigrants to ensure that they are not members of organized crime and are not terrorists or subversives.

Family Class

Canadian citizens or permanent residents may sponsor for admission to Canada as immigrants relatives who fall within the "family class." The family class includes a spouse; a son or daughter under twenty-one when the application for permanent residence is filed and the undertaking is signed and under twenty-three when the visa is issued or refused; a fiancé(e); a parent or grandparent of any age if the sponsoring relative is a Canadian citizen; a parent or grandparent over sixty years of age, widowed, or incapable of gainful employment, if the sponsoring relative is a permanent resident; an orphan relative under eighteen years of age; and a child under thirteen years of age whom the sponsor intends to adopt who is orphaned, abandoned, or placed with a child-welfare agency, where there is only one living parent, the parents are separated, or the child is born out of wedlock. If the sponsoring relative has no relatives who fall within the family class who are in Canada or who may be sponsored, that person may sponsor any relative regardless of age or relationship.

The sponsoring relative may include any dependants of the member of the family class in the application. This means, for example, that parents being sponsored may have their children under twenty-one included in the application to immigrate to Canada.

A sponsorship application is begun by having the resident relative attend at a local Canada Immigration centre to sign an undertaking of assistance, which is a promise to support the immigrating relatives for a specified period of time, if they need support. The sponsoring relatives must have a certain income in order to have the sponsorship approved. The income level is based on the number of people being sponsored and the number of family dependants in Canada for whom the sponsors are responsible. The income guidelines used are the Low-Income Cut-Off Guidelines published by Statistics Canada from time to time. These are available at any Canada Immigration centre. A spouse sponsoring a spouse where there are no children included in the application, or a parent sponsoring children alone, does not need to meet the income criteria to sponsor.

The relatives seeking to immigrate to Canada must apply for permanent residence at a Canadian visa office located in a Canadian embassy or consulate outside Canada.

Assisted Relatives and Independent Applicants

Brothers and sisters who are over twenty-one years of age or married, aunts and uncles, nieces and nephews, and parents of permanent residents under sixty years of age, who are not widowed or incapable of gainful employment, all fall within the ''assisted relative'' category. Assisted relatives are in the same position as independent applicants except for the fact that assisted relatives gain a ten-point bonus on a point assessment if there are relatives in Canada who sign an undertaking of assistance on their behalf.

Independent and assisted-relative applicants must make application at a Canadian visa office abroad. Such applicants are given a prescreening application form to complete. If it appears from this form that the applicant might pass the point assessment, an application for permanent residence is sent out and an interview with a visa officer is arranged. The visa officer assesses the applicant in the interview on the basis of specific categories for which points are given as shown in the chart below:

The Point System

1. *Education.* One (1) point for each year of education to a maximum of 12 points.
2. *Specific Vocational Preparation.* Up to 15 points for the occupation of the applicant. The points in this category

are fixed for each occupation and are based on the *Dictionary of Job Classifications*.

3. *Experience*. Up to 8 points for experience. This category is tied to the Specific Vocational Preparation category and so is determined by the applicant's occupation.

4. *Occupational Demand*. Up to 10 points for occupational demand. The points are fixed on the basis of the demand for the applicant's occupation in Canada. The Immigration Commission publishes a list of occupations for which there is a demand in Canada. This list is available at any Canada Immigration centre. It designates the number of points given for the listed occupations. In order to be approved for landing, an applicant must have at least 1 point in this category or else have arranged employment, even if the person otherwise has more than the 70 required points.

5. *Arranged Employment*. Ten (10) points if the person has an offer of employment approved by an employment counsellor at a Canada Employment centre and the person has the necessary qualifications to accept the job being offered. The employer must approach the Canada Employment centre with the job being offered. Before the job will be approved as arranged employment, the employer must satisfy the employment counsellor that there are no Canadians or permanent residents available to take the job. Once the job is approved, the approval is forwarded to the Canadian visa office closest to where the applicant lives or is staying. The applicant must then satisfy the visa officer that she has the qualifications to take the job being offered. Even if the officer is satisfied as to this, the applicant must still obtain at least 70 points on the assessment.

6. *Age*. Ten (10) points to an applicant who is between the ages of eighteen and forty-five. Two (2) points are subtracted for each year of age over forty-five.

7. *Knowledge of English or French*. Up to 15 points for the ability to read, write, and speak English or French.

8. *Personal Suitability*. Up to 10 points on a personal assessment of the applicant, by the visa officer, in the interview. Points are awarded to reflect the personal suitability

of the person and her dependants to become successfully established in Canada, based on the person's adaptability, motivation, initiative, resourcefulness, and other similar qualities.

9. *Selection Control.* Up to 10 points. This category is meant to regulate the number of immigrants coming into Canada. If there is a need for more immigrants, the level will be raised to 10 in order that more people may obtain the 70 required points. If there are already enough immigrants accepted for landing in Canada, the level control will be lowered to zero.

10. *Relatives.* As noted above, 10 points are given for relatives in Canada who sign an undertaking of assistance for the immigrant. As with sponsoring relatives, the relatives in Canada must have a sufficient income to undertake to assist the immigrating applicant and her dependants when the number of dependants in Canada the assisting relative must also support is taken into consideration. The Low-Income Cut-Off Guidelines published by Statistics Canada are used to determine the income needed. These guidelines are available at any Canada Immigration centre.

The person seeking to immigrate to Canada must make the application at a visa office first. The applicant will be advised by letter after the application for permanent residence has been assessed if her application has been refused. If she has a relative in Canada who will sign an undertaking of assistance, this relative should approach a local Canada Immigration centre to sign the undertaking. The relative in Canada will not normally be allowed to sign the undertaking without this letter. Once it is signed it is forwarded to the Canadian visa office, and the applicant will be interviewed to see if she then makes the 70 points in order to be approved for immigration to Canada.

Business Applicants

Persons who have enough money and business experience may apply to immigrate to Canada in order to establish a business or to invest in an approved investment project in Canada. There are two categories under which applicants may apply to establish a business: as *self-employed* and *entrepreneur* applicants. Since January 1986, the federal government has also established an *investor* category. If the applicant has no prior business experience, it would be difficult to be accepted in any of these categories.

A *self-employed* applicant is a person who intends and has the ability to establish or purchase a business in Canada that will create an employment opportunity for herself and will make a significant contribution to the economy or the cultural or artistic life of Canada. There is no fixed amount of money the person must invest. It depends more on the acceptability of the business.

The applicant is required to put forward a proposal setting out the specific business she intends to establish. This should be submitted to a Canadian visa office, and the applicant will be sent an application for permanent residence to complete and submit. The visa officer considering the application will normally seek an opinion of the business proposal from the provincial officials responsible for industrial and commercial development in the particular province where the applicant intends to reside. This is a very important factor in determining if the application will be approved. A self-employed applicant must still make 70 points on a point assessment, taking into consideration all of the factors used for independent applicants, except for the arranged-employment factor. Thirty points may be awarded to a self-employed applicant, in addition to the normal points given, if the visa officer feels that the applicant will become successfully established in her business or occupation in Canada.

An *entrepreneur* is a person who intends and has the ability to provide active and ongoing participation in the management of a business or commercial venture that she intends to establish, purchase, or make a substantial investment into in Canada. The business must make a significant contribution to the economy and must create a job for the entrepreneur and for one or more Canadian citizens or permanent residents. There is no fixed amount of money needed to be accepted as an entrepreneur, although larger investments are more likely to be approved.

An entrepreneur may be accepted for landing in Canada without having to provide a business proposal in support of her application for permanent residence in Canada. The visa officer may assess the entrepreneur on the basis of her past business experience and, if it is satisfactory, may issue an immigrant visa on condition that the entrepreneur establish, purchase, or invest in the business and actively participate in its management within a two-year period after landing in Canada. An entrepreneur may also provide a proposal to establish a specific business in Canada. As with the self-employed applicant, this proposal is normally referred to the appropriate provincial industry and commercial development ministry for an opinion on the viability of the business. This opinion is a very important factor considered by the visa officer. An entrepreneur need obtain only 25 points on a point assessment, taking into consideration all of the factors used to assess independent applicants, except for the occupational-demand and arranged-employment factors.

The *investor* category, as noted above, is a new category. The investor must have operated, owned, or directed a financially successful business and must have accumulated a net worth of $500,000 by her own endeavours. An investor need only obtain 25 points on assessment, considering all of the independent-applicant factors, except for the occupational-demand and arranged-employment factors. However, the investor must have invested at least $250,000 in a specific business or commercial venture or in a privately administered investment syndicate acceptable to the appropriate province, or in a government-administered venture capital fund. The investment must be irrevocable for a three-year period. It is best to check with the local Canada Immigration centre or the appropriate provincial department of industry and trade, since the kinds of projects in which investors may put their money are subject to approval by federal and provincial officials.

Retired Applicants

A person over fifty-five years of age may apply to retire in Canada. This means that the applicant does not intend to work in Canada. The retired person must make application at a Canadian visa office. An applicant in this category is not considered under the point system. Rather, the visa officer considers where the person intends to live in Canada, the presence of relatives or friends living in the locality, the potential for the person to adjust to life in Canada, her motivation, and whether she has sufficient resources to support herself and any accompanying dependants without receiving any social benefits in Canada. Financial assistance of relatives in Canada may be considered in determining if the applicant has sufficient resources to support herself.

Family Business Applications

Where a family member in Canada owns or operates a family business, she may apply to have a relative immigrate to Canada to take up a position of trust in the family business. The relative in Canada must attend at a Canada Immigration centre for an interview with documents (including year-end financial statements) to show that the business does exist, that it has been in operation for at least a year, or, if not, that it is in the process of expanding and is financially viable. She must also provide an offer of employment to the relative abroad. The immigration officer must be satisfied that the offer of employment to the relative is bona fide, that there is a need for the relative to work in the business, and that the position the relative will take involves trust. For example, the relative might be handling cash flow or supervising or controlling inventories of goods and equipment.

Once the job offer has been presented to the immigration officer, it is forwarded to the visa office closest to where the relative is living. The relative will be sent an application for permanent residence and will be interviewed by the visa officer to see if she is capable of taking the job that is offered. If so, she is evaluated on the point system, using the job offer in place of arranged employment, and receives 10 points in this category. She must still make the 70 points on the point assessment to be approved for landing in Canada.

Domestic Workers

Many women, and occasionally some men, come to Canada as domestic workers, to care for children and elderly persons. Domestic workers are temporary workers. The process for obtaining a temporary work authorization is the same as that set out above under "temporary workers." The only difference is that a shortage of domestic workers in Canada makes it generally easier to obtain approval from a Canada Employment counsellor for an offer of employment to a domestic worker. Often it is not necessary for the employer to advertise for a Canadian or permanent resident to take the job, because the employment counsellors are aware that there are not enough people in Canada who will take this kind of work.

Once approval has been obtained from the Canada Employment centre, the domestic worker must apply for the work authorization from a visa office at a Canadian embassy or consulate outside Canada. She will be assessed by the visa officer, not only on her qualifications or past experience in caring for children or the elderly or in housekeeping, but on her potential to establish successfully in Canada if she is permitted to come as a temporary worker. This is because there is a program to allow domestic workers to become permanent residents while they are in Canada. The visa officer therefore considers the domestic worker not just under the regulations for temporary workers but also under the Foreign Domestic Workers' Program. Under this program the visa officer will consider the domestic worker's education, past work experience, children and other dependants, and the presence of relatives in Canada who would assist her in becoming successfully established. The officer has to consider whether the domestic worker, over a two-year period, would be able to take courses and establish herself in order to qualify for landing in Canada under the program. If the visa officer believes that the domestic worker might be able to establish herself, then the temporary work authorization will be issued with a visitor's visa to allow the domestic worker to come to work in Canada for one year.

Once the domestic worker has come to Canada, she must work for the employer who offered her the job and who is named on her employment authorization. If the job does not work out, the domestic worker may apply to change jobs, but the new employer must obtain the approval on the job offer from the Canada Employment counsellor, and the domestic worker must then obtain a new work authorization before she actually starts working for the new employer. During this first and any subsequent years in Canada, the domestic worker should be taking part-time courses to upgrade her education or learn skills to help her in the job market in Canada. The domestic worker must obtain a student authorization from a Canada Immigration centre to study in Canada. This is done by getting a letter from the school she wants to attend and taking it to the Canada

Immigration centre for a student authorization. The domestic worker may not change schools or courses without first getting an authorization from an immigration officer to do this. It is not expected that all domestic workers will be employed for the rest of their working lives as domestics. The Immigration Commission expects that, once landed in Canada, they may well look for better-paid employment.

Before the end of the first year of working in Canada, the domestic worker's employer must renew the approval on the offer of employment at a Canada Employment centre, and the domestic worker must then attend at a Canada Immigration centre to renew her visa and to be interviewed on a first-year assessment under the Foreign Domestic Workers' Program. The immigration officer who interviews her will look to see if she has taken any courses while in Canada, how she is doing in them, whether she is fitting into the community, whether she belongs to any social clubs or a church, or otherwise has other interests beyond her courses and her work, what her goals and plans are for succeeding in Canada, and whether she is saving money. The officer is supposed to tell the domestic worker what he feels she can do in the second year in Canada to improve her chances to be landed under the Foreign Domestic Workers' Program. The immigration officer will extend the work authorization, student authorization, and visitor's visa for a second year.

Before the end of the second year the employer must again renew the approval on the offer of employment at a Canada Employment centre and the domestic worker must then attend at a Canada Immigration centre to be interviewed on her second-year assessment. At this interview the immigration officer looks to see if the domestic worker has established herself or if she has the potential to do so if she is permitted to be landed in Canada. The officer will consider the courses the domestic worker has taken and how she has done in them; what her past work experience has been; if she has stable employment in Canada—that is, if she has not changed jobs too many times and or without good reason; what her future plans are should she be landed in Canada; whether she is motivated to do well in Canada; whether she can handle the costs of support for her dependent family members, taking into consideration that older children and a husband can also work and contribute to the expenses once in Canada; how she intends to settle her family members in Canada and if relatives or friends will help her with this; how well she has integrated into Canadian society, as evidenced by her involvement in such community activities as social clubs, church activities, and volunteer work, and by whether she has made friends in Canada; how well she has managed her finances while in Canada (whether she sends money home for her family and whether she has savings); and whether there are relatives already resident in Canada who are willing to help her settle herself and any family she intends to bring once landed.

It is important at this interview for the domestic worker to provide evidence to support what she tells the immigration officer. For example, if she belongs to clubs or a church, she should get letters confirming this. If she has friends, she should get character-reference letters from them. If she has relatives, she should get letters from them confirming that they are willing to help her and her family settle in Canada. If she has sent money home, she should provide receipts or money orders to confirm this. She should bring her bank book to show her savings. She should also have a letter of reference from her employer (and any past employers, if possible), and she should get letters from her school confirming that she attended the courses and passed them.

If the immigration officer feels that the domestic worker can successfully establish in Canada, he will approve her in principle for landing in Canada. Her work authorization will be extended for a year, and during this year her application will be processed for landing in Canada. Normally, this process takes less than a year, but sometimes it may take longer. If it does, the domestic authorization and the visa will be extended for a further year to wait for the landing to be finalized.

If the domestic worker is refused landing in Canada, the work authorization and the visa will be extended for a year and she will be told to leave Canada by the expiry date on the visa.

Humanitarian and Compassionate Applications

Inland Applications

Anyone who is in Canada may make application to be landed in Canada on humanitarian grounds. The Immigration Commission will permit some people to be landed from within Canada if an immigration officer, after an interview with the person, feels that the person should be landed on humanitarian grounds and that it would be a hardship to make the person leave Canada to apply for landing in the normal manner.

Consideration for landing in Canada is given to anyone who asks for it, but approval will not be given in all cases where the request is made. There must be humanitarian reasons for approval to be given. The guidelines setting out who would and who would not likely be approved for landing in Canada are set out in the *Immigration Policy Manual*, Chapter 1, section 39. This manual is available for consultation at any Canada Immigration centre.

The kinds of applications for which approval may be given to allow for landing in Canada include:

1. Family class applicants: This includes, for example, elderly parents, young children, and spouses. If the immigration officer believes that a couple did not marry for immigration reasons, but rather because they love each other, approval will be given to land a non-resident spouse from within Canada. With spouses it is not necessary to prove that there are other humanitarian reasons existing in order to be approved for landing from within Canada.

2. Other family members: This includes for example, widowed elderly aunts or unmarried brothers or sisters who are the only family members not resident in a country other than the home country, where the parents are in Canada. Just being a last family member does not guarantee approval for landing from within Canada. It must also be established that the person would suffer hardship in having to leave Canada to make the application.

3. Difficulties with return to country of origin: This refers to persons who would face problems in returning to their country. Such people may be considered for landing on humanitarian grounds, even though they may not be refugees. For example, a citizen

of an eastern European country who has violated the terms of her exit visa may have reason for believing that she would face serious problems if she had to return to her country.

4. Long-term legal or illegal migrants: This refers to persons who have been in Canada for an extended period of time, either legally, with the exception of students, or illegally. Such people may apply to be landed on humanitarian grounds. The officer in these cases will look at how long the person has been in Canada, how successful she has been in establishing herself while here, what ties she has here with family or friends, and what hardship she would suffer if she had to return to her home country to apply for landing. Persons in Canada illegally for a long period of time take a risk in applying under these guidelines, as the guidelines are not clearly worded and immigration officers differ about whom to approve for landing. If the person illegally in Canada is not accepted for landing under the guidelines, she will be brought to an inquiry, as explained below, for removal from Canada.

Overseas Applications

Visa officers outside Canada may also consider allowing a person to immigrate to Canada for humanitarian reasons. A family member who cannot meet the requirements for landing in Canada may be permitted to immigrate here. For example, a widowed sister with dependent children, who is by herself, may be permitted to immigrate even though she cannot meet the normal selection criteria, if she has most or all of her immediate relatives resident in Canada. Unmarried sons or daughters over twenty-one years old who are the last remaining family members in their home country and who have their parents and some of their siblings in Canada may apply as a "last remaining family member" to immigrate to Canada. In this case it is not necessary to establish further humanitarian reasons for acceptance as an immigrant. Children whose parents are infirm or for some other good reason are not able to care for them, may be permitted to join relatives in Canada on humanitarian grounds.

Visa officers may also permit persons who are not admissible to Canada to come here on a temporary basis for humanitarian reasons. For example, a person in need of medical treatment may be given a minister's permit to allow her to come to Canada temporarily for treatment, if the treatment is not available in the home country. The person or relatives in Canada would, however, be expected to cover the costs of this treatment.

REMOVAL FROM CANADA

Anyone who is not a Canadian citizen may be refused permission to enter Canada or ordered removed from Canada, if she does not comply with our immigration law.

Permanent Residents

Grounds for Removal

A permanent resident has a right to enter and to remain in Canada except where it is determined that the person is in violation of the Immigration Act and regulations.

The common grounds upon which removal of a permanent resident would be sought are those involving criminal convictions: for example, providing false and misleading information; failing to admit to previous criminal convictions; failing to admit to having children or being married when applying for landing; and failing to comply with conditions of admission to Canada (e.g., a fiancée who fails to marry within the ninety-day period after landing). Failure to support oneself or dependent family members is rarely if ever used to deport a permanent resident. A prohibition against planned criminal activities is directed towards the removal of persons who are involved in organized crime, and a subversion and espionage clause is directed towards persons thought to be "terrorists" or spies of unfriendly governments.

A permanent resident cannot be refused entry to or removed from Canada without a hearing to determine if she falls into one of the categories set out in the legislation. All permanent residents who are deported from Canada for one of the above reasons may appeal to the Immigration Appeal Board on grounds of law and on the ground that, having regard to all the circumstances of the person's case, she should not be removed from Canada.

Loss of Residence

A person may lose her permanent residence in Canada if she leaves Canada with the intention of abandoning it. There is a presumption that a permanent resident who remains outside of Canada for longer than 183 days in a twelve-month period has abandoned Canada as her place of permanent residence. This presumption may be overcome if the person can convince an immigration officer or an adjudicator that she did not have an intention to abandon Canada. Factors such as family ties to Canada and ongoing links with Canada (for example, maintaining bank accounts and credit cards, filing income-tax returns, storing furniture, maintaining a home) may all be offered as evidence.

A permanent resident who wishes to remain outside Canada for longer than six months in a twelve-month period may apply for a "returning resident's permit," which would allow her to re-enter Canada within the time given in the permit. Normally these permits are given for a year at a time and may be extended if the person's reason for remaining abroad continues. Permits may be given if the permanent resident is required to work outside Canada for her employer over an extended period of time, is studying outside Canada, is upgrading her professional or vocational qualifications, or for any other reason that an immigration officer feels is appropriate. Before leaving Canada, a person may apply for a returning resident's permit at a local Canada Immigration centre or, after leaving Canada, at a Canadian visa office in an embassy or consulate.

A permanent resident who has abandoned Canada is no longer a permanent resident and is treated like any other person seeking to come into or remain in Canada. A permanent resident who has been deported also ceases to be a permanent resident.

Visitors and Others

No person other than a Canadian citizen, a permanent resident, and an Indian registered under the *Indian Act* has a right to enter or remain in Canada. Refugees claiming protection in Canada have a right to make a claim and have this claim determined, but do not have a legal right to enter or remain in Canada. The legal situation of refugees is complicated and is dealt with separately below.

Any other person may be refused admission or removed from

Canada if she has violated any of the relevant provisions of the *Immigration Act*.

Inadmissible Classes

A person may be refused admission at a Canadian port of entry, either at the border or an airport, for reasons such as serious illness, inability to support herself, a serious criminal record, or others set out in the legislation.

Persons arriving to visit in Canada are commonly refused entry if the immigration officer believes that they want to remain illegally in Canada and are not genuine visitors; or that they cannot comply with the requirements of the act or regulations either because they did not get visas before coming to Canada, as required for visitors from some countries, or because they want to immigrate to Canada and did not apply for an immigrant visa before coming to Canada as required.

Persons who fall within the above category may not be refused admission to Canada without a hearing, although in some cases the person may be allowed to leave Canada voluntarily without having to attend the hearing. Only persons who obtained a visa before coming to Canada and then are refused admission when they arrive in Canada are allowed to appeal to the Immigration Appeal Board on grounds of law or on humanitarian and compassionate grounds.

Removable Classes

A person who is already in Canada, but is not a permanent resident or a Canadian citizen may be removed from Canada on several grounds specified in the legislation, but cannot be removed without having had the opportunity to defend herself in an inquiry. Very often a person who is in violation of the immigration rules will just leave the country without reporting to the Immigration Commission in order to avoid being formally ordered to leave Canada.

Removal Proceedings

Any person who is believed to fall within one of the inadmissible or removable classes is entitled to have a hearing to determine if she has violated a provision of the *Immigration Act* and should be required to leave Canada.

The hearing is called an inquiry. The person who hears the evidence and makes a decision is the adjudicator. The Immigration Commission will be represented at the hearing by a "case-presenting officer" who acts as a prosecutor and presents evidence that the person has violated the *Immigration Act*. The person who is the subject of the inquiry has a right to attend (and, in fact, is normally required to attend), a right to have a lawyer or other counsel represent her, and a right to be told of the right to counsel at the beginning of the inquiry. If the person does not speak English or French she has a right to an interpreter, who is required to interpret all of the proceedings. Persons under eighteen years of age and persons who, in the adjudicator's opinion, are incompetent to act for themselves are entitled not only to have counsel but also to have a guardian present. In such cases the adjudicator may not proceed with the inquiry until someone volunteers or is appointed to be a guardian.

Before the inquiry, the person must be given a report setting out why it is believed that she has violated a section of the *Immigration Act* and which section she is believed to have violated. Unless she has been detained, the person must also be given a notice setting out the time and place of the inquiry. Normally, the person is given a written notice of her right to counsel and a notice that the embassy of her government may be contacted if she wishes.

At the beginning of the inquiry the adjudicator must explain the purpose of the inquiry, the possible consequences of the inquiry, the nature of the allegations against the person, and the person's right to counsel and to a guardian, if necessary. Then the case-presenting officer may call witnesses or present other evidence to prove that the person has violated the *Immigration Act*. Because the person who is the subject of the inquiry may be compelled to give evidence, normally the case-presenting officer will call the person as a witness to give evidence against herself. All witnesses giving evidence are required to take an oath to tell the truth. Once the case-presenting officer has presented his evidence, the person who is the subject of the inquiry is permitted to call witnesses and present other evidence. The case-presenting officer may call further evidence in reply. After the evidence has been presented, the case-presenting officer makes submissions as to why the adjudicator should find that the person has violated a section or sections of the act. The person concerned, or her counsel, may make submissions, and the case-presenting officer may make reply submissions. If the adjudicator does find that the person has violated a section of the *Immigration Act*, the adjudicator must decide what kind of order to make against the person. It is important to understand that when an adjudicator finds that a person has violated the *Immigration Act*, the adjudicator has no authority to let the person remain in Canada, but must decide how the person will leave Canada.

A person who was seeking to come into Canada at a port of entry but who has been found by an adjudicator to be inadmissible will, in most cases, be given an exclusion order requiring that she leave Canada. Where the person has not been allowed into Canada for some serious reason, for example, because the person has a serious criminal conviction or is a terrorist, the person will be ordered deported. A permanent resident who falls within one of the removable classes will be ordered deported from Canada, but she may appeal this order to the Immigration Appeal Board on grounds of law or on humanitarian ground, and she is allowed to remain in Canada while the appeal is pending. Any other person who was permitted to enter Canada and who then violated one of the more important sections of the *Immigration Act* (for example, because of a serious criminal conviction), will be ordered deported. Others who have violated one of the less serious sections of the act (for example, a visitor who overstayed her authorized time or worked without permission from an immigration officer), may be given a departure notice or may be deported. The adjudicator in these situations will hear evidence or listen to submissions from the case-presenting officer and the person or her counsel as to why a departure notice or a deportation order should be issued. A departure notice may only be given where the adjudicator is satisfied that the person is willing and able to leave Canada and the circumstances are such that the adjudicator believes that a departure notice should be given.

Removal Orders and Departure Notice

A *deportation order* requires the person to leave Canada and prohibits the person from ever returning to Canada without first obtaining the consent of the Minister of Immigration to do so. Where the person cannot or will not pay for her passage out of Canada the

Immigration Commission (or, in certain port-of-entry cases the transportation company that brought her to Canada) must pay for the ticket to leave.

An *exclusion order* requires the person to leave Canada and prohibits the person from returning to Canada without the consent of the Minister of Immigration for a year from her date of departure. As with a deportation order, if the person cannot or will not pay her passage from Canada, the Immigration Commission or the transportation company that brought her to Canada must pay for her ticket.

A *departure notice* requires the person to leave Canada on or before a specified date, which could be anywhere from a week to a month or longer from the date the notice was given at the inquiry. The person must pay her own passage out of Canada. There is no prohibition from returning to Canada in the future, and the consent of the Minister of Immigration is not required before her return.

Detention

Anyone who is believed to be inadmissible to or removable from Canada may be detained by an immigration or police officer. The person may be detained only if it is believed that she is a danger to the public or would not appear for examination, inquiry, or removal from Canada. The decision to detain a person must be reviewed by an adjudicator every seven days, and detention may only be continued if the adjudicator believes the person is a danger to the public or would not appear for examination, inquiry, or removal from Canada. A detention review by an adjudicator is similar to an inquiry, and the person being detained has the same right to counsel, to a guardian if a minor or incompetent, and to an interpreter if necessary.

REFUGEES

One of the objectives of the *Immigration Act* is to help refugees and displaced and persecuted persons in keeping with Canada's humanitarian tradition. There are many ways in which Canada helps people who are refugees or in refugee-like situations. The law permits a person to apply before, upon, or after arrival in Canada for protection as a "convention refugee."

From time to time there are special policies and programs that allow persons from countries experiencing serious political problems to remain in Canada on a temporary basis or to apply to become permanent residents in Canada under relaxed rules or, if already resident in Canada, to apply to bring their relatives to Canada under relaxed rules.

Convention Refugee

The *Immigration Act* (following the United Nations 1951 Convention and 1967 Protocol Relating to Status of Refugees) defines a refugee as:

> any person who by reason of a well-founded fear of persecution for reasons of race, religion, nationality, membership in a particular social group or political opinion,
> (a) is outside of the country of her nationality and is unable or, by reason of such fear, is unwilling to avail herself of the protection of that country, or
> (b) not having a country of nationality, is outside of the country of her former habitual residence and is unable or, by reason of such fear, is unwilling to return to that country.

Inland Process

Any person who arrives at an airport or border point may claim protection in Canada as a convention refugee. Any person who has already entered Canada may approach a Canada Immigration centre and claim protection. The procedure for deciding who is a convention refugee is lengthy and complicated. The refugee claimant is examined under oath by a senior immigration officer. A transcript of this examination is sent to the Refugee Status Advisory Committee in Ottawa, which recommends to the minister to recognize or not recognize a claimant as a refugee. The minister or a delegated official makes the final decision. If the claimant is not recognized, then she may apply within fifteen days to the Immigration Appeal Board for an oral hearing to have the refusal redetermined.

Overseas Process

A person may apply to a visa officer to be resettled in Canada as a convention refugee. The visa officer must consider, first, if the person falls within the definition of convention refugee, and if she would be likely to successfully establish in Canada if resettled here. The officer must assess the person on the basis of the selection criteria used for independent and assisted relatives in order to decide if the person will successfully establish in Canada, although the person does not have to make 70 points in order to be allowed to resettle in Canada.

There is provision for a group of five persons or a church or other non-profit organization to sponsor a refugee applying from outside Canada. The sponsors must attend at a Canada Immigration centre and sign an undertaking of assistance to support the refugee's application. The sponsors promise to support the refugee for one year upon arrival in Canada. The existence of a sponsoring group is a very important factor in determining if a refugee will successfully establish in Canada.

Designated Classes and Oppressed Persons

Nationals of certain countries may apply under special regulations to immigrate to Canada. The process is similar to that followed in the case of convention refugees seeking resettlement in Canada. Sponsors may undertake to provide for support of the person for a year. The visa officer must be satisfied that the person is a member of the designated class or the Oppressed Persons and Political Prisoners Class and that she will successfully establish in Canada. Sponsorship is a very important factor considered in successful establishment.

At present the designated classes include nationals, *outside* their country, of Kampuchea, the Peoples' Democratic Republic of Laos, the Socialist Republic of Vietnam, Albania, Bulgaria, Czechoslovakia, the German Democratic Republic, Hungary, Poland, Romania, and the Union of Soviet Socialist Republics.

At present the Oppressed Persons and Political Prisoners class includes nationals, *inside* their country, of Chile, El Salvador, Guatemala, Poland, and Uruguay. To fall within this class the person must have been detained for more than seventy-two hours or otherwise subjected to penal control for acts considered to be a legitimate expression of free thought or a legitimate exercise of civil rights relating to dissent or trade-union activity; or the person must have a well-founded fear of persecution for reasons of race, religion, nationality, or membership in a particular social or political group and be unwilling to avail herself of the protection of her country.

Special Programs

The Immigration Commission provides programs to permit nationals of certain countries to be landed in Canada or to be permitted to remain indefinitely in Canada on minister's permits or on visitor's visas with authorization to work or study while here. Under some of these programs, relatives resident in Canada may apply to bring close family members to Canada under relaxed criteria. Each program is different, and the different programs are put into effect and cancelled from time to time. It is necessary to check with the Immigration Commission to see if a person from a particular country would be covered by a special program. Details of these programs are published in the *Immigration Policy Manual*, Chapter 26. This may be consulted at any Canada Immigration centre.

At present there are landing or no-removal programs for nationals of at least twenty-one countries, including some of the eastern European countries, El Salvador, Guatemala, Iran, and the People's Republic of China.

PART FOUR

Women in Society—
Your Rights in the
Legal System

CHAPTER 16

WOMEN AND THE CANADIAN CHARTER OF RIGHTS AND FREEDOMS

Gwen Brodsky

Gwen Brodsky is the Litigation Director of the Women's Legal Education and Action Fund. LEAF is a national, non-profit organization, founded in April 1985 to assist women in enforcing their equality rights under the Ca-nadian Charter of Rights and Freedoms. *LEAF's primary means of achieving its objective is strategic, test-case litigation in the courts. Previously, Ms. Brodsky practised law in the firm of Acheson, Henderson and Brodsky in Victoria, British Columbia. She is the case comments ed-itor for* The Canadian Journal of Women and the Law, *a publication of the National Association of Women and the Law.*

On April 17, 1982, THE CANADIAN *CHARTER of Rights and Freedoms* was enacted. It forms part of the Constitution of Canada and, as such, is superior to all other laws in Canada. The charter creates special protection for specified, basic rights, including the right not to be deprived of life, liberty, or security of the person except in accordance with principles of fundamental justice; freedom of con-science, religion, thought, belief, and opinion; the right to be pre-sumed innocent until proven guilty; and the right to equality. Of particular significance to women are the equality rights guarantees set out in sections 15 and 28 of the charter. These equality guarantees are the focus of this chapter.

EQUALITY RIGHTS UNDER THE CHARTER

Section 15 of the *Charter of Rights and Freedoms*, which guarantees equality to the women of Canada, came into force on April 17, 1985. The section states:

15(1) Every individual is equal before and under the law and has the equal protection and equal benefit of the law without discrimination and, in particular, without discrimination based on race, national or ethnic origin, colour, religion, sex, age or mental or physical disability.
(2) Subsection (1) does not preclude any law, program or activity that has as its object the amelioration of conditions of disadvantaged individuals or groups including those that are disadvantaged because of race, national or ethnic origin, colour, religion, sex, age or mental or physical disability.

The guarantee of sex equality is reinforced by section 28 of the charter. Section 28 provides that:

28. Notwithstanding anything in this Charter, the rights and freedoms referred to in it are guaranteed equally to male and female persons.

Thanks to the efforts of our equality-seeking forebears, most obvious gender differences have been expunged from the law. In general, Canadian law is, on its face, gender-neutral. And yet women are still subordinate in Canadian society. In the paid labour force they are concentrated in job ghettos where the pay is low and opportunities for advancement few. Within the judiciary, the legislatures, and other places of institutionalized power, women are under-represented. Three out of five families supported primarily by women are living below the poverty line. Women are denigrated by pornography and sexual assault. Poor, disabled, and visible-minority women are among the most disadvantaged people in Canadian society. The elimination of obvious gender differences in the law has fallen short of creating equality in women's lives because many laws, policies, procedures, and legislative gaps, though neutral on their face, have a disparate or adverse effect on women. It is women's hope that the equality guarantees of the charter will require governments to go beyond the elimination of simple gender differences on the face of the law to address unequal effects and create real social equality.

Constitutional Status

The Charter is the most powerful equality rights law that has ever existed in Canada. Its constitutional status makes the charter superior to all other laws. Any law that conflicts with the charter is subject to constitutional attack and invalidation by the courts. The Charter has created an unprecedented opportunity for effective, strategic litigation by women. Already, it has been used on behalf of women to challenge denials of welfare benefits to single mothers, oppose mandatory retirement, secure women's rights to name their children, fight against sex discrimination in amateur sports, and oppose restrictions on the freedom of spouses of military members to assemble and associate.

An important implication of the Charter's constitutional status is that it shifts decision-making power from the legislatures to the courts. Prior to the enactment of the Charter, the courts' constitutional powers were limited to deciding which level of government— federal or provincial—was entitled to pass particular laws. As a result of the Charter the courts have the power to decide whether any government has the power to pass certain laws. As section 52(1) of the *Constitution Act, 1982* states:

> 52(1) The Constitution of Canada is the supreme law of Canada, and any law that is inconsistent with the provisions of the Constitution is, to the extent of the inconsistency, of no force or effect.

Whether transferring so much power to the courts is a positive development is a matter of debate. Some view the charter as an unwelcome threat to the authority of elected representatives to decide what will be law, a principle upon which democracy is said to rest. The counter argument is that the Charter provides necessary protection to disadvantaged groups by ensuring that their rights are determined according to principles of law and equity rather than popular prejudice. This debate, though serious, legitimate, and complex, is of little practical importance for equality-seeking groups now that the Charter is in force. If equality-seeking groups do not use the Charter effectively, it will be used against them. It has already been used in ways that are threatening to women to attack laws that impose child-support obligations on fathers, to challenge sexual-assault laws, and to protest the exclusion of men from a women teachers' federation.

The Development of Equality Rights

Even before the Charter was enacted women recognized its potential and directed their attention to it. Their work began in 1980 when the Trudeau government and provincial premiers were negotiating a new constitutional package. Though women were shut out of the formal constitution-making process, by organizing their own constitutional conference and mounting a landmark national lobby, they exerted a major influence on the formulation of the equality guarantees.

In 1980 women had legitimate cause for concern. Up to that time, the closest thing to a constitutionally entrenched guarantee of equality rights that had existed in Canada was the *Canadian Bill of Rights*, a quasi-constitutional law enacted under the Diefenbaker government in 1960. The *Canadian Bill of Rights* had produced a number of court decisions that were inimical to women's interests. *Lavell* and *Bliss* are among the more notorious *Bill of Rights* decisions. Lavell was an Indian woman whose name was struck from her band's list when she married a non-Indian man. She, along with Bedard, another Indian woman who was in the same position, used the *Bill of Rights* to challenge the provisions of the *Indian Act* that deprived an Indian woman of her Indian status upon marriage to a non-Indian man. According to the wording of the *Indian Act*, the status of an Indian man who married a non-Indian woman was unaffected. Lavell and Bedard were forced to appeal all the way to the Supreme Court of Canada, where they lost. In 1974 the Supreme Court of Canada held that the equality guarantee of the *Bill of Rights* applied only to the administration and enforcement of the law, not to its contents.

The outcome of the *Bliss* case was similar. Stella Bliss was a woman who had recently given birth and had paid unemployment-insurance premiums for the required period to qualify for ordinary unemployment-insurance benefits. According to the unemployment-insurance regulations in force at the time, a pregnant worker could qualify only for maternity benefits; to qualify, women were required to make contributions for a longer period than other workers, and Stella Bliss was refused ordinary benefits. Like Lavell and Bedard before her, Bliss launched legal proceedings, relying on the *Bill of Rights*. She too had to appeal all the way to the Supreme Court of Canada, and she too lost. In its decision rendered in 1979 the court applied the same restrictive definition of equality as in *Lavell*, and, in addition, drew a distinction between the right to equal benefits and the right to equal protections.

Initially, the equality guarantees of the Charter were drawn directly from the *Bill of Rights*. "Equality before the law and protection of the law" were guaranteed. Determined to avoid the pitfalls of the *Bill of Rights*, women, along with other equality-seeking groups, insisted on more. The words "equality under the law" and "equal benefit" of the law were added to ensure that the guarantee would apply to content, and not just enforcement and administration of the law, and to benefits, not just protections. In addition, women secured the inclusion of section 28, which entrenches sex equality as a key concept of the charter. Section 28 has been compared to the Equal Rights Amendment that American women are still fighting to secure.

The Moratorium

Between April 17, 1982, when the Charter was enacted, and April 17, 1985, there was a three-year moratorium on section 15. The stated purpose of the moratorium was to allow governments time to voluntarily bring their laws into compliance with section 15. For the most part the reforms that were implemented during this period are not significant enough to deserve comment. They are cosmetic changes, such as the substitution of the word "worker" for "workman" in workers'-compensation legislation.

During the 1982-85 moratorium women were not idle, however. Conducting equality-rights statute audits, founding a new journal of feminist legal discourse, and establishing a women's legal education and action fund were among the major projects undertaken by women during the moratorium.

EQUALITY CASES UNDER THE CHARTER

Since the close of the moratorium, some positive equality-rights initiatives have been undertaken by governments. Both the Government of Canada and the Government of Ontario have studied ways of improving their human rights legislation and have begun work on pay equity. The Government of Manitoba has enacted pay-equity legislation to cover part of the public sector. In general, however, governments continue to resist women's demands for equality, thereby forcing them to litigate.

What follows is an overview of some of the equality-rights litigation undertaken by the Women's Legal Education and Action Fund (LEAF) during the year and a half following the coming into force of section 15. It offers a picture of the range of litigation issues that confront women as they try to use the Charter to their advantage in the courts.

Names

One of the few remaining instances of blatant gender difference in the law appears in some provincial statutes dealing with the names of women and children. These statutes reflect the archaic view that the spouse and child are possessions of the male and must bear his name. On May 14, 1985, on behalf of Suzanne Bertrand, a White Horse school teacher, a challenge was brought to the Yukon Change of Name Ordinance, which denied women the right to change their surname after marriage. The ordinance stated: "A married woman, while her husband is living, cannot change her name from the one he has given her." Bertrand wished to revert to her birth name, Bertrand, because it reflected her French-Canadian ancestry.

The Yukon Supreme Court declared the challenged section of the ordinance invalid in light of the Charter guarantees of equality and awarded costs to Bertrand. Costs were specifically requested because the government, while admitting its ordinance to be unconstitutional, had not changed it during the three-year moratorium provided for the purpose, thereby requiring court action to be taken.

In Ontario, LEAF challenged the bar against giving the child of a married woman its mother's surname. The applicants wanted to give their child its mother's surname, Paul. This case, heard in the Supreme Court of Ontario on December 9, 1985, was also successful.

In Prince Edward Island, LEAF launched a similar case to the *Paul* case in Ontario on behalf of two other people who were barred by the province's legislation from giving their child its mother's surname, Stewart. In July 1986, the Prince Edward Island legislature amended its legislation, thereby bringing the *Stewart* case to a successful conclusion. The name cases have important symbolic value. They reinforce an egalitarian view of marriage as a partnership of equals rather than a patriarchal structure in which a woman's identity is required to be subsumed by that of a man. In addition, these cases are useful first building blocks for cases presenting more complex equality issues.

Spouse-in-the-House Rule

In the *Beaudette* and *Horvath* cases, LEAF challenged the constitutional validity of the requirement in Ontario's family-benefits legislation that a person must be living "as a single person" in order to be eligible for assistance.

Almost all of the recipients of family allowance are single mothers. Only a few male parents are included in the ranks of recipients. A long-standing practice of welfare administration in Ontario has been to refuse benefits to a woman who has any kind of relationship with a male, using the rationale that because of her relationship she is not living as a single person.

In the summer of 1985 LEAF reviewed the reported decisions of the Social Assistance Review Board, the tribunal that hears appeals from refusals or cancellations of family allowance. It was discovered that on the basis of the most innocent and trivial acts of friendship or help a woman could be judged to be not living as a single person: she could be disqualified for receiving help from a male friend with the deposit on her rent, phone, or utilities, so that she could get an apartment; for spending an occasional night with him; for going with him, in the company of her children, for a hamburger at McDonald's. The list is endless.

LEAF obtained a copy of the investigation guide for welfare officials. It indicated what to look for when determining whether a recipient of benefits was living as a single person. The indicators of questionable status were all aimed at discovering whether female recipients were "living with" men, but not at discovering whether male recipients were "living with" women. Here are some examples:

• men's boots, clothing, hats, tools
• lunch bucket
• wall plaques, photos
• laundry, clothes lines
• C.B. equipment
• hunting dogs
• car treads in snow early in a.m.
• traditional male hobbies

The rationale behind the regulation was extremely sexist. As soon as a woman established any kind of friendship or sexual relationship with a male, family-benefits officials believed that the man was supporting her, or that he should be. If he was not in fact doing so, they none the less treated her as if he were, by cutting her off benefits until she established that she was living as a "single person."

The courts in Ontario had delivered several strongly worded judgments deploring the practices of the administrators of family benefits. In decisions dating from 1978, the Supreme Court of Ontario had set out standards for the administrator to follow. It was clear, however, that these standards were being ignored.

Accordingly, LEAF challenged the validity of the regulation itself, arguing that history had shown this regulation to be incapable of administration in a way that preserved the equality of women. In September 1986, the Government of Ontario agreed to settle out of court. It promised to put a new family benefits model in place, that would focus on economic and legal relationships, rather than on lifestyle assumptions. As a result of the settlement a single-parent recipient should not be categorically disentitled to benefits because of a relationship with another person unless that other person lives with her and provides economic support. In accordance with the terms of the settlement the Government of Ontario has made some interim changes in the family benefits regulations, and the new model is scheduled to take effect on April 1, 1987. LEAF and other advocacy organizations are closely scrutinizing the implementation process. It is hoped that the settlement will force positive changes in family benefits law in Ontario and serve as a catalyst for reform of income-assistance programs throughout Canada.

Organizational Society of Spouses of Military Members

The OSSOMM and two individual women are challenging the provisions of the Queen's Orders and Regulations that prohibit "political activity" on military bases. The society was formed to assist spouses of military personnel, who are mostly women, in achieving basic services of importance to them and their children: a traffic light at a busy corner; better help for battered spouses; French immersion programs in base schools; a dental plan.

The Base Commander at the Penhold base in Alberta barred the society's house drop of write-in cards to be mailed back in support of the dental plan, on the ground that it was "political activity." Political activity is prohibited by Regulation 19, which reads, in part:

> 19.44—POLITICAL ACTIVITIES AND CANDIDATURE FOR OFFICE
> (1) No officer in command of a base or other unit or element shall:
>   (a) allow a political meeting to be held or a political speech to be delivered at this base or other unit or element; or
>   (b) allow a candidate in a federal, provincial or municipal election or a political agent or canvasser to visit his base or other unit or element for the purpose of carrying on political activities unless authorized by or under the *Canada Elections Act* or by service instructions or orders.

This provision appears neutral on its face. However, it is being used against a women's organization with peaceful, self-help community activity as its object. By contrast, an organization such as the Federation of Military and United Services Institutes of Canada, which has a predominantly male membership, and circulated a newsletter to elicit support for Department of National Defence initiatives such as cruise missile testing in Canada, is allowed to meet and distribute materials on Canadian bases.

The arguments in the OSSOMM case are several. It is LEAF's position that the regulation is not intended to bar community activities like OSSOMM's but rather to prevent Canada's military forces from being politically partisan. If the regulation may be interpreted to bar OSSOMM's community activities it is unconstitutional, since it denies women equality before the law under section 15 and curbs their freedom of speech and freedom of association under section 2 of the charter. There is, further, no demonstrable justification for the restrictions. Significantly, the United States, much more self-consciously militaristic than Canada, permits military families to improve conditions of military life. In fact, the American counterpart to OSSOMM makes an annual submission to Congress on matters of concern to military families.

The society and the individual plaintiffs are women of enormous courage. Refusal of the very modest ($5,000) Secretary of State grant that OSSOMM applied for to finance its meetings and communications jeopardizes the very existence of the society. Individuals have endured many threats—both veiled and explicit—of reprisals against them and their spouses.

In its report, *Equality for All*, the Boyer Commission stated its belief that spouses on military bases should not be precluded from taking part in community activities and arguing for increased services, and recommended that the Department of National Defence recognize the special concerns of the spouses of military personnel in its policies and their implementation. However, the official government response to Boyer did not endorse that recommendation, and it is expected that the case will have to be prosecuted to its full extent in order to effect any change at all.

Blainey v. Ontario Hockey Association

April 17, 1986, marked the first anniversary of the coming into force of section 15 of the charter. On this day, the Ontario Court of Appeal handed down its decision in favour of Justine Blainey. This was the first section 15 sex-equality case to be decided by an appeal court, and it is a significant victory for the women of Canada.

The court struck down sub-section 19(2) of the Ontario *Human Rights Code*, which specifically excluded sex discrimination in sports from the Code's anti-discrimination protections, thereby allowing sports organizations in Ontario to discriminate against women with impunity.

As a result of this decision sex discrimination in sports is now prohibited in Ontario. Subsection 19(2) was struck down on the ground that it denies women the right to equal benefit and equal protection of the law as guaranteed by section 15 of the charter. The court also ruled that subsection 19(2) was "grossly disproportionate to the ends sought to be served," and therefore not justified under section 1 of the charter.

Justine Blainey, a twelve-year-old girl who had been chosen to play on a hockey team in the Metro Toronto Hockey League, was barred from play by the Ontario Hockey Association (OHA). Because of subsection 19(2) of the Ontario *Human Rights Code* the Human Rights Commission refused to accept her complaint of sex discrimination.

Assisted by a lawyer provided by LEAF, Justine Blainey brought a challenge to subsection 19(2) of the code. The application heard by the Divisional Court of Ontario on September 12, 1985, was unsuccessful. Justice Steele of the Divisional Court found that although subsection 19(2) was an infringement of the equality-rights guarantee, it was one that could be justified under the rights-limiting section of the charter, section 1. Section 1 provides that:

1. The Canadian *Charter of Rights and Freedoms* guarantees the rights and freedoms set out in it subject only to such reasonable limits prescribed by law as can be demonstrably justified in a free and democratic society.

At the Divisional Court, the main argument advanced by the OHA was that subsection 19(2) of the code was necessary to prevent women's hockey from being integrated. The OHA argued that striking down subsection 19(2) would amount to "mandatory integration" of women's sports. The premise of the argument was that prohibiting sex discrimination in sports would leave women defenceless against takeover of women's sports organizations by men.

This argument ignored the force of subsection 15(2) of the charter, which protects programs designed to assist women in overcoming disadvantage. The evidence in the *Blainey* case was that Canadian girls and women are historically and currently disadvantaged in sports through lack of access to facilities, coaching, and equipment. The American courts have, in a number of cases, approved the integration of qualified women athletes into men's leagues *and* upheld the constitutionality of separate women's teams as programs necessary to help women advance in sport. Nevertheless, at the Divisional Court level the decision was against Justine Blainey and in favour of the OHA.

On January 22, 1986, the Divisional Court decision was successfully appealed to the Ontario Court of Appeal. At the appeal level, with a lawyer provided by LEAF, the Canadian Association for the Advancement of Women in Sport (CAAWS) intervened in an attempt to counteract the OHA's mandatory integration argument, and buttress Justine Blainey's case, by providing a national perspective. CAAWS had studied the circumstances of women in sport all across Canada and concluded that both access to men's teams *and* separate women's teams were essential to the advancement of women in sport.

The Court of Appeal held that subsection 19(2) discriminates directly on the basis of sex, and noted that it has a disparate impact on women. Although in theory subsection 19(2) could harm men and women equally, Dubin J.A. said that, "In substance it permits the posting of a 'no females allowed' sign by every athletic organization in this province." Judicial application of a disparate-impact analysis to a section 15 case is a positive development in equality-rights jurisprudence. As noted in the beginning, inequality may result from the effects of a provision rather than from a distinction that is apparent from the face of the provision. Many women's equality-rights cases will involve provisions that, although neutral on their face, have a disparate impact or effect on women, and success in these cases will depend upon the willingness of the courts to apply a disparate-impact analysis.

The Court of Appeal was not persuaded by the OHA's argument that striking down subsection 19(2) would amount to ringing the death knell for women's sports leagues. In the view of Dubin J.A.,

"A declaration that subsection 19(2) of the *Human Rights Code* is unconstitutional will not mandate integrated sports in this province. In the field of athletic activity, distinctions which have a different impact on participants by reason of their sex, may be reasonable, if there is a valid purpose for such a distinction." This judicial pronouncement is also a positive contribution to equality-rights jurisprudence because there undoubtedly will be situations in other areas of life besides sports where equality for women can best be achieved through different rather than identical treatment.

Finally, it is encouraging that the court applied a rigorous test in interpreting the requirements of section 1 of the charter. If the courts had taken a *laissez-faire* approach to section 1 in equality-rights cases, it could mean that though legislation was proved to discriminate, the discrimination would be judged to be a "reasonable limit" on equality.

All but one of the key positions advanced on behalf of CAAWS and Justine Blainey were accepted by the Court of Appeal. The one argument rejected by the court was that the charter applies directly to the OHA, and not only to the Ontario *Human Rights Code*. The court preferred the view that the charter's application is restricted to government laws and activities and did not accept the argument that the OHA itself either carries out a government function or acts as a government agency. The question of the scope of the charter's application is an important one for equality-seeking groups. If the reach of the charter does not extend to organizations carrying out government functions, governments may effectively sidestep the charter by permitting discrimination by its delegates. It is significant that the Court of Appeal in *Blainey* did not rule out the possibility that the charter would apply in such circumstances, but simply found that the evidence in this case did not establish such a relationship between the OHA and government.

The victory at the Ontario Court of Appeal not only overcomes the initial loss at the Divisional Court, but makes *Blainey* a stronger precedent than a win at the lower court would have been. The precedent value of *Blainey* is underscored by the fact that on June 26, 1986, the Supreme Court of Canada denied the OHA's application for leave to appeal and ordered costs against the OHA.

Cases in Which LEAF Is an Intervener

Any Charter case that raises an equality issue stands to have an impact on women. For this reason it is important that women have the opportunity to be heard in all Charter equality cases. In an equality rights case where none of the parties is speaking from the perspective of women as a group, women may be granted the right to intervene. It is in the discretion of the court to grant intervener status to a non-party who has relevant knowledge and expertise and a different perspective that may be of assistance to the court. LEAF has been granted intervener status twice, in *R. v. Seaboyer and Gayme*, and *Shewchuk v. Ricard*.

R. v. Seaboyer and Gayme

In this case two male accused persons challenged the constitutionality of sections 246.6 and 246.7 of the *Criminal Code*. These provisions, a result of years of lobbying by women's groups, limit the extent to which a complainant in a sexual-assault case may be examined about her past sexual relations with anyone other than the accused, or about her sexual reputation.

Mr. Justice Galligan of the Ontario Supreme Court ruled that these provisions offend the rights of the accused to a fair trial guaranteed by section 11 of the charter. The Attorney General of Ontario has appealed the decision to the Ontario Court of Appeal.

LEAF applied to intervene in the appeal, to argue that the provision is constitutional. On February 26, 1986, Chief Justice Howland of the Ontario Court of Appeal granted the application, and the appeal was set for the second week of January 1987.

Shewchuk v. Ricard

West Coast LEAF, along with a coalition of four other groups, intervened in this case to argue that a particular piece of discriminatory legislation should be repaired rather than struck down. Though the concept of judicial repair or extension is new to the Canadian courts, it has long been accepted in American constitutional cases. LEAF's arguments for judicial repair in this case, however, were unsuccessful.

The facts of the case are that Jerry Ricard, a male parent who had been sued for child support under the *Child Support and Pa-*

ternity Act, challenged the act on the ground that it contravenes the guarantee of sex equality in section 15. The *Child Paternity and Support Act* provides that the father of a child "born out of wedlock" may be sued for support for the child at the instigation of the mother, but does not allow a father, who has custody of a child "born out of wedlock" to initiate proceedings against the mother. An additional feature of the act is that it provides for state-paid legal counsel for the applicant.

The case went to three levels of court. At the appeal level the interveners argued that the provision does discriminate against custodial fathers and urged the court to repair the provision by extending its application to men and women equally. The repair work would have entailed changing the act to give a sole custodial father the right to seek an affiliation and maintenance order against the child's mother. The court decided that the provision discriminates, but that it is justified under section 1 of the charter, and so did not address LEAF's arguments in favour of the remedy of extension. It is regrettable that the British Columbia Court of Appeal did not seize the opportunity to lay the groundwork for the development of a Canadian doctrine of extension. Without the availability of the remedy of extension, the charter is a rather blunt instrument.

Other sex-equality cases are currently being developed or are already in the court system in which an order simply having a provision struck down could result in a net loss for women. One such example is a challenge to the federal government's Spouses' Allowance and Widows' Benefits program, presently being developed by LEAF. This is a program of financial assistance to elderly persons who are in need. In addition to need, the eligibility criteria include that the recipient must be married or widowed. Divorced and single persons are ineligible. Through its under-inclusiveness the program discriminates directly on the basis of marital status and also has a disparate impact on elderly women, who are most likely to need the assistance. Though a Charter challenge to this will be of benefit to women if the court extends the program, the result may well be that the courts will simply strike it down, leaving it up to the federal government whether to establish a new program based solely on need or drop the program completely. In a case like this, the ability of groups to follow up with concerted political action becomes a key factor in deciding whether even to proceed with the litigation.

Although in the short run it is probably preferable for women that, in the *Shewchuk* case, the British Columbia Court of Appeal saved the CPSA rather than striking it down, the reasoning employed by the court is troublesome. The court reasoned that denying a putative father the right to seek a maternity order is not as important as the state's interest in establishing paternity, and that custodial fathers may make use of the child-support provisions of the *Family Relations Act* should they need to, whereas "Legal assistance will, in many cases, be required by the mother who, by reason of her pregnancy, may have suffered loss of income, and extra expenses, and may be unable to afford the cost of application proceedings." What is disturbing about this judicial approach is that it is premised on women's need for special protection. This may be a dangerous step towards the affirmation of a theory of special protection that has been relied on in the past to deny women access to traditional male opportunities. Not so long ago the rights to vote, hold public office, own property, sue in one's own name, and join a profession were exclusively male rights. One of the justifications for excluding women from such opportunities was that women required protection against the harshness of public life.

Another important issue that arose in the *Shewchuk* case is the interpretive question of how sex discrimination is to be defined in a section 15 case. In most circumstances, distinctions based on sex serve to restrict women's legal rights rather than to advance them. It is for this reason that women's-rights advocates hope that for the purpose of section 15 cases the courts will adopt a definition of discrimination that presumes sex-based distinctions are illegal. Such a presumption should not preclude affirmative action and maternity-benefits programs designed to advance women's equality.

An alternative and much less desirable approach to sex discrimination is to define it in such a way as to presume the legality of sex-based distinctions. The difficulty with this approach is that it requires women to prove the harm and unreasonableness of sex-based distinctions on a case-by-case basis.

Other Cases in Progress

Other women's equality-rights cases in progress include challenges to:

- a lower scale of compensation for injured "housewives" than for other accident victims under Manitoba's public motor-vehicle-insurance scheme;
- exclusion of domestic workers from the protection of employment standards legislation in British Columbia and Ontario;
- unequal treatment of women in the federal penitentiary system;
- restrictive child-naming provisions in New Brunswick's and British Columbia's vital statistics legislation;
- *Criminal Code* prostitution laws;
- mandatory retirement;
- eligibility restrictions based on marital status in Ontario's Beginner Farm Assistance Program.

THE FUTURE OF EQUALITY

It is too soon to predict how successful women will be at using the charter to achieve the real social equality that section 15 promises. Success will depend upon the readiness of both the courts and the governments to take equality rights seriously. At the time of writing, the equality guarantees have been in force for less than two years, and not one case has reached the Supreme Court of Canada. This means that there is still uncertainty about how the equality guarantees will be interpreted.

Women's-rights advocates are working extremely hard to use the Charter effectively. It is hoped that the test cases initiated thus far will result in gains for women and that more cases can be developed to assist women who are doubly or multipally disadvantaged by sex, race, religion, marital status, age, disability, or sexual orientation.

The stakes in equality-rights litigation are high. A loss in the courts not only creates a negative precedent for future cases, but may also serve to reinforce discriminatory attitudes and practices. For this reason, the test cases that women have chosen to initiate have been selected, in part, for their strong fact situations. For this reason, too, litigation is seen as a companion rather than an alternative to negotiations in the political arena.

Securing the strong and broad language of section 15, along with the inclusion of section 28, was an important victory for women. Since then, some victories in the courts have been achieved, and women have demonstrated their reactive capacities by intervening in cases that threaten to erode their rights.

During the next several years the courts will establish interpretive principles that will determine the Charter's long-term usefulness as an implement of social change. The commitment to equality that women have shown in the 1980s should, on its own, be enough to persuade courts and governments that it is time to take equality rights seriously.

CHAPTER 17

CRIMES AGAINST WOMEN

Kate Andrew

Kate Andrew received her B.A. and LL.B. from the University of British Columbia. She has been actively involved in the issue of violence against women for the past ten years, worked at a women's legal clinic, as a legal consultant to the Toronto Metro Action Committee on Public Violence Against Women and Children and at the Barbara Schlifer Commemorative Clinic. She is a member of the Working Group on Sexual Violence in Vancouver, the Civil Rights and Remedies Committee in Toronto, the Board of Directors of the Emily Stowe Shelter for Women in Scarborough, and the National Action Committee on the Status of Women.

WOMEN EXPERIENCE a wide range of discrimination and violence in their lives. The continuum of sexism ranging from economic discrimination to vocational and social stereotyping to such direct forms of violence as rape, wife assault, and pornography is well covered in the various chapters of this book. The way women are taught, in school and at home; the jobs we have; the men we marry; the entertainment and media products that surround us, and the politicians we elect—all these things and many others have a bearing on the violence that women experience. In turn, the violence women encounter affects everything else in their lives.

In this chapter we will examine rape (or sexual assault, as it is legally referred to) pornography, and prostitution. Other forms of violence against women—for example, wife assault, sexual harassment, and incest—are dealt with in other chapters.

While violence against women is often an overwhelming and

depressing topic, we must realize that problems will only be solved by recognizing the issues and working together to make the world safer for all women. A great deal has been accomplished in the last twenty years towards that goal, but there is still much to do. Those interested in making contact with groups working on the issue of violence against women, or with support groups for survivors of violence, are encouraged to read Chapter 19, ''Advocacy,'' and to contact the rape crisis centre, women's centre, or transition house in their community.

SEXUAL ASSAULT

This chapter refers to the victims of sexual assault as women not because men cannot be sexually assaulted, but because it is women and female children who are overwhelmingly the victims of sexual assault. Our primary aim is to address the needs of female victims of violence, although the information may be of more general interest.

Self-Defence

Much has been written about self-defence for women. Some people suggest that there is nothing a woman can or should do to protect herself from sexual assault. Others seem to suggest that women ought to prepare themselves fully for a potential assault, and some even go as far as to insinuate that a woman is responsible for the assault if she hasn't taken all possible precautions.

It is important to remember that a sexual assault is *never* the victim's fault.

There are a number of common-sense precautions women can take and parents can teach their children that will help protect them in the event that they are assaulted or in danger of being assaulted. A list of materials and programs designed to teach these precautions is included in the resource section at the end of this book.

The Law

In 1983 the *Criminal Code* sections dealing with rape were revised. These changes were brought about in large part because of the efforts of feminists who recognized that the existing rape laws were outdated and did not represent the needs of rape victims, or of women in general.

Originally rape was seen as an offence against the property of men—much like the theft of an animal. Men who raped women would have to pay compensation not to the woman who was raped, but to her father or husband for having soiled "his" property. As a result, many myths about rape developed—all of which ignored the experience of the victims themselves. The legal system adopted many of these myths and, over hundreds of years, institutionalized them. The changes to the rape laws in Canada were an attempt to bring the laws into line with the experience of women who are raped.

The following major changes were made in the 1983 revision of the relevant sections of the *Criminal Code*:

- Rape was removed from the code and replaced with a new three-tiered offence entitled "sexual assault."
- The definition of sexual assault was broadened to include a much wider range of activities than were covered by the rape provisions. The new offences cover everything from a "stolen kiss" to sexual harassment to forced sexual intercourse, which is still often referred to as rape.
- Penetration was abolished as a requirement for rape.
- The protection husbands had previously enjoyed was done away with, so that now a husband may be charged with sexually assaulting his wife.
- A number of procedural changes were introduced with the aim of making sexual-assault trials less difficult for victims. These changes included limiting the kinds of questions defence lawyers may ask a woman about her previous sexual history, and allowing a victim to ask for a ban on publication of her name or identity.

Although the changes in the law did improve the situation for rape victims in some respects, not all the changes have been good for women. But because the courts are still interpreting the changes, it may be some time before we know the full impact of the amendments.

After an Assault

The first thing to remember after a sexual assault is that YOU ARE *NOT* TO BLAME.

A sexual assault is a traumatic event. Often the victim feels confused, upset, angry, hurt, scared, and lonely. There are people who can help. Call a friend or relative whom you feel comfortable with, or call the local rape crisis centre or crisis centre. You do not have to go through it alone.

Deciding Whether to Report to the Police

Sexual assault is a crime, but it is also a traumatic personal event. If you wish to report your assault to the police it is helpful if you do so as soon as possible. However, unless the person assaulted is a child, it is not necessary to report the assault. *It is your choice to make.* It is often helpful to have advice when you are making the decision whether to report. Rape crisis centre counsellors will give you information and details about how to report and about what the situation is in your community if you do decide to do so.

Recording Your Memories

It is often a good idea to write down everything you can remember about the assault as soon as possible so you will have a record of what happened. Put down everything—no matter how inconsequential it may seem. Especially important are any details you can remember about your attacker—little things that you might quickly forget. Date your notes and keep them handy so that if you remember more details you can write them down. Date each additional note.

Even if you do not report the assault to the police, the notes may be useful if you want to sue your assailant, apply for criminal-injury compensation, or make a "third-party report" (as described later in this chapter).

If you do report the assault, the police will take a full statement from you, but your notes may help both you and them.

Medical Care

Even if you choose not to report your sexual assault to the police, you should get proper medical care.

If you are going to report the assault, or if you think you might want to, do *not* wash, or change your clothes, or go to the bathroom before you get medical care. The doctors will have to collect specimens from you and your clothing for the police, so it is essential that you not wash up or clean up—even though it's the most natural thing in the world to want to do after an assault.

If you are reporting the assault to the police they will probably want to take your clothes for further testing, so bring an extra set of clothes to the hospital or ask someone to bring a fresh set for you.

You may want to ask a friend to accompany you to the hospital. It's a good time to have someone around. You can have your supporter in the examination room with you if you want. However, the police should not be with you when you are being examined by the doctor.

Some hospitals will provide a woman doctor if you ask for one. Don't hesitate to ask if it will make you feel more comfortable.

The doctor may ask you a number of questions in order to treat you properly for the assault. You should also be given tests for sexually transmittable diseases.

If you are not on a reliable form of birth control and want to make sure you do not become pregnant, you should ask the doctor about getting a "morning-after pill." The most recommended "morning-after pill" is Ovral. A pill called DES (for diethylstilbestrol) is sometimes used, but it is *not* recommended.

It is useful to try and write down any information the doctor gives you. Also make notes of the names of the doctor, the nurses, and anyone else you deal with after the assault. It may not be easy to remember much of what you hear right after the assault. Writing it down will help.

The doctor will probably recommend that you get a follow-up examination a week or so after the assault.

If You Decide Not to Report to the Police

Third-Party Report

If you have decided not to report the assault to the police you may still wish to have a rape crisis centre counsellor or friend make a "third-party report" to the police. This means that you authorize someone to give the police the details of your assault—except for any details that would identify you—so they can record that an assault occurred, even if an investigation isn't going to follow.

Sometimes the police will want more information. They may get in touch with the person who made the third-party report and ask to speak to you or to get more details of your assault from whoever made the report. They can't force you to speak to them.

Some police forces are more interested in taking third-party reports than others, but it is an option you may want to explore.

Human Rights Complaint

If the assault took place at your place of employment, another option you may wish to explore is making a human rights complaint. For further details on making a human rights complaint see the section on sexual harassment in Chapter 11, "Equality in Employment."

Confrontation

In some cases women who know their attacker, or know where he lives or works, choose to let him know directly what they think.

There are some things you should be careful about if you do decide to confront your attacker. You may not threaten his well-being; if you do, he could call the police and lay a charge of "threatening" against you. You may not slander him—that is, say false things that could damage his reputation. But you may confront him about what he did and how that made you feel. You may want to consult a rape crisis centre to get advice and support if you choose to confront your attacker.

Other Options

1. Even if you choose not to report your assault to the police, you are still free to sue your attacker in a civil law suit. For further details about how to go about suing your attacker see the section entitled "Civil Suits" later in this chapter.

2. Again, if you choose to report your assault you may still be able to make an application for criminal-injury compensation. For further information, please refer to the section entitled "Criminal-Injury Compensation" later in this chapter.

If You Decide to Report to the Police

Reporting to the Police
It is helpful to report a sexual assault as soon as possible so that evidence is not destroyed or lost, and so your memory about the attack is as fresh as possible.

You may call the police yourself or get someone else to call for you. If you've gone to the hospital you may ask a nurse or doctor to call the police for you.

Medical Care
If you have gone to the hospital by yourself, tell the doctor that you want to report the sexual assault, so that the doctor gets the right evidence for the police investigation. If the police have taken you to the hospital, remember that they should not be present when you are being examined by the doctor.

Police Investigation
When your assault is first reported to the police they will send out one or two police officers to investigate.

If you want a female police officer, ask for one. Some police forces try to make a female officer available to sexual assault victims, others do not.

The police officer(s) will ask you about what happened and take notes. If you are at the scene of the attack they will probably look around and take notes about the surroundings.

If you called the police before going to get medical care, they will take you to the hospital. Once you have been examined by the doctor, the police will get a copy of the doctor's report. They may also question you further in order to complete their own report.

The police should then make sure you have somewhere safe to go. If you want, the police will drive you home.

If the officers met you at the hospital, or somewhere other than the site of the attack, they will probably go to the site to collect evidence. The officers will then write up their report to give to the police who will be carrying on the investigation. In some cities there are detectives who specialize in sexual-assault investigations; otherwise it will likely be handled by a plain-clothes police officer or detective.

After a few days the officers will contact you to make arrangements for an interview. If you have physical injuries that have not been photographed you should ask the officers about being photographed. At the interview the officers will ask you to describe what happened; they will then ask you a lot of questions and take notes of everything you say. They may also tape record your interview. Some of the questions the police ask you may be very difficult or upsetting. Try to be as clear as possible about what happened. Don't ever hesitate to ask the officers to repeat or explain a question, if you don't understand or are confused. It may be embarrassing for you to talk about your assault, but remember the police have heard similar facts before, and they are there to help you.

The police will prepare a statement of everything you have told them and ask you to sign it. Read it over very carefully. If some things are wrong or left out, don't hesitate to tell the police to amend the statement.

You may be asked by the police to take a polygraph (lie-detector) test. You do not have to take the test. There is a great deal of controversy about the tests and their reliability. If you do not want to take the test you have the right to say no. If you want more information about the test, contact a rape crisis centre for information and advice.

The police may also ask you a lot of personal questions. They do this sometimes because they think it is important to let you see what kinds of questions you may be asked in court, and sometimes to see whether they think your story "holds together." You do not have to answer if the questions make you feel uncomfortable. If you feel you have been badly treated by the police, call your local rape crisis centre for support and assistance.

If you know your attacker, the police will probably have an easier time finding him than if he is a stranger. If you do not know your attacker, you may be asked to spend time with a police artist putting together a "composite" sketch of your attacker. You may also be asked to come to a police line-up to identify a suspect. The police will have the suspect and a number of other men who look like him. You will be asked to look at them from behind a one-way mirror, so that they can't see you. If you think hearing the men's voices might help you identify your attacker, ask the police to have the men say certain words. If the police don't have enough men who look like the suspect to participate in the line-up, they will put together a "photo line-up" and ask you to identify your attacker from the photographs.

Police Protection
If you feel threatened or unsafe as a result of the sexual assault, talk to the police about getting protection. While most police forces won't actually supply police protection to victims of violence, they may be able to help you protect yourself and your home. If you know your attacker, you may want a restraining order or peace bond against him. Ask the officers investigating your case about these options.

Laying the Charge
In some provinces the police decide whether to charge someone, and in other provinces the Crown counsel or Crown attorney makes the decision.

Whoever makes the decision has to review the evidence the police have collected and decide which law has been broken. If you have been sexually assaulted there are a number of different charges that might apply (Sexual Assault; Sexual Assault with a Weapon; Threats to a Third Party or Causing Bodily Harm; Aggravated Sexual Assault; Kidnapping-Forcible Confinement; Indecent or Harassing Telephone Calls; Indecent Acts; Gross Indecency; Buggery or Bestiality; Sexual Intercourse with a Female Under Age Fourteen or Between Fourteen and Sixteen). The person laying the charge has to choose the charge that is most likely to succeed in light of the facts of your case.

If you do not understand the charge that has been laid, ask the person who made the decision for an explanation. If you are still dissatisfied, talk to the superior of the person who made the decision or call your local rape crisis centre.

If the police or Crown counsel decide not to lay charges, you also have the right to question their decision. If they and their superiors continue to insist that they won't lay charges, it is possible for you to lay a private complaint. If you want to do this call your local rape crisis centre for advice and information.

Types of Charges

Many different sections of the *Criminal Code* deal with sexual offences. Some of these are "summary" offences and some are "indictable" offences. Summary offences are generally less serious charges; indictable offences are more serious and usually lead to more complex trials. Sexual assault is a "hybrid" offence, which means it can be either "summary" or "indictable." The person who decided what charge to lay will also have decided how to proceed—by summary conviction or by indictment. Only the most minor sexual assaults should be handled by summary conviction.

Bail Hearing

Once the man who sexually assaulted you has been arrested he will be brought before a judge for what is commonly referred to as a bail hearing. The legal term for bail in the *Criminal Code* is "judicial interim release."

At the bail hearing the Crown attorney will review the facts of the case—referred to as "the allegations" because they haven't yet been proved to the court—for the judge. The Crown will also make a recommendation as to whether the accused should be released, and if so on what grounds. The defence lawyer will likely deny "the allegations" on behalf of the accused and tell the judge a bit about the accused's background, education, family, employment, etc., in order to persuade the judge that it is safe to release the accused. The judge will then have to decide whether to release him and, if so, on what terms.

It is not necessary for you to attend the hearing, but if you want to, ask the police or Crown attorney to let you know when it will take place.

The *Criminal Code* outlines on what basis someone may be detained, when they should be released, and what conditions may be imposed upon them if they are released.

A number of different conditions may be imposed on an accused who is going to be released. A common condition in cases of sexual assault is that the accused have no contact with the victim or her family. If you want to make sure the Crown attorney will ask for a "no-contact" order, tell the police or Crown attorney that you want such an order. If the accused does contact you after being given a "no-contact" order as a condition of his release, he may be arrested for breaching his bail conditions. Call the police if the man who attacked you is contacting or harassing either you or your family or your friends after being released.

Interview with the Crown
Even though you are the victim of the sexual assault you are considered, for the purposes of the criminal charge, a witness for the Crown. You are referred to as the complainant.

In order to prepare for the preliminary hearing, the Crown counsel will make arrangements to interview you. The interview is to prepare you—and the Crown counsel—for the trial.

Do not hesitate to ask the Crown counsel any questions you may have about the trial procedure or about your case. Sometimes it is helpful to write things down, so you don't forget to ask them when you have a chance.

Some victims find being a "witness" to their assault at the trial an alienating experience. They feel frustrated by the loss of control over such an intimate experience. If you feel this way, or if you think the Crown counsel is ignoring your feelings, let him or her know how you feel. If you don't feel comfortable talking to the Crown counsel, get in touch with your local rape crisis centre, or ask a friend to help you.

The Preliminary Hearing
If the charge against the accused is indictable there will be a preliminary hearing. This is similar to a trial, in that the victim and all other Crown witnesses will be called to testify, and the defence will be allowed to cross-examine the witnesses. However, the hearing is intended to determine not whether the accused is guilty, but whether there is enough evidence to send him to trial. The preliminary hearing gives the defence a chance to hear the case against it before having to provide a defence. It is very rare for the defence lawyer to have defence witnesses testify at a preliminary hearing.

The Trial

Unless the accused has decided to plead guilty, a trial will follow the preliminary hearing. In summary offences the case proceeds directly to trial. If the accused has pleaded guilty, the case will go straight to a sentencing hearing.

For further general information about how a trial is conducted, see Chapter 18, ''Women and Criminal Law.''

Some aspects of trial procedure are unique to sexual-assault cases. Because much of sexual-assault law has developed from unjustified myths about rape, many of these special rules may seem unfair. However, until women manage to have the laws changed, these special rules will continue to exist.

Past Sexual History

In 1976 and 1983 Parliament put some limitations on the kinds of questions a victim may be asked about her past sexual history. However, some of these restrictions are now under attack because some courts have ruled that the restrictions are unfair to the accused. It will be some time before the law is clarified on how much, if any, of a victim's past sexual history is admissible evidence.

The *Criminal Code* currently allows a victim of sexual assault to be questioned about her past sexual history if:
• it contradicts evidence the victim has already given;
• it relates to the identity of the accused;
• it relates to sexual activity that took place at the same time as the sexual assault.

The defence lawyer must give notice of the intention to ask questions about past sexual history. The judge will then excuse the jury, if there is one, and dismiss the public from the courtroom so that a hearing can be held to determine whether the questions do fit into any of the three categories and if they are relevant. If the judge decides that the questions may be asked, the jury and public will be brought back into the courtroom and the trial will continue.

Many women think it is unfair that a victim of a sexual assault should have to answer questions about her past sexual history. The only issue at a sexual-assault trial should be whether the victim consented to sex on the occasion of the assault, not whether she has *ever* consented to sex.

Consent

Another controversial rule in cases of sexual assault is the defence of "honest belief." This means that if a woman doesn't consent to sex but the man claims that he honestly believed she was consenting, his "honest belief" will be a defence to the charge of sexual assault.

Because there is pressure on men to "perform" sexually and men are encouraged to believe that women mean "yes" when they say "no," the "honest-belief" defence has often been criticized as being an excuse for a crime that ought not be excused.

Although Parliament kept the "honest-belief" defence in the 1983 changes to the *Criminal Code*, it also introduced a sub-section that recognized some of the social pressures women are under. Section 244(3) states that consent is not obtained if the victim submits because of fraud, an exercise of authority, or the use of threats or force against the victim or a third party. These provisions are a step in the right direction in terms of recognizing the reality women often face when they are forced to have sex against their will.

Ban on Publication

Another part of the *Criminal Code* being challenged on the basis of the *Charter of Rights and Freedoms* is s. 442(3). This sub-section allows a judge to ban the publication of any evidence that would identify the victim in a sexual-offences trial.

The section was introduced to provide the victim of sexual offences a degree of privacy.

If you would like to have an order banning publication of evidence that would identify you, ask the Crown attorney when you are first interviewed what the state of the law is at the time of your trial.

Corroboration

Until 1976 a judge had to warn a jury in a trial for sexual assault that it was not safe to convict an accused on the basis of the victim's uncorroborated evidence. This is no longer the case for adult victims of sexual assault.

However, the criminal law does have special rules for children. Currently, if a child under fourteen is a witness at a trial, the judge must determine whether the child understands the nature of an oath. If the judge decides the child may testify under oath, the child's evidence is accepted. If, however, the judge decides the child may not testify under oath, the child's evidence must be corroborated. Corroborating evidence is further evidence that connects the accused to the crime and supports the "uncorroborated" evidence.

The government has recently introduced amendments to the *Canada Evidence Act* and the *Criminal Code* that would change the standards by which a judge would determine whether a child can testify. The law in this area will likely be unsettled for some time.

Similar-Fact Evidence

The rules about similar-fact evidence are not limited to sexual assault, but they are often used in this context.

Similar-fact evidence may not be introduced if its only purpose is to suggest that the accused is the type of person who would commit such an offence. It may be introduced if it is used to identify the accused, to show that he had the intention to commit the crime, or that he had used the same methods before.

This kind of evidence is often used in sexual-assault cases where the accused has sexually assaulted numerous women and is being tried for some or all of the assaults at the same time.

Marital Rape

Since 1983 a husband may be charged for sexually assaulting his wife.

There are many problems particular to being assaulted by your husband or partner. For further information about these problems, see Chapter 9, "Violence in the Family."

Witness Fees

Every province has different ways of dealing with witness fees and expenses. Check with the Crown counsel about what expenses and fee they will pay you when you testify—but don't expect much; the fees are all very low.

If you have an employer or union, check to see if your wages are paid for the day(s) you're involved in the case. Employers must give you time off if you're subpoenaed to testify, but they are not required to pay your wages.

Sentencing

At the end of the trial the judge will decide if the accused is legally guilty or not. If he is found not guilty don't blame yourself. Ask the Crown counsel about whether the Crown plans to appeal the acquittal.

If the accused is found guilty, or if he has pleaded guilty at any point after his arrest, the judge will then sentence him. There are many options in sentencing. It is often a good idea to ask the Crown counsel what sentence the Crown will be asking for and why. This will prepare you and give you some idea of what range and type of sentence is being considered.

You should also talk to the Crown counsel about preparing a "victim-impact statement," or ask to be given the opportunity to make a statement at the sentencing hearing. A victim-impact statement is a statement, either written or oral, made by the victim about how the assault has affected her life. Some Crown attorneys use victim-impact statements more often than others.

Sentences for sexual assaults vary considerably depending on the nature of the offence, the accused's background, his "prospects for rehabilitation," his previous criminal record, and his health. Sentencing options include: fines; suspended sentences or discharges, sometimes combined with a period of probation, community service, or other conditions; and imprisonment.

Appeals

After the trial or sentencing, either the Crown or the defence may appeal the conviction/acquittal, the sentence, or both.

Civil Suits

You may sue your attacker for damages as a result of a sexual assault. Damages could cover such things as nervous shock, any physical injuries you suffered, loss of wages, and loss of clothes, jewellery, etc. Suing the man who sexually assaulted you can take a very long time and can be expensive. You should consult a lawyer to discuss what your chances of success would be and what will be involved in the lawsuit.

Criminal-Injury Compensation

Another way to get compensation for an assault is through the criminal-injury compensation system. Criminal-injury compensation is paid by the provincial government in the belief that, as a matter of social responsibility, society ought to compensate the victims of violent crime. Each province has a slightly different system of compensation; check with the office in your province about how its particular system operates. If you have reported the assault to the police, you may ask the police or Crown counsel for information about the program in your area.

Some provinces have a limitation period of *one year* from the date of the offence. Make sure you know what the deadlines are in your province.

It isn't necessary to report the assault to the police to make an application for criminal-injury compensation. However, police reports and criminal proceedings are often seen as strong evidence that the assault did take place.

To make an application for compensation call the criminal-injury compensation board or branch or the government services office in your area for an application form. Application forms are usually fairly straightforward. It is not necessary to have a lawyer to apply for compensation, although some people do have a lawyer help them. Not all provinces will pay for a lawyer, so you may have to pay your own legal bill.

There are different systems for obtaining or requiring further documentation and evidence, for assessing compensation applications, and for making the decision about what award, if any, will be made. Some provinces have investigators to review claims; some assess the claim on the basis of the application and a medical examination conducted by a board doctor. Some boards have an adjudicator (usually a lawyer hired by the board) who reviews all the available evidence about your case and makes the decision about whether to make an award and how much to grant. In other provinces the board holds a hearing before one or more members to determine whether you are eligible for compensation. Consult your local criminal-injury compensation office to get information and further details about how your case will be handled.

It may be quite a while before a final award is made in a criminal-injury compensation case. This is true, for example, if you have reported the case and the trial is dragging on. If this happens, you may make a request for interim payments. These are given where there is a strong case and board personnel realize an award will eventually be made.

If you are on social assistance you should be aware that any criminal-injury compensation you receive may be deducted from your assistance. Check with your local legal-aid office or welfare-rights group about what the situation is in your area before making an application for compensation.

PORNOGRAPHY

With the development of the ''second wave'' of feminism in the sixties, more women began to talk about the violence they encountered on the streets, at work, and in the home. In response to this violence, rape crisis centres, shelters for battered women, and incest support groups began to develop across the country. As services for female victims of violence grew and more and more women began to speak out about their experiences, it became increasingly clear to feminists working in the field that pornography was an all-too-common denominator in the cycles of violence women encounter.

At the same time it became apparent that pornography was also undergoing a change; it was becoming increasingly violent and increasingly focused on the degradation and abuse of women and children. These trends were clear not only to those working directly with the victims of violence, but also to a growing number of social scientists and psychologists interested in studying the impact of pornography.

As feminists began to speak out about pornography, more women began to see what for years they had ignored or been unaware of. As the debate broadened, increasing numbers of individuals and groups became involved in the issue, and a wide range of solutions began to develop.

In response to growing pressure to do something about pornography, in June 1983 the federal government appointed a special committee to look into pornography and prostitution. Known as the

Fraser Committee, it submitted its final report to the government in February 1985.

The federal government responded to the Fraser Committee report by introducing legislation to amend the *Criminal Code* and the customs tariff sections on pornography. It is clear from the reaction to the government's proposals that it will be some time before the law on pornography is settled.

The Law

Currently there are a variety of laws, at the federal, provincial, and municipal levels, aimed at or potentially able to deal with pornography. A brief outline of the various alternative sanctions against pornography is provided here, but, as was previously mentioned, the law on pornography is going through a transition at present.

The Criminal Code

Pornography, or obscenity as it has been traditionally referred to in criminal law, is dealt with in sections 159 to 165 of the *Criminal Code*. Recent proposals to amend the obscenity provisions of the code could dramatically redefine the way the criminal law treats pornography.

If you have, or have seen, material you believe is legally pornographic, contact your local police force to lay a charge. It would be useful if you were familiar with the current definitions of obscenity—or pornography—in the *Criminal Code*, so you can tell the police which section(s) of the code you believe the material contravenes. Give the police all the information you have about the material and explain why you think it ought to be the subject of an investigation and criminal charge. The police and/or a Crown attorney will have to decide whether they believe the material meets the legal definition of pornography.

Often women have been frustrated by the way police and Crown attorneys handle cases dealing with pornography. You have the right to ask for a full explanation of their decision; if you aren't satisfied with the initial decision, ask to speak to their superiors. Remember, however, that the law is constantly evolving, with new judicial interpretations of the *Criminal Code*, so what may seem straightforward to you may, in fact, be ''legally'' something else altogether.

Once a charge has been laid it is very unlikely that you will be involved in the prosecution of the case. Partly because of this lack of citizen involvement in the prosecution of pornography cases, some women believe criminal sanctions are not the best remedy against pornography.

Canada Customs

The vast majority of pornography available in Canada is produced in the United States and Europe. As a result, effective customs regulation of the importation of pornography is viewed by many as a reasonable means of controlling pornography in Canada. While proposed changes to the customs tariff are considerably more detailed than previous customs regulations, their effectiveness, is very much in question.

If you have reason to believe pornography is being imported into the country illegally, or wish further information about customs procedures, contact your closest Customs and Tariff Branch of the Ministry of National Revenue.

Broadcasting

Much concern has been expressed recently about the amount of pornography available on television, particularly with the advent of cable and satellite transmission.

All Canadian broadcasters are subject to the control of the Canadian Radio and Telecommunications Commission (CRTC). This federal government agency is responsible for granting licences to television and radio stations and for ensuring that those stations maintain established standards.

If you are concerned that pornography is being shown on television, put your concerns in writing. Include as much detail as possible about when you saw the material and why you found it unacceptable. Send the letter to the station in question and make copies for the CRTC and Media Watch, a group based in Vancouver that monitors media portrayals of women. Media Watch also supplies complaint forms that may be used in place of letters. If the CRTC receives enough complaints about pornography on the airwaves, it may start to raise the issue at licensing and renewal hearings.

Canada Post

It is illegal to send pornography through the mail. If you receive pornography in the mail, or are aware of pornographic material that is being mailed, contact your local post office and the local police to lay a complaint.

Film and Video Classification

Unlike the previous four methods of limiting pornography, all of which are controlled by the federal government, film and video classification is a provincial responsibility. Some provinces (British Columbia, for example) classify films and videos, while others (Ontario is one) act more directly to censor films. Most provinces have not yet developed a system of control for videotapes. However, videotapes are fast becoming a prime source of pornography in Canada, and governments are looking at means of at least regulating their distribution.

If you are concerned about a film or videotape you've seen or become aware of, contact your provincial classification or censor board (most are connected to a provincial ministry of consumer and commercial relations) for further information about the board's procedures and the method of registering a complaint.

Civil Remedies

Many women concerned about pornography have come to the conclusion that civil remedies are more appropriate and effective in controlling pornography than criminal sanctions.

No existing laws in Canada effectively provide women with the right to claim compensation for damages they have suffered as a result of pornography. In the United States a municipal law that gave women this right was drafted, but it has been ruled unconstitutional and currently lies dormant.

Groups in both the United States and Canada are continuing to examine the possibility of creating legislation or adapting current human rights laws, to enable victims of pornography to claim compensation for infringement of civil rights from those who produce, distribute, and use pornography.

Non-Legal Responses

Women involved in the fight against pornography have come to realize over the years that the law will not and cannot eradicate pornography. However, individuals and groups may take the following steps to limit and attack pornography:

1. Educate yourself and your friends about the issue. The list of resources at the end of this book provides a starting place for further reading.
2. Refuse to have pornography in your home or at your workplace.
3. Refuse to shop at stores that sell pornography. Tell the store owner you will not shop at the store until the pornography is gone. Ask your friends, neighbours, and co-workers to do the same.
4. Join an anti-pornography group or women's centre to work with others concerned about the issue.
5. Let the politicians you elect know that pornography is not acceptable and that their opinion—and actions—on the issue will affect your vote.
6. Let companies who use pornography in their advertising know that you do not find it "amusing" or "entertaining," and that you will not buy their product or service until they stop using women's bodies to sell their product or service.

You can make a difference.

PROSTITUTION

Prostitution has been the focus of much controversy in Canada during the past five years. It has, of course, existed here and elsewhere for much longer.

Like pornography, prostitution is based on the trafficking of women's bodies for men's pleasure. While there has been an apparent increase in the numbers of male prostitutes in the recent past, women continue to be the major victims of prostitution.

Partly because of this connection, the federal government included both prostitution and pornography in the mandate of the Fraser Committee. The committee resisted the rising cry of police, many municipal politicians, and some citizen's groups for stiffer sanctions against street soliciting and suggested that the federal government consider implementing a series of "red light" districts across Canada.

Although the government responded more quickly to the Fraser Committee's recommendations on prostitution than on pornography, the response reflected nothing of the committee's research or thinking.

The Law

While prostitution is, in and of itself, not illegal, soliciting for the purpose of prostitution is. However, the latest amendments to the *Criminal Code* that deal with prostitution (introduced in December 1985) dramatically broadened the definition of what constitutes "soliciting" and "a public place" so as to make it much more difficult to be a street prostitute.

The amendments have come under a lot of criticism both inside and outside the courtroom. Currently there are a number of legal challenges before various courts across the country. The Supreme Court of Canada will have to pass final judgment on the legislation before the constitutionality of the amendments is settled. The appeal process may take several years.

One part of the legislation that received fairly widespread support was the removal of barriers to charging the customers with soliciting, as well as the prostitute.

In addition to criminal sanctions against soliciting, the *Criminal Code* prohibits keeping or being found in a bawdy house and procuring ("pimping"). For further information about criminal procedure if you are charged with any of these offences, please refer to Chapter 18, "Women and Criminal Law."

CHAPTER 18

WOMEN AND CRIMINAL LAW

Katherine Lippel

Katherine Lippel, LL.L., LL.MM., is a professor of law at the University of Quebec in Montreal, as well as a practising lawyer in Montreal. She practises mainly in the field of civil rights, civil disobedience, and social law. Her teaching is concentrated in the fields of social law and the construction of statutes.

WOMEN MAY BE affected by the criminal law as witnesses, as victims, as suspects, or as accused. Many issues specific to women and the criminal law are dealt with elsewhere in this book—women as victims of sexual assault or physical abuse, women charged with prostitution or procuring an abortion, and women and pornography. In this chapter you will learn your legal obligations upon witnessing a crime, your rights as a crime victim, and what you should know if you are suspected or accused of a crime.

LEGAL OBLIGATIONS UPON WITNESSING A CRIME

There is no legal obligation to report a crime to the police, although if you do witness a breach of the peace you are legally justified in interfering to prevent its continuance.

Certain provincial statutes create the legal obligation to provide assistance to a person whose life is in danger. Although this does not imply an obligation to intervene physically, calling the police when one is a witness to an assault on the street is important. You should not ignore the assault by convincing yourself that someone else has called the authorities: we are all morally if not legally responsible for the security of others when we may be in a position to help.

If you are the victim of a crime, calling the authorities may be an essential step if you later wish to claim damages from your insurance company or a criminal-injury compensation fund.

Once you have called the authorities, however, being the witness to a crime has its legal consequences. After you have filed a complaint (as a victim), or after you have told the authorities what you know (as a witness), you will most likely be obliged to testify in court.

In criminal law, once the complaint is lodged, the state, in Canada the Crown, represents the victim. The victim usually does not have her own lawyer and has little or no control of the legal proceedings once the complaint has been laid. Once proceedings have started, the decision to drop the charges is no longer up to the victim, but is in the hands of the Crown. Women who were victims of a crime have recently been imprisoned after they have refused to testify, as we shall see in a later section. The decision to prosecute is thus a serious one, and is perhaps the last decision regarding the crime a woman may make autonomously.

WOMEN AS SUSPECTS

A woman suspected of a crime is in a legal state of limbo: she feels at least a moral constraint to collaborate with the authorities, and often the police officers called upon to investigate an offence will put pressure on the subject of the investigation by implying that collaboration is the best remedy to an uncomfortable situation. Because she has not yet been accused, the suspect is not informed of her legal rights. Women are frequently raised with the desire to please and will often take the line of least resistance and provide information that they are in no way bound to offer. It is thus important to be aware of your rights and obligations.

Identification

In Canadian law there is no legal obligation to carry identification, unless one is driving a motor vehicle. You are not legally obliged to identify yourself to the police unless you are in one of three situations: driving a motor vehicle; under arrest; or when the police have reasonable and probable grounds to believe that you have committed an offence.

It is one thing to define the state of the law, however, and quite another to interpret and apply it in a given situation. If you do refuse to identify yourself and a court later decides that the police officer was in a legal position to request identification, you may be convicted of obstructing a peace officer. This is a potentially indictable offence and is often more serious than the initial suspected infraction. You should always judge the circumstances and use common sense.

A wise course is to ask the officer the reasons for the request of identification: except in a state of emergency (for example, under the invocation of the *War Measures Act* in 1970), police officers are obliged to inform a suspect if they are under arrest or, if not, of the reasons for the request. If no specific reasons are given, the police officer may not detain you and you are free to go without identifying yourself. However the most innocuous reasons (a jaywalking violation, for example) may be used to justify the request. Often it is simpler to comply.

An important exception to this principle arises when you are at the wheel of a motor vehicle. All provincial motor-vehicle legislation provides for the obligation to carry a driver's licence at all times when you are driving a car. There is, however, no obligation for the passengers of a car to identify themselves, unless they are under arrest or there exist reasonable and probable grounds to believe they have committed an offence.

If you are in a situation where you are legally obliged to identify yourself, it is sufficient to provide your name and address. However, even if it is not legally essential, providing other identifying information, if requested (for example, your date of birth or your mother's maiden name), may speed things up and avoid unnecessary friction that can lead to complications. There is no legal obligation to carry an identification card, but if you have one with you, this too may speed up the process. It is unwise to be overly technical regarding your rights unless you have a lot of time on your hands or a specific reason to avoid providing the information.

Search and Seizure

On the Street

In principle no one has the right to search you unless you are under arrest. If a request is made to search you or your belongings (clothes, purse, etc.) you should ask if you are under arrest and the nature of the charges against you. Often, a police officer who sees that you know your rights will back down. There is no reason to go out of your way to provide evidence to an over-zealous peace officer, and you may refuse to be searched if the necessary information about the charges against you has not been provided.

There exist at least two important exceptions to this principle. When the police have reasonable and probable grounds to believe that you are in possession of narcotics or an illegal weapon, they may search you prior to arresting you. Spot checks are, however, illegal. There must be reasonable and probable grounds connecting you to these offences. Without them you are not obliged to comply, although at the time of search the officer is not obliged to specify the reasonable and probable grounds being relied upon. The best advice is always to state that you object when an officer wishes to search you unless you have been informed that you are under arrest and the reasons why. If the officer refuses to provide this information, say you wish to leave. If permission to do so is refused, the wisest course of action is to submit to the search, while continuing to state your objection. Avoid a violent confrontation with the police. Any evidence obtained after an illegal search may be thrown out of court under sections 8 and 24 (2) of the Canadian *Charter of Rights and Freedoms*, if the court feels that admission of the illegally obtained evidence would bring the administration of justice into disrepute. In order to rely on the charter it must be clear that you were searched against your will: voluntary compliance with an illegal search may be a reason to admit the evidence thus obtained. If there are witnesses to your objections, these people may be useful in court, so you should try to obtain their names and addresses.

In Your Car

Driving an automobile is considered to be a privilege in Canadian law, and for this reason police powers are broader when it comes to use of an automobile. As we have already seen, a police officer may ask to see the driver's licence, even if the driver has not committed an offence. Stopping a driver does not, however, justify searching a car. Normally an automobile cannot legally be searched without a search warrant, although customs officials have special powers that permit them to do so. Looking over the visible contents of a car does not constitute a search requiring a warrant, but opening a glove compartment or a trunk normally requires a warrant. Drivers' obligations to submit to breathalyser tests will be dealt with in the section on impaired driving.

In Your Home

Although the adage "A woman's home is her castle" is not as prevalent in the case law as that pertaining to men, the principle holds that any person may refuse police officers access to her home unless the officers are in possession of a valid search warrant. If police or any other public officials wish to enter your home, ask them to show you a search warrant. If you invite them in without asking questions, evidence they may thus obtain may be used against you. If you object to their entry and they persist, take note of their names and badge numbers but do not resist: if the search is subsequently shown to be illegal, the evidence obtained may be excluded. If you resist and the search is subsequently judged to be legal, you may be convicted for obstruction and perhaps injured in the process. If no warrant is shown, refuse access politely. If the police do not comply, try to contact a lawyer and obtain witnesses.

A search warrant should specify the things to be searched for and the offence in respect of which the search is made. It should also specify the address of the premises to be searched, and the original should bear the signature of a justice of the peace. In exceptional circumstances an authorization to search may be obtained by telephone. If so, an unsigned copy of the warrant to search must be given to the occupant prior to entering the premises. The occupant may subsequently obtain a copy of the report of the search from the court clerk, whose address should appear on the search warrant.

The fundamental principle is thus that no search of a home should take place without a valid search warrant. The same principle applies to any premises, although there are more exceptions when the premises are not used as a dwelling house.

For instance, if police have reasonable and probable grounds to believe that narcotics are present in a place other than a dwelling house, they may enter and search the premises without a warrant. However, by recent amendment to the *Narcotics Control Act*, a search warrant is necessary when the place to be searched is a person's home.

Only in very exceptional circumstances will a search of a home without a warrant be justified, as in the case of "hot pursuit" of the accused by the police. However, if the police are voluntarily invited in, it is difficult to subsequently claim that they should have had a warrant. A polite question at the door may often avoid a complex legal battle later.

Under the *Criminal Code*, objects found during a search based on a valid warrant may be seized by the peace officers if they are mentioned in the warrant or if the police officers have reasonable grounds to believe they have been obtained or used in the commission of an offence. They may be restored at a later date.

Certain special legislation has been used in recent years to authorize exceptional powers to search, either because the statute specifically provides for the search, as in the case of the *Income Tax Act*, or because the statute provides for overly broad powers that may lead to abuse, as in the case of certain welfare legislation. Welfare officials have been known to enter a recipient's home without a warrant and to search sometimes among the most personal belongings. With the adoption of the *Charter of Rights and Freedoms*, most notably section 8, which protects everyone from unreasonable search or seizure, the validity of these practices is highly debatable, and certain provisions of the *Income Tax Act* have already been declared to be unconstitutional. Welfare recipients in particular tend to submit to breaches of their fundamental rights for fear of losing social assistance benefits. If the *Constitution Act, 1982* is to be of any value, people must stand up for their rights and be supported by the community when they do so.

Right to Counsel

Any person arrested or detained has the constitutional right to retain and instruct counsel without delay, and to be informed of that right. Statements made after this right has been breached may, in certain circumstances, be held to be inadmissible in evidence.

The right to counsel does not necessarily imply the right to free counsel when arrested or detained, and provincial legal-aid programs vary from one province to another. It is wise to check with your local legal-aid services about conditions of admissibility. It is also wise to know the name of a reliable lawyer who may be available in case of emergency.

If the police tell you you are not free to go, you have the right to be informed of their reasons for detaining you, and you have the right to counsel without delay. It is not necessary to be under arrest in order to have the right to counsel; it is sufficient to be detained. Not informing you of your right to counsel is in itself a breach of your rights.

Rights Upon Arrest

The police have the right to arrest you as a suspect if they have a warrant for your arrest. If they claim to have one, you may ask to see it; but if they don't produce the document, you would never-theless be unwise to resist the arrest, as they are not obliged to have a copy with them.

The police may also arrest a person without a warrant under certain circumstances. They may arrest anyone they catch in the act of committing any criminal offence. If they have reasonable and prob-able grounds to believe you have committed or are about to commit an indictable offence (a serious offence under Canadian law) they may make an arrest without a warrant even if they haven't found you actually committing the crime.

The *Criminal Code* also provides for citizen arrests in certain well-defined situations. Thus, if a citizen finds a suspect in the act of committing an indictable offence, or has reason to believe the suspect has committed an offence and is escaping from someone authorized to make an arrest, the citizen may make an arrest without a warrant and deliver the suspect to the police.

When property offences are involved, a citizen's power to arrest is even broader. Thus the owner, or the agent of the owner, of the property may arrest a suspect found committing any criminal offence in relation to the owner's property. This is the basis of the common practice of using security guards in stores to prevent shoplifting. In order for the arrest to be valid, the store's agent must have actually seen you in the act of committing the offence. The store's agent may not search you, but may detain you until the police arrive.

At the time of arrest you have the right to be promptly informed of the reasons for your arrest; the provisions regarding the right to counsel also apply. If asked, give your name and address, but do not make any other statement without consulting counsel. Any statement you make whether orally or in writing may be used against you, and often seemingly innocuous information may later prove to be incriminating.

If you are charged with a minor offence, the police will often let you go without taking you to the station if they are assured of your identity and your address. Showing an identification card at this stage may save you a lot of time. The police may release you if you sign a document entitled "promise to appear." You should sign this document, as it will not be used against you and it will facilitate your release. If the police decide to take you to the station (a usual occurrence) do not resist. In a subsequent section we will see what to expect when a suspect becomes an accused.

Recourse if Your Rights Have Been Violated

If you have been unlawfully detained, subjected to an illegal search, deprived of the right to counsel, or beaten and abused by the authorities, several legal remedies are available.

Often the simplest remedy to a breach of constitutional rights is a request that the evidence illegally obtained be declared inadmissible. Canadians often base their legal knowledge on American police dramas and thus rely on many legal myths that are inapplicable in a Canadian context.

The right to exclusion of evidence is a common example. In *Hill Street Blues*, defence attorney Joyce Davenport says the magic word "Miranda" and the case is thrown out of court. In Canada, life's not that simple. Don't feel you may say anything you want with impunity because your rights have been breached. Canadian judges may exclude evidence if it has been obtained in violation of charter rights, but they will do so only if they find that the admission of the illegally obtained evidence "would bring the administration of justice into disrepute." It's always preferable to be silent than sorry. Nevertheless exclusion of evidence is one remedy provided for by the *Charter of Rights and Freedoms*.

Other remedies include non-criminal law suits for damages resulting from the violation of civil rights. It is important to note the names and badge numbers of the officers involved. Some provinces have police commissions before which complaints may be brought against police officers free of charge. These proceedings are more of a disciplinary nature and, if successful, provide the victim of abuse of police powers with moral rather than economic satisfaction. In cases of very serious abuse—for instance, if the victim has been beaten by the police—criminal proceedings against the police should be considered.

If you feel your rights as a suspect have been violated, perhaps the best course of action is to consult a lawyer or your local civil liberties association for advice.

WOMEN AS ACCUSED

Some Prevalent Offences

Female offenders make up a very small percentage of the criminal population. Women tend to commit far fewer crimes than men, and the crimes they do commit are generally of a far less violent nature. For example, in 1980, of all women in Canada convicted of federal offences, including offences in the *Criminal Code*, 55.3 percent were convicted of non-violent crimes against property (theft, fraud, etc.), and 20.4 percent were convicted of driving while under the influence of alcohol; only 6 percent were convicted of violent crimes, including murder or attempted murder, criminal negligence, assault, armed robbery, breaking and entering, and possession of a deadly weapon.

The following discussion examines some prevalent offences that, although most often committed by men, make up the majority of the offences for which women are convicted.

Impaired Driving and Related Offences

Both federal and provincial legislation provide for offences relating to driving an automobile while under the influence of alcohol, medication, or other drugs. Although provincial legislation may vary from province to province, the *Criminal Code* is the same across Canada. Often the Crown prosecuting attorney will have the choice of proceeding under the *Criminal Code* or under provincial legislation. A *Criminal Code* conviction will lead to a criminal record. However, it is often easier to obtain a conviction under the provincial statute, and provincial legislation often provides for demerit points or other means of suspending a driver's licence. Information as to specific provincial offences may be obtained from your local motor-vehicles bureau. We shall here examine only the provisions of the *Criminal Code*.

Since December 4, 1985, Canada has cracked down on impaired driving, particularly in cases in which injury or death has occurred as a result of an accident involving an impaired driver.

You may be convicted of impaired driving either because the alcohol level found in your blood is greater than eighty milligrams of alcohol in one hundred millilitres of blood (commonly known as "over-80") or because your ability to operate a motor vehicle is impaired by alcohol or a drug. These provisions also apply to the driving of an aircraft or a boat.

In all these cases, regardless of whether you have been involved in an accident, conviction implies a minimum sentence of a $300 fine for a first offence, imprisonment for a minimum of fourteen days for a second offence, and imprisonment for a minimum of ninety days upon a third or subsequent conviction. If injury occurs to another person as a result of your impaired driving, you are liable to a maximum term of imprisonment of ten years. If death results, you are liable to a maximum of fourteen years' imprisonment.

Over and above these sentences, conviction leads to the suspension of your licence for a minimum of three months for a first offence, six months for a second offence, and one year for all subsequent offences. The judge has discretion to suspend a licence for up to three years as of the first conviction. Driving while disqualified is in itself a criminal offence.

As we have seen in an earlier section, driving an automobile is considered a privilege by the courts and, as such, is subject to far broader police scrutiny than other daily activities. Under the new legislation, a police officer may request any person having the care or control of an automobile, whether the vehicle is in motion or not, to submit to a breathalyser test if the police officer "reasonably suspects" that the person has alcohol in his or her body. It is not necessary for the police officer to have reason to believe that the suspect has consumed an excessive amount of alcohol.

Breath samples may be requested up to two hours after you have had the care and control of an automobile. It is not necessary for the police to find you behind the wheel; with reasonable and probable grounds an officer may request a breath sample within two hours after you have ceased to drive. Failure to comply with a request to submit to a breathalyser test is in itself a criminal offence.

In exceptional circumstances a police officer may request a blood sample. Such samples may be taken only under the supervision of a qualified medical practitioner. If you are unconscious, a warrant must also be obtained. Again, failure to comply with a valid request for a blood sample may lead to conviction for an additional criminal offence. Blood samples may be used to measure both alcohol and drug content.

The simple fact that you are behind the wheel and intoxicated may be sufficient to obtain a conviction, even if you never put the vehicle in motion. "Sleeping it off" in the front seat of a car may in itself lead to conviction.

The *Criminal Code* provides for other driving offences not necessarily related to alcohol or drug consumption. These include dangerous driving, criminal negligence, and failure to remain at the scene of an accident. The latter offence is prevalent and deserves our attention.

If you are involved in an accident, no matter how minor, you have the legal obligation to provide your name and address. If no one else is there (for example, if you collide with a parked car), you should leave the information in a visible place, if possible under the windshield wiper of the damaged car. If a person appears to be injured or requires assistance it is your duty to offer assistance. Failure to comply with these obligations constitutes a criminal offence punishable by a maximum of two years' imprisonment. A judge may also suspend your driver's licence for up to three years.

As we have already mentioned, provincial legislation regulating the use of motor vehicles provides for a host of infractions that we have not mentioned here. Often women are imprisoned for "crimes" as banal as unpaid parking or speeding tickets. Unpaid tickets eventually lead to arrest warrants. If you feel you may be the object of such a warrant it is worth your while to consult a lawyer to inquire about the possibility of paying off your tickets by doing community work. The possibilities vary from province to province; your local legal-aid bureau is perhaps the best equipped to answer your questions.

Drug-Related Offences

Although drug-related convictions of women are far less prevalent than those related to driving offences, they can be among the most severely punished infractions committed by women.

Two statutes govern the use and sale of illegal drugs: the *Food and Drugs Act* and the *Narcotics Control Act.*

Since drug abuse has been perceived by Parliament as a major social problem, these statutes provide for several extraordinary measures, particularly in relation to search and seizure and prosecution of those accused of trafficking in illicit substances. Since the adoption of the *Charter of Rights and Freedoms*, several sections providing for exorbitant police powers have been amended, while others have been struck down by the courts as conflicting with the presumption of innocence guaranteed in the charter.

However, in spite of much public pressure and various recommendations to government, several anachronisms have still not been corrected. Simple possession or growing of marijuana, for example, is still a criminal offence punishable by a maximum of seven years' imprisonment; by contrast, simple possession of LSD or MDA is punishable by a maximum of three years' imprisonment.

In practice the courts have become much more realistic than the statutes they apply, and it is rare to find an accused imprisoned for simple possession of marijuana or hashish. Even possession of other narcotics, (for example, cocaine) is often punished by a fine for a first offence.

Possession of any prohibited drug for purposes of trafficking is a far more serious offence. In the case of narcotics, trafficking and possession for the purpose of trafficking are punishable by life imprisonment. In practice, of course, the maximum sentence is rarely applied, but it is far from uncommon for a first offender to be imprisoned for a trafficking offence. Trafficking is defined very broadly and includes: ''to manufacture, sell, give, administer, transport, send, deliver or distribute or to offer to do'' any of the above.

Thus the legislation is so broad as to include the giving of a "joint" of marijuana to a neighbour. Broad police powers exist, and police inquiries should not be taken lightly. We refer you to the discussion of the rights of the suspect above, particularly regarding police powers of search and seizure.

Aside from murder, the most severely punished crime in Canadian law is that of importing or exporting narcotics; offences are punishable by a *minimum* sentence of seven years' imprisonment; the *maximum* sentence is imprisonment for life. Technically, taking even a small amount of marijuana across a Canadian border constitutes importing or exporting a narcotic, although prosecutorial discretion permits the authorities to lay less important charges if they choose. Transporting any narcotics across the border should be avoided.

Women are often chosen as runners or carriers, sometimes without their knowledge, to bring suitcases containing illegal drugs into Canada. If you were paid an important amount by an unknown person, it is no defence to say that you didn't know the contents of the suitcase. "No questions asked" is known in law as "wilful blindness" and will not absolve you from legal guilt.

Customs officials have very broad powers of search and seizure, including the power to perform body searches. Although some of these powers are presently being contested before the courts on the basis of the *Charter of Rights and Freedoms* it is unwise to count on legal technicalities when the consequences of a conviction are so great.

In all situations in which you are detained, particularly in relation to drugs, it is best to contact counsel immediately and to remain silent until counsel is present.

Shoplifting and Related Offences

As we have seen, non-violent theft and such related offences as fraud, the use of stolen credit cards, false pretences, and possession of stolen property are among the most common offences for which women are convicted.

What is commonly known as shoplifting is in fact theft under the *Criminal Code*, and a person convicted of shoplifting acquires a criminal record and will most likely be fined for a first offence. The courts and the department stores have cracked down on shoplifting in recent years, and many stores have hired specialized personnel to deal with shoplifters. The powers of these people have been dealt with in the section relating to the rights of a suspect.

Price-switching (changing the price tag on merchandise in order to pay less) is also a criminal offence and will be punished in the same manner as shoplifting.

Paying by cheque when you know the cheque will not be honoured is also subject to criminal prosecution.

Shoplifting is so prevalent that the courts are overloaded with such cases, and it is often extremely difficult to obtain an acquittal on a shoplifting charge; the courts have great difficulty in believing the non-payment was the result of an oversight.

Possibly because of the economic recession of recent years, many people with previously clean records have been prosecuted for stealing food, children's clothing, or even gas and electricity for heating purposes.

In Montreal in the late 1970s hundreds of welfare recipients were charged with theft under the *Criminal Code* for having consumed gas or electricity for heating purposes after the public utility had interrupted the service during the winter for non-payment. Many of the accused were single mothers who feared for the health of their children. Because of the large number of accused, and the collaboration of the accused among themselves, the majority of the charges were dropped. Sometimes only a collective defence can counterbalance the power of the Crown or the gas and electric companies.

Individuals caught stealing food or clothing are in a far worse negotiating position than utilities offenders. Many are convicted and fined, and the fine often aggravates the economic burden that caused them to shoplift in the first place. In response to this problem, a report was recently prepared for the Canadian Council on the Status of Women. The report, *A Feminist Review of the Criminal Code*, recommends that the defence of necessity be recognized as applicable to charges regarding non-violent obtaining of property for the purposes of feeding, clothing, or housing oneself or one's children.

For the moment the law does not recognize such a defence, and many women who are unable to pay the fine eventually end up in prison.

Particular provisions exist in the *Criminal Code* regarding theft between husband and wife. As long as the couple live together, the taking of each other's property does not constitute theft. If the spouses live apart, or if one is in the process of "deserting" the other, knowingly taking the other's property may constitute theft.

In practice, in all circumstances, the criminal courts seem extremely reluctant to convict a spouse, even a divorced spouse, who has taken property of the other without his or her consent. This is particularly so when no civil-court judgment has divided the matrimonial property.

Once a couple lives separate and apart, or if they were never married, it is a far preferable course of action to clarify the property situation in Family Court rather than to try to take property of your spouse against his will. Although criminal conviction is unlikely, prosecution is less so, and other remedies often provide the easiest solution.

Abuse of chequing, credit card, or other credit privileges, particularly if it is regular or systematic, is quite severely punished by the courts. Almost anyone can mistakenly pay an account with a cheque that is subsequently returned for insufficient funds. But when the cheque is refused because the account is closed, or when a pattern of bad chequing is discovered and it is unlikely that the person signing the cheques believed the cheque would be honoured, then the *Criminal Code* will be applied, with imprisonment for fraud or false pretences as a possible result.

These more systematic crimes are regarded with little sympathy by the courts; although less severely punished than violent crimes, they may quickly lead to imprisonment, which in turn often leads to a cycle of crime that is difficult to break.

Offences Relating to Social Programs

The majority of welfare recipients in Canada are women, who are often the heads of single-parent families. Welfare legislation varies from province to province and is often extremely complex, and in most cases the rates of payment are below the poverty line. Not surprisingly, recipients of welfare often have difficulty surviving on their benefits and some may do odd jobs—babysitting, for example—to help pay the bills.

In most provinces, doing undeclared odd jobs while on welfare is contrary to the provincial public-assistance legislation and may constitute an offence. A conviction under a provincial statute does not imply a criminal record. Conviction usually implies that the recipient must reimburse part or all of the welfare payments received, and must pay a fine.

In recent years the various provincial governments have been drawing a great deal of public attention to the issue of welfare "fraud," going so far as to promise, in some provinces, bounty payments for information leading to the discovery of beneficiaries receiving more than their due. The public is left with the impression of vast fraudulent schemes by welfare recipients who drive two cars, go to Florida for the winter, and draw several welfare cheques under different names.

In fact real fraud, involving the receipt of welfare money by people who are not in need, is extremely rare. Public opinion is influenced by government publicity campaigns about fraud; yet the real targets of these campaigns are those doing the odd babysitting job, or women who have boyfriends who, the state feels, should provide support.

As the section on the rights of suspects mentioned, some welfare statutes give extraordinary powers to investigators. Welfare recipients are often the most vulnerable to such invasions of privacy, as they are totally dependent on their welfare cheques and cannot risk standing up for their rights for fear of losing, even temporarily, their welfare payments. In Quebec in recent months, welfare inspectors have been conducting a campaign of terror against recipients, appearing without warning at a recipient's home, searching the home, and even, in some cases, going so far as to examine the bedsheets.

Making untrue statements to obtain welfare is, of course, illegal and may result in prosecution. Sometimes welfare investigators will threaten to prosecute the recipient for fraud under the *Criminal Code*, unless the recipient co-operates fully with the investigation. If you are being investigated by welfare inspectors, or if you are unsure of your legal rights, most provinces have welfare-rights groups that can provide information and assistance. Legal-aid lawyers may also be available for help, depending on the relevant provincial legislation.

It is relatively rare for welfare recipients to be charged with fraud under the *Criminal Code* after having obtained more than their due. If the Crown chooses to lay charges under the *Criminal Code*, judges tend to punish welfare fraud quite severely, often by a term of imprisonment. If charges are laid only under the provincial statute, treatment will be far more lenient.

In a recent case in Prince Edward Island, it was decided that criminal prosecution for fraud was not open to the Crown when the provincial statute covered an offence relating to the same behaviour. This is a new development in the case law. It is wise to obtain legal assistance if you are charged, so as to clarify your position before answering the charges.

To a lesser extent the same principles apply in the case of unemployment insurance. Making false claims constitutes an offence that may lead to a criminal record. However prosecution is almost always based on the *Unemployment Insurance Act*, and the offence is usually punished by a fine proportional to the number of weeks benefits were illegally received. Working without declaring one's earnings will result in prosecution under the *Unemployment Insurance Act*. However, collecting unemployment insurance while you are not available for work is regarded as a less serious offence and at worst will lead to the suspension of benefits.

Non-payment of income tax may lead to audits and inquiries by the Minister of Revenue. Often, if you file an income-tax statement, even an incomplete one, you can prevent prosecution, as long as you make it clear that you are lacking the information and not intentionally deceiving the tax department.

If you completely neglect to file income-tax returns, you are liable to prosecution. It is extremely rare for charges to be laid under the *Criminal Code* in income-tax matters, but the *Income Tax Act* itself contains broad powers and stiff fines. It would be foolish to take the attitude that, "if I just ignore them, they'll go away."

Protest Offences
From fighting the proliferation of nuclear arms to lobbying for day-care centres, women have become more and more active in demonstrations in recent years.

Theoretically, peaceful demonstrations are not illegal, although since the adoption of the *Charter of Rights and Freedoms*, the Supreme Court of Canada has yet to confirm that the right to demonstrate is included in the notion of freedom of speech.

Demonstrations may be regulated by provincial or municipal controls that vary from province to province, and even from city to city. From trespass legislation to zoning by-laws, literally hundreds of local rules may exist in each province, and it is wise to find out about your local situation before you organize a demonstration. One thing is certain, however: conviction under provincial or municipal legislation does not lead to a criminal record, as only federal offences are tabulated under the *Criminal Records Act*.

Protest may sometimes lead to charges under the *Criminal Code*. Anti-pornography activists have been convicted on mischief charges in recent years for doing damage to the windows of sex shops or to film posters they deemed to be offensive. Although the Crown has discretion in the mode of prosecution, charges are usually laid by summary conviction (a less serious means of prosecution, as compared with prosecution by indictment); the accused, if convicted, are often sentenced to reimburse the damages, but are rarely jailed unless they refuse to reimburse.

Sit-ins and occupations may also lead to mischief charges, as in the case of a recent occupation of a Bata shoe store in protest against Bata's investments in South Africa. Other charges may include obstruction of a police officer, or disturbing the peace (particularly if chanting is involved). Occasionally assault charges may be laid, if the protesters are considered to be trespassing. All these offences, with the exception of disturbing the peace, may be prosecuted either by indictment or by summary conviction. Disturbing the peace is a purely summary conviction offence. Usually protest charges are laid by summary conviction. The main purpose of the police is usually to find a legal justification for removing the protesters; once this has been done it is rare for the criminal law to be used in a vindictive manner, and offenders are most often fined or given probation or absolute discharges.

Immigrants without Canadian citizenship and minors are particularly vulnerable to prosecution and should avoid becoming involved in borderline protest situations unless they clearly understand the consequences.

Political defences based on necessity or international law that have sometimes been successful in the United States and Europe have been less so in Canada. It is unwise to undertake borderline protest activities, unless you are willing to accept the legal consequences of an arrest and conviction.

Criminal Procedure: From Arrest to Sentence

Arrest and Detention

We have seen in an earlier section the rights of the suspect. What are your rights once you have been arrested?

You have, first, the right to be informed promptly of the reasons for your arrest and of the specific charges against you. You should be informed without delay of your right to counsel and provided with reasonable means for exercising that right—at the very least, with access to a phone book and a telephone once you have arrived at the police station. The right to a lawyer should always be mentioned prior to questioning.

If the offence you are charged with is not very serious the police officer responsible for your case may likely release you once your identity has been established and photographs and fingerprints taken. You may speed up this process by providing an identification card and answering reasonable questions about your identity: name, address, date of birth, mother's maiden name. You are in no way obliged to answer questions about your way of life, whom you live with, or who your employer is if you choose not to divulge this information. You certainly should not answer any questions relating to the offence for which you are charged, unless you have been advised to do so by counsel. Any statement you make, orally or in writing, may be used against you. The best policy is to say as little as possible, apart from providing the necessary identification-related information.

If you are charged with a criminal offence that is liable to prosecution by indictment you must consent to be fingerprinted and photographed if requested.

If there is no warrant for your arrest, you are properly identified, you have no pending charges, and there is no reason to believe you will abscond before your trial, you will most likely be released from the police station unless you are charged with a very serious offence. You will be asked to sign a form entitled "promise to appear," by which you undertake to appear in court, and perhaps for identification purposes, on the appointed dates. Subsequent failure to appear is itself a criminal offence.

If you are not released from the police station, you should normally be brought before a judge within twenty-four hours of your arrest. If you are thus detained, be sure to contact counsel for your court appearance.

Preliminary Proceedings in Court

The first time you appear in court after an arrest is called the appearance. You will be called upon to plead guilty or not guilty. Ideally you should choose your plea on the advice of counsel, and should inquire as to your rights to legal aid if you do not have the means to pay a lawyer.

If you plead guilty at the appearance there will be no trial, and you will be sentenced immediately. If you plead not guilty, a subsequent date will be set, for trial if you are charged with a minor offence, or for a preliminary inquiry if you are charged with an indictable offence that may be tried by a jury. If you plead not guilty you may be asked to select whether you want to be tried by a judge and jury, a judge alone, or a magistrate. If you have not yet consulted counsel, always opt for trial by judge and jury: you may reopt later if necessary.

If you are detained at the time of your appearance and Crown counsel objects to your being freed, you have the right to a bail hearing. At this stage you should definitely be represented by counsel.

The next step is either the preliminary inquiry, in which the court hears evidence to ascertain if the Crown has sufficient evidence to bring you to trial, or the trial itself if you are charged with a more minor offence. It is extremely rare for the accused to testify at a preliminary inquiry, but other witnesses will likely be heard at this time.

Trial Proceedings

A criminal trial is often a stressful experience, whether you are the victim, the accused, or just a simple witness. An understanding of how a trial unfolds can demystify the judicial process.

The accused has the right to remain present throughout the trial. The victim and the other witnesses may be obliged to leave the courtroom until they are called to testify. The accused has the right to an interpreter if she or he does not understand the language in which the proceedings are taking place.

In all criminal trials the Crown prosecutor must prove the accused to be guilty of the offence charged beyond a reasonable doubt. Thus it is the Crown attorney who will call the first witnesses.

After each witness testifies for the Crown, the defence attorney may cross-examine the witness. The judge may also wish to ask questions.

When all Crown witnesses have testified, the defence may call witnesses who will in turn be questioned by defence counsel and then cross-examined by Crown counsel. The accused is never obliged to testify, but may do so if, in consultation with defence counsel, it seems preferable.

1. *Duty to testify.* All persons present in court, aside from the accused, may be called to testify. If you are subpoenaed as a witness, you must come to court; failure to do so may result in a warrant for arrest and subsequent detention. If you are present and refuse to testify, you may be charged with contempt of court and imprisoned by order of the presiding judge. In recent years two cases of contempt of court convictions against women have come to public attention.

In the first case, an Ontario rape victim refused to testify for fear of reprisals. The recalcitrant witness was jailed for seven days. In a second case, several months later, an Ontario woman was sentenced to three months in jail for refusing to testify at the trial, on charges of assaulting her, of the father of her child. Although her period of imprisonment was reduced on appeal, her conviction provoked much public outrage and prompted many citizens to call for legislative review of the judicial powers covering contempt of court proceedings against recalcitrant witnesses.

Spouses, if legally married, may not be forced to testify against each other, except regarding certain specific charges provided for in the *Canada Evidence Act*. In no case may a spouse be forced to divulge a communication received from the other spouse during their marriage. Non-married couples have no such protection. Historically the common law holds that husband and wife are one person: as one cannot be forced to testify against oneself, one cannot be forced to testify against one's spouse. The exemption does not apply to many offences, and legislation is pending that will no doubt change a number of elements of this question.

2. *Testifying in court*. When it is your turn to testify you will be called to the witness stand, sworn in, and asked to identify yourself. It is important to speak up so that the judge, jury, and counsel can hear you clearly.

You will first be questioned by the lawyer for the side that sent you the subpoena. This is called direct examination, and the lawyer will ask you broad questions that do not suggest an answer. You should listen carefully to the questions and answer to the best of your knowledge. If you do not understand a question, say so. It is normal to feel nervous; take your time when answering and don't allow yourself to get confused. If you can't remember or don't know the answer to a question, say so. The most important aspect of your testimony is your credibility; guessing answers is both irresponsible and damaging to your testimony, as one unsound answer may tarnish the credibility of your answers to all the other questions. Answer the questions put to you as completely as possible, in your own words. Do not volunteer unsolicited information; answer only the questions as asked. Often it is possible to see the lawyer who has subpoenaed you prior to the hearing to review your testimony in order to understand more clearly how the hearing will unfold. In general you may only testify as to things of which you have personal knowledge: things you saw, heard, or experienced yourself. If an objection is made to a question asked of you, collect your thoughts and wait for the judge's decision as to the objection. If told by the judge to answer, you must do so. Once direct examination is completed you will be cross-examined by the attorney of the opposing side. In cross-examination, questions may be leading, that is, they may suggest a particular answer. Often the attorney will try to confuse you. Take your time and answer the questions truthfully and patiently. Even if the questions are unpleasant or intimidating, be patient and answer them to the best of your ability. A sarcastic, impolite cross-examiner will often damage his or her own case. If cross-examination becomes abusive your attorney will object, and the judge may intervene.

After cross-examination you may be asked questions by the judge, occasionally you may be re-examined on specific points by the lawyer who subpoenaed you.

Once the evidence is completed, each lawyer will sum up the arguments about the facts and the state of the law. The judge or jury will then render a decision: sometimes immediately, sometimes days, weeks, or even months later. If you are acquitted the story is over. If you are convicted you will be sentenced.

3. *Sentencing.* The *Criminal Code* provides for a wide range of sentences, the most lenient being an absolute discharge (which implies that you are deemed not to have been convicted of an offence), the most severe being life imprisonment with no possibility of parole before twenty-five years, the mandatory sentence in the case of first-degree murder. Statistically, most women convicted of a criminal offence are usually sentenced to a fine. A delay to pay may be requested and, in extenuating circumstances, the delay may be extended by a judge upon request. Non-payment of a fine usually leads to imprisonment.

Often judges will suspend a sentence, giving probation conditions to the accused, who must keep the peace and follow the conditions of probation for the period prescribed by the judge.

More serious offences, such as drug trafficking, fraud, or theft of a considerable amount, or a second conviction on an impaired-driving charge, will likely be punished by imprisonment. Canada's women's prisons are mostly populated by two types of offenders: women condemned to pay a fine who haven't got the money to pay; and those sentenced to imprisonment for the crimes for which they were convicted. All are found in the same prison system, and all are subjected to the same conditions.

Only one federal penitentiary houses women: Kingston penitentiary in Ontario. Normally all people having prison sentences of more than two years serve their sentences in a federal penitentiary, where access to instruction and job training is supposedly available. Women offenders suffer greatly under this system. Until recently, all women offenders sentenced to more than two years were sent to Kingston, whether their home was in Newfoundland, British Columbia, or Quebec. This exile often ruptured all family ties, preventing the women from seeing their children and often depriving them of all visits; male prisoners, by contrast, could be housed in many penitentiaries across Canada.

In recent years federal-provincial agreements have been undertaken to permit long-term female offenders to be imprisoned in the provincial institutions in their regions. These undertakings have the advantage of keeping the women closer to their families. However, provincial prisons are not adequately equipped for long-term inmates: training programs are often non-existent, or at best far inferior to those available to male long-term offenders. The Quebec Human Rights Commission recently found that the conditions in Tanguay prison for women were far inferior to those in comparable institutions for men, and were, therefore, discriminatory.

A court order to do community work may sometimes be substituted for a prison sentence. Whenever possible this seems to be a preferable solution, for the accused, for her children, and for the community.

4. *After the expiry of the sentence.* All convictions under the *Criminal Code* lead to a criminal record that may render finding and keeping a job more difficult, particularly for women, who often hold jobs that involve trust (bank tellers or court clerks, for example). Even though you are not deemed to have been convicted of an offence if you receive a discharge by the judge, the fact that you have received a discharge will appear on your record.

It is possible to have a criminal record "erased," in a manner of speaking. One, two, or five years after the expiry of the sentence, including all periods of probation, a pardon may be requested by filling in the appropriate forms at the National Parole Board. The pardon is discretionary, and if it is refused you have no recourse. It costs nothing to request it and, if granted, it may help you avoid many unseen problems in the future (for example, with regard to credit checks and job evaluations). A pardon may be revoked by the Governor-in-Council if you are subsequently convicted or if you are found to be "no longer of good conduct."

CHAPTER 19

ADVOCACY: GETTING WHAT YOU WANT FROM GOVERNMENT

Heather Robertson

Heather Robertson is a lawyer in private practice with the firm of Gowling and Henderson in Toronto, where she works mainly in the area of family law. After graduating from the University of Toronto and Osgoode Hall Law School, she practised law on her own for a number of years. She has been active in a number of community associations, particularly in the areas of domestic welfare and legal aid.

MANY PEOPLE EQUATE the terms "advocate" and "advocacy" with lawyers and the legal profession. However, the words have another much broader connotation. The word "advocacy" may be used to describe the promotion of one's individual interests or needs or those of a particular group supporting a cause or issue.

We are all advocates for ourselves and others at some time. If you seek compensation from your drycleaner for damaged clothes, canvass for charity, or join a ratepayers group to oppose development in your neighbourhood you are acting as an advocate in different ways. Some people, such as community legal workers in legal-aid clinics, work directly as advocates for the interests of others.

Advocacy in this broader sense of the word may be undertaken by anyone. You do not need to be a lawyer or have a college degree in any particular field to be an effective advocate. However, it might help to know some of the skills and problem-solving techniques that lawyers and other professionals use in advocating on behalf of their clients. Many of the strategies discussed here will seem self-evident. There is no magic formula that guarantees success but, after reading this chapter, you will be better equipped and prepared for the battle than before.

In our increasingly complex society, government plays an ever-expanding role in our lives. In many cases, this leads to conflict. Whether you are defending yourself against the perceived intrusiveness of government (for example, in dealing with the police, Revenue Canada, or a children's aid society), or asserting your entitlement to rights and privileges (for example, in dealing with welfare and housing authorities), the techniques set out in this chapter should prove helpful.

These techniques may also be useful in confronting problems of other types—with consumer or tenant complaints, for example.

The focus of this chapter will be on dealing with conflicts with government in certain specific areas.

HOW TO FIGHT CITY HALL AND WIN

Dealing with any hierarchical or bureaucratic body, whether it is a government agency or large corporation, presents special difficulties. Two key words, "access" and "accountability," sum up what you are seeking in taking on such a body. You want to gain access to the proper department, agency, or process for resolving your dispute or affecting political change. And you want the proper body to be accountable—to take appropriate responsibility for dealing with the problem. In other words, you want to make the appropriate parties understand it is their problem not yours and deal with it accordingly.

Do not be misled by the apparent simplicity of the two concepts. Other skills are needed before the goals of "access" and "accountability" can be achieved.

Techniques for Dealing with the Bureaucracy

It is a disappointing fact of life that bureaucratic structures do not move quickly. To a certain extent an effective advocate can hope to make the bureaucracy relatively more responsive. But it is probably unrealistic to expect to make it move quickly in all cases.

One of the first qualities you will need, therefore, is appropriate patience. The qualifying term "appropriate" is used so that your patience will not be mistaken for doormat-like acquiescence.

There are appropriate times not to be patient, however, which leads us to the second important quality: assertiveness. The word "assertive" suggests firmness, persistence, and determination, without hysteria or abusiveness. The old adage about catching more flies with honey than vinegar is partly true. The people who work for government agencies are human. They are caught in the bureaucratic web as much as we are. They are less likely to be helpful to an applicant who is abusive, disorganized, confused, or angry at them personally. There is, therefore, an appropriate time and place to be forceful—for example, if a commitment has not been honoured by the person who promised it. This suggests a third important quality: the ability to pick your spots.

The maxim, "It's a long road that has no turning" is also apt. If you are lobbying the government for change in a particular area, you will very likely be dealing with the same bureaucrats and policy advisers over an extended period of time. It will not serve your purpose to alienate them at the outset of your campaign.

A fourth quality you will need is commitment. As an effective advocate for yourself or someone else, or for political change, you will want to minimize the delays inherent in bureaucratic systems. You will also want to maintain as much control over the process as possible. To this end you must be prepared to follow-up promises made by the government, to enforce accountability. You must also be prepared to be imaginative and innovative at appropriate times so as not to relinquish control of the issue to the other side. All of this takes time and energy. Your commitment to your issue will go a long way towards determining your results.

Before we examine "access" and "accountability" more thoroughly, we should look at two skills you will need throughout your dealings with the government: the ability to use the telephone and to write letters effectively.

Telephoning

Some general rules follow for dealing with government by telephone:
1. Always get the name of the person you are speaking to and her

job title. This helps to create accountability and, of course, gives you a handy reference or contact.

2. Always write down the phone number. This may sound silly, but if you have been making many calls to various departments and have been passed on from person to person, you may forget the extension, or, worse still, you may be cut off accidentally and forced to undertake the frustrating chore of retracing your earlier calls.

3. Always be polite on the phone. No matter how frustrated you are, or how urgent or unfair the situation is, do not become abusive with people who, however ineptly, are trying to sort out your situation.

4. Always be patient. The phone may ring more times than you think is reasonable before being answered, or your call may be rerouted through a receptionist who has no way of knowing how to find the person you are trying to reach. You may be cut off. You *will* be put on hold. You may be told no messages can be taken. This is where you should draw the line and move up to speak to the supervisor, or launch a separate campaign regarding telephone answering in the government.

5. Always express yourself as clearly and concisely as possible. Define your problem or question as succinctly as possible. (How to research an issue in order to define precisely what you need to know is discussed in a later section.) You can save much time and energy if you know exactly what you want the agency to do for you and what information you need from them. Do not make them try to interpret your needs for you.

Letter Writing

Effective letter writing also requires adherence to a few simple guidelines:

1. Always get the correct spelling of the person's name, and the correct job title, ministry or department, and full address. All of this is crucial information and will help create accountability should your correspondence go astray. If your letter was correctly directed, failure to respond is more clearly the agency's responsibility.

2. Always keep a carbon or photocopy of your outgoing correspondence.

3. Type your correspondence if at all possible. It will be much easier to read, which usually helps your case.

4. Always be as clear and concise as possible. Set out all the facts of your case. Refer to any telephone calls that have led you to this person and state your expectation of assistance.

5. Avoid rhetoric, flamboyant phrases, hyperbole, and the temptation to let off steam. The scathing phrases that express your true feelings of outrage and frustration are unlikely to impress anyone and may diminish your credibility. You may find it helpful to write a draft letter simply to vent your true feelings. Then, you can proceed more calmly to write the kind of coherent letter that will get results.

6. Always close by setting forth what you expect from the recipient (for example, that she will reply within one week, or whatever). This creates pressure and gives you a time-frame for any follow-up action.

7. It is helpful to close by suggesting that you know what your next move will be if a satisfactory reply is not forthcoming. This does not have to be a threat. Rather, you are simply letting the recipient know that you have thought through your problem or issue and have a strategy already mapped out for pursuing your goals. It is appropriate to ''advise'' that you know where to go next.

Let us now examine ''access'' and ''accountability'' more closely.

Access: How to Find the Right Person

''Access'' means finding out who can get you what you want. That is, which government, which agency, which department, and, ultimately, which person can help you resolve your problem.

Identifying the Issue

It is easier to find the right person if you have a clear idea of the issue. By analysing your situation carefully you can minimize frustration and ultimately save yourself time. This sounds simplistic: of course you know what your problem is. However, in a complex society it is easier than you might think to misidentify a problem, and this can make you particularly vulnerable to being shunted back and forth—getting "the runaround."

The following example should clarify what is meant by properly analysing your situation.

Mrs. Jones lives in public housing. She has received a letter from the Public Housing Authority telling her she must leave her unit because her children have all moved out and the unit is too large for her alone. She is also told in the letter that she must apply for a transfer to a smaller unit, and that if she has not done so by a certain date she will be evicted.

Mrs. Jones is upset by the letter. She has heard nothing of this before. She calls a tenants' self-help group and asks, "Can they evict me because my children have left home?"

She neglects to tell the tenants' group that she lives in subsidized housing.

The answers and assistance she receives will be entirely different depending on the facts and information *she* provides to the people trying to assist her.

If she had mentioned that she was in subsidized housing, she might have received the information she really needed, or at least have been referred to a group working with tenants in public housing whose rights and obligations are different from those of tenants in the private sector.

In short, Mrs. Jones failed to provide important information that would have led to proper resolution of her case.

Think your situation through carefully. Discuss it with friends. Make a list of all the factors you consider relevant. Try to assess your situation in general terms. Is it a landlord-tenant dispute? Does it involve property zoning or building by-laws? Is it primarily a problem with a welfare agency?

Identifying the Agency

Once you have identified the nature of your problem and the facts most relevant to your case, you can then start trying to obtain access to the agency that can best assist you.

In Canada there are three—and occasionally four—levels of government: federal (the Government of Canada); provincial; municipal (your local or civic government); and, in some provinces, regional (e.g., a regional municipality that governs several smaller municipalities). Each level has control over different areas of responsibility.

The division of powers between the federal and provincial governments was originally set out in the *British North America Act, 1867*, which is now incorporated in the *Constitution Act, 1982*. The division of powers between the two levels has evolved over the years so that the areas of responsibility are reasonably clear.

For example, the federal government regulates telecommunications (that is, telephones, cable and satellite television, and telegraph services). This means that the phone company is governed by federal regulations. The federal government is also responsible for national defence, ocean fisheries, and international issues.

Provincial governments have responsibility for issues that are more local in nature. Subsidized housing, consumer legislation, education, general welfare legislation, child welfare legislation, and so on, are provincial areas of responsibility.

Municipalities are created by statute and have areas of responsibility delegated to them by that statute or by other provincial legislation. Some common examples of municipal responsibility are zoning, building by-laws, road development, realty tax-assessment, administration of general welfare legislation, and general urban development. There may be areas in which the responsibilities of different levels of government overlap, and this can lead to confusion.

How then do you find out which level of government and which agency or department can assist with your situation?

1. Discuss your situation with people you know who work in the government, or are already involved in community affairs. Friends and acquaintances are good sources of information.
2. Call a local legal-aid clinic for advice. The staff will be familiar with most common situations and will be able to refer you quickly.
3. Call your local MPP, MLA, MP, or alderman. Their constituency workers are skilled in referring people to the proper agency.
4. Find out if an appropriate organization has been formed by people with similar problems. Check the phone book, the yellow pages, or a directory of community agencies for reference.
5. Obtain a copy of the provincial, municipal, or federal government directory from the government publications store or the local library and look for appropriate references.

6. The government listings in the telephone directory can be frustrating, but it might be a good idea to try them too.
7. If you are really stuck, do research in newspaper and magazine archives for the last year at the local or university library. Look for articles by journalists and the names of politicians and groups interested in the issue.

Identifying the Person

Once you have located the appropriate government department the next step is to find out *who* can get you what you want. Simply phoning the general information number for the agency may not put you in touch with the right person, however. Such calls often lead to a series of seemingly random referrals until finally you are cut off. No doubt this is the system at its worst. If you have no other option, you will have to try this route. But you will have to be extremely patient and persistent.

How do you find the right person? Again, there is no magic formula: you build on the research you did to identify the appropriate agency.

Your contacts and acquaintances are your most useful resource for locating the right person. Talk to your co-workers, your friends, your family—to anyone who might know something. You will be surprised at the number of people who will be able to give you possible leads.

Community legal workers at legal-aid clinics frequently deal with their opposite numbers in the government about problems relating to subsidized housing, welfare, and other social issues.

Use every source you can think of. It is time consuming but will ultimately work.

If you have no sources at all, you will have to look for some. Use the government phone book to find a person with a job description that seems appropriate. Call her directly to find out how accurate her job title is.

Look up recent government reports about your issue. Calling the authors and the politicians named in the report will give you a good start.

Research into newspaper and magazine files will provide similar information.

If you discover that a particular board or committee will hold power in your case, try to get information about the members of the committee to find out who can be most useful to you.

A maxim to remember during this process is: "When in doubt, go too high rather than too low." If you are having no luck at all locating someone to handle your problem, go to the top: the minister's office, the mayor's office, your alderman's office, for example. It is easier to be referred downwards than upwards.

Even if this contact does not refer you to the right person immediately, you now have a well-connected source helping you find the person you need.

Accountability: How to Get the Right Response

At the end of your search, you have found the person in the department that deals with the problem you are trying to resolve. What do you do now to ensure that he or she solves your problem? How do you make the government responsive and accountable to you?

First you should send a clear, concise, typed letter setting forth the situation and confirming your telephone conversation with the person whose job it is to resolve the problem. End the letter by confirming her promise to look into the matter and get back to you within, say, two weeks, or whatever time was agreed on. Deliver the letter yourself or send it by registered mail.

Here is an example of such a letter:

Ministry of Housing
Metropolitan Toronto Housing Authority
1324 Yonge St.
Toronto, Ontario
M5Q 2Z2

Attention: Ms. J. Smart, Tenant Placement Supervisor

Dear Ms. Smart:

Re: Susan Smith, Application for Housing No. 1234567

Further to our telephone conversation of August 5, 1986, I am writing to confirm that I am a community legal worker assisting my client Ms. Susan Smith with her application for subsidized housing.

As we discussed by telephone, Ms. Smith has been denied housing on the grounds that she and her common-law husband were previously tenants in subsidized housing and were evicted for non-payment of rent. I enclose a copy of a letter dated August 1, 1986, from Ms. K. Brown at Area Office ''A'' setting out the grounds for the refusal.

My client urgently requires housing for herself and her two children. She has been separated from her common-law spouse for several months, during which time the arrears of rent accumulated. She now resides in a women's shelter and expects to receive welfare benefits to support herself and her children. She has no responsibility for the arrears of rent.

I would be happy to meet with you to discuss this matter in more detail.

I confirm your advice that you will personally investigate this matter and review the refusal of housing.

I look forward to hearing from you by August 13, 1986, as we agreed.

Yours truly,
L. Strong
Community Legal Worker

While waiting for the reply, try to anticipate possible responses so that your next move can be made promptly.

For example, if at the end of the time stipulated in the letter you receive a reply that your client will forthwith be granted family benefits, your next move is to confirm the good news and send a letter of thanks.

If, as is more likely, you get no reply, your strategy must be designed to create pressure for a prompt response and to minimize further delay.

To do this, you will follow up the letter with a telephone call on August 13, 1986. If you make contact, which is not something to be taken for granted, you will remind Ms. Smart of her commitment to provide you with an answer and ask to know what her position is.

If she requires more time, you may have no option but to accept a postponement, pressing to keep the delay as short as possible. You must also make it clear that if she fails to meet her own deadline, you will take the matter to her supervisor, whose name you learned from your research. Again confirm your telephone conversation with a letter.

If you do not reach her by phone (I wait one day only for my calls to be returned), continue trying, but send out a follow-up letter immediately. Refer to your attempts to reach her by phone, her failure to return your telephone calls, and your expectation that you will hear from her at once. Again let her know your determination to deal with her supervisor if you do not hear from her at once.

You will have to decide on the appropriate timing of each new step for the resolution of your problem. In dealing with any bureaucratic system the reality is that immediate action is unlikely and cannot reasonably be expected. The person you are dealing with will need some time to sort out the problem.

Until you receive a response from government, your strategy and tactics are simply more of the same: more follow-up telephone calls and letters.

If no action has been taken after a reasonable time, you must move up the ladder of responsibility within the department to enlist the help of more senior people to resolve the dispute.

In your research into the issue and the government department, you will have compiled a list of people familiar with the problem and will be able to move up through the bureaucracy.

Bureaucrats must ultimately answer to politicians, and your research will also enable you to move into the political realm to seek support from elected members or their staffs.

There may be other allies you can enlist to call and write demanding the speedy resolution of your problem. Journalists, opposition members and their staffs, and other organizations interested in the issue can all assist.

Review: How to Get a Decision Reversed

What if at the end of your lobbying, the government finally makes a decision that is contrary to your interests? What do you do when you get the bad news?

The first question you must ask is: How final is the decision?

There may be internal review processes within the department or agency that you can use. The person you have been dealing with should assist you by telling you what further options you have. As well, your preliminary research and your sources can help you find out how the internal review process works.

If there appears to be no internal route, it is time to consult a lawyer or a local legal-aid clinic (listed in the phone book). If the clinic is not able to help, it will be able to refer you to a sympathetic lawyer.

The best way to locate a lawyer, however, is through word of mouth, so back you go to your sources and contacts. The law societies governing the legal profession in each province usually have a referral system, which can also be of help. This is discussed in more detail in Chapter 20, ''The Canadian Courts and Legal System.''

At this point, whether you have received a negative decision or no response at all, you should consider looking for outside help to bolster your lobbying efforts. There may be groups and individuals who will phone and write on your behalf.

Another option is to form your own lobbying group. This is discussed in more detail in a later section.

Publicity often helps create pressure to which government agencies respond. If you have learned of a journalist or free-lance writer who has taken an interest in the issue in the past, contact her to tell your story.

Other, more dramatic methods of getting media attention may be available. If you are supported by reasonably well-organized groups, or if you have formed such a group yourself, call a press conference, especially if there has been previous press coverage of the issue. If the issue is of local significance, a press conference will attract attention. However, if it fails to attract significant attention, the government may think your issue is not supported in the community and you will have additional work to counter that impression.

You do not have to be a Madison Avenue public relations expert to arrange a news conference. Draft a news release (a one-page summary of the issue), set out the date, time, and place of the conference, along with details of who will be speaking, and send it, with an invitation to attend, to the news editors of local television and radio stations, and to the local press. Follow up with a telephone call to make sure they received it and are planning to send someone.

Other more dramatic tactics include picketing or protesting. If you have marshalled significant support, you will attract media attention and will also let the government know you have support and mean business. The news often contains reports of the activities of environmental groups and nuclear disarmament groups who publicize their concern through dramatic and innovative actions.

The advocacy process has been discussed this far mainly in theoretical terms. Let's return to the example of Ms. Strong's letter to Ms. Smart about Ms. Smith's application for subsidized housing and suppose that the situation unfolds as follows:

Ms. Smart does not reply to the letter within the time limit it sets out. You reach her by telephone and she says she needs two more weeks to review the situation.

Because your client is in a women's shelter, time is critical. Ms. Smart insists that she needs two weeks.

You really have little choice but to accept her deadline, but you can go a step further and involve her supervisor at this stage. You let Ms. Smart know that you are going to speak to her boss and will be delivering copies of all correspondence to her so that a decision will be made in two weeks.

At the end of two weeks, you are told by Ms. Smart that the decision for the denial of housing was made properly in accordance with the necessary regulations and guidelines and that she will not interfere with it. She then sends you a joint letter from herself and her supervisor confirming the refusal of housing and telling you that a petition may be presented to a meeting of the board of directors of the housing authority to have the decision reviewed again.

You then investigate the petition process. You must find out when the board meets, who is on it, whether an oral or written presentation is required, when your written materials must be received in order to have your case on the agenda, and so on.

You must also focus on how to present your client's case to the board so that it will reverse a previously made decision. This means familiarizing yourself with the regulations and guidelines that govern the housing authority and also, if possible, any previously made decisions of the board that are applicable to your case.

You find out that the board will not hear witnesses other than your client, and that it wants a very brief, written presentation. Try to get a copy of the type of written presentation that is expected, either from the board or from colleagues who have made such presentations in the past.

You must also prepare your client for the board meeting by explaining the process to her and preparing her to answer questions.

At the board meeting, arrive on time. Be neatly dressed. In your presentation, speak clearly and to the point. Avoid rhetoric and "smart" remarks. Do not repeat yourself and try to stay within the allotted time limits. Set out the facts you are relying on. Remember that you are trying to persuade the board to act in your client's best interests.

At the end of the meeting, a decision is made confirming the refusal of housing unless the arrears of rent are paid, on the grounds that even though your client vacated the apartment, her name remained on the lease at the time arrears arose and she is therefore responsible for them.

At this point you have exhausted the internal review processes that are available and must look to external review by the court. You may want to consult a lawyer about the type of court application that is necessary and also to obtain her opinion about the likelihood of success.

Your role as advocate continues as you move from the bureaucratic and legal arena into the political forum. You can continue to marshal outside support to deal with this particular case, or with problems about the availability of subsidized housing in general, or with problems of women in hostels generally. There will be more about this later.

ASSISTANCE FROM GOVERNMENT AGENCIES

After you have gone through the internal review process of a particular ministry or agency but before you take your case to court or to a lawyer, you must consider whether there are any other mechanisms for review of government decisions. In certain cases, in most provinces, there are other government bodies that review government decisions and provide remedies.

Human Rights Commission

Most provinces have legislation protecting human rights and preventing discrimination on the basis of physical or mental handicap, sex, religion, race, and so forth. In Ontario, the Human Rights Commission reviews complaints against private and public bodies based on discrimination, sexual harassment in the workplace, and so on.

The commission will investigate the complaint and has very broad powers to do so.

After investigation, the commission must decide whether to proceed with the complaint if it is well founded. The commission's first option when dealing with a valid complaint is to try to negotiate a settlement between the parties. In many cases, this more informal process can be used to good effect, since the commission's views and opinions carry great weight, particularly in the case of government agencies.

If it is not possible to settle the matter informally, and the commission feels that the complaint is important, the next option open to the commission is to appoint a board of inquiry. A decision of the commission *not* to appoint a board of inquiry is reviewable by the complainant.

The board of inquiry holds a hearing, which is an adversarial process at which the complainant and the party accused of discriminatory behaviour may be represented by counsel.

After the hearing, if the board determines that discrimination has occurred, it has wide-ranging powers to effect a remedy. It may order whatever action is necessary to effect compliance with the human rights code. It may also make directions with respect to future practices. It may order monetary compensation, including damages for mental anguish, although there is a limit to the amount it may award.

The commission has further special powers relating to discrimination based on physical or mental handicap and involving review of different practices in various areas.

Either party may appeal the decision of a board of inquiry to the courts.

The commission's mandate permits it not only to deal with particular complaints but also to take preventive action in a particular field. In looking at the broad picture, the commission has the right to recommend special programs (for example, affirmative action) if problems are particularly prevalent in an area. Likewise the commission fulfils an educational role with the public and government. It exerts powerful persuasion in an informal way with the government to effect change.

Public Complaints Commission

Another special body that may exist in your province is the Office of the Public Complaints Commissioner, or its equivalent. This body deals with complaints involving police behaviour. The issues the commission deals with are wide ranging and include lack of service, rudeness, inappropriate ethnic slurs, an inappropriate or inadequate response to the victim of a crime, and use of excessive force by the police against persons accused of crimes.

When a complaint is made, generally the police are permitted the first opportunity to investigate the circumstances. In a very special case, the commission may avoid the initial police investigation and commence its own process immediately.

The commission monitors and follows the police investigation closely.

If no action is taken by the police after the investigation, the complainant has the right to request a review by the commission. The commission then conducts its own inquiry and, if it finds that the complaint is well founded, appoints a board of inquiry to hold a hearing into the issue. The standard of proof is guilt beyond a reasonable doubt, as it would be in a criminal proceeding, and the proceedings are very adversarial. The complainant is usually represented by the lawyer for the commission, and the police are represented by their own lawyers.

The commission has broad powers upon finding that there has been police misconduct. It has all the usual disciplinary actions available to it, such as suspension from the force with or without pay, reprimands, and, in extreme cases, dismissal from the force. In addition, if the wrongdoing is extreme, the commission may feel that the board of inquiry process is not appropriate and may instead recommend that criminal charges be laid. The commission may not order monetary compensation for damages.

Official Ombudsman

In most provinces there is also a provincial Ombudsman's office, which has a mandate to review government decisions. This mandate covers investigation and review of government agencies only. In Ontario much of its work involves the Workers' Compensation Board, the provincial prison system, and matters relating to government expropriation of land for the purposes of development.

The Ombudsman investigates a complaint only after every internal government review process has been exhausted.

During and after investigation, much emphasis is placed on persuading the government agency to settle with the complainant. Much of the Ombudsman's efforts involve seeking an informal settlement.

In the absence of settlement, the Ombudsman will report to the provincial legislature, setting out the relevant findings. There is often much attendant publicity and thus momentum for political change in the areas investigated by the Ombudsman.

Access-to-Information Commission

One further field that is developing both at the federal and provincial levels is that of freedom of information or access to information. In Ontario, legislation has been proposed setting forth guidelines relating to the confidentiality of and access to information in government files on individuals. It is anticipated that a regulatory agency, headed by a commissioner, will be set up to monitor and administer this system and to provide for an internal review process of the commissioner's decision regarding the release of information.

These issues are becoming more pressing as our individual involvement with the government process increases. Many of the problems addressed by government involve serious issues of confidentiality and expense. It can be very expensive to retrieve and photocopy information from government files. As well there is the risk that what is contained in government files may be embarrassing or prejudicial to the agency or ministry involved.

LOBBYING FOR POLITICAL CHANGE

There will be many situations in which, despite your efforts as an advocate, the bureaucratic and legal systems offer no solution for your client. In these cases, your role as advocate will expand, for the purpose of assisting your client and for more general purposes as well, into the realm of political lobbying—that is, action to bring about changes in government policy and/or the law.

If your lobbying is to be effective, you should consider joining forces with others who are working for the same policy change. Women have been active and effective advocates for policy changes on such issues as:

- increased day-care facilities;
- equal pay for work of equal value;
- pensions for housewives;
- family law reform;
- tax reform related to deductions for child care;
- increased social benefits and services for single mothers and elderly women;
- changes to the *Criminal Code* relating to sexual assault and child abuse;
- better access to public facilities for the handicapped;
- better access to education for the handicapped;
- improved quality of care in psychiatric facilities;
- increased community support for ex-psychiatric residents.

Forming a Pressure Group
Once you know the issue you want to address, how do you form an effective lobby group?

Research your issue thoroughly to learn about its different dimensions. Initially you will need a small core group of volunteers who are willing to work very hard.

Set long- and short-term goals. Your long-term goal will be to achieve specific changes in government policy. Your short-to-medium-term goals will be to expand membership in the group, publicize the issue, conduct research, and raise funds.

Before setting up an independent group, check into existing groups that you may be able to work with. This will save time and ultimately be more efficient. Even if all your goals do not coincide exactly with those of another group, you might be able to join forces long enough to lobby on one important issue together. A good example is the case of the 1983 municipal referendum in Toronto on nuclear disarmament. Although more than twenty groups with nuclear disarmament as one of their goals were working in Toronto, they were able to unite for the purpose of publicizing the referendum. The Toronto Disarmament Network, the result of this co-operative effort, continues to exist and provide co-ordination among the groups for various projects.

Expanding membership and support for the group is necessary, first to create reasonable work-loads, second to generate enough public support to make an impression. To drum up support and attract new volunteers, approach other groups with similar goals. An open letter sent to these groups advising them of your group and its goals will attract new members. Telephone calls to colleagues and acquaintances will also help. Write an article for a local newsletter or community publication describing your group. If you are dealing with an extremely local issue, consider putting up flyers around your neighbourhood.

Your efforts to attract other volunteers will also help to publicize your issue. Consider holding a press conference. Or hold a rally to demonstrate public support. Try to interest individual politicians in your issue. You may attract prominent support that will create publicity.

Again, there is no magic formula for creating a successful lobby group. There is much hard work and persistent following up of resources and opportunities.

One of the tasks of your group will be to develop its expertise in the area in which you want to effect reform. You want your group to be so knowledgable that its information and statistics will not be challenged and the media will contact you for your views on any story involving your area of concern.

Conduct surveys and polls. Established groups may allow you to send information to their members with their regular mailing, or alternatively, to use their mailing lists.

Direct-mail campaigns have proven very effective for political action committees in the United States. Send postcards setting out your position to be signed by sympathizer-recipients and forwarded to the minister in charge of the issue.

Prepare a brief to the government. This will provide a handy reference in the future when you are dealing with the media. It also allows you to demonstrate that you know what you are doing. After the brief is presented to the government, arrange a press conference to demand the government's prompt response.

Research is an ongoing process. Consider comparing the situation in your locale to that in other provinces or cities.

Another persistent concern will be fund raising. I hesitate to say much about the subject because it is truly an art. Whole books have been written about it, and there are many professional fund raisers in Canada. It is an issue that your group will have to address. Mailing out information to your members costs money, as do office supplies, photocopying, and so on.

Members might be willing to donate time and money. You might also approach established bodies for donations and ongoing funding. Knowing how to make grant applications and which private and public agencies have money available is the key. You will want to designate an individual or a committee to develop these special skills. Or, if you are thinking big, consider hiring a professional fund raiser on a short-term contract.

Convincing the Decision Makers

Now that your group is established and has received some publicity, how do you take on the government? What do you do to get your point across?

You want access, as always, to the person or people who can effect change and respond to your demands. You must establish contact with that person, which is usually extremely difficult. You must anticipate dealing with her staff.

In order to obtain access, you must convince the staff that there is a serious problem and that your group will become a serious problem for the ministry unless your concerns are adequately addressed. You must let them know that it is *their* problem and they must find the solution. All of this is easier said than done.

You will establish contact through telephone calls and correspondence, ultimately hoping for a meeting with the minister. This will probably take some time. The perceived level of public support and the pressure you bring to bear will determine when you can expect such a meeting.

In preparation for your meeting you must (a) establish realistic goals for what you want to accomplish, and (b) anticipate the government's counter-arguments.

Your first goal will be to create credibility for yourself and your group. Your research is vital here. You must have positive, concrete proposals for change, not just negative criticisms of the current state of affairs. You must be businesslike and assertive: you are going to be dealing with these people on an ongoing basis, and overt hostility will not help your long-term relationship.

Some of the standard positions the government might take are:
1. It is not my problem. You should be talking to Minister X, or to the provincial government.
2. Yes, it is a serious problem. We are studying the problem.
3. Yes, it is a serious problem, but there is no money.
4. It is not our problem, it is your problem. You should be doing this and that, and so on.

You must be prepared for these gambits.

Remember that inadequate funding for social programs is often a legitimate problem. The purse strings are generally controlled not just by one minister but by a committee. You must target all committee members for lobbying, not just the minister in charge of the appropriate ministry.

After you meet with the minister, hold a press conference to report on the outcome of the meeting. If the minister promised to get back to you within a few days, tell the press. This creates accountability and pressure.

Continuing the Struggle

What do you do after you have met with the government? More of the same! You keep trying to attract new members, get publicity, and exert pressure. At some point the process will seem very circular and unending. To a certain extent it is. Change does not come quickly to any government or society.

In recent years women have had a significant impact in a number of ongoing lobbying efforts. I am thinking primarily of environmental issues and the nuclear-disarmament movement.

In New Brunswick, a young woman law student and her family fought hard on behalf of residents opposed to the spraying of toxic chemicals to control spruce budworm. Using the courts and effective community organizing, this group managed to have the spraying considerably delayed, although in the end it was not reduced or eliminated.

In the nuclear-disarmament movement, the work of Dr. Helen Caldicott on behalf of disarmament is noteworthy. For two years of her life, Caldicott placed lecturing, teaching, and lobbying about the dangers of nuclear war ahead of the claims of her family and medical practice.

No matter what the issue, try to set realistic goals for yourself and your group. You will need great reserves of patience and per-severance. You will probably become discouraged and depressed. In any lobbying effort there are countless battles before the war is won. Try to focus on each individual battle or stage in the lobbying process. Most of the areas in which you are seeking change will have an impact on many other issues. There are few social issues that are not connected to or interrelated with other areas.

Much of your satisfaction from your advocacy activities will come from your participation and not from the immediate results obtained.

CHAPTER 20

THE CANADIAN COURTS AND LEGAL SYSTEM

Gillian D. Butler

*Gillian D. Butler is a graduate of Memorial University of
Newfoundland's School of Business and the University of
Alberta Law School at Edmonton. She was called to the
Bar in Newfoundland in December, 1980, and is presently
a private practitioner involved mainly in civil litigation
and particularly family law at St. John's, Newfoundland.
In addition, she is chairperson of the province's Human
Rights Commission and a Director of Family Mediation
Newfoundland/Labrador, Planned Parenthood New-
foundland/Labrador, and Planned Parenthood Federation
of Canada. She is married to David D. McKay and the
mother of one daughter, Heather.*

THROUGHOUT THE BOOK, reference has been made to the common
law and civil law, to case law and statute law, to legislation and
judicial interpretation. These terms often are bewildering to non-
lawyers and yet they are basic to understanding how our laws and
our legal system work. In this chapter you will learn about the
sources of Canadian law, the role of lawyers in our legal system,
and the structure of the courts in Canada.

SOURCES OF LAW

There are two major systems of law in the world, the common-law
system and the civil-law system. For the most part, our Canadian
legal system is based upon the common-law system of dispute res-

405

olution that had its origins in feudal England. Common law refers to the legal principles that have developed over the years from the decisions of judges in particular cases. The one Canadian exception to the acceptance of the common-law system is in the Province of Quebec, where the legal system is based on civil law, which had its origins in the French and Roman tradition of codification of law. Thus, in Quebec, there is no reliance on case-setting precedents.

Under a common-law system, if a particular legal problem is not covered by legislation, one must then rely upon the case law to resolve the issue. In advising a client in such a case, the lawyer will do research to find cases involving similar circumstances, extract the principles of law that were used in making these judgments, and determine, based upon the date of the decision and the level of the court that made the decision, how influential the case will be to that particular client.

The second source of law on which our Canadian legal system is based is statute law, which refers to legislation passed by either the federal government or a provincial or territorial government. In each case, the respective government derives its powers to make laws in relation to particular subjects from Canada's constitution.

Unlike some other countries, Canada does not have one particular document that can be called its constitution. Instead, our constitution is composed of several statutes, the most important of which, for the purposes of this chapter, are the *Constitution Act, 1867* and the *Constitution Act, 1982*. The latter contains the Canadian *Charter of Rights and Freedoms*, which is discussed in more detail in Chapter 16.

The *Constitution Act, 1867* sets out the distribution of legislative powers in Canada. In other words, it specifies which level of government may make laws pertaining to various classes of subjects. Section 91 gives Parliament, which is the federal government of Canada, the right to regulate such matters as the postal service, banking, marriage, and divorce; and section 92 gives each respective provincial or territorial government the right to regulate such matters as education, property, civil rights, and generally all matters of a merely local or private nature in the province.

In determining what legislation means, one must consider the specific words of the statute, alone and in the context of the legislation as a whole. One must also consider how courts have interpreted the legislation in previous judicial decisions and how influential these previous decisions will be in the circumstances, based on the same criteria as in a common-law situation.

Further, in interpreting legislation, courts and lawyers will often consider the policy reasons behind the statute. Consideration is given to what the legislator intended to accomplish by the legislation in question. A statute that appears on its face to be a clear declaration of the law may actually be quite complicated; consequently, often only a person with legal training or legislative experience can interpret the legislation accurately.

REPRESENTATION

Appearing Unrepresented

The Canadian *Charter of Rights and Freedoms* now provides that each individual has the right to representation in matters of both criminal and civil law. However, the need for a legal representative will vary according to the nature of the client's legal problem.

For example, in criminal matters, our *Criminal Code* and other provincial statutes distinguish between summary convictions and indictable offences. Of the two, the latter, which include such things as sexual assault, murder, and attempted murder, are the more serious breaches of the law. Summary convictions, on the other hand, attract more lenient sentences and include most breathalyser charges, and theft under $1,000.

Naturally, if you are facing criminal charges, one of the most important considerations determining whether you retain a lawyer or choose to represent yourself, will be the penalty or sentence you may face if proof of guilt is established. For this reason alone, traditionally very few offenders have chosen to appear unrepresented on an indictable charge, whereas a far greater number choose to appear unrepresented on a summary conviction offence.

Legal Aid

A second consideration if you are facing the decision to retain counsel is the estimated fee and your ability to pay. Most provinces and territories have a legal-aid system that provides for a government-funded legal-aid lawyer to be appointed to represent a client who would otherwise be unable to afford legal services. However, the guidelines for the appointment of such solicitors vary among the provinces and territories. If you are interested in seeking such assistance, check with your local legal-aid office to determine if your case qualifies for a legal-aid lawyer. In some provinces, the legal-aid rules do not provide, for example, for the appointment of a lawyer where the charge is a summary conviction matter and the client does not have any prior convictions.

In non-criminal law suits, the decision whether to attend court with a lawyer will be based on the same considerations. Here, too, the legal-aid rules provide guidance on whether a solicitor is available. For example, in at least one Canadian province, a legal-aid solicitor is not available to represent clients on a provincial maintenance application unless the other party (husband or wife) is likewise represented by counsel.

Aside from the legal-aid staff solicitors, some jurisdictions allow clients whose cases are approved by legal-aid authorities to seek outside counsel who agree to act at the legal-aid rate. Thus, it is still possible for a client who has already selected a solicitor on a private basis to ask that lawyer to take the case or handle the matter on a legal-aid certificate if approval is given.

Generally speaking, however, private solicitors' hourly rates are far in excess of the legal-aid tariffs, and only those solicitors who have committed themselves to take on legal-aid work as a community service in their daily private practice will be willing to work for the legal-aid rate. This may be a consideration for a client in the selection of a lawyer. Other considerations will include the lawyer's general fees, area of specialization, and personal manner and reputation. In today's society it is to be expected that individuals will "shop around" for legal representation or will seek referrals to lawyers whose interests and/or experience have given them expertise in the individual's particular type of legal problem.

Lawyer Referral

In some provinces the local law societies have a lawyer-referral service that acts as a guide for members of the public seeking to retain legal counsel. Readers are encouraged to check their local telephone directories under "Lawyers" or "Law Societies" for reference to such a service. This program usually guarantees a minimum fee associated with the first solicitor-client interview that flows from the referral service. Other useful guides to clients seeking assistance in domestic or family-law matters are local transition houses, unified family courts, and women's centres or shelters, which keep an up-to-date list of private solicitors well versed in the subjects in which they share a public interest.

It is trite to say that appearing without a lawyer in any cause or matter is dangerous and that it is extremely so in the more serious criminal and civil matters. A lawyer brings to the courtroom at least six years of experience and study designed to prepare him or her for the duty of representation. It would be prudent to make contact with any of the services referred to in this chapter before making the decision to appear unrepresented.

THE LAWYERS

Lawyers come from many different backgrounds. Law students are generally required to have completed a university degree program before they can apply to a Canadian law school, but in some cases, a student may be accepted to law school after having completed only two years of an undergraduate degree program. Law students must also have successfully completed the Law School Admission Test, commonly referred to as the LSAT, which tests a variety of skills, including reading comprehension and logic. Arrangements for writing the LSAT may be made through any Canadian university. Candidates for admission must also complete and forward to a university to which they are seeking entrance applications giving background information of a general nature. In addition, the university in question may require a personal interview at the expense of the applicant.

An applicant who is accepted for the study of law will then dedicate the next three university calendar years to intensive study. The first year of law school involves consideration of most of the basic subjects. In subsequent years students have some choice about which areas of law they will study. For example, family law or criminal-trial procedure are generally elective courses selected by individual students who have an interest in the subject area.

Upon successful completion of the three years of study, a student will have earned a law degree. He or she is then required to "article" with a selected law firm, Justice department or ministry, or corporation. The period of articles represents an apprenticeship period, usually spanning twelve months, in which the student is exposed to all areas of legal practice. In essence an articling student performs many of the functions of a lawyer during this period. Most provinces also have bar admission programs. The articling student is required to enrol in these for further classes during or following the period of articles in order to learn the more practical application of the law in the province in which the student intends to practise. After completing the period of articles and passing the bar admission examination, the articling clerk will then be "called to the bar" of that province or territory, and will become a barrister and a solicitor entitled both to research the law and to appear in any court of law in the province or territory in question.

Lawyers are bound by rules particular to their profession. These rules are set out by the law societies of each province or territory and by the Canadian Bar Association in its Code of Professional Conduct. These rules demand that a certain standard of professional and personal responsibility be met by all lawyers in Canada.

The present Code of Professional Conduct was developed by the Canadian Bar Association after an extensive review of legal ethics and consultation with provincial law societies and members of the profession. The code is intended as a guide for all lawyers whether in private practice or engaged in other activities. Its seventeen chapters deal with a variety of subjects, including fees, withdrawal of services, confidentiality, and preservation of clients' property. The code is designed primarily to ensure that lawyers are competent professionals who deliver high-quality services to the public with the utmost integrity.

Besides stressing the responsibility of lawyers to the public, the code also emphasizes the responsibility of lawyers to each other and to the profession in general. Breach of the code may cause a lawyer to be brought before the Law Society and may lead to temporary or permanent dismissal from the bar. Breach of the code, when it involves a lawyer-client contract, may also be cause for a law suit by the client. If the breach involves the commission of a criminal offence, the lawyer may face charges under the *Criminal Code*.

In addition to having to comply with the code, lawyers are also subject to the rules made by provincial law societies. These rules govern licensing and fees and vary from one province or territory to another.

THE LAWYER-CLIENT RELATIONSHIP

You should expect that your first interview with the lawyer you have selected will be lengthy and that fees will be discussed. This is generally so, since the initial meeting will be the best opportunity to determine the nature of the client's legal problem and to discuss the options available to the solicitor in representing your interests or protecting your rights. You should carry with you to this interview any documents in your possession relevant to the legal problem and expect to leave a copy of the documents with your lawyer.

Solicitor-Client Privilege

The relationship between solicitor and client is privileged. This means that neither oral nor written communications between them may be divulged by the solicitor. Broader still is the ethical duty of a solicitor implied in the proviso that the lawyer cannot render effective professional service unless there is full and unreserved communication between the lawyer and client.

Fees

The fees chargeable by Canadian solicitors will vary from one province or territory to another upwards from $50 an hour. The fee will be in relation to the solicitor's experience, number of years at the bar, area of specialization (if any), law office overhead, and any special circumstances, such as urgency. The Canadian Bar Association's Code of Ethics further provides that a lawyer should not ''stipulate for, charge or accept any fee which is not fully disclosed, fair and reasonable'' depending upon such factors as the time and effort spent and the results obtained.

Once the solicitor has an appreciation of the nature of the client's legal problem and is able to estimate the fees that will be charged, the lawyer will usually require the payment of a retainer as a pre-payment of the cost of the legal services to be provided. In some cases, particularly in criminal matters, the solicitor may require payment in full before proceeding. Any funds deposited in such a manner to a solicitor before an invoice is forwarded are considered trust funds and are deposited to a separate account of the law firm that is protected from the claims of the firm's creditors. When an invoice (interim or final) is presented, the solicitor may set off against the account any money held in trust for the client; but otherwise the funds are not to be used by the solicitor in any manner.

In certain provinces and territories, the law society acts permit contingent fees provided that such arrangements are fair and reasonable. The contingent fee arrangement implies that a fee will be charged only if the solicitor is successful in representing the client or protecting the client's legal rights. Customarily, the contingent fee is stated to be a percentage of the award given or settlement achieved through the lawyer's involvement and may or may not include disbursements in the stated percentage. If you are considering entering into such a solicitor-client relationship, you may wish to ask your provincial law society about the legality of such a practice in your jurisdiction.

At any stage of the solicitor-client relationship, you should be satisfied as to both the time and the manner in which the solicitor has handled your case. If you are not satisfied, you may wish to consider changing solicitors. Before doing so, however, it would be wise to contact the solicitor who was originally retained to record your dissatisfaction and provide him or her with an opportunity to address the issue. In the event of more serious dissatisfaction (for example, on grounds of negligence or breach of confidence), you may wish to lodge a complaint with the local law society, whose officers will assist you with the procedural details of doing so.

THE COURTS AT WORK

Although the common-law system is generally accepted in all provinces and territories except Quebec, the operation of the judicial system will vary from one province or territory to another as a direct result of each province's ability to legislate in matters of a merely local or private nature. However, the three major courts of the Canadian legal system do exist in all provinces and territories.

The Federal Courts

The federal courts were created by the federal government, and the judges who sit on the bench of these courts are appointed and paid by the federal government. There are two federal courts, the Supreme Court of Canada and the Federal Court of Canada. Of the two, the Supreme Court is more widely known, as it is to this court that appeals (with permission of the Supreme Court of Canada) are heard from decisions made by the Appellate Division of the Supreme Court of a province or territory.

The Supreme Court is the highest court in Canada and no appeal lies from its decisions. The Federal Court of Canada is not as well known to the general public, since its jurisdiction is limited to matters of a purely federal nature, such as claims against any federal board for a mistake made in its proceedings.

The Provincial Supreme Courts

The provincial supreme courts are given authority by their respective provincial or territorial governments but their judges are appointed and paid by the federal government. In each province or territory the Supreme Court has two divisions—a trial division and an appeal division. In some cases it may also have a lower court known as the District, County, or Surrogate Court, which may hear generally the same subject matters as the trial division of the Supreme Court. To give an example of the distinction between the District Court and the Supreme Court, Trial Division, some provinces limit the District Court's jurisdiction to claims where the amount in issue is less than $10,000, or require certain subject matters to be brought only to one court or the other. (For example, landlord/tenant matters may be required to be heard in District Court, and divorce cases in Supreme Court, Trial Division.) The current trend, however, is to amalgamate such courts with the Supreme Court, Trial Division, of each province. The role of the Court of Appeal of the Supreme Court is to hear appeals from decisions of judges sitting either at the Supreme Court, Trial Division, or the District Court level.

The Provincial Courts

The provincial courts are created under provincial law, and their judges are both provincially appointed and paid. In some jurisdictions, these judges are more commonly referred to as magistrates, and their work is restricted usually to: claims where the amount in issue is less than $1,000; criminal matters of a less serious nature; and some family and child-welfare matters.

NEW TRENDS IN OUR JUDICIAL SYSTEM

As a direct result of society's changing attitudes, customs, and standards, our law is always changing. The women's property legislation enacted by each provincial government between 1976 and 1981 is a prime example of such necessary change. However, provincial and federal governments are not the only parties responsible for changing the law. Lawyers and judges also have a role to play in recognizing shortcomings or deficiencies in both case and statute law and, in the former, advancing arguments to distinguish cases that are no longer acceptable to fair-thinking individuals in our society.

Our legal system has come a long way since the monarch's advisers in feudal England travelled through the countryside to settle both private disputes and criminal matters. Some examples of the new trends in our judicial system are set out below.

Family Court Services

Without doubt, our grandparents and great-grandparents would be shocked by the present Canadian statistics on marriage breakdown and the number of matrimonial partners who have had to rely heavily on our courts, at every level, for settlement of such issues as child custody and maintenance, property division, and so on. In direct response to a growing need in this area, some provinces, with the assistance of the federal government, have opened unified family courts or enlarged upon the services available to individuals experiencing the effects of separation, divorce, or violence in the home.

In those provinces fortunate enough to have a Unified Family Court, all services otherwise available from provincial, district, and supreme courts are provided under the same roof to clients who fall within the statutorily defined geographic territory of the court. You may refer to your local telephone directory under "Government: Courts" to determine if such a service exists in your area.

Included in the services provided by a Unified Family Court are private court hearings closed to the public, professional assessments for matters such as custody of children and household financial management, mediation, and referral.

Small Claims Court
Each province or territory has a Small Claims Court at the Provincial Court level for settlement of private disputes involving claims for loss or damage below a certain amount (from $1,000 to $10,000, depending on the province). These courts were established to meet the need for a forum in which individuals whose claims did not warrant the cost of a private solicitor could represent themselves in an atmosphere that is less adversarial than that in higher courts and where the strict rules of evidence are more relaxed.

Not all parties to Small Claims Court litigation are unrepresented, however. Since solicitors are still entitled to appear, it may be that in any given case one party is represented and the other is not. In such circumstances, the unrepresented party is at a disadvantage and may wish to reconsider the decision to do without legal representation or, at the very least, may seek a postponement in order to contact a lawyer and discuss the need for representation.

Resource Guide

In most provinces and territories there are non-government agencies who provide information on our laws and legal system. They are referred to as public legal information organizations. There are many other agencies and government departments who, as part of their overall mandate, also provide information on the law. As a starting point, we offer the following list of organizations across Canada.

Arctic Public Legal Education
Information Society
Box 2706
Yellowknife, Northwest Territories
X1A 2R1
(403) 920-2360

Calgary Legal Guidance
200 Rocky Mountain Plaza
615 MacLeod Trail Southeast
Calgary, Alberta
T2C 4T8
(403) 234-9266

Canadian Law Information Council
2409 Yonge Street
Suite 201
Toronto, Ontario
M4P 2E7
(416) 483-3802

Commission des services juridiques
2, Complexe Desjardins
Tour de l'est
Bureau 1404
Montreal, Quebec
H5B 1B3
(514) 873-3562

Community Legal Education
  Association
405 Broadway
5th floor
Winnipeg, Manitoba
(204) 945-3126/2882

Community Legal Education
  Ontario
62 Noble Street
Toronto, Ontario
M6K 2C9
(416) 530-1800

Community Legal Information
  Association of P.E.I.
Box 1207
Charlottetown, P.E.I.
C1A 7M8
(902) 892-0853

Legal Information Centre of New
  Brunswick
421 Avenue Acadie
Dieppe, New Brunswick
E1A 1H4
(506) 858-4586

Legal Resource Centre
10049 - 81 Avenue
Edmonton, Alberta
T6E 1W7
(403) 432-5732

Legal Services Society of British
  Columbia
1140 West Pender Street
Box 3, Suite 300
Vancouver, B.C.
V6E 4G1
(604) 660-4600

Public Legal Education Association
  of Saskatchewan
210-220 Third Avenue South

Saskatoon, Saskatchewan
S7K 1M1
(306) 653-1868

Public Legal Education Society of
 Nova Scotia
1127 Barrington Street
Suite 103
Halifax, Nova Scotia
B3H 2P8
(902) 423-7154

Public Legal Information
 Association of Newfoundland
Box 1064, Station C
St. John's, Newfoundland
A1C 5M5
(709) 722-2643

Yukon Public Legal Education
 Association
c/o Territorial Court Registry
Room 207, Federal Building
Whitehorse, Yukon
Y1A 2B5
(403) 667-4305

Public Legal Education Society of
 British Columbia
The People's Law School
3466 West Broadway
Vancouver, B.C.
V6R 2B3
(604) 734-1126

CHAPTER 1

Women and Credit

Further Information:
More information about credit can be obtained from the consumer affairs
department of your provincial government (check the blue pages of your

telephone directory), from women's credit unions and other financial institutions in your area, from your local public legal education association, and from the Better Business Bureau.

Further Reading:

Consumer Law: A Handbook for B.C. Consumers. Vancouver: People's Law School January, 1984.

Debts. St. John's: Public Legal Education Association of Newfoundland, 1985.

Meanwell, Catherine, and Susan Glover. *To Have and to Hold: A Guide to Property and Credit Law for Farm Families in Ontario*. Chesley, Ontario: Concerned Farm Women, 1985.

Money Problems: Your Rights and Responsibilities. Halifax: Public Legal Education Society of Nova Scotia, 1984.

Before You Go Under. Edmonton: Alberta Consumer and Corporate Affairs, 1982.

Dealing with Debts. Toronto: Community Legal Education Ontario, 1984.

CHAPTER 2

Consumer Protection

Further Information:

A great deal of information about consumer protection laws is available from the consumer affairs department of your provincial government. You may also contact:

Consumer and Corporate Affairs
   Canada
Ottawa, Ontario
K1A 0C9
(613) 997-2938

Consumers' Association of Canada
   (or your provincial chapter of the
   Consumers' Association of
   Canada)

Southvale Plaza
Level III
2660 Southvale Crescent
Ottawa, Ontario
K1P 5C4
(613) 733-9450

The Boston Women's Health Book Collective. *The New Our Bodies, Ourselves: A Book by and for Women*. New York: Simon and Schuster, 1984.

Collins, Anne. *The Big Evasion: Abortion, The Issue That Won't Go Away*. Toronto: Lester & Orpen Dennys, 1985.

Collins, Larry. "The Politics of Abortion: Trends in Canadian Fertility Policy." *Atlantis: A Women's Study Journal*. Halifax: Mount Saint Vincent University.

Dickens, Bernard M. *Medico-Legal Aspects of Family Law*. Toronto: Butterworths, 1979.

Healthsharing. A quarterly magazine published by Women Healthsharing, Box 230, Station M, Toronto, Ontario M6S 4T3.

Lexchin, Joel. *The Real Pushers: A Critical Analysis of the Canadian Drug Industry*. Vancouver: New Star Books, 1984.

McDonnell, Kathleen. *Not an Easy Choice: A Feminist Re-examines Abortion*. Toronto: Women's Press, 1984.

McDonnell, Kathleen, and Marianna Valverdo, editors. *The Healthsharing Book: Resources for Canadian Women*. Toronto: Women's Press, 1985.

Patients' Rights in Canada. Toronto: Patients' Rights Association, 1982.

Phoenix Rising: The Voice of the Psychiatrized. A quarterly journal published by On Our Own, Box 7251, Station A, Toronto, Ontario M5W 1X9.

Report on the Statute Audit Project. Toronto: Charter of Rights Educational Fund, 1985.

Rozovsky, Lorne Elkin. *The Canadian Patient's Book of Rights*. Toronto: Doubleday Canada, 1980.

Sharpe, Steven Blair. *Informed Consent: Its Basis in Traditional Legal Principles*. Toronto: Butterworths, 1979.

Storage and Utilization of Human Sperm. Ottawa: Advisory Committee to the Minister of National Health and Welfare, 1981.

Storch, J. *Patients' Rights: Ethical and Legal Issues in Health Care and Nursing*. Toronto: McGraw-Hill Ryerson, 1982.

Women's Health Products Task Force. *Women's Health Products Study*. Toronto: City of Toronto Department of Public Health, 1982.

World Inter-Action Ottawa; Inter Pares. *For Health or for Profit? The Pharmaceutical Industry in the Third World and Canada*. Ottawa: Health Action International Coalition Canada, 1984.

CHAPTER 5

Financial Planning

Further Information:
For assistance in completing your tax return and for further information about income tax law, contact your local tax information office of Revenue Canada (listed in the blue pages of your telephone directory).

Further Reading:
Chakrapani, Chuck. *Best Ways to Make Money*. Vancouver: International Self-Counsel Press, 1986.

Costello, Brian. *Your Money and How to Keep It*. Toronto: Stoddart, 1986.

Holterman, F. Marc. *Tax Law Handbook: A Guide to Canadian Court Cases*. Fourth edition. Vancouver: International Self-Counsel Press, 1985.

Hogg, R.D. and M.G. Mallin. *Preparing Your Income Tax Returns*. Revised edition. Don Mills: CCH Canadian, 1986.

Rogers, James. *Life Insurance for Canadians: How Much? What Kind? From Whom?* Vancouver: International Self-Counsel Press, 1980.

CHAPTER 6

Marriage and Cohabitation

Further Information:
Contact the public legal education association in your province for more information about your legal rights in marriage and cohabitation arrangements. Your provincial Attorney General's Office can assist you with the formalities of the marriage ceremony in your jurisdiction (check the blue pages of your telephone directory.)

Further Reading:
Bigamy. Ottawa: Law Reform Commission of Canada, 1985.

Dranoff, Linda Silver. *Every Woman's Guide to the Law*. Toronto: Fitzhenry and Whiteside, 1985.

King, Lynn. *What Every Woman Should Know About Marriage, Separation, and Divorce*. Toronto: James Lorimer, 1980.

Living Common Law. Vancouver: Legal Services Society of British Columbia, 1985.

Living Common Law. Saskatoon: Public Legal Education Association of Saskatchewan, 1985.

Marriage. Quebec: Ministère de la Justice du Québec, 1985.

Out of Wedlock. Quebec: Ministère de la Justice du Québec, 1985.

Sloss, Elizabeth, editor. *Family Law in Canada: New Directions*. Ottawa: Canadian Advisory Council on the Status of Women, 1985.

Chapter 7

Separation and Divorce

Further Information:
For further information, contact your local women's centre, community legal-aid office, or the family court office in your jurisdiction.

Further Reading:
Auxier, Jane. *Marriage and Family Law in British Columbia*. Sixth edition. Vancouver: International Self-Counsel Press, 1985.

Divorce Law: Questions and Answers. Ottawa: Department of Justice, 1986.

Gibson, Nancy. *Separation and Divorce: A Canadian Woman's Survival Guide*. Edmonton: Hurtig, 1986.

Kronby, Malcolm C. *Canadian Family Law*. Fourth edition. Toronto: Stoddart, 1986.

The Divorce Act and the ten Provincial Acts that deal with Family Property.

CHAPTER 8

Children and the Law

Further Information:

Two national organizations working in the area of children and the law are:

The Canadian Council for Children
and Youth
2211 Riverside Drive
Suite 11
Ottawa, Ontario
K1H 2X5

Justice for Children (Canadian
Foundation for Children and the
Law)
720 Spadina Avenue
Toronto, Ontario
M5S 2T9

Further Reading:

Publications available from Justice for Children include the following:

Brief on Medical Consent of Minors, February 1980.

Briefs on Special Education Legislation (Bill 82), August 1980, December 1985, and June 1986.

Brief on the Young Offenders' Act (Bill C-61), September 1981; Response to Proposed Amendments, June 1986.

Response to Ontario Consultation Paper on Implementing Bill C-61, the Young Offenders' Act, March 1982.

730 Days in Limbo: The Rights of 16 and 17 Year Olds, November 1982.

In Trouble with the Law: A Guide to the Young Offenders' Act, Second edition, July 1984.

Response to "The Children's Act: A Consultation Paper," June 1983.

Under 18: Your Rights: A Guide for Young Persons in Ontario, February 1985.

Submission on the Child and Family Services Act (Adoption Disclosure).

Response to Sexual Offences Against Children: Report of the Committee on Sexual Offences Against Children (The Badgeley Report), September 1985, and *Response to Proposed Legislation*, October 1986.

See also:
Bala, Nicolas C., Heino Lilles, and George M. Thomson. *Canadian Children's Law: Cases, Notes and Materials*. Toronto: Butterworths, 1982.

Bala, Nicolas C. *Young Offenders' Act Annotated.* Toronto: Butterworths, 1984.

Harris, Peter S. *Young Offenders' Act Manual.* Aurora: Canada Law Book Inc., 1984.

Inglis, Elizabeth. *Putting the Pieces Together: A Parents' Guide to Special Education in Ontario.* Third edition. Toronto: Ontario Association for Children with Learning Disabilities, 1983.

Child and Family Services Act Training Handbook. Toronto: Ontario Ministry of Community and Social Services, 1985.

Wilson, Jeffery. *Children and the Law.* Second edition. Toronto: Butterworths, 1986.

Law for Young People (In Trouble with the Police; You and Your Lawyer; Youth Court; The Child Witness) — 1 hour video. Justice for Children, 720 Spadina Avenue, #105, Toronto.

CHAPTER 9

Violence in the Family

Further Information:
The following may be contacted for further information and assistance: your local family services centre, emergency hospital wards, local police victims service unit, local community health centres, shelters for battered women, Victorian Order of Nurses, Regional Health Units, women's resource centres, senior citizens' centres, Alcoholics Anonymous, Alanon (for spouses and relatives of alcoholics), and Parents Anonymous (for parents who are abusers).

For films that can be used to stimulate discussion on family violence, contact:

National Film Board of Canada
Box 6100
Montreal, Quebec
H3C 3H5

For materials and lists of self-help groups in your area, and for a newsletter, contact:

National Clearinghouse on Family Violence
Health and Welfare Canada
Claxton Building
Tunney's Pasture
Ottawa, Ontario
K1A 1B5

For materials and assistance:
National Victims' Resource Centre
Solicitor General of Canada
340 Laurier Avenue West
Ottawa, Ontario
K1A 0P8

For information on the new sexual offences law:
Office of Public Affairs
Department of Justice
Justice Building
Ottawa, Ontario
K1A 0H8

For *Liaison*, a monthly journal on the criminal justice system:
Communication Division
Solicitor General of Canada
340 Laurier Avenue West
Ottawa, Ontario
K1A 0P8

Further Reading:

Foon, Dennis, and Brenda Knight. *Am I the Only One? A Young People's Book about Sex Abuse.* Vancouver: Douglas and McIntyre, 1985.

Russell, Diana. *Rape in Marriage.* New York: Macmillan, 1982.

Do You Want to Stop the Abuse and Violence in Your Life But Don't Know How? Toronto: Parkdale Community Legal Services, 1986.

CHAPTER 10

Death in the Family

Further Information:
Information about probate and letters of administration may be obtained from the surrogate court office in your jurisdiction (check under "Courts" in the blue pages of your telephone directory). To find out more about wills and estates in your province, contact the public legal education association (listed at the beginning of this resource guide).

Further Reading:
Allen, William P.G. *Estate Planning Handbook.* Agincourt: The Carswell Company, 1985.

Caroe, Laurence C. *Wills for Ontario: How to Make Your Own Will.* Seventh edition. Vancouver: International Self-Counsel Press, 1984.

Successions and Wills. Quebec: Ministère de la Justice du Québec, 1985.

Wills. St. John's: Public Legal Information Association of Newfoundland, 1985.

Wills and Estates. Sixth edition. Vancouver: The Public Legal Education Society of British Columbia, 1984.

Wills and Estates. Revised edition. Saskatoon: Public Legal Education Association of Saskatchewan, 1985.

CHAPTER 11

Equality in Employment

Further Information:
To obtain further information, contact your provincial Human Rights Commission or the women's bureau in your provincial department of labour. For information on federal matters, you may also contact:

Status of Women Canada
Ottawa, Ontario
K1A 0A6
(613) 995-9397

The Canadian Human Rights
Commission
90 Sparks Street
Suite 400
Ottawa, Ontario
K1A 1E1

Further Reading:

Backhouse, Constance, and Leah Cohen. *The Secret Oppression: Sexual Harassment of Working Women.* Toronto: Macmillan, 1978.

Canadian Human Rights Advocate. Subscription office: R.R.1, Maniwaki, Quebec J9E 3A8.

Cootes, Mary Lou. *Employment Equity: Issues, Approaches and Public Policy Framework.* Kingston: Queen's University Industrial Relations Centre, 1986.

Equality in Employment. Judge Rosalie Silverman Abella, commissioner. Ottawa: Commission on Equality in Employment, 1984.

MacKinnon, Catherine. *Sexual Harassment of Working Women.* New Haven: Yale University Press, 1979.

What Is Harassment? Ottawa: Canadian Human Rights Commission, 1984.

CHAPTER 12

Employment Rights

Further Information:

The employment standards branch of your provincial department of labour provides information about employment laws in your province. For federal information, contact:

Women's Bureau
Labour Canada
Ottawa, Ontario
K1A 0J2
(613) 997-1550

Further Reading:

Armstrong, Pat and Hugh. *The Double Ghetto: Canadian Women and Their Segregated Work.* Toronto: McClelland and Stewart, 1978.

Christie, Innis. *Employment Law in Canada.* Toronto: Butterworths, 1980.

Cornish, Mary, and Laurel Ritchie. *Getting Organized: Building a Union.* Toronto: Canadian Women's Education Press, 1980.

Guide to the Ontario Labour Relations Act. Toronto: Ministry of Labour.

Menzies, Heather. *Women and the Chip: Case Studies on the Effects of Information on Employment in Canada*. Montreal: Institute for Research on Public Policy.

Report of the Task Force on Child Care. Katie Cooke, Chair. Ottawa: Ministry of Supply and Service, 1986.

White, Julie. *Women and Part-Time Work*. Ottawa: Advisory Council on the Status of Women, 1983.

Women's Labour Project. *Bargaining for Equality: A Guide to Legal and Collective Bargaining Solutions for Workplace Problems That Particularly Affect Women*. San Francisco: Inkworks, 1980.

CHAPTER 13

Health in the Workplace

Further Information:
To obtain information about current developments in the area of occupational health and safety, contact:

Health and Welfare Canada
Brooke Claxton Building
Tunney's Pasture
Ottawa, Ontario
K1A 0K9
(613) 996-4950

Further Reading:
Bertell, Rosalie. *No Immediate Danger? Prognosis for a Radioactive Earth*. London: The Women's Press, 1985.

Chenier, Nancy Miller. *Reproductive Hazards at Work*. Ottawa: Advisory Council on the Status of Women, 1982.

DeMatteo, Bob. *Terminal Shock: The Health Hazards of Video Display Terminals*. Toronto: NC Press, 1985.

Dewey, Martin. *Smoke in the Workplace: An Action Manual for Non-Smokers*. Toronto: Non-Smokers' Rights Association, 1985.

Ison, Terence G. *Workers' Compensation in Canada*. Toronto: Butterworths, 1983.

Kaye, Lynn. *Reproductive Hazards in the Workplace*. Toronto: National Action Committee on the Status of Women, 1986.

McDonnell, Kathleen, and Marianna Valverdo. *The Healthsharing Book: Resources for Canadian Women*. Toronto: The Women's Press, 1985.

Nash, Michael Izumi. *Canadian Occupational Health and Safety Law*. Don Mills: CCH Canadian, 1983.

Reasons, Charles, Lois Ross, and Craig Paterson. *Assault on the Worker: Occupational Health and Safety in Canada*. Toronto: Butterworths, 1981.

Sexton, Patricia Cayo. *The New Nightingales*. New York: Enquiry Press, 1982.

Stellman, Jeanne. *Women's Work, Women's Health: Myths and Realities*. New York: Pantheon Books, 1977.

Stellman, Jeanne, and Susan Daum. *Work is Dangerous to Your Health: A Handbook of Health Hazards in the Workplace and What You Can Do About Them*. New York: Vintage Books, 1971.

Stellman, Jeanne, and Mary Sue Henifin. *Office Work Can Be Dangerous to Your Health*. New York: Pantheon Books, 1983.

CHAPTER 14

Organizing Your Business

Further Information:

Assistance with the filing and registration of various business forms can be obtained from your provincial department of corporate affairs (check the blue pages of your telephone directory). In addition, these government offices can direct you to a number of sources of funding and free advice offered by the government to small businesses. For information on federal programs, contact:

Corporations Branch
Consumer and Corporate Affairs Canada
Place du Portage
Tower 1
50 Victoria Street
Hull, Quebec

(Mailing address:
Ottawa, Ontario
K1A 0C9)
(613) 997-1142

Further Reading:

Amirault, Ernest. *Canadian Business Law: An Introduction to Business and Personal Law in Canada*. Third edition. Agincourt: Methuen, 1986.

Cook, Peter D. *Start Your Own Business: The Canadian Entrepreneur's Guide*. Toronto: Stoddart, 1986.

Gilbert, Taylor, et al. *Franchising in Canada*. Don Mills: CCH Canadian, 1986.

Industrial Assistance Programs in Canada. Don Mills: CCH Canadian, 1986.

James, J. D. *Federal Incorporation and Business Guide*. Vancouver: International Self-Counsel Press, 1984.

Teckert, Harry E. and Michael J. McDonald. *You and the Law: What Every Small Business Owner Needs to Know*. Toronto: Financial Post/ Macmillan, 1978.

CHAPTER 15

Immigration and Employment

Further Information:

Further information and assistance may be obtained from the following organizations:

Canadian Bar Association
130 Albert Street
Suite 1700
Ottawa, Ontario
K1P 5G4
(613) 237-2925

Citizenship Department
Provincial Government
(listed in the blue pages of your
  telephone directory)

Community Legal Clinics
(listed in your local telephone
  directory)

Employment and Immigration
Canada
Place du Portage
Phase IV
Hull, Quebec
(Mailing address:
Ottawa, Ontario
K1A 0J9)
(613) 994-2967

InterChurch Committee for
Refugees
Council of Canadian Churches
40 St. Clair Avenue East
Suite 201
Toronto, Ontario
M4T 1M9

Intercede (International Coalition
for Domestic Workers)
58 Cecil Street
Toronto, Ontario
M5T 1N6

Further Reading:

A Guide to Canada's Immigration Law. Revised edition. Saskatoon: Public Legal Education Association of Saskatchewan, 1986.

Marrocco, F.N., and H.M. Goslett. *The Annotated Immigration Act of Canada.* Second edition. Agincourt: The Carswell Company, 1985.

Segal, Gary L. *Immigrating to Canada: Who Is Allowed? What Is Required? How To Do It!* Sixth edition. Vancouver: International Self-Counsel Press, 1986.

So You're in the Refugee Backlog. Toronto Interclinic Immigration Working Group, 1986.

Sponsoring Refugees: Facts for Canadian Groups and Organizations. Ottawa: Supply and Services Canada, 1984.

CHAPTER 16

Women and the Canadian Charter of Rights and Freedoms

Further Information:

The following national organizations are concerned with the legal equality of rights of Canadian women:

National Action Committee on the
  Status of Women
344 Bloor Street West
Suite 505
Toronto, Ontario
M5S 1W9
(416) 922-3246

Women's Legal Education and
  Action Fund (LEAF)
344 Bloor Street West
Suite 403
Toronto, Ontario
M5S 1W9
(416) 963-9654

National Association of Women and
  the Law
323 Chapel Street
Ottawa, Ontario
K1N 7Z2
(613) 238-1545

Further Reading:

Bayevsky, A., and M. Eberts. *Equality Rights and the Canadian Charter of Rights and Freedoms.* Agincourt: The Carswell Company, 1985.

The Canadian Journal of Women and the Law. Published twice a year by: Canadian Journal of Women and the Law, 323 Chapel Street, Ottawa, Ontario K1N 7Z2.

Hogg, P. *Constitutional Law of Canada.* Agincourt: The Carswell Company, 1985.

Smith, Lynn, editor. *Righting the Balance: Canada's New Equality Rights.* Saskatoon: Canadian Human Rights Reporter, 1986.

CHAPTER 17

Crimes Against Women

Further Information:

For information on programs of self-defence against sexual assault, on remedies for pornography, and on prostitution-related issues, contact:

Canadian Coalition Against Media
  Pornography (CCAMP)
Box 1075
Station B

Ottawa, Ontario
K1P 5R1
(613) 230-4560

Local rape crisis centre
(check in your local telephone
  directory)

Media Watch
636 West Broadway
Suite 209
Vancouver, B.C.
V5Z 1G2
(604) 873-8511

Wen-Do Women's Self Defence
Canadian Headquarters
2 Carlton Street
Suite 817
Toronto, Ontario
M5B 1J3
(416) 977-7127
Women Hurt in Systems of
  Prostitution Engaged in Revolt
  (WHISPER)
Rockefeller Center Station
Box 5514
New York, New York
10185
U.S.A.

Working Group on Sexual Violence
2515 Burrard Street
Suite 301
Vancouver, B.C.
V6J 3J6
(604) 734-0485

Canadian Organization for the
  Rights of Prostitutes (CORP)
Box 274
253 College St.
Toronto, Ont.
M5T 1R5

Further Reading:

After Sexual Assault: Your Guide to The Criminal Justice System. Ottawa: Ministry of Justice, 1986.

Barry, Kathleen. *Female Sexual Slavery*. Englewood Cliffs: Prentice-Hall, 1979.

Boyle, Christine. *Sexual Assault*. Agincourt: The Carswell Company, 1984.

Brownmiller, Susan. *Against Our Will: Men, Women and Rape*. New York: Simon and Schuster, 1975.

Clark, Lorenne, and Debra Lewis. *Rape: The Price of Coercive Sexuality*. Toronto: Women's Education Press, 1977.

Delacoste, Frederique, and Felice Newman, editors. *Fight Back: Feminist Resistance to Male Violence*. Minneapolis: Cleis Press, 1981.

Dworkin, Andrea. *Pornography: Men Possessing Women*. New York: Pedigree Books, 1981.

Ellis, Megan. *Surviving: Procedures for After a Sexual Assault*. Vancouver: Press Gang Publishers, 1986.

Lederer, Laura, editor. *Take Back the Night: Women on Pornography*. New York: Bantam Books, 1980.

Millett, Kate. *The Prostitution Papers*. New York: Basic Books, 1971.

Russell, Diana. *The Politics of Rape: The Victim's Perspective*. New York: Stein and Day, 1975.

Sanford, Linda Tschirhart, and Anne Fetter. *In Defence of Ourselves: A Rape Prevention Handbook for Women*. Garden City: Doubleday/ Dolphin, 1979.

CHAPTER 18

Women and Criminal Law

Further Information:

The following organizations may be contacted for further information and assistance:

Canadian Association of Elizabeth Fry Societies
151 Slater Street
Suite 302
Ottawa, Ontario
K1P 5H3
(613) 238-2422
(local societies are listed in your telephone directory)

Canadian Civil Liberties Association
229 Yonge Street
Suite 403
Toronto, Ontario
M5B 1N9
(416) 363-0321

Community Legal Clinics
(listed in your local telephone directory)

Further Reading:

Adelberg, Ellen. *A Forgotten Minority: Women in Conflict with the Law*. Ottawa: Canadian Association of Elizabeth Fry Societies, 1985.

Boyle, Christine, et al. *A Feminist Review of the Criminal Code*. Ottawa: Status of Women Canada, 1985. Includes an extensive bibliography.

Brian Lawrie, and Ian MacLean. *Pull Over Please: What to do When the Police Stop You*. Toronto: Doubleday Canada, 1985.

CHAPTER 19

Advocacy

Further Information:

A number of provincial government departments should be able to provide assistance. Check in the blue pages of your telephone directory for the office of the ombudsman, public complaints office, social services department, and legal-aid office.

Further Reading:

Advocacy Guide for the Physically Handicapped. Halifax: Public Legal Education Society of Nova Scotia, 1985.

All About Welfare. Rexdale: Rexdale Community Information Directory, 1985.

Howell, Shelley, editor. *How to Fight for What's Left of the Environment*. Toronto: Canadian Environmental Law Association, 1985.

Incorporating a Non-Profit Corporation. Toronto. Flemingdon Community Legal Services, 1985.

Mental Health Law: The Advocate's Manual. Toronto: Community Legal Education Ontario, 1986.

No Big Secret: Social Assistance Information for Advocacy Workers in Nova Scotia. Halifax: Public Legal Education Society of Nova Scotia, 1984.

Non-Profit Organizations: A Nova Scotia Guide. Halifax: Public Legal Education Society of Nova Scotia, 1983.

Vayda, Elaine J., and Mary Satterfield. *Law for Social Workers: A Canadian Guide*. Agincourt: The Carswell Company, 1984.

Young, Joyce. *Fundraising for Non-Profit Groups*. Vancouver: International Self-Counsel Press, 1981.

CHAPTER **20**

The Canadian Courts and Legal System

Further Information:
For lawyer referrals and community legal information, contact the law society of your province. For assistance in filing claims, contact the small claims court office of your province (listed in the blue pages of your telephone directory). For other information on the legal system, contact:

The Canadian Bar Association
130 Albert Street
Suite 1700
Ottawa, Ontario
K1P 5G4
(613) 237-2923

Further Reading:
Alberta's Court System Kit. Edmonton: University of Alberta Legal Resources Centre, 1985.

Code of Professional Conduct. Ottawa: Canadian Bar Association, 1974.

Common Law for Common Folk. Second edition. Saskatoon: Public Legal Education Association of Saskatchewan, 1986.

The Courtwatcher's Manual. Revised edition. Vancouver: Legal Services Society of British Columbia, 1985.

Gall, Gerald L. *The Canadian Legal System.* Agincourt: The Carswell Company, 1977.

Gibson, Dwight L., Terry G. Murphy, and Fred Jarman. *All About Law: Exploring the Canadian Legal System.* Second edition. Toronto: John Wiley and Sons Canada, 1984.

Handbook on Courts in Saskatchewan. Saskatoon: Public Legal Education Association of Saskatchewan, 1986.

Taking Your Case to Small Claims Court. Halifax: Public Legal Education Society of Nova Scotia, 1985.

GLOSSARY

Administrator (administratrix) a person appointed by the court to settle the estate of a person who died without a will or without naming an executor

Advocate anyone who defends or pleads the cause of another person

Affidavit a signed statement sworn before a commissioner for oaths

Annuity a fixed yearly amount of money, payable for a specific period of time

Annulment a decree of the court invalidating a marriage retroactively

Appeal application to a higher court to review the decision of a lower court

Appraise to estimate the value of property

Arbitration the process whereby a dispute is referred to a neutral person for a decision

Bar originally a bar or rail across the courtroom separating the court officials from the public; lawyers must be "called to the Bar" in a formal ceremony before they can practise law

Beneficiary a person named in a will or trust to receive money or property

Bequest a gift of personal property in a will

Bona fide in good faith

Cause of action the recognized legal reasons for a lawsuit

Chattel mortgage a mortgage of personal property, such as cars, furniture or equipment

Civil action a lawsuit dealing with private, or civil rights and obligations

Codicil an addition or amendment to a will, executed with the same formalities as a will

Cohabitation living together as husband and wife without being legally married

Collusion a secret agreement or understanding to deceive a third party

Common law that part of the law not written in statutes; it is based upon the principles developed in earlier court decisions

Connivance a plan to arrange or bring about the necessary grounds for divorce

Conveyance a transfer of an interest in real property

Creditor an institution or person who lends money for a debtor

Defendant the accused party; the person sued by the plaintiff

Devise a gift of real property under a will

Domicile a person's permanent legal residence

Estate all of the property and assets owned by a person at the time of death

Executor (executrix) a person appointed by will to carry out the administration of the estate

Fee simple outright ownership of real property

Garnishment a legal procedure for recovering a debt from someone by having their employer pay part of their wages to the creditor or having the debt paid out of their bank account

Guarantee a promise to be responsible for another person's obligations

Holograph will will written and signed entirely in the testator's own handwriting; witnesses are not required

Indictment a formal charge against a person accused of a serious crime

Intestate a person who dies without a will

Joint tenancy ownership of property by two or more persons with equal interests; upon the death of one joint tenant, the property passes automatically to the remaining joint tenant(s)

Legacy a gift of personal property or money by a will

Liability a legal responsibility

Lien a claim against a person's property for an outstanding debt

Mortgage a legal document transferring an interest in real property as security for a debt

Ombudsman an official appointed to investigate complaints against the government

Personal property tangible items of property, such as money, furniture, cars, jewellery but not including real property

Plaintiff the person who brings a lawsuit against the defendant

Probate the procedure by which a court determines that a will is valid

Real property the legal term for real estate or land and buildings

Remedy legal redress; the options open to a court to rectify a wrong

Residence the place where a person lives either temporarily or permanently; a person may have several residences but only one domicile

Secured loan a loan giving the creditor the power to claim against the borrower's property if the loan payments are not made

Statute a written law passed by a provincial or federal government

Summons a notice to an accused in a criminal trial or to a defendant in a civil action to appear in court to answer the charges

Surrogate court the court dealing with probate of wills and the administration of estates

Testator (testatrix) the person who makes a will

Trust a responsibility to hold property for the benefit of another person

Warranty a guarantee or promise that goods or services meet a certain standard

INDEX